Between
Two Worlds

Jaguar Books on Latin America

Series Editors

WILLIAM H. BEEZLEY, Neville G. Penrose Chair of Latin
American Studies, Texas Christian University
COLIN M. MACLACHLAN, Professor, Department of History,
Tulane University

Volumes Published

John E. Kicza, ed., *The Indian in Latin American History: Resistance,
Resilience, and Acculturation* (1993). Cloth ISBN 0-8420-2421-2
Paper ISBN 0-8420-2425-5

Susan E. Place, ed., *Tropical Rainforests: Latin American Nature and
Society in Transition* (1993). Cloth ISBN 0-8420-2423-9
Paper ISBN 0-8420-2427-1

Paul W. Drake, ed., *Money Doctors, Foreign Debts, and Economic
Reforms in Latin America from the 1890s to the Present* (1994).
Cloth ISBN 0-8420-2434-4 Paper ISBN 0-8420-2435-2

John A. Britton, ed., *Molding the Hearts and Minds: Education,
Communications, and Social Change in Latin America* (1994).
Cloth ISBN 0-8420-2489-1 Paper ISBN 0-8420-2490-5

Darién J. Davis, ed., *Slavery and Beyond: The African Impact on Latin
America and the Caribbean* (1995). Cloth ISBN 0-8420-2484-0
Paper ISBN 0-8420-2485-9

David J. Weber and Jane M. Rausch, eds., *Where Cultures Meet: Frontiers
in Latin American History* (1994). Cloth ISBN 0-8420-2477-8
Paper ISBN 0-8420-2478-6

Gertrude M. Yeager, ed., *Confronting Change, Challenging Tradition:
Women in Latin American History* (1994). Cloth ISBN 0-8420-2479-4
Paper ISBN 0-8420-2480-8

Linda Alexander Rodríguez, ed., *Rank and Privilege: The Military and
Society in Latin America* (1994). Cloth ISBN 0-8420-2432-8
Paper ISBN 0-8420-2433-6

Gilbert M. Joseph and Mark D. Szuchman, eds., *I Saw a City Invincible:
Urban Portraits of Latin America* (1996). Cloth ISBN 0-8420-2495-6
Paper ISBN 0-8420-2496-4

Roderic Ai Camp, ed., *Democracy in Latin America: Patterns and Cycles* (1996). Cloth ISBN 0-8420-2512-X   Paper ISBN 0-8420-2513-8

Oscar J. Martínez, ed., *U.S.-Mexico Borderlands: Historical and Contemporary Perspectives* (1996). Cloth ISBN 0-8420-2446-8 Paper ISBN 0-8420-2447-6

William O. Walker III, ed., *Drugs in the Western Hemisphere: An Odyssey of Cultures in Conflict* (1996). Cloth ISBN 0-8420-2422-0 Paper ISBN 0-8420-2426-3

Richard R. Cole, ed., *Communication in Latin America: Journalism, Mass Media, and Society* (1996). Cloth ISBN 0-8420-2558-8 Paper ISBN 0-8420-2559-6

David G. Gutiérrez, ed., *Between Two Worlds: Mexican Immigrants in the United States* (1996). Cloth ISBN 0-8420-2473-5 Paper ISBN 0-8420-2474-3

Between Two Worlds

Mexican Immigrants in the United States

David G. Gutiérrez
Editor

Jaguar Books on Latin America
Number 15

A Scholarly Resources Inc. Imprint
Wilmington, Delaware

Scholarly Resources Inc.
104 Greenhill Avenue
Wilmington, DE 19805-1897

Library of Congress Cataloging-in-Publication Data

Between two worlds : Mexican immigrants in the United States /
    David G. Gutiérrez, editor.
        p.   cm. — (Jaguar books on Latin America ; no. 15)
    Includes bibliographical references.
    ISBN 0-8420-2473-5 (alk. paper). — ISBN 0-8420-2474-3 (pbk. :
alk. paper)
        1. Mexican Americans. 2. Mexicans—United States. 3. Immi-
grants—United States. 4. United States—Emigration and immigration.
5. Mexico—Emigration and immigration. I. Gutiérrez, David (David
Gregory) II. Series.
E184.M5B493   1996
973'.046872—dc20   95-26564
                                                                          CIP

⊛ The paper used in this publication meets the minimum requirements
of the American National Standard for permanence of paper for printed
library materials, Z39.48, 1984.

Acknowledgments

Completion of this project was greatly facilitated by the efforts of several friends and colleagues. I am particularly indebted to Greg Rodríguez for his research assistance and for his expert help in preparing the manuscript and to José Jiménez, Luis Murillo, and Susie Porter for their outstanding research assistance. Thanks also to Bill Deverell and Pamela Radcliff, my colleagues at the University of California, San Diego, for their incisive critiques of early versions of the introduction and to series coeditor Bill Beezley for his patience, encouragement, timely advice, and good humor.

About the Editor

David G. Gutiérrez is associate professor of history and codirector of the Southwest History Project at the University of California, San Diego (UCSD). He received a B.A. in history and Chicano studies from the University of California, Santa Barbara, and M.A. and Ph.D. degrees from Stanford University. He has taught history and ethnic studies at the University of Utah, Stanford, and UCSD.

Gutiérrez's research interests include regional immigration history, ethnic politics, and recent social movements. He is the author of *Walls and Mirrors: Mexican Americans, Mexican Immigrants, and the Politics of Ethnicity* (1995) and has published numerous articles on the history of ethnic Mexicans in the United States. His research has been supported by fellowships from the Dorothy Danforth Compton Foundation, the Ford Foundation and National Research Council, the John Randolf Haynes and Dora Haynes Foundation, and the Chicano Fellows Program at Stanford University. His essay on the emergence of the contemporary Mexican immigration debate won the Bolton-Kinnaird Prize of the Western History Association in 1992. Gutiérrez is currently at work on a comparative study of ethnicity and citizenship in the United States since 1945.

Contents

Introduction

On the eve of the twenty-first century, the phenomenon of transnational migration has become one of the most vexing and complicated issues facing both industrial and developing nations. With millions of people around the world moving across political borders seeking work, reunification with family members, or refuge from religious or political persecution, no nation is immune from the pressures wrought by the mass movement of populations from one place to another. Such pressures in the United States have contributed to the eruption of one of the most intense waves of anti-immigrant sentiment in recent American history. Symbolized by the long-simmering debate over federal immigration policy, the passage of California's controversial Proposition 187 in November 1994, and the recent resurgence of restrictionist and nativist political movements, the contentious debate over immigration will almost certainly continue to rage for years to come.

Although immigrants enter the United States from virtually every nation, Mexico has long been identified in the public imagination as one of the primary sources of the economic, social, and political problems associated with immigration. The popular association of Mexicans with the immigration controversy has complex origins. Clearly, much of the animosity stems from a long history of Mexican migration across a two-thousand-mile border. Beginning with the thousands of Sonoran miners who moved to California soon after the United States annexed Mexico's northern provinces following the U.S.-Mexican War, and intensifying after the turn of the century, the number of these migrants increased gradually throughout the nineteenth century. Drawn by the concomitant economic development of northern Mexico and the southwestern United States in the late 1870s and 1880s (largely facilitated by the extension and eventual linkage of the American and Mexican national railroad systems), at least one hundred thousand Mexicans had migrated across the border by 1900. The outbreak of the Mexican Revolution in 1909–10 intensified the movement of people within Mexico toward the United States, but the patterns of both internal and international migration northward had already been established.

Americans historically have tended to place the onus of these migration patterns on Mexican immigrants themselves, but the relationship between American employers and Mexican workers has been much more symbiotic than most people generally have wished to acknowledge. For more than a century, these employers and their allies in government have worked in close partnership to ensure the availability of a large pool of Mexican laborers within U.S. boundaries. Beginning in the 1870s and 1880s and continuing to the present day, American employers have considered Mexican workers a vital component of the labor market. Filling jobs in the agricultural, mining, railway, and construction industries in the Southwest, laboring as agricultural, automobile, and mill workers in the Midwest, and sometimes venturing as far as Alaska to find employment as fishery and cannery workers, Mexicans had been fully integrated into the the lower rungs of the American economy by the late 1920s.

The employment of this first large group eventually stimulated the first of many fierce public debates in the United States. American workers and nativist groups protested against Mexican laborers on both economic and cultural grounds, arguing that foreign labor eroded the wages and working conditions of citizen workers and that the influx of foreigners threatened the integrity of American cultural and political institutions. Employers attempted to blunt this growing public concern by developing an elaborate rationale to explain their use of Mexican labor. Although the specific components of this rationale varied, beginning soon after World War I these employers launched an intensive public relations campaign designed to convince their countrymen that Mexican workers were both culturally and biologically suited to perform the back-breaking jobs that were "beneath" American workers and, more important, that unlike previous immigrants, Mexicans had no intention of settling permanently in the United States.

Nativist groups continued to exert pressure on Congress, but, for four decades between 1890 and 1930, employers' lobby groups were able to convince U.S. government officials that hiring Mexicans was crucial for many industries. Laying the foundation for what one scholar has termed a "system of ad hoc exemptions," policymakers established an intricate patchwork of mechanisms including administrative exemptions, executive orders, and, most commonly, extended periods of "informal" nonenforcement of extant immigration and labor statutes to ensure American employers maximum flexibility in regulating the flow of Mexican migrants and immigrants into the United States.[1] Consequently, although the general trend in American immigration law between the 1880s and the Great Depression was the gradual imposition of increasingly tight restrictions on the entry of persons considered to be a threat to the nation's cultural and political integrity, between the mid-1880s and the late 1920s Mexicans were consistently exempted from these laws.

For its part, Mexico's government has been deeply ambivalent about the mass migration of its citizens to the United States. Although the exodus of workers has long been a source of consternation and embarrassment to Mexican nationalists and government officials, they have also been compelled to recognize that, in many ways, labor migration has served as an important safety valve for social and political unrest in their country. Thus, since the 1910 revolution, Mexico's emigration policy traditionally has been predicated on attempting to protect the rights of its citizens abroad (largely through diplomatic channels and through the efforts of the consular corps in the United States); maintaining a sense of patriotism among expatriates by sponsoring observances of national holidays in ethnic Mexican communities in the United States; and encouraging, and at times actively fostering, the eventual repatriation of Mexican nationals abroad.

The steady growth of the United States' ethnic Mexican population—that is, the combined number of resident nationals and the expanding population of American citizens of Mexican descent—before the Great Depression provides stark evidence of the extent to which Mexican acquiescence and the imperatives of regional economic development worked in concert with U.S. labor and immigration policies to stimulate and sustain transnational migration patterns. Although historical migration statistics for the border region are notoriously inaccurate because of inconsistent enumeration techniques, changing methods of ethnic and racial classification in the United States, and the cyclical movement of uncounted thousands of undocumented migrants in and out of U.S. territory, extrapolation from both countries' census sources provides a sense of the magnitude of population movements over the past hundred years. In 1890 the number was probably no more than 78,000. By 1900, however, the number of Mexican citizens living in the United States jumped to 103,000, more than doubled to 222,000 in 1910, and then doubled again to 478,000 in 1920. By 1930 the number of Mexican-born residents of the United States is conservatively estimated to have increased to at least 639,000. Estimates of the total migratory flow for this period vary widely, but most historians believe that at least one million, and as many as 1.5 million, entered the United States between the late 1880s and 1929.[2]

Despite a brief reversal of migration flows during the Great Depression (when in-migration virtually ceased and an estimated 350,000 to 500,000 Mexican nationals and their U.S.-born children were "encouraged," or compelled, to return to their homeland), migration trends were quickly reestablished in the 1940s. Again, U.S. labor policy decisions provided the major impetus for the renewal of mass migration from Mexico at this juncture. Facing a significant farm labor shortage as a result of conscription and war mobilization, the United States made overtures in early 1942 concerning the creation of a temporary bilateral labor agreement.[3]

Historian Manuel García y Griego notes in Chapter 3 that although the Mexican government was reluctant to enter into any kind of agreement without first gaining assurances that workers' rights and interests would be protected, in August 1942 the two nations came to terms on what was announced as a temporary labor program. Under the specifications of the Emergency Farm Labor Program (soon unofficially dubbed the Bracero Program, after the Spanish term for field laborer), Mexico's government was assured that its workers would be provided with certain minimum wage levels and working conditions as well as food, housing, and travel back to their country upon the expiration of their contracts. The accord also stipulated that braceros would be shielded from discrimination while in the United States.

The establishment of the Bracero Program in the early 1940s had several important effects. On the most fundamental level, it reopened the border to large-scale Mexican labor migration. Although the program was established as an emergency wartime measure, employers successfully convinced Congress to renew it several times after the war, and as a consequence the use of bracero labor gradually became an institutionalized component of the American agricultural labor market, replacing many of the informal labor recruitment mechanisms employed earlier in the century. At the program's peak in 1959–60, braceros represented fully 26 percent of the U.S. migrant labor force. By the time the Bracero Program was finally terminated in 1964, nearly five million contracts had been issued.

The recruitment and employment of large numbers of Mexican contract workers also had the largely unanticipated effect of stimulating both sanctioned and unsanctioned migration to the United States. By reinforcing communication networks between these contract workers and their friends and families back home, many Mexicans were able to gain firsthand knowledge of the labor market conditions north of the border. Consequently, the number of Mexicans seeking legally to emigrate to the United States increased steadily in the 1950s and 1960s, but, perhaps more important, over the long run the Bracero Program also served as a catalyst stimulating a dramatic new influx of unsanctioned labor migration.

Drawn to the prospect of improving their material condition (either as temporary sojourners or as permanent emigrants), thousands of Mexicans chose to circumvent the formal bracero contract process and entered the United States surreptitiously. In the mid-1940s the U.S. Immigration and Naturalization Service (INS) reported apprehending an average of 159,000 undocumented Mexican workers each year. By the mid-1950s, however, this number had risen to more than 590,000 per year. Although apprehensions of undocumented migrants tapered off for several years after the INS's infamous Operation Wetback of 1954 (when a reported 1,075,168 Mexicans were apprehended and repatriated), the institutionalization of foreign labor recruitment programs helped establish patterns of sanctioned and unsanctioned northward migration that continue to the present day.

Since 1960 more people have legally and illegally emigrated to the United States from Mexico than from any other single nation. As a result, between 1960 and 1980 the number of ethnic Mexicans in this country grew from about 2.3 million to 8.7 million. In 1990 an estimated 4.4 million Mexican nationals resided in the United States, and the combined population of Mexican Americans and Mexican immigrants had grown to an estimated 13.4 million.[4]

Although few Americans seemed to recognize it as it happened, migration of this magnitude set into motion forces that gradually transformed the contours of social relations in a large region of the United States. In a territory stretching from southern California to the Gulf of Mexico, and extending northward to the agricultural and industrial centers of the Midwest, Mexicans migrated and settled in large numbers, drawn to the jobs, wages, educational opportunities, and social services that generally were not available at home. In the process, these immigrants (at first predominantly single men and later entire families) and their U.S.-born children helped to expand existing ethnic enclaves such as those in Los Angeles, Tucson, El Paso, San Antonio, and the lower Rio Grande Valley, or created new ones in places such as Washington's Yakima Valley, Chicago, Detroit, and northwestern Ohio. Complete with a complex and growing infrastructure of diverse small businesses, owner-occupied homes, restaurants, bars, bordellos, newspapers, record shops and recording studios, and various organizations and associations, the expansion of these ethnic communities represented in some important ways the development of a parallel society in the United States. Of course, continuous exposure to elements of American popular and material culture powerfully influenced the evolution of these syncretic hybrid communities, but the constant influx of both permanent immigrants and sojourners helped to sustain the

distinctive cultural atmosphere of Mexican and Mexican-American enclaves in cities, towns, and rural communities in the Southwest and Midwest.

Historians, social scientists, journalists, and politicians have been
deeply divided about how to interpret these postwar developments. More
optimistic observers viewed the growth of a permanent Mexican immigrant population in the same way that they interpreted the history of European immigrants to the United States, arguing that Mexicans would
eventually "become American" as previous immigrants had. Encouraged
to think along these lines by the leaders of prominent Mexican-American
civil rights organizations such as the League of United Latin American
Citizens (LULAC) and the American G.I. Forum (who argued that such a
process was already occurring among U.S.-born Mexican Americans),
many scholars adopted the view that the history of Mexican immigration
represented just one more chapter in the continuing saga, which had begun in the seventeenth century, of the peopling of the United States by
immigrants.

This is not to argue that American scholars uniformly assumed that
the process of adaptation worked smoothly with Mexican immigrants.
On the contrary, beginning with the first serious studies conducted in the
1920s and continuing until the mid-1960s, many of these scholars noted
with concern the slowness with which ethnic Mexicans were becoming
"assimilated" into the mainstream. Some viewed this "lag" as a natural
outgrowth of the proximity of Mexico to the United States. Most reseachers
of this era concluded that certain Mexican cultural traits, such as their
supposed "clannishness," "fatalism," or "presentmindedness," both hindered the assimilation process and explained many of the social problems
in the ethnic communities. Still, most of these scholars seemed to believe
that once Mexicans learned to adopt more "American" social and cultural
practices, they would gradually become integrated into society as had
previous immigrant groups.[5]

Others have not been nearly so optimistic about the inevitability of
the "assimilation" and "Americanization" of Mexican immigrants, particularly those who have entered the United States since the 1970s. Indeed, if the current debate over immigration is any gauge, many Americans
seem to have lost faith in the ability of society to absorb such large numbers of immigrants. Echoing fears similar to those expressed in earlier
periods of large-scale immigration, increasing numbers of people in this
country have argued in recent years that immigrants from Mexico (and,
by extension, from other Latin American nations as well) are stealing
jobs, undermining wage rates, committing crimes, threatening public
health, and straining the already overburdened social welfare and public

education systems. Others share these concerns but are even more alarmed by what they see as the cultural implications of the rapid expansion of the ethnic Mexican and pan-Latino population that had grown to some twenty-two million by 1990 and is projected to grow to as many as forty million in the year 2010.

Insisting that the sustained growth of a Spanish-speaking population seemingly committed to preserving "foreign" cultural and linguistic practices is antithetical to the U.S. tradition of the melting pot, Americans from all walks of life have demanded that the federal government (and, in some cases, state governments) take immediate steps to limit and control the number of both "legal" and undocumented immigrants allowed to enter the country now and in the future. Moreover, in light of the recent passage of California's Proposition 187 (which, if upheld by the courts, would deny education, health care, and other tax-supported public services to undocumented residents and their children), it is difficult not to view the current backlash against Latino migrants at least partially as a reaction to demographic changes that have already fundamentally transformed states such as California, Arizona, Texas, and Illinois.

Anyone who has maintained even a passing interest in the immigration issue over the past ten or fifteen years readily recognizes these arguments. However, such publicity has helped to obscure the extent to which traditional interpretations, both of the Mexican diaspora and of the immigration process generally, have been reassessed, revised, and, in many cases, rejected by immigration scholars. This process of reassessment and revision has been under way for some years. Growing out of a slowly evolving sense among some researchers that traditional theoretical models not only were outmoded but also were actually helping to distort key aspects of the phenomenon of international migration, since the 1970s scholars in a variety of disciplines have called for the development of more complex approaches to the study. Criticisms of the old models have been as varied as the scholars raising them, but such critiques have several general points in common.

Perhaps the most important was the broad critique of the "assimilationist" or "melting pot" model of American immigration history. As mentioned above, although traditional scholars acknowledged the many difficulties that immigrants faced in their efforts to adjust and reestablish themselves in a new and often hostile society, many researchers assumed that, given enough time, immigrants (and their U.S.-born children) would gradually become assimilated into American life in a progressive, linear, and largely unambiguous fashion. Researchers also assumed that by slowly shedding their former traditional cultural norms and practices and adopting modern ones in the United States, it was only a matter of time before immigrants and their children would melt into the mainstream of social, cultural, and political life in this country.

By the early 1970s scholars influenced by the so-called new social history began to develop different approaches to the study of international migration generally, and Mexican immigration to the United States specifically. Although researchers stressed various elements in the individual conceptual frameworks they built, in general these immigration scholars sought to replace the assimilationist perspective with analytical models that stressed the complexity and variability of the immigrant experience and emphasized the agency of immigrants themselves. For example, whereas assimilationist theorists often had interpreted U.S. immigration history within a framework that portrayed immigrants as passive subjects waiting to adapt, adjust, and reorient themselves as "Americans," revisionist scholars insisted that immigrants had much more varied motivations for their actions and exerted much more control over the pace—and direction—of their "adaptations." While theorists acknowledged that in fact some immigrants attempted to follow what they understood to be assimilationist prescriptions for their inclusion into American society (for example, by learning English, becoming citizens, voting, or joining the U.S. armed forces), scholars emphasized that such strategies represented only one of many possibilities open to them as they tried to shape their future and that of their children.

The logic of this more open conceptualization led humanist and social science scholars to reassess their views on many other elements of human migration. For example, if older approaches to the study of immigration had tended to emphasize the experiences of uprooted, atomized, and (literally) alienated individual immigrants moving from one distinct society to another, and to stress similar bipolar oppositions (such as the distinctions between "citizens" and "aliens," "traditional" and "modern," "rural" and "urban," "backward" and "progressive"), one of the hallmarks of newer scholarship is its attentiveness to the evolution of transnational migration networks in which migrants move back and forth between communities in two or more nation-states, maintain strong ties to both their natal communities and their "adopted" ones, and continue to maintain their own cultural practices at the same time that they selectively incorporate elements of the culture of the "host" society.

The implications for the study of Mexican migration of the current reconceptualization of the general processes of international migration and immigration are far-reaching. Transnational models obviously call attention to the ambiguities of citizenship and the nation-state by emphasizing the permeability of territorial boundaries to international flows and linkages of capital, communications, and populations. But, by extension, such perspectives also call into question the constructed nature of other heretofore commonly accepted social boundaries and categories such as those demarcating "races," "ethnic groups," and "classes." By highlighting the ways in which contemporary transnational migrants' daily lives and extended multinational social networks make a mockery of these traditional, narrowly bounded systems of classification, transnational analyses provide new insights into the increasingly complicated phenomenon of human migration from Mexico to the United States, and back again. The fact that virtually any resident of the border region either personally knows or can easily imagine extended or even nuclear families composed of American citizens of Mexican descent, Mexican citizens who are in the country "legally," Mexican citizens who are in the country "illegally," and U.S.-born children whose parents might be categorized in any of the above-mentioned statuses provides graphic evidence of the almost infinitely intricate and fluid social and cultural matrices in which individual and collective identities have evolved among ethnic Mexicans in the United States.

Drawing on some of the insights provoked by recent trends in immigration research, the essays in this anthology provide an overview of some of the most important current trends in the interpretation of historical and contemporary dimensions of the Mexican diaspora. In addition, in compiling this anthology, particular interest was focused on bringing together selections that would provide a sense of the changing significance of the U.S.-Mexico border over the past 150 years, as people on both sides of the international frontier sought to create and sustain social space for themselves on this fiercely contested terrain.

In the first chapter, Sister Mary Colette Standart explores the social history of Sonoran migrants to California during the Gold Rush, the earliest example of large-scale immigration from Mexico to the United States. The experiences of these first migrants provided strong clues about how interethnic and intraethnic relationships would evolve in California and the greater Southwest in the last half of the nineteenth century. Standart's account gives important insights into the social conditions of the northern Mexican frontier, the motivations of the Sonoran migrants, and the complexity and volatility of interethnic interactions in the California goldfields.

As Standart illustrates, although Anglo-Americans were themselves recent interlopers into the region, their abiding belief in their nation's Manifest Destiny contributed to a general sense among them that Mexicans represented a degenerate "race" and culture and, by extension, that the region's natural resources were theirs to exploit exclusively. Such attitudes not only led to the widespread physical and juridical harassment of Mexican and other Spanish-speaking miners in the 1840s and 1850s but also helped to reinforce pernicious stereotypes about these newcomers as "greasers"—an image that would stubbornly persist until well into the twentieth century.

Standart also perceptively notes that the Sonoran migration helped illuminate sources of intraethnic conflict between Spanish-speaking Californians and more recent Mexican migrants, a theme that until recently scholars have tended to overlook. Although most nineteenth- and early twentieth-century Americans did not recognize any meaningful distinctions between the estimated one hundred thousand people annexed along with the Mexican Cession and those who emigrated to this territory later, Mexican Americans and Mexicans were sensitive to the many social and cultural differences that had evolved between their countrymen on the northern frontier and those in central Mexico. Just as regionalism continues to play a significant role in shaping individual identities in present-day Mexico, local attachments and loyalties, class differences, and subtle variances in customs and language patterns helped to stratify the ethnic population in the nineteenth century.

As noted, most Americans failed to appreciate the internal heterogeneity of the ethnic Mexican population. Indeed, if anything, as the nineteenth century progressed, awareness of a Mexican presence in the United States steadily declined. Transformed into a tiny minority by the mass westward migration of Americans and forced into shrinking urban barrios and isolated rural settlements, Mexicans seemed to have disappeared from the social landscape of the Southwest by the 1870s. This situation would change at the turn of the century, when thousands of migrants crossed the border into the United States, greatly expanding the ethnic communities and contributing to a florescence of Mexican culture north of the Rio Grande.

Given the long history of racial and cultural antipathy toward Mexicans in the southwestern United States, it may seem surprising that they were allowed to enter the country in such numbers in this period. Historian Mark Reisler explores this apparent contradiction in Chapter 2. In his view, the key to understanding the paradox lies in comprehending the ways in which American employers were able to manipulate existing stereotypes about Mexicans to rationalize their use in the labor market. Of course, the linchpin of the lobbyists' rationalization was that these workers were employed only in those menial occupations that American citizens tended to avoid. Citing Mexicans' inherent indolence, tractability, and cultural backwardness, employers insisted that they were ideally suited to do this kind of work. But, as Reisler argues, labor migration of this magnitude probably would not have been tolerated if employers and their lobbyists had not also been successful in convincing the public and Congress that Mexicans were temporary "birds of passage" who had no interest in settling permanently but had come only to earn a stake before eventually returning to their homeland. By propagating this "myth of return," American employers and their representatives helped to reinforce the notion that it was completely appropriate for Mexicans to work in the United States while being systematically excluded from entering into the civic culture of the country. The fact that they could be, and periodically were, compelled to return to Mexico during economic slumps added force to this rationale and significantly contributed to the widespread perception among many citizens of the "naturalness" of their inferior position in the American social hierarchy.

In many ways the logic that helped determine Mexicans' tenuous status in American society between 1900 and 1930 was elaborated and reinforced by the formalization of "temporary" labor importation schemes. As historian Manuel García y Griego argues in his richly detailed contribution (Chapter 3), the creation of the 1942 Emergency Farm Labor Program and its successors helped to rationalize and institutionalize both economic and social practices that American employers had experimented with since the late nineteenth century. Although the Bracero Program extended guarantees to contract laborers that were designed to protect their rights and interests while working in the United States (and in many cases exceeded protections granted American workers in similar occupations), these provisions proved almost impossible to enforce. Thus, patterns of widespread exploitation and abuse of Mexican workers that had been common earlier in the century were reestablished on an even broader scale in the 1940s and 1950s.

More important, by instituting a flexible system of what the labor activist Ernesto Galarza termed "managed migration," over the long run American employers and their allies in government were able to perpetuate the fiction of the "temporary" Mexican laborer in the United States. By maintaining the myth of legal, temporary bracero labor while generally tolerating the extensive employment of even cheaper undocumented Mexican labor, the government convinced the public that the integrity of a clear distinction between American citizens and alien workers was being maintained. No doubt, it was occasionally necessary to demonstrate that such distinctions had meaning. Thus, in 1954, in an episode that closely mirrored the great repatriation campaigns of the 1930s, the INS made a great show of its efforts to "regain control of the nation's borders" by launching Operation Wetback, a highly publicized series of "sweeps" in which undocumented migrant laborers were compelled to repatriate to Mexico.

Although U.S. government officials crowed about their success in reasserting national sovereignty, ethnic Mexican activists such as Galarza of the National Farm Workers Union perceptively observed that the most important effect of Operation Wetback was that it simultaneously helped to discipline undocumented workers and further helped rationalize the systematic exploitation of both legal and "illegal" workers at the expense of American farm laborers. Stating as much before a Washington congressional subcommittee after Operation Wetback had ended, Galarza noted that, "while one agency of the U.S. government rounded up illegal aliens and deported them to Mexico, . . . [an]other . . . was busily engaged in recruiting workers in Mexico to return them to U.S. farms."[6]

Galarza's comments serve as a good barometer of the extent to which some Mexican-American activists had come to recognize, and begin to take action against, the manipulation of the immigration issue. Like most activists associated with major Mexican-American advocacy and civil rights organizations, Galarza was vehemently opposed to both the use of contract labor and policies that had the effect of winking at undocumented labor migration when it suited U.S. economic interests. However, his analysis of the migration phenomenon reflected the deep ambivalence that permanent Mexican immigrants and their U.S.-born children felt toward the immigration controversy.

As historian Mario García notes in Chapter 4, such tensions and ambiguities have characterized Mexican-American and Mexican immigrant relations ever since the border was established in 1848. Confronted with the political reality that at the stroke of a pen arbitrarily separated Mexicans into two nationalities, the new international frontier helped to sharpen many of the distinctions that had been drawn between *norteños* and the rest of society earlier in Mexico's history. As García points out, although Mexican Americans' perceptions about Mexico and its people varied widely, their attitudes tended to fall somewhere between two poles of opinion. One side was occupied by those who continued to identify strongly with Mexico and therefore felt strong affinities with Mexicans "from the other side." Although Mexican Americans who subscribed to this viewpoint were painfully aware that subsequent immigrants from below the border often directly competed with them for scarce jobs and housing in the United States, they believed that similarities between them outweighed any invidious distinctions that others might make.

García demonstrates that not all Mexican Americans held these views. Indeed, over time, many ethnic Mexicans permanently residing in the United States came to adopt nearly opposite opinions. While they, too, generally acknowledged the deep historical, cultural, and kinship ties that bound them to Mexico and Mexicans, from their point of view the border had created an unbridgeable gap between them. Thus, while they might be sensitive toward Mexico's problems and sympathize with its immigrants, they reluctantly concluded that the needs and interests of American citizens of Mexican descent had to take precedence over those of recent arrivals. As García argues, the divisions among ethnic Mexicans in the United States deeply influenced the contours of their political actions for more than 150 years.

Chapter 5, a speech delivered by labor activist Luisa Moreno in 1940, illustrates the essential elements of the arguments advanced by ethnic Mexicans in the United States, who viewed immigrants from their homeland with empathy and in solidarity. A founding member of the militant Spanish-Speaking Peoples' Congress, Moreno insisted that the long-standing U.S. practice of recruiting and employing such workers had helped transform the meaning of citizenship and community in American society. Departing from the views of more conservative civil rights organizations such as LULAC, Moreno and the Congress advanced the proposition that not only had Mexican workers earned the right to live and work in the United States but also that they should be considered fully vested members of American society, even if they chose not to become naturalized citizens. Basing this rather startling proposition on their belief that anyone who had worked, sacrificed, invested in property and homes, and raised children in the United States should be afforded the benefits of that society, members of the Congress anticipated positions that ethnic Mexican activists would advance during the height of the Chicano movement nearly forty years later.

Although perhaps not as eloquent or impassioned as Moreno, other ethnic Mexicans lived their daily lives in a manner that was completely consistent with her description of them. As historian Vicki Ruiz notes in Chapter 6, while the material and popular culture of the United States deeply influenced Mexican immigrants, they often reacted to the forces of "Americanization" in complicated and unexpected ways. Focusing her study on women, Ruiz examines the roles played by the mass media (especially newspapers and movies), employment experiences, and public education in shaping Mexican culture in the United States in the important period between the 1920s and the 1950s. Ruiz presents a nuanced analysis of cultural change and cultural resistance that explores the ways that Mexican and Mexican-American women attempted to negotiate the contradictions raised by their daily existence as members of a racialized and gendered minority. Ruiz notes that, while sometimes accommodative, sometimes appropriative, sometimes oppositional, and always

transformative, the means these women employed to adjust to their changing circumstances deeply influenced the evolution of Mexican-American
families and thus their communities in the United States.

Such social, cultural, and political negotiations manifested themselves
in different ways from one community to another, as ethnomusicologist
Manuel Peña demonstrates in Chapter 7. Exploring the evolution of two
styles of popular music—the *orquesta*, a hybrid style combining elements
of traditional Mexican music with elements of American big-band "swing";
and the *conjunto*, a polka-like style built around the accordion that was
(and remains) particularly popular among the working classes—Peña provides a fascinating glimpse of the ways that the growing diversity of the
resident ethnic Mexican population was symbolically played out in the
realm of popular music. He stresses that the growing schisms between
aficionados of each style symbolized deeper, even more significant splits
between the increasingly Americanized and upwardly mobile Mexican-
American middle class and members of the *mexicano* working class, who
doggedly attempted to maintain a sense of *mexicanidád* (Mexicanness)
and thus pointedly rejected the "*jaitón*" style of the *orquesta*. Like Ruiz
and García, Peña interprets this widening intraethnic rift as one of the
defining characteristics of twentieth-century Mexican-American social
and cultural history.

As political historian David Gutiérrez argues in Chapter 8, such rifts
manifested themselves even more dramatically in the turbulent decade of
the 1960s. Although the apparent decrease in the migration of undocumented workers in the late 1950s and early 1960s and the demise of the
Bracero Program in 1964 seemed to signal the beginning of an era in
which the ethnic Mexican population in the United States might stabilize,
by 1967 it was clear that migration was again on the rise. Occurring at the
same time that young Mexican Americans were beginning to reconceptualize their ethnic identity and commencing a series of protests that eventually coalesced as the Chicano movement, the reemergence of the
immigration debate helped accentuate some of the social cleavages explored in different historical contexts by Standart, García, Ruiz, and Peña.
Gutiérrez points out that although few Chicano militants immediately
recognized it at the time, the renewal of the immigration controversy soon
raised a series of questions about the relationship between Mexican Americans and Mexican immigrants, the sources of "Chicano" identity, and the
appropriateness of pursuing rigidly ethnically based political strategies
that in many ways remain unanswered.

The essays that make up the concluding portion of this anthology
focus on more contemporary dimensions of Mexican migration to the
United States. The section begins with two provocative, and contrasting,

interpretations of the potential future of these migratory flows. In Chapter 9, sociologist Saskia Sassen attempts to broaden the context in which Mexican migration is analyzed by comparing recent patterns to similar developments in other parts of the world. Reflecting a growing trend in the study of transnational migrations, Sassen contends that by failing to acknowledge forthrightly that modern population movements are intrinsically related to the emergence of multinational labor markets and to the fundamental internationalization of huge areas of human enterprise (including communication, trade, capital flows, and technology exchanges), the current debate over U.S. immigration policy is deeply flawed. Sassen refutes the long-held assumption that modern labor migration from Mexico and other nations is necessarily driven exclusively, or even primarily, by economic disparities among nations. She insists instead that recent migration trends may well be the result of fundamental transformations associated with foreign investment strategies by advanced industrialized powers such as the United States. Thus, in Sassen's view, the habit of U.S. politicians to frame the immigration debate in isolation from policy decisions in these other areas virtually guarantees that many of the policies ostensibly designed to curb labor migration are doomed to failure. Indeed, Sassen agrees with other analysts who have argued that, in many cases, immigration policies devised by the United States and other industrial powers since World War II may have had the paradoxical effect of stimulating international migration rather than controlling and discouraging it.

Although employing a similar analytical approach, in Chapter 10, Dolores Acevedo and Thomas Espenshade come to significantly different conclusions in their analysis of the probable effects of the North American Free Trade Agreement (NAFTA) on Mexican migration patterns. Adhering to a conceptual framework criticized by Sassen, Acevedo and Espenshade contend that the contiguity of Mexico to the United States along a long border, combined with significant and persistent disparities in economic growth between the two nations, largely explains post-World War II migration trends. In their analysis of the contemporary period, the authors address negotiators' failure during the NAFTA talks to consider labor and migration questions openly in conjunction with their discussions of the movement of goods and services across existing borders. The authors believe that this unwillingness to deal with these vexing issues has helped mask the probability that the only development likely to slow out-migration from Mexico is a marked and sustained long-term improvement in that country's economy. Moreover, they note that, in the short term, economic development and restructuring in Mexico may well increase labor migration. The current volatility of the Mexican economy—

and the social and political unrest that volatility has spawned—will un-doubtedly test the predictive power of Sassen and Acevedo and Espenshade in the months and years to come.

Roger Rouse's essay (Chapter 11) serves as an appropriate coda to the collection because it refocuses our attention on the many human dimensions of international migration trends. He accomplishes this by paying close attention to the ways that intricately linked international economies, deeply rooted transnational migration circuits, and multilingual systems of representation and communication have disrupted the integrity of nation-states and corresponding national identities to the extent that current efforts to reassert such arbitrary distinctions (for example, California's Proposition 187) may be hopeless. While many Americans clearly view such disruptions with alarm, Rouse argues that analysis of the widespread decentering of traditional, bifurcated conceptual categories, such as those demarcating "citizens" and "aliens," may help us develop useful new ways to map and comprehend the rapidly changing and contested social landscape that migrants and permanent residents share.

Part of a growing body of scholarship that seeks to reconceptualize and reorient the study of human migration in a manner that takes seriously the accelerating trends toward what he terms "national disarticulation," Rouse's essay provides a clear example of the direction of some of the most promising work in diaspora studies. One can only hope, along with Rouse, that such work will help to dismantle invidious stereotypes about transnational migrants and contribute to a recasting of immigration research in ways that encourage reflection on—if not complete comprehension of—the increasingly crucial social, cultural, and political implications of transnational human migrations.

Notes

1. Ellwyn R. Stoddard, "Illegal Mexican Labor in the Borderlands: Institutional Support of an Unlawful Practice," *Pacific Sociological Review* 19, no. 2 (1976): 175–210.

2. For discussion of the growth of the ethnic Mexican population between 1890 and 1930, see Arthur F. Corwin, "Quien Sabe? Mexican Migration Statistics," in *Immigrants—and Immigrants*, ed. Arthur F. Corwin (Westport, CT, 1978), 108–35; José Hernández Alvarez, "A Demographic Profile of the Mexican Immigration to the United States, 1910–1950," *Journal of Inter-American Studies* 8 (July 1966): 471–96; Thomas J. Boswell, "The Growth and Proportional Distribution of the Mexican Stock Population in the United States, 1910–1970," *Mississippi Geographer* 7 (Spring 1979): 57–76; and Lawrence A. Cardoso, *Mexican Emigration to the United States, 1897–1931* (Tucson, AZ, 1980).

3. For discussion of the repatriation campaigns of the 1930s, see Mercedes Carreras de Velasco, *Los mexicanos que devolvió la crises, 1929–1932* (México,

D.F., 1974); Abraham Hoffman, *Unwanted Mexican Americans in the Great Depression: Repatriation Pressures, 1929–1939* (Tucson, AZ, 1974); George J. Sánchez, *Becoming Mexican American: Ethnicity, Culture, and Identity in Chicano Los Angeles, 1900–1945* (New York, 1993), 209–26; and Francisco E. Balderrama and Raymond Rodríguez, *Decade of Betrayal: Mexican Repatriation in the 1930s* (Albuquerque, NM, 1995).

4. See Frank D. Bean and Marta Tienda, *The Hispanic Population of the United States* (New York, 1987); David E. Lorey, ed., *United States-Mexico Border Statistics since 1900* (Los Angeles, 1990); John R. Weeks and Roberto Ham-Chande, eds., *Demographic Dynamics of the U.S.-Mexico Border* (El Paso, TX, 1992); U.S. Bureau of the Census, Current Population Reports, Series P-20, No. 455, *The Hispanic Population in the United States: March 1991* (Washington, DC, 1991); and Phillip Martin and Elizabeth Midgley, "Immigration to the United States: Journey to an Uncertain Destination," *Population Bulletin* 49, no. 2 (September 1994).

5. For early examples of scholarship discussing the putative Mexican cultural traits affecting their potential "assimilation" into American society, see Victor S. Clark, *Mexican Labor in the United States*, U.S. Bureau of Labor Statistics Bulletin, No. 78 (Washington, DC, 1908); Emory S. Bogardus, *The Essentials of Americanization* (Los Angeles, 1923), and *The Mexican in the United States* (Los Angeles, 1934); Roy L. Garis, *Immigration Restriction: A Study of Opposition to and Regulation of Immigration to the United States* (New York, 1928); Helen Walker, "Mexican Immigrants as Laborers," *Sociology and Social Research* 13 (1928): 55–62; and Rensen Crawford, "The Menace of Mexican Immigration," *Current History* 31 (February 1930): 902–7. For more recent examples, see William Madsen, *Mexican-Americans of South Texas* (New York, 1964); and Celia S. Heller, *Mexican American Youth: Forgotten Youth at the Crossroads* (New York, 1968).

6. See testimony of Ernesto Galarza in U.S. Congress, House of Representatives, Committee on Agriculture, *Hearings on Mexican Farm Labor Program*, 84th Cong., 1st sess., 1955, 172. For similar analyses, see James Cockcroft, *Outlaws in the Promised Land: Mexican Immigrant Workers and America's Future* (New York, 1986), 67–86; and Michael Kearny, "Borders and Boundaries of State and Self at the End of Empire," *Journal of Historical Sociology* 4, no. 1 (March 1991): 52–74.

I

Historical Antecedents

1

The Sonoran Migration to California, 1848–1856: A Study in Prejudice

Sister Mary Colette Standart

Although Mexicans did not begin migrating to the United States in great numbers until the late nineteenth century, significant numbers of immigrants and sojourners began to cross the newly established international frontier soon after the American conquest of the Mexican north in 1848. Sister Mary Colette Standart, an historian affiliated with the Dominican College in San Rafael, California, explores the challenges faced by this first group of Mexican migrants in California during the Gold Rush.

Skillfully placing the Sonoran migration in the context of the dizzying social changes that transformed California virtually overnight, Standart demonstrates that the first Mexican migrants to the United States often felt nearly as much prejudice and hostility from the Mexican Californios as they did from the Anglo-American immigrants who poured into the region during the Gold Rush. Both the Californios and the Sonorans would soon discover, however, that most Americans recognized few, if any, meaningful distinctions between them. Thrown together in a volatile sociopolitical milieu in which these migrants were considered inferior aliens by definition, and Mexican Americans were stigmatized and relegated to the lower rungs of the emerging social hierarchy, both groups found themselves defined as outsiders in American society.

By October 1848 miners from Sonora, Mexico, were emigrating in considerable numbers to the Southern Mines of California.[1] The great Sonoran migration of 1848–1856 had begun. This first of a long series of movements north from Mexico to California foreshadowed a century of Mexican migration characterized by social conflict, economic competition, and racial prejudice. The 1848 exodus received its impetus from the discovery of gold in California. Among those attracted by the

From *Southern California Quarterly* 57 (Fall 1976): 333–57. Reprinted by permission of the *Southern California Quarterly*.

discovery were some of the more resourceful and skilled of the Sonoran miners: men who had left a country that deplored their departure for one in which their welcome was less than enthusiastic. They settled first in the area between the Stanislaus and Tuolumne Rivers at the "Sonorian Camp" and then spread throughout the Southern Mines. . . .[2]

It is difficult to determine how many Sonoran '48ers came at this time directly from Mexico and how many from southern California. The great migration got under way in October 1848 when the first organized caravan of *gambusinos* (miners working without capital or assistance) left Hermosillo and when the Mexican newspapers carried the first accounts of the discovery.[3] The news also spread by word of mouth and by letters, such as one written by María Antonia Pico from Monterey, November 14, 1848, to her son Manuel, in Mexico, in which she told him of the discovery at Sutter's Mill, the success of the placers, and the fact that several members of the family had mined with profit during the two months previous.[4]

If the migration started slowly, it soon reached stampede proportions. Janssens, at his ranch near the Santa Inés Mission, saw as many as five hundred travelers some days: Sonorans, Yaquis, foreigners, all going north to the placers; while Moerenhout, from his vantage point in Yerba Buena in late November, estimated the number of immigrants in California, which increased every day, to be between five and six hundred from Lower California and Sonora alone. In January 1849, he stated that more than three thousand Sonorans had already arrived and that more than twenty thousand were expected in April or May.[5]

Moerenhout's estimates seem excessively optimistic, but even during the severe winter of 1848, the exodus from Mexico continued. To Colonel Cave Johnson Couts, writing on December 17 from his camp on the west bank of the Colorado River, it seemed that the whole state of Sonora was on the move. He wrote that he saw Sonorans passing "in gangs" daily, and that they said that they had not yet started.[6] At the same time, Sonoran officials interjected a warning and deplored what they called exaggerated tales from California, which seemed to them to have been written with the express and vicious objective of drawing off Sonora's already scant population.[7]

This movement would, however, not begin to reverse itself effectively until August 1849. For nearly eight months, the great majority of the Sonoran goldseekers traveled north, many of them taking their families with them.[8] As a protection against Indians en route, they went chiefly in caravans which varied in size from groups of thirty or forty to sixty as a general rule. A convoy of seven hundred men, women, and children that General John C. Frémont met near the Colorado River was the exception rather than the rule.[9] In any case, the total numbers were relatively large. By mid-February 1849, Moerenhout wrote that it appeared that the entire population of the northern provinces of Mexico was ready to start for the mines; and by May he stated that in the past two months over ten thousand men, women, and children had passed within a few leagues of Monterey and that more kept coming.[10]

California watched the migration with interest; the Mexican government, with dismay. Governor Manuel María Gándara told the Sonoran Congress at Ures on January 18, 1849, that both the frontier of the state and some places in the interior were being depopulated, that more than a thousand persons had already emigrated to California, and that he estimated that four thousand more would leave within a month.[11] From Hermosillo came official reports that in January and February, one thousand Sonorans had left taking over two thousand animals with them, and later seven hundred persons had come through from other states en route to California.[12] Both interim-governor Juan Bautista Gándara in February, and Governor José de Aguilar in May 1849, issued circular letters deploring the continual threats and the attacks by the Apache on the frontier and pointing out that the problem was compounded by the depopulation resulting from the migration of so many Sonorans to California.[13] In fact, conditions were so bad by May that some towns in Sonora did not have enough adult males in residence to fill the vacancies in municipal offices; while in Altar, town officials could not raise a sufficient force of able-bodied men to punish four American bandits there.[14]

It is easier to determine why the Sonorans left for California than it is to discover exactly how many left. Passports were required for departure, but some emigrants certainly did not obey the regulation.[15] José Velasco, writing in 1850, pointed out that the population of Sonora was diminishing daily due to emigration. He estimated that possibly between five thousand and six thousand, and certainly not less than four thousand, Sonorans had already left.[16] Other estimates, besides Moerenhout's ten thousand from Sonora and Lower California in 1849, include Bayard Taylor's statement that in the summer of 1849, ten thousand Sonorans came into the country in armed bands. Taylor's estimate, as well as those of many Americans in the mines, must be considered with caution since the Yankee often tended to group together all Spanish-speaking foreigners—Spaniards, Peruvians, Chileans, Mexicans—without attempting to identify them. In some cases, native Californians were included in the count.[17]

In any event, a large proportion of the mining population was Sonoran and because the loss of so many of its citizens exacerbated conditions at home, the Mexican press, directly or indirectly, kept up a continuous campaign in 1849–50 aimed at stopping the exodus. They argued that although life in Mexico might be difficult, conditions in California were as bad if not worse. The editors stressed the severity of the California winter, the high cost of living in the diggings, the horror of living in a country without laws or courts, the injustices committed by the American government against foreigners, the difficulty of traveling from place to place in the mines, the prejudice and intolerance towards the Spanish race, the dangers to life and property from flood, fire, and robber, and even the threat from hostile Indians.[18] But in spite of all this adverse publicity, there is little doubt that many Sonorans preferred to take their chances in California rather than face life at home, where they had no reason to believe that conditions would improve. The Mexican press also appealed to its citizens to stay in Sonora and work the rich deposits of gold and silver, which would pay as well or better than those of California and which at the same time would enable the Mexicans to stay close to family and friends while enjoying the protection of their own government.[19] The Sonorans, however, influenced by experience, took a very dim view of what their government could do for them. Neither funds to help fortify the frontier nor an effective armed force ever materialized in spite of the fact that from 1848 throughout 1851 the Mexican Congress repeatedly discussed the problem of the Indian attacks and debated possible solutions.[20]

During this same period, the Sonoran government also attempted to solve the problem by urging its citizens to populate the frontier and by proposing to set up and to support its own military force there.[21] But Sonora was obviously too poor to carry out the plans and, when the California migration reversed itself for a time late in 1849, those returning home found conditions as bad as they had been when they left.[22]

Many Sonorans found it prudent, if not absolutely necessary, to return to Mexico in late 1849. Conditions in California may not have been so uniformly dismal and hopeless as the Mexican press described them, but they were often very bad. Moreover, frequent attacks and continual friction in the mines between Americans and foreigners made life in the diggings uncomfortable, even dangerous, especially for the Spanish-speaking people. The more successful the foreign miner, the more unpopular he became, and the Sonoran was notably successful. In fact, some observers maintained that it was Sonorans who found the best pay dirt, recognized the gold first, and dug up the biggest nuggets.[23] To add insult to injury, they, along with other Mexicans, were accused of carrying the gold out of the country, thus depriving the Americans of their rightful property.[24]

It was a combination of factors, however, that accounted for the reversal of the 1849 migration. Those who had not found much gold, those who had lost their earnings at the gambling tables, those who feared the rigors of a California winter, all headed for home.[25] On the other hand, as Thomas Butler King made clear in his 1850 report to the secretary of state, there was increasing friction and antiforeign activity in the mines, which resulted in the Mexicans' departing in great numbers either through fear or because they had satisfied their cupidity.[26] No doubt industry and perseverance had paid off for many Sonorans who were satisfied enough with their profits to leave the placers for the time being, but the hostility of the Americans was an even more persuasive factor and one which could not be ignored by the majority.[27]

Antiforeign activity was widespread in the Southern Mines by 1849. Coronel (who should have known since he was on the scene in 1848–49 and well aware of conditions both in the Dry Diggings of the Northern Mines and in the Stanislaus placers) stated that the reason for most of the antipathy towards the Spanish-speaking was the fact that they were Sonorans, men used to gold mining and consequently successful. He wrote that in the spring of 1849, notices were posted in the Dry Diggings telling all that were not U.S. citizens to leave the area within twenty-four hours, and that while the eviction was not actually carried out, some of the weak were despoiled of their claims by the stronger.[28] In some other sections of the mines, eviction became a reality. Sonorans were ordered out of the Tuolumne, Stanislaus, and Mokolumne River placers in the summer of 1849, and Bayard Taylor noted that many of the ten thousand Sonorans working in the district left, although some returned as soon as things quieted down.[29] A number of camps in the Southern Mines also passed resolutions ordering Chileans and Mexicans out, but the movement did not reach anything like the proportions that would develop in 1850.[30]

Those Sonorans who were hired to work for Anglo-Americans at this time naturally fared better and were able to mine in relative safety. Frémont, in January 1849, contracted with a group of fifty Sonorans to work his Mariposa mines in return for protection and 50 percent of the gold. The results were excellent and satisfactory to both parties; and when, after several months, the Sonorans wanted to return home, the profits were amicably divided.[31] A similar agreement was made between Thomas Martin and forty Sonorans whom he employed for several months both in the Mariposa mines and in the diggings near Agua Fría.[32] In fact, in the Mokolumne River placers many Americans used Sonorans and Indians to dig for them in return for half the gold and for necessary supplies and provisions. Generally speaking, whether they worked for themselves or for others, the Sonorans do not appear to have fared too badly during their first season in the mines.[33]

As they shuttled between Mexico and California and back again to Mexico, the Sonorans were both exploited and feared. Some of them, without funds and short of supplies, thought nothing of taking whatever they could pick up along the way. From Isaac Williams's well-stocked ranch near Los Angeles, the Sonorans who passed daily to and from the mines habitually stole his horses and ate his bullocks to what amounted to a $50,000 loss between July and the end of 1848. It is not at all strange that Williams reputedly "hated them with a holy hatred."[34] Another victim of their depredations was Thomas Blanco, who had a ranch in the Salinas Valley. While he was away in the mines in the summer of 1849, Sonorans carried off all his vegetables, stole his mules, and threatened his wife and sister.[35] Nor was it uncommon for emigrants who traveled the Gila route to tell of meeting great numbers of Sonorans, some of whom tried to steal their mules and provisions.[36]

On the other hand, as they traveled by the Yuma route across the Colorado River, or along the Camino Real to and from the mines, the Sonorans themselves were frequently victimized by both the Yankee and the Californian. During 1849, a company of American soldiers constructed a rope ferry at the crossing of the Colorado River for the convenience of emigrants whom they charged fifty cents each to cross. But Mexicans, besides paying ferriage, were also required to pay a 10 percent tax on the gold they were taking out of the United States, with a forfeiture of all their gold as a penalty for concealment. In spite of repeated indignant protests on the part of the Mexican press, this practice continued well into 1851.[37]

Nor were the native Californians averse to taking advantage of the situation. To them, the Mexican was of a lower social order, a peon or *cholo*, on whom many Californians looked with contempt. The Sonoran, moreover, was easily identified by his dress, especially by his white trousers; he was consequently nicknamed *calzonero blanco* and considered fair game by the Californian. One of the latter, an alcalde at San Luis Obispo, established himself at a point on the road near the Mission and charged a fifty-cent per capita toll on all Sonorans who passed that way.[38]

As they journeyed back to their homes, either with or without gold, the Sonorans faced serious problems. Those without funds had to shift for themselves even though the Mexican government, as early as August 1849, suggested that, in light of conditions in California developing from hatred of Mexicans, Chileans, and Chinese, the Sonoran government should take the steps to do everything possible to aid its citizens in their efforts to return home—even to subsidizing them if necessary.[39] But Governor Aguilar did not act on the proposal. He pointed out that Sonorans were beginning to return to their families, that about three hundred had already come back, and that others were arriving daily. He added that although there was insecurity and violence in the California placers, most

Sonorans came back satisfied with the bonanza and claimed that only some of the camps were excluding noncitizens. As a result, many intended to go back next season, and Aguilar predicted correctly that the second exodus would be greater than the first.[40]

In the interim, however, Sonora profited by the influx both of manpower and of gold. By the end of 1849, conservative estimates put the number of returnees at approximately twenty-four hundred persons, who probably brought back with them over 2 million pesos in gold.[41] As a result, Sonora's chronically depressed economy got a real, albeit temporary, lift not only from the added wealth but also from the return of so many of the emigrants. They included her ablest, most enterprising, and hard-working citizens, who, upon returning, engaged in farming, commerce, or industry for a season at least.[42]

The prosperity was temporary, however, since the Sonoran miners planned from the beginning to return to the California bonanza, either with or without their families.[43] The climate of opinion must have been influenced in part by the obvious success of so many who had taken part in the first migration. But it was certainly also clear to many that it was still futile to expect real and lasting improvement in conditions at home. The total picture was particularly bleak in 1850: Sonora was plagued not only by Indian attacks but also by a severe cholera epidemic, by high prices, and by the machinations of a dishonest judiciary and an unstable government.[44]

In 1850, the hazardous conditions on the northern boundary were aggravated by the constant Indian raids and by the fact that Anglo-American emigrants on their way to California at times joined the Apache in plundering isolated and defenseless frontier settlements.[45] Nor were conditions any better in the interior where the Indians attacked continually, levying contributions on the smaller pueblos and on unprotected ranches and haciendas. By late 1850 all the haciendas between the Sonoran capitals, Ures and Hermosillo, had been destroyed, the inhabitants murdered, the cattle carried off, and the few troops in the district helpless to take any effective action since they had no cavalry support.[46]

To make matters worse, the severe cholera epidemic of 1849 continued into 1850, and although it lessened temporarily by April, some Sonorans left for California hoping to escape its ravages.[47] Moreover, excessively high prices, especially for meat, and generally great dissatisfaction with the administration of justice also caused repeated protests.[48] Since conditions did not improve, the migration continued, and by April, the 1850 exodus had already exceeded the totals of the whole previous migration. As a result, the Sonoran authorities continually deplored the situation. They were especially aroused when *El Sonorense* published the official emigration figures from the towns of Ures, Arizpe, Hermosillo, San Ignacio, and Montezuma, listing a total exodus of 5,893 of which 99 were women and 100, children.[49]

It was, of course, almost impossible for the Sonoran government to check on those citizens who left the state without passports, but in the spring of 1850 the legislature made an attempt to stop the practice. A decree was promulgated stating that anyone who left without official papers would lose citizenship rights, be excluded from all public employment or office, and be deprived of all legal rights. He would, however, still be required to bear arms and to pay taxes.[50] This order was naturally difficult to implement: Sonora had an unstable and inept government at best, and in the early 1850s it was occupied with power struggles among political factions; moreover, the immigration of 1850 involved not hundreds, but thousands of its citizens. An American, who arrived in California in May, reported that the accounts of the numbers leaving Sonora were not exaggerated. He himself had passed thousands on the road, and he added that many towns in northern Mexico were completely deserted.[51] These figures are supported by the 1850 San Pedro Memorial to the U.S. Congress petitioning that a customhouse be established at San Pedro since at least ten thousand Sonorans passed through Los Angeles on their way to the mines each spring, generally returning to Mexico in the fall.[52]

In light of all this, it is not at all strange that the extreme nativism that developed in the Southern Mines early in 1850 was especially directed against the Spanish Americans. They were numerous, relatively aggressive and successful, and increasingly competitive. The Sonorans were particularly unpopular since they were not only everywhere, but doing everything: mining, freighting, selling goods and supplies, and generally offering very real competition in both trading and mining.[53] As a result, as the mines became more crowded and it became increasingly difficult to find gold easily, a very real xenophobia, directed at first against the Spanish-speaking people, developed not only among the Americans but among other foreigners as well.[54] Irish, English, Australians, even the Germans who could scarcely speak intelligible English, all attacked the Spanish-speaking miners.[55] To many, the mining population at this time was either "greaser" or "gringo," and the tendency was to place all Spaniards and Latin Americans in the "greaser" category and most of the others in the "gringo."[56]

If exploitation of Latin American miners had been the keynote in 1849, eviction and expulsion became more and more common in 1850. Sonorans, who were already frequently victimized by American miners as well as by much adverse local legislation, were especially affected by the Foreign Miners' Tax law of April 1850. The law, which made specific reference to "culprits of Mexico and South American states," levied a tax of twenty dollars a month on noncitizens who engaged in mining in California.[57] Although both Americans and foreigners protested the law as illegal, unjust, and exorbitant, it was upheld by the California court, and as soon as tax collectors appeared in the diggings, trouble began in the Tuolumne placers where the Sonorans were concentrated.

In May 1850, large numbers of Mexicans, Chileans, and some French were mining near Sonora and Columbia. Hoping to avert enforcement of the law, some of them marched in a body to Sonora in an attempt to influence the tax collector, Lorenzo A. Besancon, to consider something more reasonable than the twenty-dollar tax.[58] They failed to reach an amicable agreement, and their show of force at Sonora on May 19, and at Columbia the day following, roused the Americans to action. The latter professed to believe that an insurrection was threatening, and since the majority of the Americans were U.S. citizens who had the support of the authorities and of the law, the foreigners accomplished nothing. Those who persisted in refusing to pay a tax they rightly considered unreasonable were ordered out of the mines. Many of them packed what they could carry and left at once, some for home, some to find employment with Americans, while some scattered throughout the countryside, where they became outlaws or bandits.[59]

Those Sonorans who were forced out of the Southern Mines in the summer of 1850 took the river route from Stockton to San Francisco or traveled south by the overland trails, crossing the river ferries at the Stanislaus, Tuolumne, and the San Joaquin. The Stockton waterfront was crowded with Mexicans, Sonorans, and Chileans who left in companies of twenty to fifty men, and, in at least one case, a group of one hundred Sonorans and other Mexicans purchased a schooner to take them and their families home.[60] Perkins and others maintained that about five hundred Sonorans left the Sonora-Columbia area at that time.[61] In fact, by August, between fifteen and twenty thousand Mexicans were reported to have left the diggings, either to avoid paying the tax or because they were being run out by those who accused them of responsibility for the crimes being committed throughout the Southern Mines.[62] Enos Christman, a resident of Sonora, estimated that by August, three-fourths of the Mexicans who had been working in the district had returned to their homes in Sonora, Mexico, with rather a bad opinion of the Yankees. But he also pointed out that Americans were similarly prejudiced against Sonorans due to the murders and robberies attributed to bands of Mexican guerrillas.[63]

There is no doubt that some of the Mexicans and Chileans, resentful of the injuries they had suffered and angered at the loss of their claims and property, took to the hills and became outlaws. During the summer and fall of 1850, they carried on a reign of terror, robbing travelers, attacking isolated claims and camps, and often murdering those who offered resistance.[64] In July 1850, Sonora (California) reported numberless robberies as well as twenty murders committed within the space of twenty-five days. Most of the crime was attributed to Mexicans and Chileans.[65] On the other hand, lawless elements among the "gringos" took advantage of the situation, formed armed bands, attacked "greasers" wherever they could be found, and ran them out of the country. Frequently too, late in the season, the most peaceful Mexicans, working quietly and in possession of a legal license, had their claims jumped by Americans who were finding it difficult to strike pay dirt through their own efforts.[66]

In spite of abuse, injustice, and outright persecution, some Sonorans refused to leave the mining region at a time when the diggings were still paying so well. A considerable number hired out to Americans as day workers in return for protection and wages.[67] Others continued to come into the country from Mexico. They refused to be intimidated by the accounts of mistreatment, eviction, and loss of arms and property reported by their countrymen, or by the knowledge that even payment of the license tax might not guarantee their rights.[68] William Hutton met large numbers of miners from Sonora, Mexico, near San Luis Obispo in May 1850. They were en route to the placers, determined to defy the American authorities even to [the point of] refusing to pay the twenty-dollar tax.[69] At McLean's Ferry, not far from Sonora, forty to fifty Mexicans were crossing daily by the end of August, and foreigners continued to pour into Tuolumne County from San José and from southern California.[70] The *Stockton Times* noted that up to August 15, the ferry crossings of the Stanislaus, Tuolumne, and San Joaquin Rivers reported that the numbers leaving the mines exceeded those coming in, but that after that date the reverse was true and the crossing was almost entirely towards the mines.[71] Some of those who left, of course, never returned, and to the chagrin of the Americans, they took considerable gold out of the country with them.[72]

Not all Americans, however, were unfriendly to foreigners in California, nor were all in agreement with the foreign miners' tax policy adopted by the state legislature. Some felt that the policy would jeopardize American interests and in the long run do more harm than good. This judgment was supported by a letter written from Mexico City on September 25, 1850. The writer stated that a great many Sonorans had already returned from California with considerable wealth and that the foreign miners' tax had actually benefited Mexico doubly: the bad characters had stayed in California; the good, hardworking Sonorans had returned home.[73]

Although a small group of Americans felt that the Mexicans should be allowed to work unmolested, that they were a good, peaceful, industrious people, the majority of those who defended their rights were moved by economic self-interest.[74] Merchants, traders, gamblers, and saloon keepers all felt the consequences of a decline in business and a loss of revenue.[75] In May 1850, shortly before the foreign miners' tax went into effect, Tuolumne City on the San Joaquin River was carrying on a prosperous trade with Sonorans who were crossing the ferry there by the hundreds.[76] By the end of the month, however, Stockton merchants, as well as those in the Tuolumne mining towns, were complaining of a drastic decline in business—complaints that would continue until the repeal of the tax in March 1851.[77] But both as a source of revenue and as a solution to the problem of foreign competition in the mines, the tax was a relative failure and the repeal actually did little to improve the situation.

Several other factors also helped to account for the decline and end of the first great Sonoran migration. Sonorans, both in California and in Mexico, were aware of the increasing hostility of the Yankee; at the same time, they suspected that the mines were beginning to pay less and to require hard work and expensive machinery.[78] By 1851–52, moreover, there were definite indications that the Mexican government was, at long last, beginning to take some real and effective action against the Indians, and that a genuine attempt was being made to colonize the frontier areas.[79] As a result, many Sonorans returned to Mexico determined this time to stay.[80]

The great migration was practically over by the spring of 1851, although some Sonorans continued to come into the Southern Mines either to hire out as day laborers or to work the quartz mines or to obtain grazing or farm lands.[81] In March 1851, the *Alta California* reported that eight thousand Sonorans had reached Los Angeles ready to migrate to the Southern Mines; the following month the editor noted that ten thousand Mexicans had arrived in the Mariposa and Tuolumne regions.[82] In 1852, a large group of Sonorans [was] causing trouble in the Merced River placers near Agua Fría, and the following April, Judge Benjamin Hayes noted that twelve hundred Sonorans were expected to pass through Los Angeles headed for the mines.[83] Even as late as 1854–55, if reports from Los Angeles are accurate, Sonorans, still trying to escape the Apache, continued into the Southern Mines in a steady stream.[84] But by late 1855, the migration had slowed almost to a halt. A good number of the Sonorans who left the placers at this time returned to Mexico; others settled in the area in and around Los Angeles, where there was still a Latin American majority. There they worked as domestics, vaqueros, tradesmen, gamblers, or at anything that came to hand.[85]

There was in 1855–56, however, at least one fairly well-publicized attempt on the part of the Californians themselves to establish an organization to aid destitute Sonorans and dissatisfied Californians by subsidizing their emigration to Sonora, Mexico. "The Society for the Promotion of the Emigration of Native Californians to Sonora" held its first meeting at the St. Francis Hotel in San Francisco on February 7, 1855.[86] Ex-governor Juan Bautista Alvarado presided. The secretary, Francisco Casanueva, noted that the organization proposed to help Sonorans, as well as Californians, emigrate to Mexico. For that purpose, the society planned to send Don José Islas, a native of Mazatlán and an unsuccessful California miner, to Mexico City and to Sonora to negotiate for a land grant in Sonora, for supplies, and for privileges for settlers.[87]

The colonization society got off to a slow start. The organizing junta was primarily interested in the problems, not of the Mexican miners, but of the Californian rancheros whose complaints stemmed from disputed land titles, the squatter invasion of their property, the law's delay, heavy taxes, and other oppressive acts.[88] But in spite of their dissatisfaction, most Californians were averse to joining the movement. Some, like Andrés Pico, were holding public office and felt a consequent loyalty to the United States; others wanted to remain on their native soil at any cost.[89] By August 1855, however, Islas had successfully negotiated with the Mexican government for a grant of land in Sonora with the subsoil rights. He had also obtained a promise from Ures of a donation of wheat and cattle, and from a "wealthy citizen" of northern Mexico, a loan of money.[90]

Nevertheless, Islas had trouble finding emigrants ready and willing to join his movement. When in May 1856, two months or more behind schedule, he finally led a small group of would-be settlers from San José to Los Angeles, he did so hoping that more would join his colony in the south.[91] But shrewd and knowledgeable Californians were quick to point out that Mexico would not be able to support a colony and that ubiquitous Apache and the undisciplined military would continue to offer problems to settlers in Sonora. They also reminded the emigrants that Los Angeles had always been the asylum of the inhabitants of Sonora and that Sonorans would do better to stay there rather than leave the country.[92] On the other hand, *El Clamor Público* admitted that Los Angeles in the late 1850s was not the whole answer to the Sonorans' problems: a double standard of justice oppressed Latin Americans there as well as in the mines; they were often falsely accused, victims of prejudice, and misunderstood.[93] But in spite of all the pressure from vigilantes, from indifferent justice, and from the depression and bad times following 1855, very few Sonorans or Californians joined the Islas colony.[94]

Although organized emigration did nothing to solve the problems facing the Latin Americans at this time, American antagonism towards those still in the Southern Mines lessened considerably. Their numbers had decreased to such an extent that they had ceased to offer real economic competition in the diggings. As early as 1852 there was a growing antipathy towards the Chinese in the mines; and from that time on, discrimination was directed against them rather than at the Spanish-speaking. Those Sonorans who had not returned to Mexico or settled in southern California began to mine for wages or continued to operate mule freight lines or hired out as mule drivers for Americans.[95] They no longer competed directly for a major share of the mineral wealth. And, more importantly, as far as Mexico was concerned, her citizens were no longer migrating to the mining regions of California in great numbers.

Notes

1. Antonio F. Coronel, "Cosas de California," MS, Bancroft Library (hereafter cited as BL), Berkeley (México, D.F., 1938), 238; Walter Colton, *California Diary* (Oakland, 1948), 162, 166; Eduardo Villa, *Compéndio de historia del estado de Sonora* (México, D.F., 1938), 238.

2. *San Francisco Alta California* (hereafter cited as *AC*), May 13, July 2, 1849; Thomas Butler King, "California: The Wonder of the Age," in Bayard Taylor, *Eldorado, or, Adventures in the Path of Empire* (2 vols. New York, 1850), 2: 237; Thomas R. Stoddart, *Annals of Tuolumne County*, ed. Carlo M. De Ferrari (Sonora, CA, 1963), 54; Jonas Winchester to Susan Winchester, August 25, 1850, Letters, California Historical Society Library, San Francisco.

3. José Francisco Velasco, *Notícias estadísticas del estado de Sonora* (México, D.F., 1850), 281; Villa, *Compéndio de historia*, 238; *El Siglo XIX* (México, D.F.), October 24, 1848.

4. María Antonia Pico to Manuel Pico, in "Documentos para la historia de California," MS, BL, 1: no. 505.

5. Augustín Janssens, *The Life and Adventures of Don Augustín Janssens*, ed. William H. Ellison and Francis Price (San Marino, 1953), 143; A. P. M. Nasatir, trans. and ed., "French Consulate in California, 1843–1856," *California Historical Society Quarterly* 13 (March 1934): 275–76; Thomas Larkin to Faxon Dean Atherton, 19 January 1848. Larkin writes that he believes that ten thousand will come from Sonora, Mexico, alone and about six thousand from the rest of Mexico. *The Larkin Papers*, ed. George P. Hammond (10 vols.; Berkeley, 1951–1960), 8: 103.

6. Cave Johnson Couts, diary, December 17, 1848, BL, 113. Although some Sonorans came by sea, the majority traveled overland along the old Anza trail, which was in common use by Mexicans in the 1850s. *AC*, July 2, 1849; Charles Lambertie, *Voyage pittoresque en Californie et au Chile* (Paris, 1853), 258; Jack Forbes, "Development of the Yuma Route before 1846," *California Historical Society Quarterly* 43 (June 1964): 111–13.

7. *El Sonorense*, December 22, 1848.

8. Ibid.

9. Jessie Benton Frémont and Francis Preston Frémont, "Great Events During the Life of Major General John C. Frémont . . . and of Jessie Benton Frémont," MS, BL, 1891, 97. See also *AC*, May 13, 1849. *El Universal*, June 5, 1849, mentions a caravan of four hundred persons near Altar.

10. Nasatir, "French Consulate," 356, 363. Many of the parties were made up of Mexican peons grouped together under a patron who paid their expenses in route in exchange for half the profits in the mines. Frémont, "Great Events," 97; Carl Meyer, *Bound for Sacramento* (Claremont, CA, 1938), 73–74; Coronel, "Cosas," 152; Couts, diary, 117; Samuel A. Damon, *A Journey to Lower Oregon and Upper California: 1848–1849* (San Francisco, 1927), 72; Daniel Woods, *Sixteen Months in the Gold Diggins* (New York, 1851), 47.

11. *El Sonorense*, February 2, 1849.

12. Ibid., March 2, 1849.

13. Alphonse Pinart, "Colección de documentos impresos y manuscritos de los estados del norte de México," MS, BL, 2: 995, 1012; *El Universal*, February 13, April 13, 1849.

14. *El Sonorense*, May 4, June 15, 1849; *El Universal*, July 13, 1849.

15. Hubert Howe Bancroft, *History of the Northern Mexican States and Texas* (2 vols.; San Francisco, 1889), 2: 671n. *El Sonorense* lists a total of 737 passports issued in seven Sonoran towns between February and April 1849. It is interesting to note that the great majority of the applicants described themselves as day laborers or field workers and that relatively few identified themselves as miners. *El Sonorense*, March 7, 23, 28, 30, April 15, May 11, 1849.

16. Velasco, *Notícias*, 289, 295.

17. Taylor, *Eldorado*, 1: 102; *AC*, May 13, June 21, July 2, 1849. See also William Perkins, *Three Years in California: William Perkins' Journal of Life at Sonora, 1849–1852*, ed. Dale Morgan and James Scobie (Berkeley, 1964), 143. Mario Vallejo noted that Americans tended to classify as Chileans anyone who came into California by boat from Valparaíso. Mariano G. Vallejo, "Recuerdos históricos y personales tocante a la Alta California . . . , MS, BL, 1875, 5: 22–223.

18. *El Universal*, January 22, 26, February 14, March 4, 15, May 3, 16, 22, 24, June 5, 20, August 25, 1849; April 24, May 24, July 18, August 4, 27, 1850; *El Siglo XIX*, January 16, July 25, August 27, 1850; *El Sonorense*, May 2, June 22, 1849; *La Palanca* (México, D.F.), June 24, September 4, 1849; February 14, 1850.

19. *El Universal*, January 26, 31, February 14, March 11, 15, 1849; *El Sonorense*, June 29, 1849; *El Siglo XIX*, February 5, June 9, August 9, 16, 1850.

20. Vicente Manero, *Documentos interesantes sobre colonización* (México, D.F., 1878), 36; *La Palanca*, March 9, 12, 14, 16, 1850; *El Universal*, November 25, 1848; April 27, November 2, 1849; March 28, April 3, July 18, September 4, 8, 10, 1850; *El Siglo XIX*, July 30, 1850.

21. *El Sonorense*, April 19, October 25, 1850; *El Siglo XIX*, June 9, 1850.

22. *El Sonorense*, April 22, 1848; March 28, 1849; *El Siglo XIX*, February 5, 8, March 10, 1850; Velasco, *Notícias*, 315.

23. Colton, *California Diary*, 131, 157, 174; Friedrich Gerstacker, *Gerstacker's Travels* (London, 1854), 207; *Stockton Times*, March 16, 1850; Lewis R. Price, "Mazatlán to the Estanislao," ed. W. Turrentine Jackson, *California Historical Society Quarterly* 39 (March 1960): 46. In October 1849, Price was at Wood's Creek in the Southern Mines, where he observed that the adventurers from Sonora (Mexico) were more successful than any other miners, since they had been accustomed from infancy to life among the "placers."

24. Colton, *California Diary*, 203. Colton, among others, maintained that relatively little gold left California in the hands of Sonorans. In May 1849 he wrote, "I have been in a camp of five hundred Sonorans, who had not gold enough to

buy a month's provisions—all had gone, through their improvident habits, to the capacious pockets of the Americans." Ibid. See also *AC*, May 31, 1849; *El Siglo XIX*, September 12, 1849; Lambertie, *Voyage pittoresque*, 258; Perkins, *Three Years*, 118, 213; Theodore Johnson, *California and Oregon, or Sights in the Gold Region* (Philadelphia, 1851), 179–80; Thomas Allsop, *California and Its Gold Mines* (London, 1853), 80.

25. *El Universal*, June 12, 1849; *El Siglo XIX*, September 12, October 29, December 25, 1849; Perkins, *Three Years*, 107.

26. King, "California," 2: 244.

27. *AC*, July 26, August 2, October 1, 25, 1849; Johnson, *California and Oregon*, 225; Damon, *Journey*, 72; J. D. Borthwick, *Three Years in California* (Oakland, 1948), 312.

28. Coronel, "Cosas," 166, 169.

29. Taylor, *Eldorado*, 1: 102.

30. Lambertie, *Voyage pittoresque*, 259; *AC*, July 26, October 1, 25, 1849; Charles A. Kirkpatrick, journal, October 14, 18, 1849, MS, BL. Robert McKane at Big Bar on the Mokolumne acted as chairman of a miners' meeting which drew up resolutions ordering all Mexicans to cease mining there. In retrospect, McKune found the action regrettable as one against "a laborious and peaceful people." *Pioneer and Historical Review*, December 29, 1877.

31. Frémont, "Great Events," 97, 125.

32. Thomas Martin, "Narrative of John C. Frémont's Expedition to California, 1845–1846 and Subsequent Events in California to 1853," MS, BL, 1878, 54.

33. Taylor, *Eldorado*, 1: 87, 102; *El Sonorense*, October 26, 1849. See also *El Universal* for June 12, 1849, which reported that some Mexicans were writing from the Stanislaus placer complaining of scant returns and of much hard work, but that the greater number of Sonorans who wrote from there spoke of California in much more favorable terms than did the Guadalajarans.

34. Couts, diary, January 8, 1849.

35. Taylor, *Eldorado*, 1: 133.

36. Ibid., 1: 151. With the reputation that Sonorans had in southern California, it is not surprising that many believed the report circulating in August 1849 that Sonorans, in revenge for being turned out of the mines, were about to attack under the leadership of General José Urrea and kill all the Americans in Los Angeles. William R. Hutton, *Glances at California, 1847–1853* (San Marino, 1942), 30. See also *San Francisco Daily California Courier*, September 13, 1850.

37. C. E. Pancoast, *A Quaker Forty-niner* (Philadelphia, 1930), 254–55, 258; *El Sonorense*, November 22, 1850; *El Siglo XIX*, December 25, 1850; Cave Johnson Couts, *From San Diego to the Colorado in 1849: The Journal and Maps of J. Cave Couts* (Los Angeles, 1932), 47–48.

38. J. M. Guinn, "The Sonoran Migration," *Historical Society of Southern California Annual, VIII* (1909–1911): 32.

39. *El Sonorense*, October 26, 1849.

40. Ibid. See also Alphonse Pinart, "Documents for the History of Sonora," MS, BL, 4: 174–75. Velasco, who agreed with Aguílar, wrote in 1850 that of 4,000 Sonorans who went to California, at least 2,667 returned intending to remain at home, but they changed their minds and decided to go back with their families. Consequently, Velasco predicted that the second migration would be greater than the first; Velasco, *Notícias*, 295.

41. Ibid., 290, 295. In 1850, Velasco stated that between August and the beginning of December 1849, between 2 and 3 million pesos of gold were brought into Sonora, Mexico, the result of only a little more than three months' work. Most authorities agree with these figures although it is impossible to discover exactly how much gold was smuggled in. Villa stated that 2,400 Sonorans returned with 2,337,080 pesos in gold. *Compéndio de historica*, 239. *El Sonorense* of January 18, 1850, concluded that 2 million pesos of gold had been brought into Sonora from California. Bayard Taylor observed that although the Sonorans left great amounts at the gambling tables, they took back home with them $5 million in gold. *Eldorado*, 1: 87. See also *El Siglo XIX*, October 29, December 25, 1849.

42. Villa, *Compéndio de historia*, 239; *El Universal*, September 11, 1849.

43. *El Siglo XIX*, February 5, 1850.

44. Ibid., February 5, June 23, 1850; May 23, 1851.

45. William Manning, ed., *Diplomatic Correspondence of the United States Inter-American Affairs* (Washington, DC, 1937), 9: 355.

46. *San Francisco Daily Pacific News*, October 11, 1850, which quotes a Mexico City correspondent. See also *San Francisco Evening Picayune*, December 2, 1850, for another letter from Mexico City dated November 4, 1850, which stated that the greater part of the area of Sonora under Indian attack was inhabited only by women, since the men had gone to California.

47. *El Siglo XIX*, June 27, 30, 1850.

48. Ibid., June 23, 1850.

49. *El Sonorense*, April 26, 1850. In evaluating these statistics, it is pertinent to note that Arizpe lost 941 citizens at this time and that, ten years previously, Duflot de Mofras had found there a population of only fifteen hundred already decreasing due to Indian raids and emigration. Duflot de Mofras, *Travels on the Pacific Coast*, ed. Marguerite Wilbur (2 vols.; Santa Ana, 1937), 1: 107. Even more striking is the report of John Audubon, who in his journal for August 22, 1849, noted that Ures, the capital at that time, was no more than an adobe village with a governor, some soldiers, and about four thousand Indians. John W. Audubon, *Western Journal, 1849–1850* (Cleveland, 1906), 139. *El Sonorense* of April 26, 1850, noted the departure of 1,606 from Ures.

50. *El Universal*, May 26, 1850.

51. *Stockton Times*, May 11, 1850.

52. Guinn, "Sonoran Migration," 33.

53. *Stockton Times*, May 11, 1850; Perkins, *Three Years*, 147; Narciso Botello, "Anales del sur de California," MS, BL, 1878, 175; *El Siglo XIX*, January 16, June 28, 1850; William Shaw, *Golden Dreams and Walking Realities* (London, 1851), 147. See also a letter to Peter Burnett from Chileans, Sonorans, and other Mexicans of Jesus Maria, Calaveras County, May 1, 1850, Burnett Letters, MS, California Historical Society Library (hereafter cited as CHSL); Eugene Upton, "Letter to the Boston Traveller," June 12, 1850, Scrapbook No. 7, CHSL. There are repeated references to the fact that Sonorans were very numerous in the Southern Mines. At times they were listed separately from other Mexicans, but it is possible that some Americans used the terms "Sonoran," "Sonoranian," and "Sonorense" loosely and applied them to all Mexicans. A. Lascy, "Sketches of the Early History of Calaveras County," May 1850, MS, BL.

54. *AC*, May 28, 1850; *Stockton Times*, July 30, 1850. The antiforeign resolutions adopted at Sonora (California) on July 21, 1850, referred specifically to

"the peons of Mexico, the renegades of South America, and the criminals of the British Empire." Herbert Lang, *A History of Tuolumne County* (San Francisco, 1882), 44–45.

55. Zoeth Skinner Eldredge, *The Beginnings of San Francisco from the Expedition of Anza, 1774 to the City Charter of April 15, 1850* (5 vols.; New York, 1912), 3: 706.

56. Perkins, *Three Years*, 143–44, 222; Frank Marryat, *Mountains and Molehills, or Recollection of a Burnt Journal* (New York, 1855), 236, 293–94.

57. Statutes of California, 1st sess. (San Jose, 1850), 221.

58. Stoddart, *Annals*, 133, n. 1; Perkins, *Three Years*, 153–55. Besancon sent Governor Burnett a brief account of the events of May 19 in Sonora. He pointed out that a tax of ten or twelve dollars would have been more equitable and would have realized greater revenue. Besancon to Burnett, May 22, 1850, Burnett Letters, CHSL. See also *AC*, July 10, 1850; George Jewett, journal, 1849, MS, BL, 28.

59. Stoddart concluded that three-fourths of the foreign population left when the tax went into effect and that Sonora never really recovered from the loss. *Annals*, 131. Columbia was practically deserted by June 1850. *Stockton Times*, June 22, 1850. See also Edmund Booth, *Edmund Booth, Forty-niner* (Stockton, 1953), 27; *AC*, August 9, 1850; *El Sonorense*, September 20, 1850; *San Francisco Daily Pacific News*, August 28, 1850.

60. *Stockton Times*, July 20, 1850.

61. Perkins and others estimated that five hundred Sonorans left for Mexico at the time. Perkins, *Three Years*, 156; *Alta California*, June 3, 1850.

62. *San Francisco Evening Picayune*, October 14, 1850; J. Heckendorn and W. A. Wilson, *Miners and Business Men's Directory* (Columbia, 1856), 183. The directory noted that one-half to three-fourths of the Mexicans had left by September 1850.

63. Enos Christman, *One Man's Gold, the Letters and Journal of a Forty-niner* (New York, 1930), 173, 183.

64. Riley Senter to his cousin, July 7, 1850, Letters, BL; Booth, *Edmund Booth*, 27; *AC*, July 10, 1850; *Daily California Courier*, July 27, 1850.

65. Ibid. See also Stoddart, *Annals*, 139. Carlo De Ferrari states that the attacks by Mexican outlaws following the enactment of the foreign miners' tax were unequalled at any other time in the Tuolumne Diggings. Ibid., 145, n. 4.

66. *San Francisco Daily Pacific News*, November 20, 1850; Manning, *Diplomatic Correspondence*, 9: 129, 133, 153, 346, 432, 568. There were repeated protests on the part of the Mexican government regarding the treatment of its nationals in the California mines. Perkins felt that the crimes committed by Americans were actually more numerous and more outrageous than those of the Mexicans. *Three Years*, 175.

67. Woods, *Sixteen Months*, 59; *Daily California Courier*, October 18, 1850; *Stockton San Joaquin Republican*, October 4, 1851.

68. *Marysville Herald*, August 30, 1850; *El Sonorense*, August 16, September 13, 1850; *AC*, August 19, 1850. March 7, 1851; Jewett, journal, 29.

69. Hutton, *Glances*, 44. Benjamin Deane, who was mining on the Tuolumne River in May, saw great numbers of Sonorans crossing at the ferry near Merced City. Benjamin Deane, journal, May 1850, MS BL.

70. *AC*, September 2, 1850.

71. *Stockton Times*, September 21, 1850.

72. Ernest de Massey, *A Frenchman in the Gold Rush*, ed. Marguerite Wilbur (San Francisco, 1927), 153; *AC*, October 21, 1850.

73. Ibid.; *El Siglo XIX*, September 25, 1850. Mexican accounts naturally place the blame for the trouble on Yankee greed, which was attempting to eliminate all competition by means of the tax and by slandering persons of Spanish origin. Ibid., August 26, September 17, 1850.

74. *Stockton Times*, August 3, 1850; *AC*, August 19, 1850; *Daily California Courier*, November 21, 1850; Jewett, journal, 27; Thomas Wiggins et al. to Burnett, May 1, 1850, Burnett Letters, CHSL.

75. *Stockton Times*, May 25, June 1, 22, 1850; Christman, *One Man's Gold*, 178. The *AC* for January 26, 1851, noted that if had not been for the tax on foreign miners, which had driven off ten to fifteen thousand Mexicans, the gambling establishments of Stockton would flourish.

76. *Stockton Times*, May 11, 1850.

77. *AC*, March 7, 15, 21, 1851; *Stockton Times*, May 24, 25, June 8, 22, 27, 29, August 3, 10, November 23, 1850; March 5, 8, 12, 15, 20, 22, 1851. For the act repealing for foreign miners' tax see *Statutes of California*, 2nd sess. (1851), 424.

78. *El Sonorense*, August 16, September 16, 1850; *El Siglo XIX*, August 26, September 17, 1850; *AC*, May 29, November 2, 1850; *San Francisco Evening Picayune*, November 16, 1850; Perkins, *Three Years*, 181; William Downie, *Hunting for Gold: Reminiscences of Personal Experiences* (San Francisco, 1893), 81. See also William Town Smith to Burnett, in which Smith writing from Double Springs in the Southern Mines on November 4, 1850, informed the governor that numbers of foreigners who had conformed with the requirements of the law had been prevented from mining (Burnett Letters, CHSL).

79. *El Siglo XIX*, January 2, 19, March 11, 1851; *San Joaquin Republican*, June 7, 1851; September 22, 1852; *AC*, June 8, August 28, 1852.

80. *El Siglo XIX*, September 7, October 4, 11, 25, 1850; *La Voz del Pueblo* (Ures, Sonora), July 23, September 10, 1851; *San Joaquin Republican*, September 23, 1852.

81. Jonas Winchester, Diary, June 13, 1851, MS, CHSL.

82. *AC*, March 17, April 21, 1851.

83. *Pioneer and Historical Review*, March 24, 1877; *Stockton Journal*, June 29, July 23, 1852; *San Joaquin Republican*, June 30, 1852; Benjamin Hayes, "Notes on California Affairs, A Chronicle, 1769–1861," April 16, 1853, MS, BL, Folder No. 8.

84. *San Joaquin Republican*, May 9, 1854; February 11, 1855; *AC*, November 27, 1855; *San Francisco Daily Herald and Mirror*, November 7, 1854.

85. *Los Angeles El Clamor Público*, May 17, 1856.

86. *San Francisco Daily Herald and Mirror*, February 9, 1855; *Sacramento Union*, February 12, 1855.

87. *Los Angeles El Clamor Público*, October 23, 1855; *San Joaquin Republican*, January 25, March 14, 1855.

88. *San Francisco Daily Herald and Mirror*, February 9, 1855; *Sacramento Union*, February 12, 1855.

89. Andrés Pico to Juan Bautista Alvarado, March 3, 1855, in "Documents for the History of California," MS, BL, 49: 381; *AC*, March 8, 1855.

90. *Los Angeles El Clamor Público*, February 16, 1856.

91. Ibid., June 15, 1855; May 10, 1856.

92. *Los Angeles El Clamor Público*, May 17, 24, 1856.
93. Ibid., August 7, September 11, 1855.
94. Ibid., May 1, 1856.
95. Perkins, *Three Years*, 147; *Hutchings California Illustrated Magazine* 1 (December 1856): 114.

2

Always the Laborer, Never the Citizen: Anglo Perceptions of the Mexican Immigrant during the 1920s

Mark Reisler

The intensity of the current debate over Mexican immigration often makes it seem as if the controversy is of very recent origin. However, as independent historian Mark Reisler makes clear, most of the dimensions of the contemporary public debate were already in place by the 1910s and 1920s. Exploring the origins and early evolution of the discussion over what was commonly referred to in the 1920s as the "Mexican Problem," Reisler helps to explain why so many Mexicans were encouraged to enter the United States during a period in which other "undesirable" national groups were systematically barred from immigrating.

In recounting the saga of the peopling of the United States, historians have tended to focus on the movement of people across the Atlantic and neglect another significant aspect of American immigration: the migration of workers across the Rio Grande. Perhaps as much as 10 percent of Mexico's population, approximately one and a half million people, trekked northward to the United States between 1900 and 1930.[1] Only in the past few years have such scholars as Rodolfo Acuña and Matt Meier and Feliciano Rivera, in their surveys of Chicano history, and Abraham Hoffman and Mercedes Carreras de Velasco, in their monographs on repatriation during the Great Depression, begun to delve into the history of the Mexican immigrant in the twentieth century.[2] While these scholars and others have noted in a general way the attitudes of Americans toward Mexicans, we still do not have a detailed inquiry into the nature of Anglo perceptions of Mexican immigrants during the 1920s, the decade when

From *Pacific Historical Review* 45, no. 2 (May 1976): 231–54. © 1976 by the Pacific Coast Branch of the American Historical Association. Reprinted by permission of the University of California Press Journals.

the political controversy over Mexican immigration reached fever pitch. Based upon opinions expressed in the periodical press, in congressional hearings, and in heretofore untapped archival material, this study attempts to explore systematically how Americans, both those favoring and those opposing unrestricted entry, viewed Mexican workers. In addition, this investigation analyzes the manner in which popular perceptions of this immigrant group were translated into public policy as well as the role pressure groups played in influencing federal action on the Mexican immigration issue.

Major Mexican immigration began shortly after the turn of the century, a result of the pull of attractive American wages and the push of Mexican poverty. The arrival of Mexican workers took place very quietly. Of all the non-Anglo-Saxon groups entering the United States in large numbers, Mexicans were probably the most inconspicuous. At first they were obscured not only by the huddled masses landing at Ellis Island but also by the location of their employment opportunities in the Southwest, where they were hidden from sight in the boxcars, tents, and shacks of railroad and migrant farm labor camps.

After World War I, however, Mexican immigration became more visible as the number of legal entrants increased dramatically to a peak of about ninety thousand during fiscal year 1924.[3] But Immigration Bureau figures tell only a fraction of the story, for those statistics do not include a large but undeterminable number of Mexicans who entered surreptitiously in order to evade literacy tests, head taxes, and visa fees. The large number of legal and illegal immigrants were now coming in response to the demands of southwestern farmers and midwestern industrialists. By the early 1920s Mexican workers were appearing in the steel and meat packing plants of Chicago, the automobile factories of Detroit, and on the track maintenance crews of most of the nation's major railroads. As Mexican immigrants became increasingly urbanized and dispersed geographically, Americans gradually grew conscious of the alien tide from below the border. "When it gets into the cities and gets in a mess," announced Representative Albert Johnson of Washington, the nationally renowned restrictionist who chaired the House Committee on Immigration and Naturalization, "then we begin to hear of it."[4]

The intrusion of Mexicans into new areas and new occupations prompted Americans for the first time to ponder seriously the nature of the Mexican immigrant, his relationship to American society, and his possible place within it. Most Americans already harbored grave doubts about the wisdom of ethnic heterogeneity, and these doubts provoked both conscious and unconscious comparisons of Mexicans to other alien and nonwhite groups in the United States. How Anglos perceived Mexicans can best be illuminated by analyzing the stereotyped view which gained currency during the 1920s.

During that decade a lengthy and bitter debate raged over legislative proposals to restrict immigration from Mexico, but both proponents and opponents of restriction accepted a remarkably similar Mexican stereotype. Both camps believed that most Mexican immigrants were Indian peons whose characteristics and potentialities were racially determined. Both groups, as well as many social scientists interested in immigration, described Mexicans as docile, indolent, and backward. They clashed only over the question of whether permitting such people to labor in the United States would prove ultimately advantageous or disadvantageous to the nation. Those in opposition to Mexican immigration—nativists and labor leaders—viewed docility, indolence, and backwardness as antithetical and threatening to the values upon which the United States was founded. Those favoring Mexican immigration, however, considered these characteristics to be splendid prerequisites for the type of labor they required.

From the earliest appearance of Mexicans on the railroads and farms of the Southwest, Anglos commented on their seeming docility, and employers cheerfully contemplated the benefits of having an easily manipulated labor supply. The Mexican, reported economist Victor S. Clark in 1908, "is docile, patient, usually orderly in camp, fairly intelligent under competent supervision, obedient, and cheap. If he were active and ambitious, he would be less tractable and would cost more. His strongest point is his willingness to work for a low wage."[5] Twelve years later a representative of the South Texas Cotton Growers' Association assured a congressional committee that "there never was a more docile animal in the world than the Mexican."[6] Farmers attributed this trait to the Mexican's lack of mental development, to the belief that "the Mexican is a child, naturally."[7] Like children, Mexican workers, if handled with understanding, could be coaxed into behaving properly. Their alleged tractability made them superior employees in the eyes of southwestern growers. "They are content with whatever you give them," declared a Texas cotton grower. "The whites want more water, etc., and are troublemakers. If there is a labor shortage they want exorbitant prices. Yes, the Mexicans do it some. But you can handle the Mexicans better; they're more subservient, if that's the word."[8] In the mid-1920s, S. Parker Frisselle of California, who later helped organize the Associated Farmers and combated Mexican strikers during the depression, candidly voiced the view of most large growers: "The Mexican is . . . a man who gives us no trouble at all. He takes his orders and follows them."[9]

Those favoring the curtailment of immigration from Mexico agreed with the farmers that the Mexican was, by nature, extremely tractable.

Kenneth Roberts, a leading restrictionist as well as a historical novelist, maintained that the Mexican "is probably the most docile and gullible of all the immigrant arrivals that the United States has ever seen."[10] But if employers considered meekness and simplicity to be ideal traits for farm workers, restrictionists believed them to be serious dangers. Docile Mexicans would willingly accept inferior living conditions and thereby be the cause of hygienic and social problems.[11]

Not only were Mexicans docile, according to the serotype, they also possessed a "birthright of laziness."[12] Most Americans, both those favoring and opposing restriction, believed that Mexicans, coming from a country that economist Walter Weyl (a future editor of the *New Republic*) called "the land of mañana," cared little whether they worked or not and never planned for the future.[13] It was not difficult for Anglos to imagine that the Mexican carried his homeland's "mañana spirit" with him to the United States.[14] "The Mexican peon dislikes work," observed an Americanization teacher in California. "Work is work; Joy is joy. The two are not the same. There is joy in play, in music, in color, in rest, in the dance, but not in work. There is no such thing as the joy of working at difficult tasks. One does disagreeable work for money, not joy."[15]

Sociologist Emory Bogardus, one of the more scholarly commentators on Mexican immigration, also stressed sloth in his evaluation of Mexican work habits, although he, unlike most restrictionists and employers, identified cultural heritage rather than heredity as the source of the Mexicans' negative qualities. Wrote Bogardus: "Unskilled Mexicans as a class require supervision. Without someone directing them, they are likely to take time off freely. They live so largely in the present that time has no particular meaning to them."[16] Employers generally agreed that Mexican workers were indolent and tended to quit their jobs and loaf once they had accumulated a little money. Consequently, advised growers, the wages of the Mexicans must be kept low.[17]

Having invested the Mexican with the qualities of indolence and submissiveness, many Anglos found it easy to characterize him as generally backward or, to use the favored term of the period, "unprogressive." Unprogressive groups, as a result of racial or cultural traits or a combination of the two, were out of step with the ever-forward movement of American civilization. They lacked thrift, ambition, intelligence, and strong moral fiber, qualities upon which the past accomplishments and the future improvement of the nation rested. To most Americans, Mexicans fit the criteria of an unprogressive group since they were seen as prodigal, illiterate, and nomadic, and, therefore, unable to rise in occupational status and contribute to community stability.[18] Due to their backwardness, they would always remain in an inferior status. According to a Texas grower, "good white laborers save up their money and go into farming for themselves and don't labor anymore for others. The Mexicans will spend what they make; they will spend $1 a yard for silk for a dress, and sleep on a dirt floor. . . . What's the use of trying to help them save money? They won't do it anyway. They're laboring people. You know what the Bible says about the hewers of wood and drawers of water; the poor we always have with us; they're not progressive."[19]

Many Anglo observers related the alleged negative work habits of Mexican immigrants to their experience in the old country. Because most Mexicans had been servile laborers on large estates and entrapped in a system of debt bondage, they had become, as Emory Bogardus phrased it, "hacienda-minded."[20] As a peon, the Mexican had no opportunity to exercise independence, initiative, or responsibility.[21] Since landlords expected him to be patient and obedient, he became improvident and irresponsible, rather than self-reliant. "Their ideals and ideas," noted the progressive Republican senator from Idaho, William E. Borah, "are quite different from ours."[22]

In discussing Mexican immigrants, Anglos, both those pro and con on restriction, often employed the term "peon" as a synonym for "Mexican."[23] Just as Americans' perceptions of the Chinese became inextricably linked to the image of the coolie, so their concept of the Mexican melded with the image of the peon. Unlike the peasant immigrants from Germany and Scandinavia, who rapidly achieved farm ownership, and the Irish and eastern and southern Europeans, who generally became industrial workers, most Mexicans in the United States continued to be landless field workers. "The Mexican," remarked sociologist Max Handman, "comes as a laborer and remains a farm laborer, and that of a unique kind— unique for America. For he comes in the majority of cases as a peon."[24] Classifying them as peons, Americans could comfortably view Mexicans as a caste, distinct from and below the rest of society—and destined to remain so.

Although during the 1920s there existed an implicit consensus among restrictionists, employers, and most social scientists that the peon image aptly captured the negative qualities of the Mexican immigrant, there was a small number of Americans who refused to think in terms of stereotypes.[25] This group consisted primarily of Protestant missionaries who, while attempting to convert the Mexican workers, also recognized and sympathetically described the value of the Hispanic culture. Like the exponents of cultural pluralism, these missionaries believed that all ethnic groups possessed a distinctive and important cultural heritage which could make a valuable contribution to the development of American civilization. They emphasized the Mexican's artistic and musical ability and his love of beauty, and implied that the United States could learn much from the Mexican.[26] But those Anglos who celebrated the Mexican's potential cultural contributions composed a tiny and lonely minority. In the eyes of most people, the Mexican could contribute little but brawn.

The influx of Mexican immigration during the twenties coincided with a period of immense popularity for pseudoscientific racial explanations of cultural differences. Led by Madison Grant, chairman of the New York Zoological Society, racists taught that mankind was neatly divided into distinct breeding stocks whose unequal potentials were determined by the fixed quality of their genes.[27] In accordance with this theory, many Americans believed that the disreputable characteristics they saw in the Mexican stemmed from his inferior racial background. Mexicans were not white, they argued, but rather Indians and mestizos.[28] As proof, they cited figures from the Mexican census, which indicated that Mexico's population was about 60 percent mestizo, 30 percent Indian, and only 10 percent white. Princeton University economist Robert Foerster noted that, historically, very few Spanish women ever emigrated to Mexico so "beyond a doubt the most frequent unions of Spanish men were with Indian women."[29] To some Anglos, the Spanish conquest clearly demonstrated the inferiority of Mexican Indians. A stronger race would not have been defeated, nor would it have allowed itself to fall into a state of peonage. A few went so far as to argue that only the most unfit of Mexico's native population, those "low-grade Indians who did not fight to extinction but submitted and multiplied as serfs," had survived the Spanish conquistadores.[30] And now their progeny was inundating the United States. "More Indians," declared one observer, "have crossed the southern border in one year than lived in the entire territory of New England at the time of the Plymouth settlement. This movement is the greatest Indian migration of all time."[31]

The appearance of a large Indian population in the United States raised perplexing social questions. How would Mexican Indians fit into the racial patterns of American society? Could Mexicans be accepted as whites? If not, could they easily be relegated to the subordinate position of blacks? Sociologist Max Handman of the University of Texas, a close student of Mexican labor throughout the 1920s, warned of the problems created by immigration from below the Rio Grande. America, he advised, "has no social technique for handling partly colored races. We have a place for the Negro and a place for the white man: the Mexican is not a Negro, and the white man refuses him an equal status. What will result from this I am not prophet enough to foretell, but I know that it may mean trouble." "Are we," asked Handman, "creating for ourselves a social problem full

of dismal prospects, of race hatreds and bruised feelings and social ostra-
cisms and perhaps lynchings and the race wars of a twentieth century
American city?"[32]

Although a few staunch restrictionists, such as Representatives
John C. Box of Texas and Thomas A. Jenkins of Ohio, maintained that
Mexicans "have a strain of negro blood derived from black slaves carried
to Mexico from Africa and the West Indies," most Americans seemed to
agree with Handman that Mexicans were not black.[33] Yet Mexicans were
not recognized as simply another alien white nationality group like the
Poles and Italians. Throughout the country Anglos utilized the term "Mexican" to distinguish immigrants from south of the border from both whites
and blacks.[34] A Texas congressman in 1921 noted that "the word Mexican
is used to indicate race, not a citizen or subject of the country. There are
probably 250,000 Mexicans in Texas who were born in the state but they
are 'Mexicans' just as all blacks are Negroes though they may have five
generations of American ancestors."[35] When questioned as to the race of
Mexicans, a Chicago chamber of commerce official responded: "No, they
are not regarded as colored, but they are regarded as an inferior class. Are
the Mexicans regarded as white? Oh, no!"[36] Some Americans could apparently feel comfortable only when attributing a specific color designation to Mexicans, such as "little brown peons," "chocolate-colored
Mexican peons," or "copper-colored men." Others simply referred to
Mexicans as "half-breeds" and "mongrels."[37] In almost all cases, "Mexican" became a racially loaded term.

Those most concerned with the racial implications of Mexican immigration were the nativists who had already struggled to protect the nation
from the non-Anglo-Saxon aliens from Europe and Asia. In the mid-1920s
these race-conscious restrictionists stood at the forefront of a crusade to
limit the entry of Mexicans, a crusade which had gained the backing of
organized labor by the end of the decade. Defending the Mexican against
efforts to bar him were the growers and railroads which relied upon his
labor. The battle over restriction raged in the committee rooms of Congress and the popular periodical press. The rhetorical ammunition employed by both sides played heavily upon the peon image of the Mexican.

Passage of the 1921 Immigration Act and the 1924 National Origins
Act marked the triumph of restrictionists over those who favored an open
immigration policy. The United States for the first time placed quantita-
tive limits on the admission of European aliens. In this legislation Congress accepted the nativist axiom that a wise immigration policy must not
only limit the total number of newcomers but also discriminate among
prospective immigrants on the basis of biological heritage. As a result,

Congress established the quota principle, which favored aliens from western and northern Europe over those from the eastern and southern parts of the continent, the source of non-Anglo-Saxon immigrants.[38]

Nativists took great pride in their achievement. They looked forward to both an absolute decline in immigration and the exclusion of inferior peoples. But as they examined the results of their handiwork in the mid-1920s, they were shocked to learn of a serious omission. The legislation of 1921 and 1924, in giving special consideration to the Pan-American neighbors of the United States, excluded Western Hemisphere nations from the quota principle. Thus, aliens from Canada and Mexico, the two leading sources of New World immigrants, continued to flow unabated into the United States. Canadian immigrants, nearly all of whom were white, did not concern nativists as much as the "Indian peons" from Mexico.[39] Prior to the passage of the legislation, nativists scarcely noticed the movement of workers from Mexico, overshadowed as it was by the multitudes arriving from Europe. During the first decade of the century Mexicans comprised only 0.6 percent of the total number of legal immigrants. Between 1911 and 1920 the percentage rose only to 3.8 percent.[40] With the passage of the National Origins Act, however, the Mexican percentage increased dramatically. The number of Mexicans lawfully admitted during fiscal year 1924—some 87,648—equaled about 45 percent of the year's entrants from eastern and southern Europe and 12.4 percent of the total number of newcomers.[41]

Race-conscious restrictionists reacted with horror to this news. Unrestricted immigration from Mexico would negate their years of painstaking effort to save the purity of America's genetic pool. Surely the same vital racial reasons which necessitated the enactment of the National Origins Act, nativists argued, also required that Mexico be placed under the act's provisions. It had been the height of folly to restrict European immigration and at the same time leave the "side doors" to this country "wide open."[42] "From the racial point of view," asserted Madison Grant, America's most influential nativist, "it is not logical to limit the number of Europeans while we throw the country open without limitation to Negroes, Indians, and half-breeds."[43] The small portion of white blood flowing through the veins of Mexicans did little to enhance their biological worth, according to nativists, because it stemmed from Spanish sources, and the Spanish, being of "Mediterranean" rather than "Nordic" origin, were among the most undesirable Europeans.[44] The addition of hundreds of thousands of "low-grade" Indian-Spanish hybrids could result only in disaster for the nation's future racial integrity. Mestizo, Indian, and black stock, warned Robert Foerster in a study sponsored by the U.S. Department of Labor, "does not attain the race value of white stocks, and therefore . . . tend[s] to lower the average of the race value of the white population in the United States."[45] Nativist spokesmen like Harry H. Laughlin, a eugenics "agent" of the House Immigration and Naturalization Committee, argued that the National Origins Act represented a momentous policy decision to choose newcomers on the basis of "race biology," rather than labor need, and that continued Mexican entry undermined that policy. Observed Laughlin: "We can now, if we desire, recruit our future human seed stock from immigrants of assimilable races, who will also improve our existing hereditary family stock qualities. We conserve and improve our domestic plants and animals, why not our human seed-stock also?"[46]

Not only would the nation have to cope with the immediate race problems caused by unassimilable Mexican immigrants, explained nativists, it would also have to grapple with an even more acute situation in the future due to the backward peon's "indefinite powers of multiplication."[47] Although Mexican males in the United States outnumbered females, observed Robert Foerster, there were enough Mexican women available to influence the "permanent race stock" of the nation. Moreover, he noted, as the volume of Mexican immigration had climbed, the proportion of female arrivals had also likely increased.[48] With Mexican immigration reaching peak levels in the 1920s, nativists became obsessed with what they termed the "excessive fecundity" of Mexicans. In the pages of *World's Work*, C. M. Goethe, a California nativist, urged Americans to ponder the kind of future their great-grandchildren would face in a country overrun by Mexicans. "The average American family," he declared, "has three children. Mexican laborers average between nine and ten. . . . At the three-child rate a couple would have twenty-seven great-grandchildren. At the nine-child rate 729 would be produced. Twenty-seven American children and 729 hybrids or Amerinds!" With odds like twenty-seven to one, asserted Goethe, the offspring of Mexicans would overwhelm that of Americans.[49] Borrowing the race suicide theme originally developed by nativists opposing European immigration, Samuel J. Holmes warned that the pressure of the burgeoning Mexican population would become so intense that Americans would cease reproducing. "You cannot let a foreign group into a country," the Berkeley zoologist explained, "without its having the effect of keeping a great many thousand, perhaps millions, of our native population from being born. Are you going to sacrifice our children for the sake of assimilating the Mexican?"[50]

In addition to fearing a booming Mexican birth rate, nativists anxiously contemplated the possibility of miscegenation. Because Mexicans themselves were the product of intermarriage among whites, Indians, and blacks, argued Representatives John Box and Thomas Jenkins, they harbored a casual attitude toward interracial unions and were likely to mix

freely with both whites and blacks in the United States. To the congressmen, "such a situation will make the blood of all three races flow back
and forth between them in a distressing process of mongrelization." "No
other alien race entering America," Box told his colleagues, "provides an
easier channel for the intermixture of blood than does the mongrel Mexican. . . . Their presence and intermarriage with both white and black races
. . . create the most insidious and general mixture of white, Indian, and
negro blood strains ever produced in America."[51] Thus, the presence of
Mexicans would encourage violation of the nation's most inviolate racial
taboo. Harry Laughlin, the eugenics agent of the House Immigration and
Naturalization Committee, warned ominously that "if the time ever comes
when men with a small fraction of colored blood can readily find mates
among white women, the gates would be thrown open to a final radical
race mixture of the whole population." "The perpetuity of the American
race," he explained, depended totally upon the "virtue" of American
women.[52] Apparently, nativists believed that the exclusion of nonwhites
was a much wiser policy than reliance upon feminine virtue to guarantee
the nation's race purity. If race mixing, or "mongrelization," were allowed
to occur, cautioned Samuel J. Holmes, the United States would decline to
the substandard social and cultural levels of South America.[53] C. M. Goethe
further admonished that whenever a people of superior blood interbred
with inferiors, the decay of civilization was the outcome. "Does our failure to restrict Mexican immigration spell the downfall of our Republic,
with all its hopes of betterment for all humanity? Athens could not maintain the brilliancy of the Golden Age of Pericles when hybridization of
her citizenry began. Rome fell when the old patrician families lost their
race consciousness and interbred with servile stocks."[54]

Nativists objected to Mexicans on social as well as racial grounds
and often fused the two types of arguments. Being Indians, immigrants
from below the border had no appreciation of even the most elementary
standards of cleanliness and decency. As a result, Mexicans contributed
greatly to crime, health, slum, and welfare problems. The cost of Mexican labor to greedy employers might be low, nativists argued, but the cost
to American society was immeasurable. At the same time that municipalities were forced to subsidize Mexican farm workers during the off-
season, the presence of those very workers threatened the well-being of
taxpayers who supported them.[55]

Not only would Mexican immigration engender immediate and severe social problems, nativists asserted, but it would also have detrimental long-range effects upon American society. Due to racial differences,
Mexicans would comprise an undesirable element in the nation's social
structure, a caste "to fill an underworld of millions who cannot share in

the impulses and best hopes of American life."[56] Nativists disapproved of
the creation of another color caste in the United States for a variety of
reasons. First, as already noted, a distinct Mexican class would mean further social division and thereby violate the cherished nativist dream of a
more homogeneous America. Second, the existence of a servile group
was likely to undermine the moral fiber and will to work of Americans. "I
don't believe that it is safe to divide America into an upper and an under
world," said Congressman John C. Box. "I don't believe it is good to
have thousands of millions of people among us who can have no part or
parcel with us except as our menial servants. . . . If we do have great
numbers of such people with us, we will have a conditions such as some
of the older nations had when there were millions of slaves and few citizens. I think it tends to destroy democracy. I think it tends to make our
own people helpless."[57] Finally, nativists insisted that a caste system did
violence to the traditional American ideals of liberty and equality. Mexican immigration had led, in the words of Madison Grant, to the establishment of "an exploited peasant class unconformable with the principles of
American civilization."[58] A superintendent of schools in Colorado's sugar
beet region expressed well the dilemma which the presence of Mexican
workers posed to nativists. "Only two things present themselves as alternatives as I see it. Either the two peoples will amalgamate, which for my
part I must waive aside as absolutely repulsive, or we must create a caste
system. If we create a caste system, it will be worse upon us, the aristocracy, than upon the Mexicans in their serfdom. We would be sacrificing
the ideals which our fathers worked so hard to establish and preserve and
which we are morally bound to perpetuate."[59]

Like those who had attacked slavery on principle but simultaneously
favored the return of blacks to Africa, nativists desired to preserve both
their ideological and their racial purity. They refused to recognize any
contradiction between opposing a caste system on ideological grounds,
on the one hand, and refusing equality to some men on the basis of race,
on the other. To protect their veneer of idealism and to avoid the anxiety
which might arise should their democratic values be put to the test, nativists saw only one course of action—exclusion of the Mexican.

Nativists portrayed a Mexican caste as an economic menace to both
farmers and urban workers in the United States. A continued influx of
Mexican laborers, they charged, would bring about the perpetuation of a
plantation-type agricultural system in the Southwest and the destruction
of the family farm system in the South. It was not honest, hard-working
yeomen who desired Mexican labor, but the large, often corporate, growers of the Southwest. These growers, said Kenneth Roberts, thought only
of selfish gain in demanding cheap labor. To them, sneered Roberts, "fifty

thousand chimpanzees a year would admittedly be acceptable, if they knew how to pick cotton."[60] By using Mexican workers, southwestern cotton growers, whom nativists depicted as "plantation lords" rather than true farmers, could undersell small cotton operations in the South. As a result, the living standard of American farmers would plummet to a peon level, and the nation's independent, highly individualistic agricultural structure would be transformed into a decadent Old World feudal system. Rather than submit to the living conditions of a "pauper peasantry," Americans would abandon their farms, leaving the country's cherished agriculture in the hands of the Mexican. Invoking the agrarian myth, Madison Grant, the Manhattan patrician, predicted that Mexican immigration would destroy the nation "since the maintenance of American civilization depends largely on the maintenance of a healthy and prosperous farm population."[61]

According to the nativists, Mexican immigration represented a danger to American workers as well as farmers. Just as cheap peon labor would grind down the yeoman, so it would hurt the American factory, transportation, and construction worker. Mexicans, due to their racial heritage and experience with poverty in Mexico, were able to live on next to nothing, explained nativists. "No self-respecting white laborer," wrote Robert DeCourcy Ward of the Immigration Restriction League of Boston, "can compete with a Mexican peon who works for a small wage and exists in poverty and wretchedness."[62] The Mexican laborer would replace the American, not because the peon was a superior worker, but simply because he was cheaper. Since Congress protected white men from the competition of Oriental coolies, it should also shield them from Mexican peons. The restriction of Mexican workers, nativists concluded, was consistent not only with the nation's policy of Oriental exclusion but also with its tariff policy. Since Congress designed the tariff to protect American workers from cheap foreign labor abroad, it followed logically that such labor must not be permitted to compete within the nation's borders.[63]

No one could agree more heartily with nativists that Mexicans constituted a menace to American workers than leaders of organized labor. Union spokesmen for the American Federation of Labor [AFL] and the Railroad Brotherhoods charged that "cheap peon labor" admitted to the United States for farm work inevitably made its way to cities, where it drove down wage levels, replaced American workers, and contributed to unemployment. The "stupid and ignorant" Mexican, said labor officials, accepted low wages and "un-American" living conditions which white wage earners were unable to tolerate.[64] While the main thrust of their objections to Mexican immigration centered on jobs and wages, labor leaders often voiced racial arguments that echoed those of the nativists. After maintaining that the AFL had "the kindest feeling toward the Mexi-

can people," union representatives warned Congress that aliens from below the border were of Indian rather than Spanish stock. As such, they
constituted an unassimilable group which "would bring another race problem."[65] Edward H. Dowell, vice president of the California State Federation of Labor, asked members of the U.S. Senate Immigration Committee
whether they desired a nation filled "with a mongrel population consisting largely of Mexicans and Orientals." Because of the Mexican's Indian
background, argued AFL representative William C. Hushing, no American "would care to have any member of his family intermarry with the
general run of these immigrants—peons."[66]

In an effort to block the combined nativist and union drive for restriction, southwestern growers, railroads, and mining interests joined with
midwestern sugar beet companies in a vigorous coordinated defense of
Mexican immigration.[67] At the urging of their southwestern affiliates, the
National Grange and the American Farm Bureau Federation publicly opposed any precipitous change in Mexico's nonquota status.[68] Similarly,
the U.S. Chamber of Commerce, in deference to its members with close
ties to agriculture, objected to limiting the entry of aliens from below the
Rio Grande.[69]

While almost all employers of Mexican labor claimed to support the
general principle of immigration restriction and defended the quota acts
as being in the national interest, they nevertheless pleaded that an exception be made for Mexican workers. Unlike the European immigrant, employers explained, the Mexican did not compete with American workers,
but, rather, took only those jobs which Americans could not or would not
perform.[70] Grower representatives claimed that the Mexican's racial background made him perfectly suited, both biologically and psychologically,
for monotonous, backbreaking stoop-labor in desert heat. The use of
Mexicans, they argued, would spare whites the "serious physical consequences" of manual labor in the Southwest.[71] Employers also contended
that only the Mexican could supply agriculture's unskilled labor needs.
Observed Fred H. Bixby, a representative of the American Cattle Raisers'
Association: "We have no Chinamen; we have not the Japs. The Hindu is
worthless; the Filipino is nothing, and the white man will not do the work."
The restriction of Mexican aliens, proclaimed Bixby, "will stop half of
the farming on the other side of the Missouri River."[72] To curtail the labor
supply now, growers maintained, would not only doom heroic pioneering
efforts to transform the Southwest from a barren desert to a flourishing
garden but would also mean the waste of hundreds of millions of federal
dollars which had been spent on reclamation projects and farm loans.[73]

By using financial arguments such as these, employers had some
success in countering the economic contentions of restrictionists, and in

doing so they staved off speedy congressional action on the Mexican immigration issue. They had greater difficulty, however, in refuting the racial and social arguments against Mexicans. Because growers and their business allies generally accepted the same peon image as their restrictionist adversaries, they could not contend that Mexicans possessed the character from which this country could fashion acceptable citizens. Instead, employers tried to manipulate the stereotype in such a way as to demonstrate that Mexicans would not have a detrimental impact on American society. They argued that the Mexican's inborn traits made him a lesser racial menace than any other unskilled labor group. Because Mexicans were inherently tractable, growers asserted, they minded their own business, willingly separated themselves from whites, and caused few social problems. "They are a very docile people," said Congressman John Nance Garner of Texas, the future vice president. "They can be imposed on; the sheriff can go out and make them do anything. That is the way they are."[74] C. S. Brown, an Arizona cotton farmer representing his state's Farm Bureau, testified that southwestern growers were naturally endowed with skill in the handling of Mexicans. Just as southerners were particularly adept at controlling blacks, so "we of the Southwest . . . know the Mexican; we know how to please him and how to get him to please us."[75]

To further bolster their position, employers contended that in the event Congress curtailed Mexican immigration, they would be compelled to turn to far more undesirable groups—blacks, Puerto Ricans, or Filipinos—to meet the Southwest's unskilled labor needs.[76] "The American negro we all know," said Ralph Taylor, a grower spokesman. "Are we Americans, with a full knowledge of the very serious racial problems which he has brought to the South and other parts of America, willing deliberately to spread him over the rest of the country in ever increasing numbers?"[77] The Puerto Rican represented a racial menace even more insidious than the Negro, according to George Clements, director of the Los Angeles Chamber of Commerce's agricultural department. "While they all have negro blood within their veins, the greater part of them are without those physical markings which can only protect society. They are red-headed, freckle-faced, thin-lipped negro hybrids with the vicious qualities of their progenitors."[78] Filipinos, too, presented a serious danger to the purity of the nation's bloodstream and the chastity of its womanhood. "I dread the day when we get filled up with Filipinos," shuddered Congressman Arthur M. Free of California. "With them comes the sex problem. This is what makes the race problem become acute on the Pacific coast."[79]

Unlike blacks, Puerto Ricans, and Filipinos, maintained the antirestrictionists, Mexicans presented no miscegenation problem. Harry Chandler, who published the *Los Angeles Times* and owned a large amount of California farmland, assured congressmen that the Mexicans "do not intermarry like the negro with white people. They do not mingle. They keep to themselves. That is the safety of it."[80] Mexicans, antirestrictionists argued, were less dangerous than other nonwhites because they did not desire white women. Cattle raiser Fred Bixby expressed confidence that his three daughters were totally safe "riding the range with . . . the kind of people who are working for me, and they are Mexicans. Do you suppose we would send them out with a bunch of negroes? We should never think of such a thing."[81]

In addition to asserting that Mexican workers constituted neither racial nor social nor economic threats, antirestrictionists employed a final argument against demands for a quota. The Mexican alien, they pointed out, lived just a short distance from his homeland. In the event that labor demand diminished or the Mexican did create serious racial or social problems, he, unlike blacks, Puerto Ricans, and Filipinos, who were not legally aliens, could easily be deported. With such insurance, employers concluded, restrictive legislation was superfluous.[82]

Congress, however, did not accept this position. In 1930 the restrictionist pressure which had been building up during the twenties triumphed over all employer arguments. The Senate passed a quota bill singling out Mexico alone of all Western Hemisphere nations. A similar measure had strong support in the House, but was killed by Republican leaders of the Rules Committee at the behest of the Herbert Hoover administration.[83] The administration was attempting to improve relations with Mexico at the time, and Secretary of State Henry L. Stimson believed that the quota measure, which Mexico viewed as blatantly discriminatory, would both undermine reconciliation efforts and be "prejudicial" to "the very considerable American interests" south of the border.[84] The executive branch was able to thwart restrictive legislating only because the State Department, as early as 1928, had begun to reduce Mexican immigration drastically by administrative means. In the hope of forestalling congressional action, the department had instructed American consuls in Mexico to adhere strictly to existing immigration regulations in issuing visas. Due to this policy, legal immigration was cut to a trickle as almost all Mexican workers were denied entry under the public charge, literacy, or contract labor clauses of the 1917 Immigration Act.[85]

While restrictionists may have been denied a formal victory—a quota law applicable to Mexico—they had largely succeeded in stopping legal Mexican immigration by compelling the State Department to undertake a novel form of administrative regulation. In their drive against aliens from below the Rio Grande, restrictionists had been able to use to good advantage the pervasive stereotype of Mexican as Indian peon. They continually stressed a dual theme: the Mexican's Indian blood would pollute the nation's genetic purity, and his biologically determined degenerate character traits would sap the country's moral fiber and corrupt its institutions. Given their acceptance of the Mexican's inferiority, antirestrictionists found it impossible to affirm that the United States could mold the "peon" into a worthwhile citizen. Thus, they defended their position by relying on specious racist arguments purporting to prove that the Mexican constituted a lesser racial evil than did other nonwhites, an evil that could be erased at will by deportation. Most Americans, by the 1920s, had lost all faith in the country's power to assimilate non-Anglo-Saxon newcomers and had become fixed in their devotion to the chimera of an ethnically homogeneous society. Perhaps nothing better illustrates this than an editorial in the *New York Times*, a newspaper with no crucial stake in the Mexican immigration issue. "It is folly to pretend that the more recently arrived Mexicans, who are largely of Indian blood, can be absorbed and incorporated into the American race."[86] Few Americans dissented from this view. To most Anglos, the immigrant from south of the border was always the peon laborer and never the potential citizen.

Notes

1. Carey McWilliams, *North from Mexico* (Philadelphia, 1949), 163. This work stood for two decades as the only comprehensive history of Mexican immigration.

2. Rodolfo Acuña, *Occupied America: The Chicano's Struggle toward Liberation* (San Francisco, 1972); Matt S. Meier and Feliciano Rivera, *The Chicanos: A History of Mexican Americans* (New York, 1972); Abraham Hoffman, *Unwanted Mexican Americans in the Great Depression* (Tucson, 1974); Mercedes Carreras de Velasco, *Los mexicanos que devolvió la crisis, 1929–1932* (México, D.F., 1974). For a discussion of recent historical literature on Chicanos, see Arthur M. Corwin, "Mexican-American History: An Assessment," *Pacific Historical Review* 41 (1973): 269–308.

3. U.S. Department of Labor, *Annual Report of the Commissioner-General of Immigration* (Washington, DC, 1924), 8. In 1900 there were about one hundred thousand Mexican-born individuals in the United States. By 1930 there were nearly 1.5 million first- and second-generation Mexicans living in the United States.

4. House Committee on Immigration and Naturalization (hereafter cited as HCIN), *Hearings on Seasonal Agricultural Laborers from Mexico*, 60th Cong., 1st sess., 1926), 240.

5. Victor S. Clark, "Mexican Labor in the United States," *Bulletin of the Bureau of Labor*, no. 8 (Washington, DC, 1908), 496.

6. Senate Committee on Immigration (hereafter cited as SCI), *Hearings on the Admission of Mexican Agricultural Laborers*, 66th Cong., 2d sess. (1920), 4.

7. Ibid., 23; HCIN, *Hearings on Seasonal Agricultural Laborers from Mexico*, 107.

8. Quoted in Paul S. Taylor, *An American-Mexican Frontier* (Chapel Hill, 1934), 130.

9. HCIN, *Hearings on Seasonal Agricultural Laborers from Mexico*, 21.

10. Kenneth L. Roberts, "Mexicans or Ruin," *Saturday Evening Post*, 200, February 18, 1928, 15.

11. Samuel J. Holmes, "Perils of the Mexican Invasion," *North American Review* 227 (May 1929): 617. See also the statement submitted by Robert DeC. Ward of the Immigration Restriction League of Boston in SCI, *Hearings on the Restriction of Western Hemisphere Immigration*, 70th Cong., 1st sess. (1928), 187.

12. Roberts, "Mexicans or Ruin," 15.

13. Walter Weyl, "Labor Conditions in Mexico," *Bulletin of the Bureau of Labor*, no. 38 (Washington, DC, 1902), 17.

14. Emory S. Bogardus, *The Mexican in the United States* (Los Angeles, 1934), 47.

15. Helen W. Walker, "Mexican Immigrants and American Citizenship," *Sociology and Social Research* 13 (1929): 466.

16. Emory S. Bogardus, "The Mexican Immigrant," *Sociology and Social Research* 11 (1927): 478, 488.

17. Taylor, *An American-Mexican Frontier*, 127.

18. U.S. Immigration Commission [Dillingham Commission], *Abstract* (Washington, DC, 1911), 1:683–90, and *Reports of the Immigration Commission, Immigrants in Industries* (Washington, DC, 1911), part 25, vol. 2, 59; Jeremiah Jenks and W. Jett Lauck, *The Immigration Problem* (New York, 1913), 227–28; Samuel Bryan, "Mexican Immigrants in the United States," *Survey* 28 (September 7, 1912): 730.

19. Taylor, *An American-Mexican Frontier*, 300.

20. Bogardus, *The Mexican in the United States*, 16–17, 46.

21. Robert F. Foerster, *The Racial Problems Involved in Immigration from Latin America and the West Indies to the United States* (Washington, DC, 1925), 55; Walker, "Mexican Immigrants and American Citizenship," 466; Roberts, "Mexicans on the Run," 15.

22. William E. Borah to W. G. Swendsen, June 9, 1928, Box 288, Borah Papers, Library of Congress, Washington, DC.

23. Both proponents and opponents of Mexican immigration used "peon" interchangeably with "Mexican." See, for example, the statements of Congressmen John C. Box and John Nance Garner, in HCIN, *Hearings on Seasonal Agricultural Laborers from Mexico*, 43, 189. This "peon" image pervaded the popular American mind. Emory S. Bogardus, *Immigration and Race Attitudes* (Boston, 1928), 20.

24. Max Handman, "The Mexican Immigrant in Texas," *Southwestern Political and Social Science Quarterly* 7 (1926): 35.

25. The most significant of the social scientists who refused to do so was economist Paul S. Taylor, whose classic studies of Mexican labor in various parts of the United States during the late 1920s and early 1930s are eminently objective. See, for example, *Mexican Labor in the United States, Bethlehem, Pennsylvania* (Berkeley, 1931); and other studies by Taylor cited below.

26. Robert N. McLean, "Mexican Workers in the United States," *National Conference of Social Work Proceedings* (Chicago, 1929), 536–38; Charles A. Thompson, "Mexicans—An Interpretation," *National Conference of Social Work*

Proceedings (Chicago, 1928), 499–503; Vernon M. McCombs, *From over the Border* (New York, 1925), 59–61.

27. John Higham, *Strangers in the Land* (New York, 1966), 155–57.

28. Clark, "Mexican Labor in the United States," 501; Dillingham Commission, *Dictionary of Races or Peoples* (Washington, DC, 1911), 96; " 'Little Mexico' in Northern Cities," *World's Work* 48 (September 1924): 466.

29. Foerster, *Racial Problems Involved in Immigration from Latin America*, 9–10; Paul S. Taylor, *Mexican Labor in the United States, Migration Statistics* (Berkeley, 1929), 238–39.

30. Speech of Republican John C. Box before an immigration conference held on January 18, 1928, in Memorial Continental Hall, Washington, DC, in *Congressional Record* (hereafter cited as *CR*), 70th Cong., 1st sess. (1928), 2817–18.

31. Glenn E. Hoover, "Our Mexican Immigrants," *Foreign Affairs* 8 (October 1929), 107.

32. Max Handman, "Economic Reasons for the Coming of the Mexican Immigrant," *American Journal of Sociology* 35 (January 1930): 609–10; Handman, "The Mexican Immigrant in Texas," 37–41.

33. HCIN, *Hearings on Western Hemisphere Immigration*, 70th Cong., 2d sess. (1930), 410, 419, and *Hearings on Temporary Admission of Illiterate Mexican Laborers*, 66th Cong., 2d sess. (1920), 192.

34. Paul S. Taylor, "Crime and the Foreign Born: The Problem of the Mexican," in U.S. National Commission on Law Observance and Enforcement, *Report on Crime and the Foreign Born*, no. 10 (Washington, DC, 1931), 200.

35. James L. Slayden, "Some Observations on Mexican Immigration," *Annals of the American Academy of Political and Social Science* 93 (January 1921), 125.

36. Paul S. Taylor, *Mexican Labor in the United States, Chicago and the Calumet Region* (Berkeley, 1932), 235.

37. Lothrop Stoddard, *Re-forging America* (New York, 1927), 214; Kenneth Roberts, "Wet and Other Mexicans," *Saturday Evening Post*, 200, February 4, 1928, 137; HCIN, *Hearings on Temporary Admission of Illiterate Mexican Laborers*, 143; HCIN, *Hearings on Immigration from Latin America, the West Indies, and Canada*, 68th Cong., 2d sess. (1925), 345; HCIN, *Hearings on Western Hemisphere Immigration*, 75.

38. Higham, *Strangers in the Land*, 308–11, 316–24; Robert A. Divine, *American Immigration Policy, 1924–1952* (New Haven, 1957), 8–18.

39. HCIN, *Hearings on Immigration from Countries of the Western Hemisphere*, 70th Cong., 1st sess. (1928), 680.

40. William S. Bernard, *American Immigration Policy* (New York, 1950), 40.

41. U.S. Department of Labor, *Annual Report of the Commissioner-General of Immigration* (Washington, DC, 1924), 9. From 1925 to 1927, Mexicans were second only to Germans as the nationality most frequently admitted. Mexicans accounted for 11.2 percent of the total number of immigrants to the United States during the decade from 1921 to 1930. California Governor C. C. Young's Mexican Fact-finding Committee, *Mexicans in California* (San Francisco, 1930), 20–23; Bernard, *American Immigration Policy*, 40.

42. "Effects of the Immigration Act: Third Annual Report of the Committee on Immigration of the Allied Patriotic Societies, Inc.," sent to President Calvin Coolidge by Dwight Braman, president of the Allied Patriotic Societies, February 27, 1926, Calvin Coolidge Papers, Library of Congress, microfilm reel 79, file 133.

43. Madison Grant, "America for the Americans," *Forum* 74 (September 1925): 355.

44. Foerster, *Racial Problems Involved in Immigration from Latin America*, 44; Roberts, "Wet and Other Mexicans," 11.

45. John C. Box, speech in *CR*, 70th Cong., 1st sess. (1928), 2817–18; Foerster, *Racial Problems Involved in Immigration from Latin America*, 57.

46. HCIN, *Hearings on Immigration from Countries of the Western Hemisphere*, 705, 712, 722.

47. Testimony of Henry DeC. Ward, in ibid., 15.

48. Foerster, *Racial Problems Involved in Immigration from Latin America*, 4. According to the 1920 census, there were 276,526 Mexican-born males and 209,892 Mexican-born females residing in the United States.

49. Holmes, "Perils of the Mexican Invasion," 616. Kenneth Roberts said that Mexicans breed "with the reckless prodigality of rabbits." "The Docile Mexican," *Saturday Evening Post*, 200, March 10, 1928, 41. See also C. M. Goethe, "Peons Need Not Apply," *World's Work* 59 (November 1930): 47–48; Goethe, "Other Aspects of the Problem," *Current History* 33 (August 1928): 766–68; Goethe, "The Influx of Mexican Amerinds," *Eugenics* 2 (January 1929): 8–9.

50. Samuel J. Holmes, "An Argument against the Mexican Immigration," *Transactions of the Commonwealth Club of California* 21 (March 23, 1926): 27. For a discussion of the development of Francis A. Walker's "race suicide" theory, see Higham, *Strangers in the Land*, 147–48: and Thomas F. Gossett, *Race: The History of an Idea in America* (Dallas, 1963), 302–3.

51. HCIN, *Hearings on Western Hemisphere Immigration*, 75, 410.

52. HCIN, *Hearings on Immigration from Countries of the Western Hemisphere*, 709.

53. Holmes, "An Argument against Mexican Immigration," 27.

54. C. M. Goethe to Senator Arthur R. Gould, January 16, 1930, SIC Records, file: "S.51 Harris," Record Group 46, National Archives.

55. Holmes, "Perils of the Mexican Invasion," 615–22; Albert Bushnell Hart, "The Natural Origins Plan," *Current History* 30 (June 1929): 481; Goethe, "Other Aspects of the Problem," 768.

56. Testimony of John C. Box in SCI, *Hearings on Emergency Immigration Legislation*, 66th Cong., 3d sess. (1921), 231; Chester H. Rowell, "Why Make Mexico an Exception?" *Survey* 66 (May 1, 1931): 180.

57. SCI, *Hearings on Emergency Immigration Legislation*, 230.

58. Madison Grant, *The Conquest of a Continent* (New York, 1933), 327.

59. Quoted in Paul S. Taylor, *Mexican Labor in the United States, Valley of the South Platte, Colorado* (Berkeley, 1929), 220.

60. Roberts, "Mexicans or Ruin," 145.

61. Grant, *Conquest of a Continent*, 328–29. For a discussion of the agrarian myth, see Richard Hofstadter, *The Age of Reform* (New York, 1958), chapter 1.

62. SCI, *Hearings on the Restriction of Western Hemisphere Immigration*, 188.

63. Madison Grant to Albert Johnson, April 1, 1928, HCIN Records, file 70A–F14.3, Record Group 233, National Archives. See also Richard Strout, "A Fence for the Rio Grande," *Independent* 120 (June 2, 1928), 518; HCIN, *Hearings on Immigration from Countries of the Western Hemisphere*, 682.

64. Arizona State Federation of Labor, *Proceedings of the Annual Convention* (n.p., 1929), 34; testimony of Edward Dowell, vice president, the California State Federation of Labor in SCI, *Hearings on the Restriction of Western Hemisphere*

Immigration, 6–11; testimony of A. F. Stout, representing the Railroad Brotherhoods, in HCIN, *Hearings on Western Hemisphere Immigration*, 365–66; testimony of AFL legislative representative Edgar Wallace, in HCIN, *Hearings on Seasonal Agricultural Laborers from Mexico*, 297.

65. Testimony of AFL legislative representative William Hushing, in HCIN, *Hearings on Western Hemisphere Immigration*, 365–66; testimony of AFL legislative representative Edgar Wallace, in HCIN, *Hearings on Seasonal Agricultural Laborers from Mexico*, 297.

66. SCI, *Hearings on the Restriction of Western Hemisphere Immigration*, 12; HCIN, *Hearings on Western Hemisphere Immigration*, 366. See also AFL, *Proceedings* (Washington, DC, 1930), 333.

67. "Mexican Immigration and the Farm," *Outlook* 957 (December 7, 1927): 423; SCI, *Hearings on the Restriction of Western Hemisphere Immigration*, 111, 118–22; *CR*, 71st Cong., 2d sess. (1930), 7218–19.

68. HCIN, *Hearings on Immigration from Countries of the Western Hemisphere*, 160; and *Hearings on Western Hemisphere Immigration from Countries of the Western Hemisphere*, 342; National Grange, Patrons of Husbandry, *Journal of Proceedings* (Cleveland, 1927), 144.

69. Chamber of Commerce of the United States, *Fifteenth Annual Meeting* (Washington, DC, 1927), 52; HCIN, *Hearings on Immigration from Countries of the Western Hemisphere*, 268; and *Hearings on Western Hemisphere Immigration*, 76–77.

70. SCI, *Hearings on the Restriction of Western Hemisphere Immigration*, 47–49; HCIN, *Hearings on Immigration from Countries of the Western Hemisphere*, 268.

71. HCIN, *Hearings on Western Hemisphere Immigration*, 231–32; and *Hearings on Immigration from Countries of the Western Hemisphere*, 276.

72. SCI, *Hearings on the Restriction of Western Hemisphere Immigration*, 26–30.

73. HCIN, *Hearings on Western Hemisphere Immigration*, 228; SCI, *Hearings on the Restriction of Western Hemisphere Immigration*, 45, 60; C. C. Teague, "A Statement on Mexican Immigration," *Saturday Evening Post*, 200, March 10, 1928, 170.

74. HCIN, *Hearings on Seasonal Agricultural Laborers from Mexico*, 190; George Harlan, president of the Ventura County, California, Farm Bureau to William Borah, March 4, 1926, box 268, Borah papers.

75. SCI, *Hearings on the Restriction of Western Hemisphere Immigration*, 148.

76. HCIN, *Hearings on Immigration from Countries of the Western Hemisphere*, 323; C. B. Moore, "Why New Laws to Restrict Immigration?" *Western Grower and Shipper* (February 1930): 36; George Marvin, "Monkey Wrenches in Our Mexican Machinery," *Independent* 120 (April 14, 1928): 352.

77. HCIN, *Hearings on Western Hemisphere Immigration*, 238.

78. George Clements to Representative W. E. Evans, December 28, 1928, House Immigration and Naturalization Committee, file 70A–d10, Record Group 233, National Archives.

79. Senate Committee on Agriculture and Forestry, *Hearings on Agricultural Labor Supply* 71st Cong., 2d sess. (1930), 84–85.

80. HCIN, *Hearings on Western Hemisphere Immigration*, 61–69.

81. SCI, *Hearings on the Restriction of Western Hemisphere Immigration*, 30.

82. George Clements to W. E. Evans, December 27 and 28, 1928, House Immigration and Naturalization Committee, file 70A–D10, Record Group 233, National Archives; HCIN, *Hearings on Western Hemisphere Immigration*, 238; and *Hearings on Immigration from Countries of the Western Hemisphere*, 325; Teague, "A Statement on Mexican Immigration," 170.

83. *CR*, 71st Cong., 2d sess. (1930), 8842–44; Albert Johnson to V. S. McClatchy, June 5, 1930, House Immigration and Naturalization Committee, file 71A–F16.4, Record Group 233, National Archives; Francis Kinnicutt, "Immigration: Stalemate in Congress," *Eugenics* 3 (July 1930): 279. For an analysis of the legislative fight over the Mexican quota and the role of executive departments in the issue, see Mark Reisler, "Passing through Our Egypt: Mexican Labor in the United States, 1900–1940" (Ph.D. diss., Cornell University, 1973), chapter 9.

84. Henry L. Stimson to James J. Davis, September 23, 1929, U.S. Conciliation Service Records, file 165–223B, Record Group 280, National Archives.

85. *New York Times*, January 16, 1929, 9; James H. Batten, "New Features of Mexican Immigration," *National Conference of Social Work Proceedings* (Chicago, 1930), 486; Paul S. Taylor, "More Bars against Mexicans," *Survey* 64 (April 1, 1930): 26–27.

86. *New York Times*, May 16, 1930, 2.

3

The Importation of Mexican Contract Laborers to the United States, 1942–1964

Manuel García y Griego

It can be argued without exaggeration that the Bracero Program that ran from 1942 to 1964 helped to establish the major contours of modern Mexican migratory flows and to create many of the economic, political, and cultural issues that dominate debate over immigration at the present time. Although the program was originally viewed as a temporary measure designed to alleviate labor shortages in the United States during World War II, the bracero soon became an institutional feature of the American labor market after employers successfully convinced the U.S. Congress to renew the program repeatedly. However, as Manuel García y Griego, a professor of political science at the University of California, Irvine, argues in this richly detailed chapter, the institutionalization of the widespread use of Mexican labor had profound consequences. On the most basic level, the program helped to stimulate a renewed influx of both legal and unsanctioned immigrants. More important over the long run, the Bracero Program helped to reestablish and reinforce transnational migration circuits that in many ways still persist today.

The bracero program, also known as the Mexican contract-labor program, was a mechanism by which Mexicans were sent to work in certain agricultural areas of the United States under a series of bilateral agreements with Mexico that spanned two decades. It began in 1942 as an emergency program to satisfy perceived labor shortages created in agriculture by World War II. By the time this growing and increasingly controversial program reached its peak in the late 1950s, it had become an institutionalized feature of U.S. and Mexican agriculture.

From *The Border That Joins: Mexican Migrants and U.S. Responsibility*, ed. Peter G. Brown and Henry Shue (Totowa, NJ: Rowman and Littlefield, 1983), 49–98. Reprinted by permission of Rowman and Littlefield.

Although the contract-labor program was not renewed after 1965, it left an important legacy for the economies, migration patterns, and politics of the United States and Mexico. Since 1980, the possibility of again admitting temporary workers from Mexico has become a significant element in the ongoing debate over the direction of U.S. immigration policy. Various interpretations of what occurred during the program have figured prominently in arguments raised for and against the future admission of temporary workers. This chapter will describe the operation and development of the program in historical context and assess its legacy for the current policy debate.

An overview of the history of twentieth-century Mexican migration to the United States before 1942 suggests that four themes may be stressed: (a) the characterization of much of the flow as the movement of temporary or seasonal laborers; (b) the operation of formal labor recruitment systems; (c) the utilization of established repatriation mechanisms at selected points in time, especially during U.S. economic slowdowns; and (d) the involvement of U.S. and Mexican government agencies in influencing the nature and volume of the flow. . . .

Mexico's official position on emigration emerged from the 1917 Constitutional Convention, where legislation was passed in the form of Article 123 of the Constitution to provide safeguards for emigrant workers. Popular views in Mexico correctly held that emigrant workers in the United States suffered serious abuses. In the late teens, Mexican border officials were ordered to discourage the departure of workers who did not have labor contracts meeting the standards of the newly enacted legislation. The consulates in the United States were directed to become more active in protecting the rights of Mexican citizens, which they did, to a limited extent. Throughout the 1920s, the Mexican government exhorted emigrants to stay at home and provided return transportation to others with the hope that the return migration would be permanent.[1]

By 1929, it had become abundantly clear that Mexican unilateral efforts to restrain emigration had failed.[2] From this failure, and from the sudden realization in the early 1930s that the U.S. economic downturn— and not Mexican government policies—was causing emigrants to return in record numbers, emerged a view that the emigration of unemployed Mexicans was a "safety valve" for Mexico's polity.[3] In a move that would foreshadow the institution of the bracero program a decade later, the Mexican government in 1929 proposed to the United States that it consider an international agreement for the purpose of jointly managing the flow of workers between the two countries. The proposal was ill timed and not acted upon.[4]

In contrast, the changing policies of the U.S. government seemed to be a function of fluctuating economic conditions. In 1909, when there was apparently a need for sugar beet workers in Colorado and Nebraska, Presidents Taft and Porfirio Díaz arrived at an executive agreement authorizing the migration of a thousand Mexican contract laborers to those states. In 1917, as the United States entered World War I, the prohibitions against contract labor that had just been legislated were suspended for about seventy-three thousand Mexican workers.[5] Some authors have referred to the World War I temporary admissions as the "first bracero program."[6] The program begun in 1942 drew from the United States' experience with the unilateral recruitment of workers during this earlier period. . . .

Wartime Cooperation, 1942–1946

On August 4, 1942, the governments of the United States and Mexico embarked upon a program unprecedented in the history of both nations: the large-scale, sustained recruitment and contracting of temporary migrant workers under the aegis of an international agreement. This agreement was renewed several times during World War II, and in 1946, a year after the war ended, its termination was proposed by the State Department. Also in 1946, Congress provided the first legislative authority for a postwar contract-labor program. Since the succeeding international agreement, that of March 10, 1947, introduced some substantial changes in the operation of the program, 1946 marks an appropriate terminus for what may be considered the first and simplest phase of the bracero program.

What the 1942 agreement did was to create a labor recruitment and contracting system administered by a number of government agencies on both sides of the border. On the Mexican side the program first involved the Dirección General del Servicio Consular, the Oficialía Mayor and, later in the 1950s, the Dirección de Asuntos de Trabajadores Agrícolas Migratorios (DATAM) of the Secretaría de Relaciones Exteriores (SRE); officials of the Secretaría de Gobernación, and the Secretaría del Trabajo y Previsión Social; the offices of the state governors; and the *presidentes municipales* of counties where migrant workers resided. First an agency of Gobernación, then DATAM served as the principal administrative center, where operating decisions were made and information relative to Mexico's role in the international agreements was gathered. This agency was also responsible for assigning quotas to the Mexican states and for making sure that the requisite number of workers assembled at the recruitment centers (Mexico City during 1942–1944 and Guadalajara and

Irapuato during 1944–1947). The functions of some of these agencies changed several times during the life of the program.[7]

On the U.S. side, four departments were involved in the administration of the program: State, Justice, Agriculture, and Labor. The federal agencies most actively involved were the U.S. Employment Service (USES) of the Department of Labor (DOL) and its state branches, and the Immigration and Naturalization Service (INS) of the Department of Justice. The principal administrative responsibility was signed initially to the DOL in 1942; this was quickly transferred to the Department of Agriculture in 1943 and then returned to the DOL at the end of the war.[8]

The Mexicans who were accepted by their government as bracero candidates were turned over to the Department of Labor representatives, who, acting as agents for employers, selected those they thought fit for agricultural work. Next, INS officers took fingerprints and prepared documentation for those accepted, and the candidates were transported to U.S. contracting centers at the border. There they were screened by the U.S. Public Health Service and were left to be considered by visiting employers and their agents.[9]

This process of labor recruitment and distribution, created during the war, remained in operation for twenty-two years. To be sure, the names and duties of the government agencies involved changed throughout this period; for several years after World War II, the labor contracts were made directly between U.S. employers and Mexican workers, and the bureaucratic machinery to enforce their provisions was scaled back drastically. But even then, the program was operated within the framework of an international agreement, and either one or both governments were involved in the recruitment and distribution of workers. Thus, the wartime program represented the beginning of a process Ernesto Galarza aptly calls "managed migration"—a process sustained virtually without interruption from 1942 to 1964. In a number of other respects, however, the period 1942–1946 is unique. First, World War II represented a period of extraordinary growth in the demand for labor in the United States. Yet, by comparison to the years after 1946, the number of workers involved in the wartime program was the smallest ever. Another feature of the period 1942–1946 is that contract laborers were employed in activities other than agriculture. Finally, it was the only sustained period during which the Mexican government seems to have had the upper hand during the bilateral negotiations.

A felt need for labor and the critical importance of certain agricultural products in wartime were the essential elements which provided the justification—from the U.S. point of view—for the creation of the wartime emergency contract-labor program. Whether labor "shortages" actually existed or not is a matter of definition, but the labor market had definitely begun to favor the worker.

It is noteworthy, however, that the number of workers imported during the critical years of World War II was smaller than the number contracted for any comparable postwar period. Depending upon whether one uses Mexican or U.S. statistical sources, the average number of contract workers that entered per year during 1943–1946 was forty-nine thousand or eighty-two thousand.[10] Regardless of which of these two numbers is correct, or what precisely each data set indicates, there is no doubt that the wartime period involved the smallest volume of recorded bracero migration. During the later period of 1947–1954, the average annual number of contracts issued was at least 116,000 and could have been as high as 141,000. During the final ten years of the program, the average annual number of contracts recorded was 333,000. Of the total 4.6 million contracts issued during the life of the program, about 72 percent occurred between 1955 and 1964, whereas the wartime program involved only 4–7 percent of all such contracts.[11]

Indicators of Mexican Labor Migration to the United States, 1942–1964

Year[a]	Mexican contract workers departed, according to Mexican authorities[b] (Col.) 1	Contracts issued to Mexican workers by U.S. authorities[c] 2	Mexican immigrants admitted to U.S.[d] 3	Deportable Mexicans apprehended[e] 4
1942	4,152	4,203	2,378	na
1943	75,923	52,098	4,172	8,189
1944	118,059	62,170	6,598	26,689
1945	104,641	49,454	6,702	63,602
1946	31,198	32,043	7,146	91,456
1947	72,769	19,632	7,558	182,986
1948	24,320	35,345	8,384	179,385
1949	19,866	107,000	8,083	278,538
1950	23,399	67,500	6,744	458,215
1951	308,878	192,000	6,153	500,000
1952	195,963	197,100	9,079	543,538
1953	130,794	201,380	17,183	865,318
1954	153,975	309,033	30,645	1,075,168
1955	398,703	398,650	50,772	242,608
1956	432,926	445,197	65,047	72,442
1957	436,049	436,049	49,154	44,451

1958	432,491	432,857	26,712	37,242
1959	444,408	437,643	23,061	30,196
1960	319,412	315,846	32,684	29,651
1961	296,464	291,420	41,632	29,817
1962	198,322	194,978	55,291	30,272
1963	189,528	186,865	55,253	39,124
1964	179,298	177,736[f]	32,967	43,844

[a]Calendar years of column 1, fiscal years for all other columns.

[b]*Anuario Estadistico de los Estados Unidos Mexicanos*, 1943–1954, 1964, and unpublished data collected by the Dirección General de Estadística, summarized in Moisés González Navarro, *Población y sociedad en México (1900–1970)* (México: Facultad de Ciencias Políticas y Sociales, UNAM, 1974), vol. 2, table opposite p. 146.

[c]U.S. Department of Labor, summarized in Congressional Quarterly, *Congress and the Nation, 1945–1964* (Washington, DC: Congressional Quarterly Service, 1965), p. 762.

[d]For the period 1942–1954, the immigrants admitted refer to persons of Mexican citizenship, and beginning in 1955, to persons born in Mexico. U.S. Bureau of the Census, *Statistical Abstracts*, summarized in González Navarro, *Población y sociedad*, pp. 133–34.

[e]Prior to 1960 these refer to actual apprehensions; afterward, to deportable Mexicans located. INS *Annual Reports*, summarized in Julian Samora, *Los Mojados: The Wetback Story* (Notre Dame, IN: University of Notre Dame Press, 1971), p. 46.

[f]After 1964, the following number of contract workers were admitted under P.L. 414: 20,286 in 1965, 8,647 in 1966, 7,703 in 1967, and zero thereafter. U.S. Department of Labor, in *Mexican Workers in the United States: Historical and Political Perspectives*, ed. George C. Kiser and Martha Woody Kiser (Albuquerque: University of New Mexico Press, 1979), p. 219.

The only nonagricultural industry to succeed in establishing that a labor shortage existed was the railroad. The employment of contract laborers by this industry, particularly in tasks related to the maintenance of way, was unique to the wartime period and an aberration in the history of the bracero program.[12] Its administration by U.S. officials was entirely separate from the farm-labor program; and many of its logistical functions, such as defining the specifications and requirements for labor, securing food and transportation facilities, carrying out recruitment and interviewing workers, and issuing Individual Work Agreements and cards, were the responsibility of a quasi-labor agency, the Railroad Retirement Board.[13] Moreover, at the end of the war there was an immediate effort to repatriate the contract workers and terminate the program, an effort which suffered relatively minor delays.

In April 1943, when contracting for the railroad program began, the agency responsible for supervising the program, the War Manpower Commission, approved the use of construction and maintenance-of-way workers for the Southern Pacific; the Atchison, Topeka, and Santa Fé; and the Western Pacific railroads. The privilege of utilizing Mexican contract workers was extended the following year to twenty-one other railroads. By the time the contracting stopped in 1945, thirty-five railroads were involved. The majority of the railroad "braceros" worked in Montana, Washington, Oregon, California, Nevada, and southern Arizona; over half of them worked for the Southern Pacific or the Atchison, Topeka, and Santa Fé lines. At the peak of the railroad program in March 1945, sixty-nine thousand workers were employed.[14]

The position of the Mexican government on the creation and operation of the contract-labor program during the cooperative era of 1942–1946 was influenced to a great extent by its prior experiences with the repatriations of Mexican citizens, and with the unorganized recruitment that had been carried out by *enganchadores* (labor contractors) and private employers during the preceding decades. Controls over the international contracting of its citizens had been written into the Ley de Migración of 1932.[15] Mexico was also influenced by domestic public opinion, which opposed labor emigration to the United States,[16] and by the ideas of Manuel Gamio, a leading anthropologist who had written a seminal work on the subject in 1930.[17]

The preparation that went into the negotiation of the agreement, and the reluctance to enter into the contract-labor program in 1942, reveals the Mexican government's sensitivity to these factors and explains why it expressed serious reservations about the emigration of its citizens.[18] In addition to these concerns, opposition to the program was based on the notion that Mexican agricultural production would be harmed by labor emigration to the North.[19] Nevertheless, it is probable that emigration was perceived in some quarters of Mexican government as a potential safety valve for rural unemployment even as early as 1942. Adherents of this point of view held that the U.S.-Mexican agreement would facilitate the labor exodus in a controlled manner, one which would allow the Mexican government to influence its management. Moreover, it seems that the bracero agreement was initially conceived by Mexico as part of a package that included wartime cooperation in other areas in exchange for U.S. concessions on Mexico's foreign debt and the settlement of claims arising from the recently expropriated oil industry.[20]

In any event, when in 1942 Mexico expressed its willingness to consider an international labor agreement with the United States, it did so on the basis of a number of conditions.[21] First, recruitment would be based on a written labor contract. Second, the administration of the program would be carried out by both governments, and contract compliance would be guaranteed by the same. Third, recruitment would be based on need, i.e., Mexican laborers would not displace domestic labor or lower its wage.[22] Fourth, employers or the U.S. government would pay transportation and subsistence costs between the recruitment center in Mexico and the work site. Fifth, contract workers would need to be permitted to remain permanently in the United States. Finally, racial discrimination, of the type in which Mexicans were turned away from "white" restaurants and public facilities or sorted by color on buses, was unacceptable. Its occurrence in a U.S. community would constitute grounds for excluding braceros from that community. In the view of the Mexican government, adherence to these conditions would allow the migration to take place without the serious abuses it perceived had occurred in the past.[23]

The agreement, signed on July 23, 1942, and made effective by an exchange of diplomatic notes on August 4, incorporated all the above elements and provided contract workers with certain labor guarantees not then available under U.S. law to domestic workers. This outcome suggests a relatively strong Mexican negotiating position in 1942,[24] a further indication of which was the initial reaction by U.S. growers to the contents of the agreement. The president of the American Farm Bureau complained about the extensiveness of the program's regulations, expressed the view that they were unnecessary, and recognized that informal recruitment mechanisms already existed: "Why not just let the growers go into Mexico and get the workers they needed as they had done in the past?"[25]

Another indication of Mexico's bargaining strength was its refusal to certify braceros for employment in the state of Texas—a position it justified by reference to the discriminatory treatment historically suffered by Mexicans in that state. In response, Texas appointed its Good Neighbor Commission and lobbied strongly to be included among the areas receiving contract laborers. It was unsuccessful in effecting a change in Mexican policy throughout the war, however, and not until March 10, 1947, did Mexico lift its ban on Texas.[26] During the period when the bracero agreement was not in force in Texas, its agricultural employers relied on Mexican workers who entered without any documents at all—known then as "wetbacks."

Although the Mexican government's practice of unilaterally blacklisting Texas—and other U.S. areas where discrimination occurred—may not have reduced the discrimination its citizens suffered in the United States, it did promote a greater awareness, at some embarrassment to U.S. officials, of the problem. The Mexican government could also point to the blacklisting, in justifying the program to domestic constituencies, as a sign of its willingness to establish some limits on the abuses suffered by Mexican workers in the United States. Nonetheless, the practice became a serious bone of contention, and it ended during the negotiations for the 1949 agreement.

Despite occasional tension over the conduct of the program, the two governments managed to play down the conflicts that occurred and put the best possible light on the situation. Some of those incidents, however, were indicative of underlying tensions that were to erupt in the postwar period, during a time when the management of conflict between the two governments was to receive less attention.

One source of tension was the previously mentioned Mexican insistence that contract laborers not be sent to Texas because of ongoing discrimination against Mexicans in that region. Nevertheless, Texas growers needed labor, and they made their needs felt when Congress, in the spring of 1943, enacted Public Law 45, which gave legislative approval to the executive agreement negotiated months earlier. The act included a section authorizing the commissioner of immigration to lift then-existing restrictions on the entry of farm laborers so that under certain conditions an "open border" could be unilaterally declared by the United States, much as had occurred during the temporary admissions of World War I. On May 11, 1943, regulations were issued authorizing Mexican laborers waiting at the border to enter for a period of one year. According to one source, Texas farmers, "harried by fears of insufficient labor to meet spring needs, rushed across the border to recruit the necessary workers." This process evidently undermined the bilateral program upon which the Mexican government had staked so much, and on May 28 it threatened to abrogate the agreement. After a series of meetings between U.S. government officials and farm groups "in which some of the participants bluntly advocated disregarding Mexico's wishes," the State Department announced that the section of Public Law 45 providing for unilateral recruitment did not apply to Mexico.[27] What in 1944 might have boiled over as a crisis was averted by the adoption of a U.S. position that assigned a greater weight to assuring Mexico's cooperation in keeping the program intact than to assuaging the special interests of Texas growers in getting access to labor on their own terms.

Another source of tension was the management—or mismanagement—of the so-called wetback problem. When contract laborers and unilaterally recruited workers were banned from Texas, in order to assure a labor supply to the growers of that state the U.S. government acquiesced in the use of "wetback" labor by Texas farmers. An assistant commissioner of immigration wrote: "At times, due to manpower shortages and critical need for agricultural production brought on by the war, the Service officers were instructed to defer the apprehension of Mexicans employed on Texas farms."[28] This practice brought Mexican protests that the United States do something about the employment of undocumented workers, and U.S. countercharges that Mexico itself was not doing enough to prevent illegal migration and to return expelled migrants to the interior.

In June 1944, the two governments agreed on a set of joint policies to address the problem, which included border enforcement by both countries.[29] According to U.S. sources, Mexico did not carry out its part of the agreement. The United States did increase enforcement by the INS, but to minimize its expense, it expelled the migrants through the nearest border community; those apprehended in California were expelled through Mexicali and Tijuana, which were virtually isolated from the rest of Mexico at the time because of limited transportation facilities. These INS actions apparently created severe problems for those Mexican border communities, and in December 1944 the Mexican government unilaterally closed those two ports to the return of expelled migrants. The U.S. government responded by redirecting some of those expelled migrants to other border ports more accessible to the Mexican interior.[30] As in the previous example, this series of events suggests a superior Mexican bargaining position.

During 1945 and 1946, Mexico and the United States continued to make limited efforts to improve the management of the legal program and to address the problem of workers who entered illegally. By this time, however, it was becoming clear that without spending additional money on enforcement—and perhaps [not even] then—these objectives would not be met. For whatever reasons, neither government increased its allocation of resources significantly. When the war came to a close, conditions were perceived to have worsened. The Mexican government refused to transport expelled migrants to the interior, U.S. officials slackened efforts to deport migrants, and unemployed Mexicans congregated in the border towns of both countries. Domestic groups in the United States, which had not been vocal during the war, began to speak out against the importation of foreign labor.[31]

At the end of 1946, the posture of the U.S. government, though ambiguous, seemed to indicate that the bracero program was coming to an end. To be sure, Public Laws 521 and 707, enacted that year, extended the appropriations of the program to 1947 and provided legislative authority for what could no longer be considered an emergency, wartime program. Nevertheless, the nonagricultural component of the bilateral agreement was terminated noisily, and the State Department formally proposed an end to the agricultural program within the time frame originally established. Similarly, although two years earlier a Mexican source had indicated that the emigration of workers had been a palliative for Mexico's unemployment, the secretaría de trabajo unofficially communicated its desire that the program come to an end.[32] Thus, during the closing weeks of 1946 it appeared that the four-year program, with several hundred thousand contracts issued, was about to pass into history. It would have been difficult to imagine that eighteen more years of existence and 4.3 million more contracts lay ahead.

Turbulence and Transition, 1947–1954

Almost all the significant changes that occurred in the contract program between the early war years and the late contracting system of the 1960s took place during the eight-year period 1947–1954. During these eight years, the bracero program evolved from a wartime to a peacetime activity where key interests and power politics were given a freer hand, the consequences of which are examined below.

A useful approach to the issues of that time is to divide them into two broad categories: (a) the general problem of illegal, or "wetback," immigration, and (b) certain specific issues of dispute between Mexico and the United States. These problem issues resulted in a number of confrontations, two (October 1948 and January 1954) of which merit discussion as events that both shaped and laid bare the reaccommodation of postwar U.S.-Mexican power relationships.

The Postwar Wetback Invasion

The entry and presence of undocumented Mexicans became an important issue that drew increased national attention and public hostility in the United States during the postwar years.[33] Since undocumented migration is a clandestine phenomenon, the public perception of the growing problem was based on data that could be only a rough index of its volume, and on its interpretation by public officials. At that time as now, this data consisted of the number of deportable aliens apprehended by the INS. A rapidly growing number of such apprehensions led the [U.S.] President's Commission on Migratory Labor to argue in 1951: "The number of deportations and voluntary departures has continuously mounted each year. . . . In its newly achieved proportions, [the wetback traffic] is virtually an *invasion*."[34] The magnitude of the arrests increased rather than declined after the commission's report, and in 1954, an INS official characterized the phenomenon as "the greatest peacetime invasion complacently suffered by a country under open, flagrant, contemptuous violation of its laws."[35]

The views expressed by the commission in 1951 reflected a position that was slow to develop in the United States. Earlier, public opinion had countenanced the illegal entry and employment of undocumented Mexicans. Thus, some of the proposals of the commission—the imposition of penalties for those who harbored, concealed, or transported illegal aliens; fines and imprisonment for employers of deportable aliens; prohibitions against interstate shipment of products made with the labor of undocumented aliens[36]—seemed novel or harsh. The recommendations of the commission were largely ignored. Only the criminal sanctions against "harboring" deportable aliens were approved, and at the insistence of the Texas congressional delegation, the so-called Texas Proviso was inserted in the 1952 antiwetback legislation, which explicitly exempted the act of offering employment from its penalties.[37]

By contrast, since the early 1940s the Mexican government had expressed the view that the extralegal emigration of its workers was a threat to the bracero system, to domestic agricultural production, and to the agricultural interests who wanted assured access to an ample domestic labor supply. Early in the operation of the program Mexico pressed the United States to effectively penalize employers of undocumented labor. It also promoted cooperative efforts to control the clandestine migration to the North, but it stopped short of costly enforcement measures.[38]

Critics of Mexican antiwetback policies have pointed out that other than consistently to pressure the United States to penalize employers, Mexico itself did little to stop the undocumented flow.[39] The reasons for this have yet to be adequately explored. Certainly, Mexican officials were juridically correct in pointing out that Mexican legislation on this issue provided the government with few legal instruments to interfere with the free transit of its citizens. Also, Mexican policymakers probably had not forgotten that there were limits to the effectiveness of Mexican government intervention in this process, as evidenced by the failure of Mexican efforts in the 1920s to stop labor emigration. Moreover, the thrust of Mexican government actions throughout the bracero program suggests an awareness by political elites that the government had little domestic "policy space" in this issue area.[40] But there is also evidence, as is mentioned below, to show that Mexico's stake in the continuation of emigration to the United States seems to have become more visible in the postwar years, raising the question [of] whether it was consistent with its objective interests to stop the clandestine flow. Nevertheless, Mexico's perceived interests, as well as its formal position, were consistently expressed in opposition to the uncontrolled emigration of its citizens.

The United States was more equivocal. "Even in 1952 and 1954, when the wetbacks were in full tide," wrote Ernesto Galarza, "senators and representatives from the border states took the lead in cutting back appropriations for the Border Patrol. With the purse half shut the gate could remain half open."[41] Testimony of Border Patrol officers indicates that immigration law enforcement, particularly along the Texas border, was deliberately lax and selective. As early as 1949, Senator Clinton P. Anderson of New Mexico had introduced a bill (S. 272) arguing for an "open border" and virtually unrestricted recruitment from Mexico.[42] The following year, the chief inspector at the port of Tucson, Arizona, testifying before the President's Commission on Migratory Labor, noted that he "received orders from the District Director at El Paso each harvest to stop deporting illegal Mexican labor."[43] A report from south Texas at about the same time indicates that a senior officer kept his force of Border Patrolmen away from certain farms and ranches in his district.[44] The explanation for this flexible approach to the enforcement of immigration law was expressed in testimony before Congress in 1951 by the chief INS official responsible for this enforcement in a bald-faced assertion of authority to enforce the law selectively: "We do feel we have the authority to permit to remain in the United States aliens who are here as agricultural workers whether they are here legally or not."[45]

U.S. policy responses to undocumented migration can be divided into two categories: mass legalization (1947–1951) and mass expulsion accompanied by legalization (1954–55). Both processes involved the transformation of illegal to legal (contract) labor migration. During this period, therefore, the flow of Mexican labor was not stopped; it was regularized. The first process was called "drying out the wetbacks"; the second was a campaign run by the Border Patrol called "Operation Wetback."

Legalization was a process by which deportable Mexicans who had been in the United States for a certain number of weeks were given bracero contracts, usually to work for the same employer, without the laborer having to return to Mexico and undergo the screening process in the interior, or the employer having to pay transportation to the United States. It first occurred as a result of the 1947 bilateral agreement, when fifty-five thousand undocumented Mexicans in Texas (which up to that time had received no contract laborers) were legalized as braceros.[46] According to the President's Commission on Migratory Labor, during the years 1947–1949, 74,600 Mexican contract laborers were imported, and 142,200 deportable Mexicans already in the United States were legalized and put under contract.[47] During fiscal year 1950, only 19,813 new bracero contracts were issued; but 96,239 undocumented Mexicans already here were "dried out" as a result of the international agreement.[48] Thus, in the years following the war, more legalized "wetbacks" were contracted by employers than braceros were imported from within Mexico. By the time the commission's report was written in 1951, it had·become evident that mass legalization was not curbing illegal immigration; as a result, its abolition was successfully recommended.[49] Nevertheless, the practice did convince many employers that bracero labor could be used as a substitute for undocumented labor when deportation raids threatened to interrupt access to such labor.[50]

The organization of Operation Wetback followed a tour of inspection of the U.S.-Mexican border in August 1953 by Attorney General Herbert Brownell.[51] In April 1954, retired army general Joseph Swing, a personal friend of President Eisenhower, was named INS commissioner, and a military-style expulsion campaign was in the process of formulation.[52] After much fanfare in the United States, Operation Wetback formally began on June 17 with the deployment of eight hundred Border Patrol officers in Mexican communities and ranches throughout southern California. The immigration authorities were able to count on the support of local and state authorities, including the police, and the local press, who created the impression that an "army" of Border Patrolmen was "invading" the area. The patrol had impressive logistical support, including the use of aircraft and boats. Most important, in California they were able to count on the farmers who employed the aliens.[53] Many were not expelled to the border as was customary, but were transported by air, sea, and land to the Mexican interior with financial support provided by the Mexican government.[54]

In the months following, the operation moved to the Midwest and Pacific Northwest, and to Texas, where it received some resistance in farm communities.[55] Operation Wetback was sanctioned by U.S. public opinion, which blamed "wetbacks" for the propagation of disease, labor strikes in agriculture, subversive and communist infiltration, border crimes, low retail sales in south Texas, and adverse effects on domestic labor.[56]

Operation Wetback was viewed by its organizers as a test upon whose outcome the future of the Border Patrol might rest.[57] Fortunately for the leadership of the INS, the action was immediately successful in restoring credibility and morale to an agency which had a serious image problem with Congress.[58] The campaign had been under way for barely a month when Congress, which had cut the INS's budget from the previous year, rewarded the agency with a supplemental appropriation of $3 million.[59]

Contrary to popular opinion, Operation Wetback was not merely a mass-expulsion campaign, although the deportation drives were the most visible part of this action. Had it been, history suggests that it would have accomplished little. Instead, the relative success of Operation Wetback in reducing the volume of illegal migration seems to have rested upon a unique strategy of combined rewards and punishments mostly directed at the employers of such workers. Important elements in this strategy were INS activities designed to (a) convince employers that they faced an increased risk of having the INS interrupt their use of undocumented labor,[60] (b) facilitate access to contract labor for these employers,[61] and (c) "streamline" the contract-labor program and eliminate those provisions to which employers objected most seriously.[62] Another element that seems to have been important in effecting changes in employer attitudes toward the *status* of their workers (though not toward their need for Mexican labor) was the more general pattern of antiwetback public opinion.[63] These factors, taken together, provide plausible reasons why Operation Wetback was successful in regularizing much of the flow of Mexican labor to the United States.

As early as 1955, the INS could take credit for having eradicated the "wetback problem." In his annual report of that year, Commissioner Swing wrote: "The so-called 'wetback' problem no longer exists. . . . The border has been secured."[64] The number of apprehensions of Mexicans dropped precipitously after 1954, and by 1958 the Mexican newspaper *Excélsior* was implicitly editorializing that "the era of the 'wetbacks' [had passed] into history."[65] Hindsight tells us, of course, that they editorialized too soon, but it is evident that the flow of undocumented labor was reduced substantially for a decade from what appearances suggest it had been before 1954.

The costs of this achievement were not immediately apparent.[66] One of the consequences of the "success" of Operation Wetback, as was noted, was the substitution of bracero labor for undocumented workers. In order to persuade employers to effect the substitution, the protections of the contract-labor program were dropped—formally, through negotiation with Mexico, and informally, by reduced U.S. enforcement of contract provisions.[67] In other words, after 1954 the bracero program became little more than a formally sanctioned recruitment system for the employment of "wetbacks" in U.S. agriculture.

Diplomacy and Dispute on Selected Issues

The period 1947–1954 witnessed a series of sharp confrontations between the governments of the United States and Mexico and a growing public debate on the formal aspects of the contract-labor program. The disputed issues, to be discussed below, were (a) the location of the recruitment centers in Mexico, (b) the practice employed by the Mexican government of unilaterally blacklisting areas and employers from receiving contract workers, (c) the wages earned by contract laborers, and (d) the relative merits of government-to-government and employer-to-worker agreements. To varying degrees, each of these issues led to breakdowns in negotiations during this eight-year period, and each contributed to the mounting tensions immediately preceding the two border incidents and diplomatic confrontations.

Out of this turbulence, three major and interconnected themes emerge: the progressive deterioration of the Mexican government's bargaining position, the assertion of control over the program by U.S. farm organizations, and the increasing importance to the Mexican government that it maintain the program for what was perceived to be a "safety valve" for domestic rural unemployment. As a result of these processes, by 1954 U.S. farm groups had managed to institutionalize a labor-recruitment program largely paid for by the Mexican and U.S. governments, which supplied them with labor on favorable terms. Also apparent by 1954 was a willingness on the part of the Mexican government to compromise, almost at any cost, its position on the operation of the program and to look the other way when the contract guarantees it had worked so hard to achieve became diluted.

The U.S. position on the location of the recruitment centers, which was largely determined by the interests of agricultural employers, was that recruitment should be done as close to the border as possible. A nearby recruitment center was attractive because it meant lower transportation and subsistence costs to the employer who participated in the program.[68] This position also recognized that, since Mexican northward migration to the border had been self-sustained since the 1920s, there was no need for a formal recruitment system to absorb the expense of transporting workers from their communities of origin.

The Mexican position held that recruitment centers should be located in the interior, hundreds of miles from the border. This position seems to have been determined by two principal considerations: first, that the labor supply of large-scale Mexican agriculturalists in the northern states of Sonora, Chihuahua, and Sinaloa might be adversely affected by border recruitment, and second, that the degree of Mexican control over the migration process was directly proportional to the distance the centers were located away from the border.[69] This position recognized that the contract-labor program was a system of managed migration; in order to reduce the effects of *stimulating* undocumented migration, the centers should be located *away* from the border, where such effects would be less pronounced.

The location of the recruitment centers gradually shifted northward. During the war, Mexicans were recruited in Mexico City, Guadalajara, and Irapuato. During the 1947–1954 period, new centers were located closer to or at the border: Monterrey, Chihuahua, Zacatecas, Tampico, Aguascalientes, Hermosillo, and Mexicali. Beginning in 1955, Mexican statistics show that some braceros were officially contracted at the border, and Empalme, Sonora, also appeared as a new recruitment center location.[70]

The demise of the Mexican negotiating position on this issue had occurred as early as 1950, even though it may not have been evident to the public at the time. On August 18 of that year, the Mexican government did not seek to prevent the issuance of work certificates to Mexicans at the border. "Although Mexico expressed concern about the total withdrawal of wetback restraint," wrote Peter Kirstein, "there was no abrogation, there was no protest note—just a request that publicity of the Mexican-supported open order 'be restricted.' "[71]

Similarly, the practice of blacklisting certain areas in the United States by the Mexican government to bar the use of braceros was another source of international conflict in which Mexico's position was gradually undermined. These bars were motivated by Mexican perceptions that employers in those areas had not lived up to the terms of the agreements, and by concerns that Mexican citizens in those places were subjected to discrimination. The first concern led to a brief ban upon eight midwestern and northwestern states in 1946 because of reported violations of the agreement by sugar beet employers.[72] The second concern led to the prohibition of Mexican contract labor in Texas until the legalization in 1947 of undocumented workers already there.[73] Mexico's perception that Texas farmers proceeded to violate the terms of the contracts conferred upon them with the acceptance of legalized labor led to its decision to close Texas to further bracero contracting on September 26 of that year.

The Mexican position during the January–February 1949 negotiations held that a blacklisted area would not be allowed to receive contract workers until guarantees were offered by local authorities that discrimination would stop. In the event that these guarantees were violated, the appropriate Mexican consul was to request the participation of the USES in a joint investigation. But "if the USES and the Mexican consul differed as to the presence of discrimination, the issue was to be unilaterally resolved by the Mexican foreign minister."[74]

The United States argued for joint determination of blacklisted areas and made the execution of its part of the bargain to enforce laws against "wetbacks" contingent upon Mexico's removal of the Texas ban. By the summer of 1949, the Mexican government had given in, and the bracero program was salvaged by an agreement to determine such bans jointly.[75]

Disputes between the United States and Mexico concerning the wages to be paid to braceros by farm employers go to the heart of the conflict over the administration of the program itself. The President's Commission correctly characterized the negotiation of the agreements as a "collective bargaining situation" where Mexico represented its workers and the United States its employers. And the SRE, wrote Galarza, "had never concealed its polite indignation over the low wages prevailing in the Southwest."[76] According to Galarza, Mexican pressures to raise the wages paid to braceros led to the two open-border incidents that occurred in 1948 and 1954. Mexican motives for wage increases seem to have been linked to domestic pressure by labor organizations in Mexico and the awareness that they would improve the foreign-exchange earnings of the contract workers. The U.S. response was to accuse the Mexican consuls of attempting to set the wages at rates higher than those prevailing, to blame the "wetback" influx upon Mexican intransigence, and to insist that "if farm employers were to be persuaded to give up hiring illegals 'certain modifications in the agreement and in the work contract are imperative.' "[77]

The original Mexican position during the 1942 agreements was that Mexican labor was to be paid the "prevailing wage" in the communities where braceros were sent. As the Mexican government began to realize that the prevailing wage was whatever the employers decided it would be, it developed the position that the wages paid were negotiable.[78] Its attempt to raise wages for cotton pickers in 1948, however, was unsuccessful. The death knell of the new Mexican position was sounded by the terms of the 1951 agreement, which stated that the U.S. secretary of labor would have the exclusive responsibility for determining the prevailing level of wages.[79] After the second major diplomatic confrontation in 1954, the Joint Determination signed that year reaffirmed the same principle.[80]

A final issue that grew out of the conflicts of the years 1947–1954 was the relative merits of government-to-government and worker-to-employer agreements. The wartime agreements were of the former type: they required close governmental supervision over recruitment, selection, transportation, the issuance of contracts, the investigation of complaints, and the assurance of contract compliance. The 1948 agreement introduced some changes that moved the program in the direction of the latter type of agreement: Individual Worker Contracts were issued on a worker-to-employer basis, and the responsibility of the INS and USES for assuring compliance was removed.[81] Experimentation with a less formal version of the bracero program continued until congressional approval of Public Law 78 in 1951.

The passage of Public Law 78 had come partially as a result of Mexican insistence that a formal structure for the execution of bilateral agreements be created, and that there be a return to a government-to-government program. In pressing its demands, the Mexican government took advantage of the conjuncture afforded by the Korean War. Its position was strengthened by the President's Commission, whose report was issued as the enactment of Public Law 78 was being debated, and which also argued for an end to the worker-to-employer experiment.[82] Mexico's insistence that the experiment come to an end was motivated by the perception that U.S. employers frequently violated the terms of the agreements negotiated between 1948 and 1951. Placing the responsibility for enforcing the agreement on the shoulders of the U.S. government was perceived to be the most feasible way to assure compliance.[83] Mexican pressures for assuring accountability therefore could be expressed through the familiar channels of diplomatic protest and bilateral negotiation.

The passage of Public Law 78 and the end of the informal period of contracting could be narrowly construed to be a victory for the Mexican vis-à-vis the U.S. position.[84] However, during the postwar years the U.S. position shifted from one exclusively determined by powerful agricultural interests to one influenced by other segments of the U.S. public. These latter segments demanded that the United States assert some control over contract-labor migration and not leave it exclusively in the hands of the employers. Their views were typified by those of the President's Commission. Even so, the influence that employers had on Congress can be discerned from the fact that, despite the pressure of antiwetback forces, the Mexican government, and others, Congress refused to legislate any penalties against employers for hiring "wetbacks."

The adoption of Public Law 78 was a hollow victory for the Mexican government. To be sure, the mechanisms to ensure contract compliance were formally in place once again, but by this time the Mexican negotiating position had so deteriorated that it mattered little. The years after the 1951 agreement, and particularly after 1954, are marked by Mexican acquiescence in a program whose specifics would have been rejected out of hand at any time prior to 1947.[85]

An important event that influenced Mexican policy responses to bracero emigration was the increasing Mexican stake in maintaining the contract-labor system. This grew out of the perception, which came to dominate the views of Mexican policymakers sometime after World War II, that bracero emigration provided much-needed dollar income[86] and "probably spared Mexico a great deal of social unrest and upheaval."[87] Juan Ramón García argues: "Even if Mexico had discontinued the program at the end of World War II, it is quite doubtful that large-scale emigration to the United States could have been prevented. . . . [A]n international agreement, reasoned Mexican officials, would allow for some protection of their citizens while in the United States. If mass emigration seemed inevitable, then let it occur under government auspices."[88] While it is not clear just when the view that emigration was "inevitable" became prevalent among policymakers, it evidently gained currency in the postwar years. At the same time, emigration was becoming a source of acute embarrassment, because it was associated with the failure of the regime's land-reform program.[89]

Thus, the relationship between the Mexican government and the labor program began to be framed in the form of a dilemma for Mexican policymakers. On the one hand, the program was perceived to be increasingly important as a safety valve for domestic political and economic troubles and as an interim strategy for managing Mexico's economic underdevelopment. On the other hand, Mexico's participation in the program was itself viewed as an admission of failure in providing domestic solutions for unemployment problems and as an activity that abetted the exploitation and discrimination suffered by Mexican workers in the United States. Thus, the Mexican government found itself caught between what it perceived to be a growing stake in keeping the labor program in operation and the political heat resulting from its participation in it—particularly the criticisms leveled at it by leftist opposition groups.[90] It acted to reduce the impact of negative publicity arising from the program and adopted public and private negotiating positions that were increasingly inconsistent.[91] As Mexico's maneuvering room with respect to the United States was shrinking as a consequence of the domestic political process, its bargaining capacity vis-à-vis its neighbor was deteriorating steadily. These complex, interrelated processes set the stage for the diplomatic confrontations of 1948 and 1954.

Two Open-Border Incidents

In the summer of 1948 the U.S. government pressured Mexico to allow recruitment along the border; Mexico yielded partially by agreeing to establish a recruitment center in Mexicali and by proposing that centers be established in interior cities of other border states. Nevertheless, according to a secret study uncovered by Peter Kirstein in the Truman Library, representatives of the DOL, the INS, and the State Department met to discuss the pros and cons of opening the border to illegal entrants, thereby unilaterally disrupting the 1948 agreement. The meeting, mediated by the White House, seems to have resulted in the position that the agreement would be adhered to.[92]

Between October 13 and 18, however, the border port of El Paso was opened to several thousand undocumented Mexicans waiting to enter the United States: "The *braceros* . . . waded the shallow river in sight of the

Border Patrol, which received them with formality, herded them into temporary enclosures and immediately paroled them to the cotton growers, who trucked the men at once to the fields."[93] The Mexican government responded by abrogating the 1948 agreement, formally announcing that it would reserve the possibility of filing claims for damage inflicted upon its agricultural production in the North from the uncontrolled exodus of border resident laborers. The United States formally apologized for the incident days later.[94]

As a result of his review of the secret study, Kirstein concluded that the order to open the border did not emanate from the White House, but was a decision made within the INS and USES. He made a point to note that no disciplinary action was taken against the officials who created the "El Paso incident," as it became known, and that the United States used the incident to place new conditions on the table when negotiations were reopened during January–February 1949.[95]

In any event, the planning for the second incident clearly involved the highest levels of the U.S. government.[96] On January 15, 1954, the Departments of Justice, State, and Labor issued a joint press release announcing that braceros would be contracted unilaterally until a binational accord was reached. Mexico responded sharply by announcing that braceros could no longer be legally contracted to work in the United States and by exhorting Mexican laborers to stay at home.[97]

The situation in 1954 would seem anomalous today: the United States was advocating an "open border" at its neighbor's expense. During the last week of January, hundreds of Mexican workers gathered at Mexican border cities with the expectation of entering the United States, despite the call of their government to stay at home. Mexican local police converged upon mobs, attempting to disperse them and to prevent their entry to the United States. As some of the men raced across the line they were snatched back into Mexico, while Border Patrol officers extended a helping hand from the other side. Other undocumented migrants already in the United States were brought to the border, told to step across briefly to meet the legal requirement of having been expelled, and then to reenter so they could be admitted as contract workers by INS officials. The resulting commotion was illustrated graphically in a photograph published in February 1954, depicting a bracero pulled in a tug of war between a Mexican border official and a U.S. officer.[98]

Mexico countered with a show of force designed to prevent the emigration of its citizens. The government deployed troops to Ensenada, Nuevo Laredo, Nogales, and other points near the border. Border guards repelled the rush of illegal crossers with clubs, fists, water hoses, and shots fired into the air. In Mexicali, five hundred would-be braceros marched on the governor's palace demanding jobs or food; soldiers turned them back with fire hoses. As President Ruiz Cortines received reports that the international confrontation was turning into a domestic crisis at the border, he ordered Mexican troops withdrawn and instructed Mexican officials not to use force to oppose any citizen attempting to cross illegally. Mexico had been beaten in its brief attempt to use dissuasion and force to prevent the emigration of its workers.[99]

The Mexican defeat in January 1954 merely laid bare the end result of a process that had been unfolding for several years. On the one hand, as close observers had known for some time, Mexico lacked either the political will or the policy instruments to withhold the labor of its workers on whose behalf it was negotiating, and its "cooperation" with the United States in this and other issue areas was no longer vital. On the other hand, domestic criticism was forcing Mexico to adopt positions which it could not sustain.[100] When it refused to compromise further its position in the fall of 1953, it apparently miscalculated in assuming that the United States would not adopt a position of unilateral recruitment.[101] Once the confrontation was in process, little could be done to salvage Mexico's position or credibility.

A number of deliberately conciliatory signals sent by Mexico during the crisis were suggestive of Mexico's limited "policy space." It unilaterally extended the life of the agreement which had expired, and Ruiz Cortines made a public statement that the affront by the United States was "not a problem but only an incident that could be resolved within the norms of the good neighbor policy."[102] Simultaneously, the Mexican ambassador in Washington quietly made a request that negotiations be resumed, to which Eisenhower publicly acceded on February 11. Since the Mexican government needed a face-saving device, this was played up as a victory in the Mexican press.[103]

In the aftermath of the diplomatic crisis it was discovered that the U.S. government had no legal authority to spend federal funds on unilateral recruitment; Congress therefore passed Joint Resolution 355 on March 3, which amended Public Law 78 to provide for U.S. unilateral recruitment.[104] Although the implications of this were not lost on the Mexican negotiators (a U.S. congressman characterized it as a means of seeking an agreement "with a pistol in their backs"),[105] the Mexican government publicly played down this legislative defeat.[106] Two days later, the Mexican government announced that the negotiations for a new agreement were proceeding satisfactorily. To allow Mexico some domestic maneuvering room, Eisenhower postponed signing Resolution 355. A new bilateral accord, in which Mexico in essence ceded all its demands, was reached on March 10, and on March 16 Eisenhower signed the resolution into law.[107] Perhaps to strengthen Mexico's position before its domestic critics, or because the U.S. president had an appreciation for irony, he explained that signing Resolution 355 was "necessary for the United States government to provide Mexican braceros with the protection of its laws." Not surprisingly, Mexico publicly ignored the resolution and instead played up its "success" in reaching the labor agreement, which in actuality "contained little to satisfy the Mexican demands that had prompted termination of the agreement a few months earlier."[108]

The crisis of January 1954 was a rude awakening for the Mexican public. A columnist in a Mexico City newspaper in February seemed to express this when he wrote that thanks to the "safety valve afforded by emigration, the failure of the regime's agrarian-reform policies had not provoked another revolution."[109] Another columnist wondered: "Is it possible to prevent the emigration of braceros?"[110] The answer from the Mexican public seemed to be "no." In his State of the Union address in September 1954, Ruiz Cortines "deplored the migration of laborers but concluded that it was unavoidable because the country did not have enough work to hold the braceros."[111] This view was to hold among Mexican political elites for many years after the crisis of 1954.[112]

Apogee and Demise, 1955–1964

By 1955 the bracero program was well into what Richard Craig calls the "era of stabilization"—a period with no serious disagreements between Mexico and the United States or substantive changes in the formal operation of the program. It was also a time when the "adverse effects" of the importation of foreign workers, particularly in the agricultural labor market, emerged as a domestic issue in the United States, which ultimately led to the end of the contract-labor program.

Early opposition to the importation of foreign workers, in 1947–1949, was based on claims that it undermined strikes, working conditions, and farm wages. So claimed the National Association for the Advancement of Colored People, which issued public statements to that effect; and the National Farm Labor Union, affiliated with the American Federation of Labor, enlisted the support of the Federal Advisory Council of the Bureau of Employment Security with the DOL. This position apparently had limited acceptance at that time, however; although the President's Commission showed that the increased use of braceros correlated negatively with rising agricultural wages, it did *not* propose an end to the program. Instead, it argued for modifications which would assure that certifications of need would be based on actual shortages.[113] This view implicitly recognized that the realities of U.S. domestic politics did not allow for any successful opposition to the farm bloc in Congress and assumed that if the program could be held to some standard of compliance, adverse effects could be avoided.

Growers opposed such interpretations of the contract-labor program with arguments which essentially held that there were no serious adverse effects and that the labor contracts were being complied with. They argued that braceros were more efficient than native workers, and that far from constituting a source of cheap labor, they were more expensive than domestic workers since employers were responsible for transportation costs, insurance, bonds, and the like.[114] It appears that the thrust of the growers' arguments—that bracero laborers were more expensive in terms of gross outlays—would have been correct if the contracts had actually been complied with. Evidence suggests that contract compliance was most frequently observed during the wartime program, the period when the labor program was least attractive to employers.[115] Nonetheless, as contract compliance declined and the program was made more attractive to employers (after the postwar period of worker-to-employer agreements and during Operation Wetback), adverse effects from the importation of contract laborers became more visible.[116] As the number of workers involved in the program expanded, growers resorted to the fiction that bracero workers were more expensive—as indeed they had been at the beginning of the program[117]—to defend the program against those who attacked it as a means for importing "cheap labor." In assessing this expanding bracero labor force, Galarza wrote: "Contrary to the iron laws of supply and demand, which are nowhere more ironic than in agriculture, the dearer type of labor was driving out of the market the cheaper."[118]

The substitution of contracted labor for domestic labor proceeded apace throughout this final phase of the program. California farm-labor statistics tell part of the story. From December 1949 to September 1959, the peak number of braceros at work in the state shot up from seventy-five hundred to eighty-four thousand. Peak employment of local domestic seasonal workers for the same years declined from 150,000 to 131,500. In certain crops, such as sugar beets, and certain areas, such as San Diego and Imperial counties, noncontract labor had virtually disappeared. Comparisons to out-of-state or nonlocal workers are more illustrative. In 1949 there were more than three noncontract workers for every contract laborer; in 1959 there were six contract laborers for every three noncontract workers. "Plainly," asserted Galarza, "the native inter-state migrant, about whose peripatetic misery a copious and sympathetic literature had accumulated, was close to extinction in California."[119]

As the number of contract workers involved in U.S. agriculture increased, so did the perception among agricultural labor organizers that the importation of farm labor had adverse effects upon the domestic labor force. Wages in the agricultural areas where they worked remained constant or dropped. Some domestic farm wages, largely determined by the employers in advance of the harvest, never got much higher than "wetback" standards in the 1950s; it was possible—and common—to find domestic, contract, and undocumented workers in the same crews.[120] Wage depression in the 1950s was facilitated by the importation of labor during a period when increased mechanization of certain crops also lowered the demand for casual labor. Given the relative immobility of many domestic farm workers between rural and urban occupations, and the absolute immobility of contract workers, it appears that increasingly both were competing for less. The National Agricultural Workers Union, a group that was persistent in its attempts to organize California agricultural workers, thus directed most of its energies not toward attacking the growers directly, but toward stopping the Mexican contract-labor program.[121]

The emphasis that the National Agricultural Workers Union gave to exposing the evils of the bracero program found expression in a research project directed by Ernesto Galarza, which was published in 1956 under the title *Strangers in Our Fields*. This report recorded the abuses of the bracero system with depth and perception, often by reproducing interviews held with the braceros in and out of work camps in California. Galarza's interviews and his review of pay stubs and receipts for camp meals and other deducted charges led him to conclude that "in almost every area covered by the International Agreement, United States law, state law, and the provision of the work contract, serious violations of the rights of Mexican nationals were found to be the norm rather than the exception."[122]

The response to *Strangers* by agricultural interests was predictably negative. The official response by the DOL, however, was silence, and its unofficial response constituted the beginning of a reassessment of its position of the contract-labor program.[123] By exposing employer noncompliance with the terms of the labor agreement, Galarza had raised the painful issue of whether the bracero program was having adverse effects on the domestic labor market.

The year that *Strangers* was published also marked the beginning of a new effort by the DOL to tighten its administration of Public Law 78 and to adopt a more skeptical attitude concerning employer compliance with the agreements. In December 1956, the department improved the standards applied to bracero housing; in the summer of 1958, a new formula for determining wages and assuring a minimum hourly rate was applied. In October 1959, the findings of what was known as the Consultants' Report were released; the study recommended that the secretary of labor take action to reduce the adverse effects of the importation of braceros. In November, the DOL issued new regulations that set minimum standards for the wage and working conditions of domestic workers recruited through the farm placement service of the Labor Department. During the period, the actions of the department and the records of its private meetings indicate the reluctant admission that many of the allegations in *Strangers* were true.[124]

As early as 1957, farmers in the state of California began to sense that opposition to the program created by Public Law 78 was mounting and that the contract-labor system was being seriously threatened. Local grower associations began to exhort their members to "not turn down domestic labor applicants," and one demanded that its members sign a pledge of honest compliance, or be dropped. Caught between the DOL's increasingly forceful attempts to ensure compliance and minimize adverse effects and a public opinion shifting against the bracero program, farmers became more uncomfortable with a system they had worked to create. Mechanization of the harvest, particularly for those engaged in cultivating cotton, became a sought-after alternative.[125]

Beginning in 1960, opposition to the bracero program mounted in Congress. During the session of that year, acrimonious debate postponed the vote on the extension of Public Law 78 until the last day, at which time a six-month extension was secured. This was the first effective attack on the program in Congress. In 1961, the program was extended for another two years; the antibracero forces had gained in strength, although they were unable to bring the program to an immediate end. In 1962 the Kennedy administration openly opposed the Public Law 78 program, and in 1963 the program was extended one final time.[126]

The final extension of the program was obtained only after pro-bracero advocates revealed that there was substantial opposition by the Mexican government to its abrupt termination. A diplomatic dispatch from the SRE dated July 21, 1963, summarized the Mexican position: to end the contracting system would not end the underlying migratory process; in other words, bracero emigration functioned as a substitute for illegal migration. In the view of Mexican political elites, the termination of the program would have serious effects on Mexico's unemployment; the dispatch argued for more time so that Mexico could reabsorb approximately two hundred thousand persons to "stave off the sudden crisis" that would result.[127] The dispatch was placed into the *Congressional Record* on August 15, and the program was extended for a final year.[128] On December 31, 1964, the Mexican contract-labor program formally came to an end.[129] Mexico did not experience a political upheaval; crops in the

U.S. Southwest did not rot in the fields. Whatever were the effects of the termination of the program, they were not immediately apparent.

The Legacy of Debate

A phenomenon of the magnitude and duration of the Mexican contract-labor program does not end without leaving traces of its impact. The effects of the bracero program on the migration process itself have not been adequately researched, although inferences can be drawn from available data. The importation of laborers under contract largely reinforced the characteristic features of pre-bracero migration: the seasonal migration of laborers as opposed to permanent settlement, a regional concentration of migrants from about six or seven states in the north-central region of Mexico to selected areas of the U.S. West and border areas, and the concentration of Mexican workers in agriculture and in "stoop" labor. It is no surprise that post-1964 "illegals" come from the same regions, work for many of the same employers in the United States, and often work only a few months before returning to Mexico.[130] Clearly, the migration of braceros established continuity between the first wave of Mexican migrants during the first four decades of the century and the more recent immigration of undocumented persons during the 1960s and 1970s.

The migration of workers stimulated and regulated by the contract-labor program is not an aberration in the history of Mexican immigration to the United States. To be sure, the large-scale importation of contract labor from Mexico under the auspices of a binational agreement has not occurred before or since, but to dwell on the formal aspects of administered migration is to miss the point. The bracero migration not only continued the labor migration of the earlier period, it reaffirmed the notion that the northward movement of Mexicans is a single process. Braceros and undocumented (and, to a limited extent, legally admitted) immigrants were substituted for each other. After 1954, the "success" of Operation Wetback signified the substitution of braceros for "wetbacks"—at labor standards substantially below those afforded by contract-labor guarantees. After 1964, some braceros were replaced by "wetbacks" and others by machines; the elite within the bracero labor force immigrated legally and became either permanent residents or "green card commuters."[131] Thus, throughout the contract-labor period and since then, the formal conditions of Mexican labor migration—i.e., the labels assigned to it—varied from time to time, but the informal patterns of migration persisted.

The termination of the contract-labor program had a pronounced effect on Mexican policymakers. One result was the creation of additional jobs in Mexico, presumably for the ex-braceros who after 1964 could not work legally in the United States. Most frequently cited in this connection is the Border Industrialization, or Maquiladora, Program—a system of unique binational concessions principally to U.S. corporations that located manufacturing assembly plants in northern Mexico border towns and whose production is exported entirely to the United States.[132]

A number of factors had already laid the basis for the Maquiladora Program before the end of the contract-labor recruitment, but the Mexican government gave it additional stimulation in 1965. Mexican concessions involved making a number of exceptions in its legislation to allow for wholly owned foreign subsidiaries to enter the country. This action had perceived and objective benefits to certain sectors of Mexico's society, but it also involved some risk to the government. The Maquiladora Program has been criticized within Mexico as an abandonment of revolutionary goals with respect to the control of foreign direct investment and to limitations upon landownership by foreigners; it has also been attacked as the de facto transformation of the country into a free-production zone. That Mexican political elites would knowingly embark upon such a program is in part a reflection of how seriously they viewed the elimination of the safety valve afforded by the labor program.

The border industries have not hired ex-braceros, however; instead, they have hired a young female labor force who had attained a level of education superior to the men among local residents. This outcome apparently was unforeseen by the Mexican architects of the program. Thus, if the Maquiladora Program has acted as a substitute safety valve, it has not done so directly.

Another set of Mexican responses to the termination of the bracero program was to seek its renewal, an effort sustained over a period of ten years. These efforts were made for a twofold purpose: to reestablish the safety valve, and to adopt a control measure to manage what was perceived to be a growing problem of undocumented migration (apprehensions of deportable Mexicans grew at a geometric rate of about 25 percent per year in the late 1960s and early 1970s). These efforts culminated in a public admission by President Echeverría in his 1974 State of the Union address that Mexican attempts to secure a labor agreement with the United States had failed. In his 1972 and 1974 addresses Echeverría stressed several familiar themes: that emigration was in part due to the lack of domestic opportunity and that development efforts were addressing that problem; that Mexican workers in the United States received inhumane treatment; and that Mexico expressed its concern that this be corrected.[133]

By 1975, Echeverría's position changed, to the surprise of many, when he publicly announced that Mexico did *not* want a labor agreement. According to Jorge Bustamante, a meeting between Echeverría and Galarza shortly before his announcement had persuaded the president to change his posture.[134] In his 1976 State of the Union address, Echeverría explained: "We reject the idea of a new migrant worker agreement, for such agreements have never succeeded in preventing undocumented emigration in the past."[135] This reflected a new interpretation of the potential effects of a renewed contract-labor program—one which stressed the stimulation, rather than the substitution, effects of such a program with respect to undocumented emigration.

Echeverría's sudden change in policy threw open a debate—largely conducted within government circles and the Mexico City press—which has continued to this day. The sudden deemphasis of a search for a binational temporary-worker program may be consistent with Mexican domestic and foreign policy objectives, but it has left that government with few alternatives. Generating additional employment within Mexico continues to be an important goal of the regime, but even if drastic changes in Mexico's development model, placing more emphasis on labor-intensive activities, were to be made, the domestic employment problem would not be even close to solution during this century.[136] In falling back upon a position which stresses domestic job generation and in protesting the ill treatment of undocumented Mexicans in the United States, Mexican policymakers have continued to demonstrate that emigration touches upon sensitive domestic issues, and that it continues to be perceived as a "safety valve." This fallback position also reveals that the Mexican government has few options in this issue area that can yield short-term results.

In the United States, the termination of the bracero program has set in motion several processes which have also demanded policy responses. Three of these have been mentioned—the increased flow of "commuters" across the border, increased undocumented immigration, and the export of jobs through "runaway plants" that have relocated on the Mexican border. Thus, the termination of the program ended the legal importation of workers, but not the U.S. domestic controversy over Mexican labor migration. Of these post-bracero program issues, the perceived increase of undocumented immigration has provoked the sharpest debate and presented U.S. policymakers with a serious issue on which there seems to be no national consensus about how to proceed.[137]

It is no surprise that the policy proposals most frequently suggested to address the "illegal alien problem"—increased enforcement at the border, mass roundups of deportable aliens in the interior, penalizing employers for hiring such aliens, legalizing undocumented persons already here, and instituting a temporary-worker program—are not new. Today's proposals are but variants of those measures adopted or actively considered during the "wetback invasion" of the early 1950s. The participants in the present debate seem to be unaware of the past, however; those who advocate "sealing" the border, for example, seem to be aware neither that such options have been considered before nor of the reasons why such responses have not been pursued in the past. Proponents of "police-type" solutions apparently do not know that no such measure has ever successfully stopped migration; at best, in the aftermath of Operation Wetback, the flow was only regularized. Even then, the mass roundup of 1954 created new problems as it temporarily solved an old one. Those who argue that the United States bears no responsibility to Mexican migrants who recently have entered illegally ignore the long-standing involvement of U.S. employers in promoting this flow, and of the U.S. government in encouraging the violation of its immigration laws in order to accomplish its foreign policy objectives. To embark upon paths that repeat errors of the past does not speak well for the capacity of this society and polity to learn from historical experience.

One area that has generated recent discussion is temporary-worker programs.[138] Early in its term the Reagan administration itself proposed a "pilot program" by which fifty thousand Mexican nationals would be admitted each year for temporary work in the United States.[139] It is noteworthy that while this proposal was included within a package of other far-reaching immigration policy proposals, it is the temporary-worker plan that has generated the most discussion thus far. That temporary-worker proposals are in themselves controversial is a legacy of a program which itself expired almost two decades ago.

It may be true, as David Gregory argues, that "the historical perspective of Mexican participation in earlier programs such as the *bracero* programs acts as an impediment to our current search for a policy to effectively deal with contemporary migration movements."[140] Certainly, current interpretations of that experience have led many to equate all temporary-worker program proposals with the bracero program, and to assume that the evils and/or benefits of the earlier program automatically carry over into the present. It is in this sense that Gregory seems to be arguing against the drawing of close parallels between the earlier experience and the present situation.

Nevertheless, it is also true that the historical experience derived from the bracero era is indispensable for an understanding of the current debate and for the formulation of an appropriate U.S. policy response to undocumented migration. The experience of the contract-labor program may not give us answers regarding what a proposed temporary-worker program will accomplish, but it does offer a framework for posing some important questions. An examination of the proposals made thus far suggests that many of these questions have received little public attention or scrutiny.

Perhaps the first question to be posed in the current debate is, to what extent is the proposed program simply a copy of the contract-labor program, and to what extent does it diverge significantly? For example, the so-called H-2 program, which currently operates through §101 (15) (H) (ii) of the Immigration and Nationality Act, is essential a unilateral bracero program. It involves the importation of temporary workers who are admitted to work for a specific employer, largely in agriculture. The principal difference between this and the Mexican contract-labor program is that the Mexican government is not directly involved in its design or administration.

Other questions which might be considered are: if the temporary-worker program is designed to serve as a substitute for undocumented migration, what evidence is there to suggest that it will function as planned? (The earlier experience suggests that the contract-labor program functioned alternatively as a stimulator and as a substitute for undocumented migration, depending upon the circumstances.) Moreover, what additional measures will be needed to get the proposed program to function as a substitute for undocumented migration? (The earlier experience suggests that widespread employer participation in any temporary-worker scheme is necessary for it to function as such a substitute.) Will a temporary-worker program be accompanied by an expulsion campaign, a new version of Operation Wetback? Will the design of the program be such that it will constitute little more than legitimizing the current situation in which undocumented workers are employed? Will the operation of the program have the necessary safeguards for working conditions and wages, or will it result in the kinds of abuse and exploitation that occurred previously, particularly during the 1950s?

The answers to such questions will be debated for some time. The discussion about the future direction of U.S. immigration policy with respect to Mexico will unavoidably focus on undocumented migration, on temporary-worker program proposals, and on conflicting interpretations of the contract-labor program of 1942–1964.

Notes

1. For a discussion of Mexican policies to restrain or return emigrants during the years 1910–1940 and Mexican perceptions of abuses suffered by Mexican workers in the United States, see Lawrence Cardoso, *Mexican Emigration to the United States, 1897–1931: Socio-economic Patterns* (Tucson: University of Arizona Press, 1980), 64, 107, 113–15; Arthur F. Corwin, ed., *Immigrants—and*

Immigrants: Perspectives on Mexican Labor Migration to the United States (Westport, CT: Greenwood Press, 1978), 179–84, 187–88; Moisés González Navarro, *Población y sociedad in México (1900–1970)*, vol. 2 (México, D.F.: Facultad de Ciencias Políticas y Sociales, UNAM, 1974), 38–41, 46, 49, 153, 207-10, 245-239; Harvey A. Levenstein, "The AFL and Mexican Immigration in the 1920s: An Experiment in Labor Diplomacy," *Hispanic American Historical Review* 47, no. 2 (May 1968): 212–14.

2. González Navarro, *Población y sociedad*, 208.

3. This view was expressed by José María Dávila, a member of Congress, in 1932. González Novarro, ibid., 163.

4. Cardoso, *Mexican Emigration*, 117.

5. John Martínez, *Mexican Emigration to the U.S., 1910–1930* (San Francisco: R & E Associates, 1971), 18; George C. Kiser and Martha Woody Kiser, eds., *Mexican Workers in the United States: Historical and Political Perspectives* (Albuquerque: University of New Mexico Press, 1979), 9–29; Mark Reisler, *By the Sweat of Their Brow: Mexican Immigrant Labor in the United States, 1900–1940* (Westport, CT: Greenwood Press, 1929), 24–42.

6. Kiser and Kiser, *Mexican Workers*, 3–4.

7. Ernesto Galarza, *Merchants of Labor: The Mexican Bracero Story* (Charlotte, NC: McNally and Loftin, 1964), 80–81; Henry P. Anderson, *The Bracero Program in California* (New York: Arno Press, 1976), 5–9. Another source, Johnny Mac McCain, "Contract Labor as a Factor in United States-Mexican Relations, 1942–1947" (Ph.D. diss., University of Texas, Austin, 1970), 179–80, shows that the Secretaría del Trabajo y Previsión Social was involved in the assignment of labor quotas within Mexico for the recruitment of railroad contract workers during World War II. During the 1950s, the principal agency on the Mexican side responsible for negotiating the agreement was the Dirección de Asuntos de Trabajadores Agrícolas Migratorios (DATAM) of the SRE. The agency responsible for operating the recruitment centers in Mexico was the Oficina de Trabajadores Emigrantes of the Secretaría de Gobernación. See México, SRE, *Memoria de la Secretaría de Relaciones Exteriores; septiembre de 1951—agosto de 1952* (México, D.F.: Talleres Gráficos de la Nación, 1952), 188; José Lázaro Salinas, *La emigración de braceros: Una visión objetiva de un problema mexicano* (México, D.F.: [Cuauhtémoc], 1955), 66–89.

8. Agencies within the Departments of Agriculture and Labor that were responsible for the administration of the program during the war were the Farm Security Administration, the Extension Service, the War Food Administration, and the War Manpower Commission (Galarza, *Merchants of Labor*, 80).

9. Ibid., 82–83; Anderson, *The Bracero Program*, passim.

10. The 1942 recruitment season began late and is excluded from the calculation of the average. According to the table, U.S. statistics indicate that 195,765 contracts were issued during 1943–1946, and in the same period, Mexican sources registered 329,821 departures (*salidas*) of contract laborers. In interpreting these figures, the reader should keep in mind that they represent an approximate measure of the *flow* of Mexican contract workers to the United States for the years indicated; they do not indicate the number of such workers in the United States at any given time (stock). Contract extensions, renewals, and multiple entries by individual workers make these numbers somewhat deceptive. The reader should also note that, as yet, no one has explained the difference between the U.S. and Mexican statistics on the flow of braceros. (U.S. secondary sources cite U.S.

statistics, and Mexican sources cite one of two sets of Mexican statistics; up to this point apparently no researcher has even acknowledged that the disparity existed.) There are a number of possible explanations for this disparity, but their discussion exceeds the scope of this essay. For the present case, the precise number of contracts issued in any given year is not important, and both sets of numbers will be used to indicate [the] range of possible values.

11. According to U.S. statistics, 1,128,990 contracts were issued between 1947 and 1954; according to Mexican statistics, this number was 929,964. Mexican statistics for 1955–1964 indicate that 3,327,601 braceros departed; U.S. statistics record 3,317,241. The total for the program, according to U.S. sources, is 4,646,199; the same total, according to Mexican data, is 4,591,538.

12. My research indicates that only railroad workers were employed through the nonagricultural labor program, although attempts to use them in the San Diego naval yards and as forge and foundry workers, food workers, sawmill operators, and in other capacities, almost succeeded. McCain, "Contract Labor as a Factor," 182–92.

13. Peter N. Kirstein, *Anglo over Bracero: A History of the Mexican Worker in the United States from Roosevelt to Nixon* (San Francisco: R & E Associates, 1977), 28; McCain, "Contract Labor as a Factor," 174.

14. Galarza, *Merchants of Labor*, 54; Kirstein, *Anglo over Bracero*, 32–33.

15. Galarza, *Merchants of Labor*, 46; SRE, *Memoria de la Secretaría de Relaciones Exteriores; septiembre de 1952–diciembre de 1953* (México, D.F.: Taleres Gráficos de la Nación, 1953), 331.

16. Mexican domestic opposition to the initiation of the wartime program and to Mexico's continued participation had several motivations and can be gleaned from a number of sources. See, e.g., a letter from a labor organization representing Mexican workers in the United States which argued against bracero emigration in April 1942, reproduced in: *Boletín del Archivo General de la Nación*, Tercera Series 4, no. 4 (October–December 1980): 22–23.

17. Manuel Gamio's participation in the design of the contract-labor program still has to be adequately researched. His proposal for a temporary-worker program to substitute for the northward movement of legal immigrants is expressed in his book *Mexican Immigration*, 182–83. Evidence that his involvement was crucial in the formulation of a Mexican position in 1942 is provided in a reference made by Robert D. Tomasek, "The Political and Economic Implications of Mexican Labor in the United States under the Non-Quota System, Contract Labor Program, and Wetback Movement," (Ph.D. diss., University of Michigan, 1957), 29, to an interview with a Mexican official. For other evidence of Gamio's involvement in the wartime program, see his confidential report to Avila Camacho, reproduced in *Boletín* (1980): 38–40.

18. McCain, "Contract Labor as a Factor," 77; Otey Scruggs, "The United States, Mexico and the Wetbacks, 1943–1947," *Pacific Historical Review* 30, no. 2 (May 1961): 152. For a discussion of the interagency preparation for the agreement among the Departments of State, Justice, Labor, and Agriculture in the United States and SRE, Secretaría de Gobernación and Secretaría del Trabajo y Previsión Social, as well as Mexico's initial reluctance to participate in the program, see McCain, "Contract Labor as a Factor," 6–23; Juan Ramón García, *Operation Wetback: The Mass Deportation of Mexican Undocumented Workers in 1954* (Westport, CT: Greenwood Press, 1980), 21–23; Tomasek, "Political and Economic Implications," 53–54.

19. The view that emigration harmed Mexico's rural economy seems to have emerged soon after the program began. González Navarro (*Población y sociedad*, 215) reports that at the outset of mass labor migration, the authorities of [the] two states most severely affected—Jalisco and Guanajuato—sought to prevent it "because of the economic damage it caused." He also notes (p. 163) that in 1943, as bracero emigration increased, a shortage of agricultural labor developed in parts of Mexico.

20. Centro de Estudios Históricos, *Historia general de México*, vol. 4 (México, D.F.: El Colegio de México, 1976), 197–98, 164–65.

21. These are summarized from the list presented in Galarza, *Merchants of Labor*, 47.

22. One should keep in mind that "needs," like agricultural labor "shortages," are not absolutes, even though the initial Mexican position—accepted by the United States—assumed that they were. In a path-breaking analysis of the California harvest labor market, Lloyd Fisher noted that labor demand is best expressed not in terms of numbers of laborers, but in labor hours. Since farmers had an interest in minimizing the risks of disease, bad weather, and spoilage, and because farm labor was paid piece-rate and the farmer could not experience diminishing returns to labor, the agricultural labor market experienced sharp peaks in labor demand for short periods. Had farmers been willing to accept those risks and some unevenness of quality in the product harvested, Fisher argues, labor demand would have been lower and the harvest season longer. Thus, a labor "shortage" in this type of agriculture is a relative, not an absolute, concept (Lloyd H. Fisher, *The Harvest Labor Market in California* [Cambridge, MA: Harvard University Press, 1953], 6, 123, 151–60).

23. The first and fourth conditions mentioned are explicitly derived from Article 123 and pertinent Mexican labor legislation. The second, third, and fifth conditions are explicitly mentioned in Manuel Gamio's proposal, outlined in 1930 (*Mexican Immigration*, 182–83). The sixth condition reflects an old concern by the Mexican public and government dating to the teens and twenties.

24. McCain, "Contract Labor as a Factor," 32; Richard B. Craig, *The Bracero Program: Interest Groups and Foreign Policy* (Austin: University of Texas Press, 1971), 434–45; González Navarro, *Población y sociedad*, 240–42.

25. García, *Operation Wetback*, 26.

26. Jorge del Pinal, "Los trabajadores mexicanos en los Estados Unidos," *El trimestre económico* 12, no. 1 (April–June 1945): 30–31; Galarza, *Merchants of Labor*, 56; Kirstein, *Anglo over Bracero*, 71.

27. Kiser and Kiser, *Mexican Workers*, 86–87.

28. Quoted in Scruggs, "The United States, Mexico and the Wetbacks," 152. The author further notes (p. 153) that in 1944, "In conversations with State Department officials, an immigration officer confessed that the Service [the INS] was deporting only those workers not engaged in harvesting perishable crops."

29. Ibid., 154, 158.

30. Ibid., 154–55.

31. Ibid., 156–57; Tomasek, "Political and Economic Implications," 51.

32. Tomasek, "Political and Economic Implications," 158, 171; del Pinal, "Los trabajadores mexicanos," 33. Tomasek (p. 83) cites a number of Mexican sources which opposed the extension of the program and implies (p. 84) that only the president and the SRE preferred to continue with the program.

33. Many articles in the national media, in such publications as *Time, Newsweek, Life,* the *New York Times,* the *Saturday Evening Post, Business Week,* and the *Washington Post,* drew attention to the "wetback" problem in the postwar years, especially during 1951–1954. These articles stressed the threat, real or imagined, that undocumented Mexicans represented for the United States. Since the vast majority of the U.S. population did not have contact with "wetbacks" in their daily lives, it is generally agreed that these articles—and the allegations of antiwetback groups reported therein—were instrumental in the shaping of U.S. public opinion on issues relating to undocumented migration.

34. U.S. President's Commission on Migratory Labor, *Migratory Labor in American Agriculture* (Washington, DC: GPO, 1951), 69 (emphasis added).

35. Willard F. Kelley, "The Wetback Issue," *I & N Reporter* (January 1954): 38–39.

36. President's Commission, *Migratory Labor,* 88.

37. Tomasek, "Political and Economic Implications," 253–54; Galarza, *Merchants of Labor,* 62; Corwin, *Immigrants—and Immigrants,* 152–53.

38. Richard B. Craig, *The Bracero Program: Interest Groups and Foreign Policy* (Austin: University of Texas Press, 1971), 94–99; McCain, "Contract Labor as a Factor," 300; Tomasek, "Political and Economic Implications," 204–5, 224, 239, 241–42, 248–54; Kiser and Kiser, *Mexican Workers,* 129, 155–58; SRE, *Memoria, 1951–52,* 17, 184.

39. Tomasek, "Political and Economic Implications," 224.

40. Indications of this are that, when Mexico used force to prevent emigration to the United States, as in August 1953, there was a virtual news blackout on the action. The only reference I was able to find was a four-paragraph article in the Mexico City official newspaper: "Impídese que sin contrato salgan muchos braceros; centenares, detenidos en la frontera norte," *El Nacional,* August 18, 1954. (Compare Tomasek, "Political and Economic Implications," 257.) By the same token, when Operation Wetback was launched a year later, Mexico's active participation in it received practically no notice in Mexico City newspapers during June, July, or August 1954. (Again compare Tomasek, "Political and Economic Implications," 271.)

41. Galarza, *Merchants of Labor,* 61.

42. McCain, "Contract Labor as a Factor," 268–89; Kirstein, *Anglo over Bracero,* 73–74; García, *Operation Wetback,* 111, 122.

43. Kirstein, *Anglo over Bracero,* 90. See also President's Commission, *Migratory Labor,* 75–76; Tomasek, "Political and Economic Implications," 141.

44. American G.I. Forum and Texas State Federation of Labor (AFL), *What Price Wetbacks?* (Austin: [Allied Printing], 1953), 42.

45. Quoted in Galarza, *Merchants of Labor,* 63. See also García, *Operation Wetback,* 111.

46. President's Commission, *Migratory Labor,* 52.

47. Ibid., 53.

48. Galarza, *Merchants of Labor,* 63.

49. President's Commission, *Migratory Labor,* 88, 180.

50. Hundreds of agricultural employers joined farm-labor associations during the years 1951–1954 on the condition that deportable Mexicans in their employ would be approved for bracero contracts (Galarza, *Merchants of Labor,* 64).

51. Craig, *The Bracero Program,* 127; Galarza, *Merchants of Labor,* 70; García, *Operation Wetback,* 158; Tomasek, "Political and Economic Implications," 267.

52. Craig, *The Bracero Program*, 128.

53. Ibid., 129; Galarza, *Merchants of Labor*, 70, 255; Julian Somora, *Los Mojados: The Wetback Story* (Notre Dame, IN: University of Notre Dame Press, 1971), 52; Tomasek, "Political and Economic Implications," 270. For a discussion of employer cooperation with Operation Wetback and substitution of legally imported labor for "wetbacks," see Kiser and Kiser, *Mexican Workers*, 101; Tomasek, "Political and Economic Implications," 269–70.

54. García, *Operation Wetback*, 175–76, 186, 220–21; Tomasek, "Political and Economic Implications," 271.

55. García, *Operation Wetback*, 214–15; Tomasek, "Political and Economic Implications," 270.

56. American G.I. Forum, *What Price Wetbacks?* 17–25, 28–32, 34–36; Craig, *The Bracero Program*, 126, n. 80; Galarza, *Merchants of Labor*, 70; González Navarro, *Población y sociedad*, 199; García, *Operation Wetback*, 159.

57. Commissioner Swing reportedly told the chief of the Border Patrol that whether or not there would be a patrol in the future depended upon the success of the campaign (García, *Operation Wetback*, 178).

58. The negative-image problem and low morale of the Border Patrol in the early 1950s are discussed in a number of sources. See García, *Operation Wetback*, 113, 116–17, 218–19; Tomasek, "Political and Economic Implications," 140.

59. Tomasek, "Political and Economic Implications," 150, 267–68, 270. He notes (p. 256) that appropriations for the Border Patrol had been reduced such that in 1952 it had 1,200 men compared to 1,450 ten years earlier, when the number of apprehensions was much smaller. In early 1953 the force was further reduced to one thousand men.

60. Indicative of this were the howls of pain raised by many growers, particularly in Texas, and the creation (accompanied by some initial grumbling) of new organizations in the lower Rio Grande Valley, Arizona, and Imperial Valley to contract braceros. See García, *Operation Wetback*, 219; Tomasek, "Political and Economic Implications," 99.

61. García, *Operation Wetback*, 219.

62. "Streamlining" the program involved changing provisions that the Mexican government had insisted on from the outset of the program. Mexico dropped its requirement of a minimum contract work period of six weeks for "special cases," and lowered it to four weeks two days after Operation Wetback began in Texas. See SRE, *Memoria, 1954*, 694; García, *Operation Wetback*, 212. In 1955, the INS unilaterally instituted a simple border-crossing card that "allowed braceros to proceed immediately to contracting centers and to bypass procedures set up by the Mexican government" (García, *Operation Wetback*, 219). "Streamlining" also involved relaxing DOL provisions designed to reduce the "adverse effects" of braceros on domestic labor, such as the contracting of specialized contract workers (ibid., 219). It was not immediately apparent how much of an impact this had on U.S. farm workers, but Tomasek ("Political and Economic Implications," 274) notes the substitution of domestic migrant labor for the same. In the lower Río Grande Valley contract laborers increased from three thousand to seventy thousand; domestic workers only increased from nineteen thousand to thirty-two thousand. Compare García, *Operation Wetback*, 208, 209.

63. Galarza, *Merchants of Labor*, 70.

64. Quoted in García, *Operation Wetback*, 225.

65. "La época de los 'espaldas mojadas' pasa a la historia," *Excélsior*, August 24, 1958. Craig (*The Bracero Program*, 129) also notes that when the United States and Mexico concluded an agreement relating to illegal migration in April 1955, "the wetback had, for all practical purposes, ceased to exist."

66. One of the "costs" rarely discussed in the writings on Operation Wetback, which cannot be elaborated on here but is nevertheless important, is the violation of civil rights—particularly of persons of Mexican origin—that the campaign entailed. References to the tremendous social costs borne by the Mexican community in the United States as a result of this action can be found in García, *Operation Wetback*, 194–99, 216, 218, 230–31.

67. Tomasek, "Political and Economic Implications," 274.

68. Craig, *The Bracero Program*, 104; García, *Operation Wetback*, 39; Kirstein, *Anglo over Bracero*, 67.

69. Galarza, *Merchants of Labor*, 77; García, *Operation Wetback*, 39: González Navarro, *Población y sociedad*, 248.

70. Galarza, *Merchants of Labor*, 52, 81; González Navarro, *Población y sociedad*, table opposite p. 146.

71. An internal document prepared during the Truman and Eisenhower administrations summarized the communication between the U.S. and Mexican governments on this issue during 1948–1953. This document was entitled *The Secret Study* by Kirstein, who discovered it (Kirstein, *Anglo over Bracero*, 76).

72. McCain, "Contract Labor as a Factor," 330–34.

73. Ibid., 274, 278–79, 284, 288–89.

74. Kirstein, *Anglo over Bracero*, 70.

75. Ibid.

76. President's Commission, *Migratory Labor*, 50; Galarza, *Merchants of Labor*, 77.

77. Galarza, *Merchants of Labor*, 77–78.

78. Prevailing wages were determined at preharvest-season meetings, where farmers agreed in advance on what wages would prevail. See American G.I. Forum, *What Price Wetbacks?* 50; Fisher, *The Harvest Labor Market*, 91–116; Galarza, *Merchants of Labor*, 111; President's Commission, *Migratory Labor*, 59–60.

79. This provision was agreed to as a compromise solution, since the growers actually wanted the Agricultural Extension Service to determine farm wage levels.

80. Galarza, *Merchants of Labor*, 77–78.

81. Kirstein, *Anglo over Bracero*, 65; Scruggs, "The United States, Mexico and the Wetbacks," 159; Tomasek, "Political and Economic Implications," 224–26.

82. Tomasek, "Political and Economic Implications," 239–42.

83. Galarza, *Merchants of Labor*, 75; Salinas, *La emigración de braceros*, 11–29.

84. García, *Operation Wetback*, 121.

85. Tomasek, "Political and Economic Implications," 226, 228–29, 241–42, 248–55, 262.

86. Tomasek (ibid., 84), notes that the economic importance of bracero remittances and income brought by returning migrants was an argument offered by a Mexican government official as an explanation for the desire of the Alemán administration to renew the program in 1947, notwithstanding domestic opposition

to its continuation. It is doubtful, however, that bracero earnings ever had a substantial impact on Mexico's exchange of goods and services with the United States. Bracero remittances (which do not include amounts brought back by returning contract workers) reached a peak relative value of 20 percent of the U.S.-Mexican trade balance in 1955. In other years it fluctuated between 10 and 16 percent, and occasionally dropped to lower levels.

87. García, *Operation Wetback*, 58–59. Referring to the years 1948–1951, Richard Craig writes: "One needs little imagination to visualize the extent of rural discontent that Mexico was spared as a result of the legal and clandestine northern flow during these years" (Craig, *The Bracero Program*, 60).

88. García, *Operation Wetback*, 59.

89. González Navarro, *Población y sociedad*, 154–56.

90. Craig, *The Bracero Program*, 22–23; García, *Operation Wetback*, 70–73; 79–80; Scruggs, "The United States, Mexico and the Wetbacks," 152, 155, 163; Tomasek, "Political and Economic Implications," 65–171.

91. García (*Operation Wetback*, 32) notes: "In confidential letters, memos, and telegrams, Mexican officials often expressed concern about problems plaguing the program, including discriminatory acts against Mexican nationals, physical abuse, inadequate grievance procedures, and violations of civil rights and contract guarantees. When news of such incidents did become public, Mexican officials wrote with concern about how such news proved damaging to their efforts to keep the contract labor program in a positive light. They informed officials of the United States that, when news of abuses of secret agreements leaked out, it placed Mexico in a difficult situation, forcing [it] to take harsher stands than [it] ordinarily might."

92. Kirstein, *Anglo over Bracero*, 67.

93. Galarza, *Merchants of Labor*, 49.

94. Craig, *The Bracero Program*, 69; Galarza, *Merchants of Labor*, 50; *Hispanic American Report* 1, no. 1 (November 1948): 3; Kirstein, *Anglo over Bracero*, 68; Tomasek, "Political and Economic Implications," 232–35.

95. Kirstein, *Anglo over Bracero*, 70, 76.

96. Craig, *The Bracero Program*, 105–6.

97. Ibid., 109–10; Galarza, *Merchants of Labor*, 66; *Hispanic American Report* 7, no. 1 (January 1954): 8; Salinas, *La emigración de braceros*, 11–14; Tomasek, "Political and Economic Implications," 259.

98. Craig, *The Bracero Program*, 112–13; Galarza, *Merchants of Labor*, 66; Tomasek, "Political and Economic Implications," 206.

99. Craig, *The Bracero Program*, 112–13; Galarza, *Merchants of Labor*, 68; Tomasek, "Political and Economic Implications," 260; "A pesar de la excitativa oficial, empezó la fuga de braceros," *Excélsior*, January 23, 1954.

100. Tomasek, "Political and Economic Implications." For a discussion of that criticism, see 166–79, 257–58.

101. Craig, *The Bracero Program*, 119; García, *Operation Wetback*, 81–82.

102. Quoted in Tomasek, "Political and Economic Implications," 260. Compare Craig, *The Bracero Program*, 112.

103. Craig, *The Bracero Program*, 117; Tomasek, "Political and Economic Implications," 261.

104. Craig, *The Bracero Program*, 114, 117–18; Tomasek, "Political and Economic Implications," 262.

105. Quoted in Craig, *The Bracero Program*, 115, n. 52.

106. Ibid., 115–19; García, *Operation Wetback*, 95–96; Tomasek, "Political and Economic Implications," 261.

107. García, *Operation Wetback*, 95; Tomasek, "Political and Economic Implications," 262.

108. Quoted in García, *Operation Wetback*, 95–96.

109. Cited in González Navarro, *Población and sociedad*, 177.

110. Fernando Robles, "¿Será posible detener la emigración de los braceros?" [opinion column], *El Universal*, February 9, 1954. For a discussion of the internal debate in Mexico about the causes of emigration, see Craig, *The Bracero Program*, 118–21. Compare SRE, *Memoria de la Secretaría de Relaciones Exteriores; 1 de enero a 31 de diciembre de 1957* (México, D.F.: Talleres Gráficas de la Nación, 1958), 391; ibid., *Memoria de la Secretaría de Relaciones Exteriores; 1 de enero a 31 de diciembre de 1958* (México, D.F.: Talleres Gráficas de la Nación, 1959), 308.

111. Galarza, *Merchants of Labor*, 244.

112. Official references explained the inevitability of emigration in terms of "supply" and "demand." Instead of expending futile efforts to prevent it, both governments should regulate and control it. See González Navarro, *Población y sociedad*, 222–23.

113. Ernesto Galarza, *Farm Workers and Agri-business in California, 1947–1960* (Notre Dame, IN: University of Notre Dame Press, 1977), 114; Kirstein, *Anglo over Bracero*, 74, 83; President's Commission, *Migratory Labor*, 56–59, 63, 66. Tomasek ("Political and Economic Implications," 120–25) also discussed the early opposition of a number of ethnic-group, social-welfare, and religious organizations. Compare McCain, "Contract Labor as a Factor," 338; Congressional Quarterly, *Congress and the Nation, 1945–1964* (Washington, DC: Congressional Quarterly Service, 1965), 764.

114. Galarza, *Merchants of Labor*, 103–4.

115. García, *Operation Wetback*, 45.

116. Tomasek ("Political and Economic Implications," 226–27) notes that, after the war, the number of contract laborers grew and the number of U.S. and Mexican compliance inspectors declined. After 1951 some fifty DOL compliance officers were responsible for overseeing contract guarantees for some thirty thousand farmers who used Mexican contract labor. Compare García, *Operation Wetback*, 45–48.

117. The issue of the relative costs of contract and "wetback" labor was fraught with controversy throughout the duration of the program. It cannot be resolved here. It seems clear, however, that (a) braceros were generally more productive than domestic workers and (b) bracero labor became cheaper as the program wore on, such that after 1954 the wages and benefits of contract workers were equivalent to—perhaps worse than—those of "wetbacks," a fact which facilitated their employment as substitutes.

118. Galarza, *Merchants of Labor*, 106.

119. Ibid., 94–95.

120. Ibid., 101, 105.

121. Galarza, *Farm Workers and Agri-business*, 356–57.

122. Ibid., 252–53.

123. Ibid., 253–56.

124. Craig, *The Bracero Program*, 151–54; Galarza, *Farm Workers and Agri-business*, 272–73.

125. Craig, *The Bracero Program*, 151, 176, 180–81; Galarza, *Farm Workers and Agri-business*, 271–72; Kiser and Kiser, *Mexican Workers*, 100, 110–11.

126. Craig, *The Bracero Program*, 155–85; Kirstein, *Anglo over Bracero*, 104. In Kiser and Kiser (*Mexican Workers*, 111–14, especially p. 111), a split among agricultural interests is noted between those who found mechanization a viable alternative and those who did not.

127. The text of the diplomatic note is reproduced in Kiser and Kiser, *Mexican Workers*, 120–23.

128. Craig, *The Bracero Program*, 186–87.

129. Contract labor continued to be admitted for three more years under Public Law 414 (the Immigration and Nationality Act of 1952). The number of such workers was small.

130. Not all Mexicans who currently enter illegally into the United States fit the pattern of contract-labor migrants. But one of the subpopulations in this flow—temporary, illegal, long-distance migrants—is essentially a continuation of the bracero migration. See Wayne A. Cornelius, Leo R. Chávez, and Jorge G. Castro, *Mexican Immigrants and Southern California: A Summary of Current Knowledge*, A Report to the Human Resources Committee of the Los Angeles Chamber of Commerce (La Jolla, CA: Program in U.S.-Mexican Studies, UCSD, 1981), 5–7.

131. The responses of California agricultural producers to the termination of the bracero program varied widely, as discussed in David Runsten and Phillip LeVeen, *Mexicanization and Mexican Labor in California Agriculture*, Monographs in U.S.-Mexican Studies, no. 6 (La Jolla, CA: Program in U.S.-Mexican Studies, UCSD, 1981). For a discussion of the "green card commuters" who reside in Mexican border cities and work in the United States, a group that seems to have expanded significantly since 1964, see Kiser and Kiser, *Mexican Workers*, 215–56.

132. See María Patricia Fernández Kelly, *Women and Multinational Corporation: The Ciudad Juárez Maquiladoras* (Albany: SUNY Press, 1983); Kiser and Kiser, *Mexican Workers*, 257–84; Antonio Ugalde, "Regional Political Processes and Mexican Politics on the Border," in *Views across the Border*, ed. Stanley R. Ross (Albuquerque: University of New Mexico Press, 1978), 109–11; Mitchell A. Seligson and Edward J. Williams, *Maquiladoras and Migration: A Study of Workers in the Mexican-United States Border Industrialization Program* (Tucson: University of Arizona, Department of Political Science, 1980), a study prepared for the Employment and Training Administration of the DOL.

133. See Jorge A. Bustamante, "La migración mexicana en la dinámica de las percepciones" (paper presented at the Seminar on Economic and Social Aspects of Relations between the United States and Mexico, Stanford University, Stanford, CA, November 15, 1980), 19–29; and Corwin, *Immigrants—and Immigrants*, 157, 197–99. Excerpts from Echeverría's State of the Union addresses in 1972 and 1974 are reproduced in Kiser and Kiser, *Mexican Workers*, 124, 196.

134. Bustamante, "La migración mexicana," 28; Corwin, *Immigrants—and Immigrants*, 198–99; Kiser and Kiser, *Mexican Workers*, 125–26.

135. Kiser and Kiser, *Mexican Workers*, 126.

136. Wayne A. Cornelius, "Immigration, Mexican Development Policy, and the Future of U.S.-Mexican Relations," in *Mexico and the United States*, ed. Robert H. McBride (Englewood Cliffs, NJ: Prentice-Hall, 1981), 113–14.

137. See U.S. Select Commission on Immigration and Refugee Policy, *Immigration Policy and the National Interest* (Washington, DC: GPO, 1981), 331–419.

138. See, e.g., Edwin Reubens, "Immigration Problems, Limited-Visa Programs, and Other Options," in *The Border That Joins: Mexican Migrants and U.S. Responsibilities*, ed. Peter G. Brown and Henry Shue (Totowa, NJ: Rowman and Littlefield, 1983), 187–222; David Gregory, "A U.S.-Mexican Temporary Workers Program: The Search for Co-determination," in *Mexico and the United States*, 158–77; Warren C. Sanderson, "The Problems of Planning for the Expected: Demographic Shocks and Policy Paralysis" (paper presented at the Seminar on Economic and Social Aspects of Relations between the United States and Mexico, Stanford University, Stanford, CA, November 15, 1980); Wayne A. Cornelius, "Legalizing the Flow of Temporary Migrant Workers from Mexico: A Policy Proposal," Working Papers in U.S.-Mexican Studies, No. 7 (La Jolla, CA: Program in U.S.-Mexican Studies, UCSD, 1981), and "Statement of Cornelius Position on Guest-Worker Programs" (May 5, 1980, Program in U.S.-Mexican Studies, UCSD), where he clarifies some of the distinguishing features of his proposal.

139. See "White House Asks a Law to Bar Jobs for Illegal Aliens," *New York Times*, July 31, 1981, pp. 1, 9, and "Plan on Immigrants," p. 9, in the same issue. See also "Testimony of William French Smith before the Senate Subcommittee on Immigration and Refugee Policy and the House Subcommittee on Immigration, Refugees, and International Law," July 30, 1981. A critique of the Reagan proposals, including the temporary worker plan, is discussed in Wayne A. Cornelius, "The Reagan Administration's Proposals for a New U.S. Immigration Policy: An Assessment of Potential Effects," *International Migration Review* (December 1981): 769–78.

140. Gregory, "A U.S.-Mexican Temporary Workers Program," 160.

II

Political and Cultural Contestation

4

La Frontera: The Border as Symbol and Reality in Mexican-American Thought

Mario T. García

Many Americans maintained strongly ethnocentric views concerning Mexican immigrants' suitability for membership, much less citizenship, in American society. For ethnic Mexicans in the United States, however, questions of citizenship, personal and collective identity, and national and cultural loyalty were much more complicated matters. Having grown up in demographically complex communities in which it was not at all uncommon to find Mexican nationals (both "legal" and "undocumented"), third- or fourth-generation Mexican Americans, and the U.S.-born children of all these groups living in close proximity, the meanings of potentially crucial distinctions such as those between native and foreigner, citizen and alien, and "American" and "Mexican" became increasingly vague and ambiguous.

Historian Mario García, a professor of history and Chicano studies at the University of California, Santa Barbara, traces the sources and explores the implications of some of the most vexing social, cultural, and political issues facing ethnic Mexicans living on the north side of la frontera. *Focusing on three Spanish-language newspapers published in the United States in three distinct eras, García analyzes the ways different groups of Mexican Americans and Mexican immigrants attempted to negotiate the tensions inherent in being part of an ethnic minority in an often hostile environment.*

For almost a century and a half the U.S.-Mexican border has influenced the Mexican-American experience. The result of the U.S. conquest of northern Mexico during the midnineteenth century, the border

From *Mexican Studies/Estudios Mexicanos* 1, no. 2 (Summer 1985): 195–225. © 1985 by The Regents of the University of California. Reprinted by permission of the University of California Press Journals.

separated some Mexicans from the motherland and made them part of a new and significantly different society. Hence, people of Mexican descent, in what became the American Southwest, have had to relate in one degree or another to the border. It is both symbol and reality in the Mexican-American experience and has confronted each generation with questions: What does it mean to be a Mexican in the United States? How should Mexican Americans relate to the continual influx of Mexican immigrants? How much of Mexican culture and identity should one retain? How should Mexican Americans relate to Mexico? These and other questions assume relevance because of the propinquity of Mexico and the heavy concentration of Mexican Americans in the Southwest and along the U.S.-Mexican border. How each generation has responded has determined particular political strategies for coping with the ethnic, race, class, and cultural positions Mexican Americans have occupied in different historical periods. An examination of the concept of the border in Mexican-American thought provides a view of the changing nature of ethnic and cultural nationalism among Mexicans in the United States. The meaning and ramifications of the border have varied in Mexican-American history depending on historical epoch, whether one is an immigrant or not, levels of acculturation, and class position and consciousness. . . .

The Immigrant Era

Between 1900 and 1930 about a million Mexicans crossed the border seeking work or political refuge from the Mexican Revolution of 1910. Of course, Mexicans resided in the Southwest before the turn of the century, but their settlements were small and scattered. Experiencing the initial consequences of the Anglo-American conquest involving loss of lands, racial oppression, labor exploitation, and second-class citizenship, these nineteenth-century Mexicans reacted in different ways. Some refused to submit to conquest and defended themselves against Anglo control. Others, however, accommodated themselves to the transformation. Nevertheless, both groups maintained a Mexican cultural, political, and economic presence until [their numbers were] reinforced by extensive Mexican immigration. Capitalist economic development in the region and the need for cheap labor triggered this reinforcement, which in turn overwhelmed the earlier Mexican settlements, with the exception of northern New Mexico and certain locations in South Texas. Nineteenth-century Mexican communities now became predominantly immigrant ones. At no other time in Mexican-American history, as during the thirty years between 1900 and 1930, have Mexican immigrants and refugees so totally dominated the Spanish-speaking Mexican condition in the Southwest and elsewhere.[1]

La Opinión, founded in Los Angeles in 1926 by publisher Ignacio Lozano, proved to be among the most articulate voices of the immigrant era. Ten years earlier Lozano had established *La Prensa* in San Antonio. Together, *La Opinión* and *La Prensa* became the most widely circulated and read Mexican daily newspapers in the United States although exact circulation figures no longer exist. A middle-class Catholic who had supported the overthrown dictator Porfirio Díaz, Lozano rejected the Revolution and from his sanctuary north of the border critiqued the succession of revolutionary governments. Lozano spoke for the émigré opponents of the Revolution and expressed a distinct bourgeois philosophy steeped in political and cultural nationalism. While hardly representative of the thousands of poor immigrant-workers who flocked to the United States, Lozano nevertheless helped shape Mexican public opinion north of the border through his newspapers.[2]

As a creator and expressor of immigrant and refugee political thought, *La Opinión* related to the presence of the border. It recognized, for example, the reality of a political division between Mexico and the United States. Mexican immigrants temporarily inhabited a foreign land. Cognizant of the historic Mexican tradition in the Southwest, *La Opinión* did not consider this region, as later some Chicanos would, as an extension of Mexico or as "Occupied Mexico."[3] Mexicans were not strangers in their own land, but strangers in another land.[4] José Vasconcelos, the noted Mexican philosopher, observed in *La Opinión* that Mexicans did not regard Texas as another Alsace requiring restoration to the mother country.[5] Instead, *La Opinión* accepted the loss of these former Mexican lands to the gringos. *La Opinión*, however, believed that Mexican ethnicity and culture transcended the border. Ethnically, culturally, and intellectually, Mexicans in the United States formed an extension of Mexico even though residing in another land. *La Opinión* considered all Mexicans, including those born north of the border, as an organic part of Mexico. They were *México de Afuera* (Mexico of the Outside) or *México flotante* (floating Mexico).

La Opinión correctly understood that almost all Mexicans who crossed the border had no intention of surrendering their Mexican citizenship. It applauded and encouraged this frame of mind. Most Mexicans believed that they would soon return to *la patria* once they had saved enough money and once political stability was restored. Hence, crossing the border rather than breaking with one's nationality and culture instead reaffirmed them.[6] Although *La Opinión* misread the similar ethnic and cultural persistence of European immigrants to the United States, it nevertheless suggested that whereas Europeans were prepared to renounce their nationality and culture, Mexicans were immune to this condition owing to their shorter overland migration and the proximity of Mexico. Mexicans deflected Americanizing tendencies and consequently were less acceptable to Americans. Retaining their ethnic distinctiveness, Mexicans unfortunately encountered more exploitation and discrimination.[7]

La Opinión regretted this disadvantage of the Mexican immigrant experience, but also saw benefits in it. Immigration and ethnic retention helped dissolve provincialism among Mexicans. "In effect," the paper stated, "here in the United States before anything else we are Mexicans." Mexicans could remain proud of the region of their birth, but once across the border such distinctions made no sense. To help and protect one another, immigrants formed not regional but national organizations. The very names of their mutual societies, for example, smacked of national rather than regional pride: Sociedad Mexicana de Bellas Artes, Hijos de México, Cruz Azul Mexicana, Confederación de Sociedades Mexicanas. Immigration produced a "melting pot" where Mexicans lost their provincialism, but instead of becoming Americans they united as Mexicans.[8] The immigrant experience also dissolved the political and religious differences that had so badly hampered nationhood in Mexico. "We have the right to be whatever we want," *La Opinión* concluded, "but we also have the obligation above everything else to be Mexicans."[9]

Moreover, such ethnic unity transcended nationality and citizenship. *La Opinión* considered all Mexicans, whether holding Mexican or U.S. papers, to be one people. All were part of the Mexican nation. *La Opinión* commentator Rodolfo Uranga noted that no prejudices should mar relationships between Mexican nationals and Mexican Americans. Rather, friendship and solidarity should be promoted. "All are members of the same *raza*," he observed. While those "*de aquí*" were legally U.S. citizens, they retained the same religion, language, and customs as Mexican nationals. "In spirit they are Mexicanos." Anglos, of course, lumped all Mexicans together, and hence Uranga encouraged a united Mexican front against discrimination.[10] He allowed that among Mexican Americans diverse opinions existed concerning Mexican immigration. Some supported restrictions. All, however, denounced the racism against Mexicans voiced by supporters of the Box Bill intended to place Mexicans on immigrant quotas. Uranga stressed the imperative of ethnic defense. He cautioned Mexican nationals not to criticize Mexican Americans for speaking incorrect Spanish or for using certain Anglicisms in their vocabulary. Mexican nationals should correct Mexican Americans through example and not by ridicule. In fact, many Mexican Americans spoke better Spanish than some Mexicans. "On the whole, there is no difference between them and us. We all speak, think, and feel the same."[11]

Unlike those in Mexico who viewed the immigrants and refugees as traitors for leaving their homeland, *La Opinión* regarded them as true patriots. Rather than taking something away from Mexico, Mexican immigrants contributed much value to *la patria*. They would return having learned new skills and work discipline that Mexico desperately needed for its development. They might face much hardship in the United States, but *La Opinión* encouraged immigrant-workers to sacrifice for the sake of what they could offer to Mexico. *La Opinión* almost interpreted Mexican life north of the border as a form of purgatory. One suffered temporarily here, but paradise awaited upon return. Mexican immigrants would also be a vanguard bringing political salvation to Mexico. Having learned how to reconcile their political, religious, and regional differences while living in another country, repatriated Mexican immigrants and refugees would introduce an often missing ingredient in Mexican politics: tolerance. Consequently, the border and its crossing by Mexicans symbolized for *La Opinión* not despair but hope for Mexico's future.[12]

This future, however, needed nurturing. *La Opinión* recognized that Mexican political and cultural nationalism in the United States could only be sustained in the short run. It did not worry about the immigrant generation that had displayed no inclination to discard its Mexican citizenship and pride in being Mexican. Indeed, those few who became U.S. citizens were regarded as traitors. Yet, as the immigrant experience became prolonged and a new generation of U.S.-born Mexicans appeared, Americanization would begin to take its toll. This would occur due to involuntary circumstances as well as conscious efforts by Americanizing institutions.[13] *La Opinión* warned against the consequences of "de-Mexicanization." It considered naive, for example, a suggestion by Mexican labor leader Luis Morones that Mexican workers in the United States seek protection under the American Federation of Labor. Mexican workers might be exploited, *La Opinión* contended, but they were better off than in Mexico. More importantly, the newspaper found it unacceptable for Mexican workers to move toward becoming U.S. citizens—a prerequisite for AF of L membership—in return for union benefits. *La Opinión* believed that the best solution for Mexican immigrant-workers lay in a marked improvement in Mexico's economic and political fortunes that would permit Mexicans to return home.[14]

La Opinión admonished Mexican workers to beware of American welfare organizations that, in return for assisting Mexicans, expected them to accept Americanization. This would involve loss of both citizenship and religion. The paper observed that such conversion ironically would not lead to a better status for Mexicans since they would still be treated as inferior aliens.[15] These were hardly alarmist warnings, Uranga stressed. Americanization had already spilled over onto the Mexican side of the border with unhealthy results. Havens of Mexican culture in the past, these bordertowns had now adopted questionable U.S. tastes in architecture, music, dance, and even the use of *chicle*, chewing gum. Unfortunately, while many Mexicans equated Americanization with superior civilization, Mexican bordertowns, rather than becoming more civilized, had become barbaric. In contrast, Mexican immigrants had civilized bordertowns on the U.S. side by their infusion of Mexican culture.[16] However, retaining a strong Mexican cultural influence north of the border would not be easy. Adults had to remember that while they might not fall under Americanizing influences, their children and grandchildren would. If the diaspora lasted long enough, succeeding generations would be lost forever to Mexico.[17]

To prevent this, Mexicans in the United States had to promote their culture. Uranga noted the success of Jewish immigrants in retaining their identity and encouraged Mexicans to do likewise by establishing their own cultural institutions.[18] He promoted, for example, the formation of Spanish-language libraries either through private donations or by the Mexican government through its consulates.[19] Libraries, however, would not be enough. Uranga and *La Opinión* applauded the opening of such schools throughout the Southwest where children could learn Mexican cultural traditions and absorb a love of Mexico.[20] In reporting the inaugural of the José María Morelos School in Burbank, California, Uranga observed that, despite its modest appearance, what mattered was its rich spirit. At the same time, he disputed those who believed that Americans objected to separate Mexican schools or who felt it unwise for Mexicans to duplicate good American schools. Uranga argued that in fact Americans supported such schools and that in no location had these Mexican schools caused problems. Of course, he admitted, Americans would object to anti-Americanism. But this would not be the case. Mexican schools would acknowledge the benefits to be derived from the United States and would stress the value of Mexican culture rather than the dangers of Americanization. Uranga agreed that U.S. public schools were good, but that as more Mexicans crossed the border no reason existed why they could not form a comparable system.[21]

In educating Mexican children north of the border, *La Opinión* considered indispensable the retention of the Spanish language. "We who are proud of our nationality," it noted, "should understand and always keep fresh in mind this incontrovertible truth: nationality begins with language and language either strengthens or weakens nationality."[22] Hundreds of thousands of Mexicans now lived in the United States, and *La Opinión* worried that within many families young children received their primary schooling in English and expressed themselves outside the family in that language rather than in Spanish. *La Opinión* saw nothing wrong in their learning English, but not at the expense of the mother tongue. The speaking and writing of Spanish had to be fostered.[23]

Cultural retention or "boundary maintenance" also involved other expressions. Uranga, for example, sponsored Mexican music. He publicized the organization of Mexican bands and promoted Mexican musical concerts. Music, he believed, kept alive the spirit of the culture. "It Mexicanizes our sentiment." Moreover, Mexican music exposed Anglos to the refined cultural tastes held by Mexicans. Anglos knew about political instability and economic underdevelopment in Mexico but, unfortunately, little about its music and culture. "Let us make the music of Mexico," he exhorted, "a second religion."[24]

Viewing the immigrant experience as an opportunity to create a "new" Mexican, *La Opinión* believed that barrios needed to be self-reliant political and cultural enclaves. In this process, the Mexican government had to play a major role through its consuls. Immigrants and refugees looked to Mexico City, not Washington, for protection and redress of grievances. Uranga called on Mexican consuls to sponsor less commerce and more protection and services for Mexicans regardless of political or religious beliefs.[25] He lamented that in many communities consuls spied on their conationals and bred discord. "The diversions that exist within our country," Uranga stressed, "should not go beyond our borders, and if they do, they should not persist."[26] Instead, consuls needed to provide ethnic self-protection and [have] their consulates transformed into centers of Mexican unity. *La Opinión* likewise encouraged mutual societies to assist Mexicans in times of need. Uranga suggested that Mexicans build and maintain their own clinics and hospitals. Mexicans needed to show compassion toward their "compañeros." Uranga scolded Mexicans in Colorado who, knowing about a worker named Antonio Casillas who had been sentenced to die for a crime, refused to visit him or attempt to convince officials to commute his execution. As the Great Depression dawned, *La Opinión* called on Mexicans to protect one another from increased efforts to deport them across the border [and from pressure] to turn over their jobs to unemployed Anglos. To avoid mass deportations, it cautioned its readers in Mexico about entering the United States and urged the Mexican government to institute economic incentives to encourage Mexican repatriations.[27]

Until they returned, Mexicans in the United States had to conduct themselves honorably. Recognizing their vulnerability as aliens as well as insisting on law and order, *La Opinión* lectured Mexicans on obeying U.S. laws. By so doing they hopefully would eliminate certain grounds for prejudice against them and create respect for Mexicans. Uranga noted that Anglos accused Mexicans of possessing three vices: thievery, delinquency, and uncleanliness. He considered such charges to be on the whole false, but conceded that they contained a germ of truth. "It is impossible, we know, for 'México de Afuera' to be imperfect; it is formed by humans, and all humans—without exception of race or color—are far from being perfect." Mexicans could better themselves. Uranga especially urged Mexican business and professional leaders to uplift their poorer compatriots. In addition, *La Opinión* cautioned Mexicans to avoid U.S. domestic politics. Reflecting its own aversion to "radicalism," the newspaper frowned on Mexican involvement in Los Angeles's disturbances concerning the controversial Sacco-Vanzetti case. *La Opinión* warned that those arrested in such disorders could not expect much help from either the newspaper or the consul. It concluded that the most appropriate decorum for Mexicans consisted of staying out of trouble, obeying the laws, and, above all, working hard.[28]

If *La Opinión* favored Mexican nationalism north of the border, it also encouraged its version of Pan-Americanism. Vasconcelos explained that Mexicans in the United States, having experienced a *choque*—the shock of accommodating to Anglos and other ethnic groups—had, as a result, not only become more Mexican but more "Latino"—Latin American. "One hears more about '*latinidad*' in *México de Afuera* than in *México de Adentro*, 'Mexico of the Inside.' " Vasconcelos believed in identifying with the rest of Latin America.[29] *La Opinión* displayed a hostility to Yankee material and cultural imperialism not from a Marxist perspective, but from a conservative elitist one that stressed Hispanic cultural superiority. It called on Mexicans in the United States to be proud of this legacy and to associate with *La Raza*—the people of Latin America. Mexicans had to counter Anglo-American hegemony by counterpoising Latin American unity. The "Colossus of the North" had to be checkmated by the "Colossus of the South." *México de Afuera* formed the frontline defense.[30] While speaking from a conservative émigré point of view, *La Opinión*, nevertheless, reflected certain realities of Mexican life north of the border. Mexican immigrants for the most part saw their experiences as transitory. They hoped to return to *la patria* and a better life. Theirs was a "Mexican Dream," not an "American Dream." They accommodated to life in the United States by attempting to reproduce a Mexican world for themselves. Consequently, *La Opinión*'s political and cultural nationalism appealed to many immigrants. Unfortunately, many never returned, including Ignacio Lozano himself. As *La Opinión* feared, the longer Mexicans remained apart from Mexico the more acculturation threatened them, especially their children. If the border proved to be centripetal for most immigrants, it was centrifugal for many of the succeeding generation.

The Mexican-American Era

The 1930s witnessed a new and expansive generation of U.S.-born Mexicans who came of political age. They utilized various terms of self-definition, including Spanish American and Latin American, but increasingly identified as Mexican American. They saw themselves in relationship to life north of the border. Mexican Americans, certainly through their leadership and major organizations such as the League of United Latin American Citizens (LULAC), the American G.I. Forum, and even more militant groups such as the Spanish-Speaking Congress and the Asociación Nacional México-Americana (ANMA), broke with an immigrant consciousness while upholding a tradition of ethnic defense. Politics for Mexican Americans meant the politics of U.S. citizenship and not the politics of Mexico. More acculturated than immigrants, Mexican-American leaders demanded civil rights and equal opportunities. World War II created increased labor demand in the Southwest. By providing Mexican Americans with access to more skilled jobs, exposure to unionization, and even breakthroughs into lower-middle-class professions, the war only served to accelerate Mexican-American aspirations for a better life in the United States. Seeking a place in American society, Mexican Americans pursued a pluralistic world view that would allow them to be accepted as U.S. citizens while remaining proud of their ethnic origin.[31]

Ignacio L. (Nacho) López was among the best-known journalist-intellectuals of the Mexican-American era. Born in Guadalajara but nationalized and raised in the United States, López published and edited *El Espectador* from 1933 to 1960 in the Pomona Valley of Southern California. A weekly tabloid, *El Espectador* could not compete with *La Opinión* in circulation. Still, it played an influential role in mobilizing Mexican-American political action in the Pomona Valley as well as presenting an alternative viewpoint to *La Opinión*, which, despite its continued publication after 1930 (it is still publishing today), has historically directed itself more to recent arrivals from Mexico and to those who remain largely *Mexicano* in sentiment. By contrast, through his editorials, essays, and general direction of *El Espectador*, López reflected and shaped a Mexican-American consciousness.[32]

López, like *La Opinión*, accepted the political reality of the border. He, however, recognized that a new generation of Mexicans in the United States permanently resided north of it. Mexico, not the United States, was foreign to many Mexican Americans. While *La Opinión* saw Mexicans on both sides of the border as an organic whole, López discerned political, cultural, and economic cleavages separating Mexican Americans both from Mexico and from Mexican immigrants. Mexican Americans were not *México de Afuera* but "Americans of Mexican descent."

The border and the return to Mexico held no attraction for López. For Mexican Americans, there was no retreat to Mexico. The more enterprising aspired to the "American Dream." López appreciated the permanency of Mexican Americans in the United States. Having attended American schools, he desired to make something of himself in his adopted country. López absorbed the values and ideals of the United States. He did not at the same time reject his Mexican cultural traditions. Yet a U.S. experience, not a Mexican one, shaped much of his politics. López and many of the Mexican-American activists and intellectuals of his generation can be seen as political sons and daughters of the New Deal era and of the U.S. involvement in World War II. As part of a generation engaged in a campaign to overturn obstacles to full equality, López helped advance the notion that the Mexican-American struggle lay north of the border. By participating in Mexican-American issues, such as the desegregation of public facilities and schools plus the movement into electoral politics, López spoke more for the attainment of the fruits of the American Revolution than of the Mexican Revolution. Hence, the sense of permanency—the United States as home country—influenced the political ideology and activism of Mexican Americans.

As permanent residents of the United States, López and other Mexican Americans in the Pomona Valley waged protracted struggles against discrimination and segregation. Prejudice, of course, affected all Mexicans, and López did not differentiate between Mexican Americans and Mexican nationals in the securement of equal treatment. He did believe, however, that Mexican Americans had more at stake in desegregation. Besides combating affronts to their ethnic dignity, Mexican Americans saw desegregation as a means to [achieve] equal opportunities with Americans and recognition as full-fledged U.S. citizens.

Unlike *La Opinión*, López understood that Mexican Americans could not reconcile their exploited conditions by believing that a better life awaited in Mexico. Mexican-American life might be a purgatory, but heaven would be found north, not south, of the border. *La Opinión*'s caution about Mexicans not engaging in civil conflict in the United States had no relevance to Mexican Americans. López preached direct action to combat prejudice. He challenged discrimination in public facilities such as movie theaters, swimming pools, and restaurants as among the most objectionable forms of separation. In 1939, for example, López person-

ally lead a boycott of the Upland Theater in Upland, California, for seg-
regating Mexicans in the first fifteen rows. The boycott succeeded, and
the theater agreed to complete integration. "In this manner the first step
is taken," López noted, "in the Mexican community's defense of its dignity and in its struggle for civil rights."[33]

Both *La Opinión* and *El Espectador* advocated education for Mexican children north of the border. However, where *La Opinión* supported a
separate Mexican system to prevent acculturation, López encouraged
Mexican Americans to integrate the public schools. He believed in ethnic
pride and cultural retention, but appreciated that in order for Mexican
Americans to advance they had to learn English and have access to quality education. This could only be achieved by dismantling the dual public
school system of the Southwest that relegated Mexican children to inferior public "Mexican schools" and instead integrating both Mexicans and
Anglos in same schools. Writing in *El Espectador* Eugenio Nogueras also
pointed out the contradiction of "Mexican schools" in California. Such
schools belonged in Mexico, not the United States.[34] Moreover, López
upheld school integration not only as a right but as pedagogically correct.
Integration facilitated the learning of English; segregation impeded it.
Integration also socialized children to live with one another and to respect each other. López saw in integrated public schools the perfect ve-
hicle for achieving democratic rights for Mexican Americans.[35]

El Espectador supported ethnic solidarity, as did *La Opinión*, but not
at the expense of equal opportunities for Mexican Americans. While *La
Opinión* had supported self-sufficient Mexican enclaves that would breed
Mexican nationalism, López rejected what he considered self-segregation.
He opposed, for example, any form of segregated housing. In 1950 he
editorialized against construction of a housing tract in Whittier exclusively for Mexican-American veterans. He admitted that some Mexican
Americans supported such housing because it meant better homes, but
aligned himself with those who opposed it on the principle that segregation was unacceptable. The housing tract constituted an effort to pacify
Mexican Americans while denying them the opportunity to purchase homes
in Anglo neighborhoods. Offended at such discrimination, especially when
the country asked for unity because of the Korean conflict, López concluded: "It is not the Anglo-Saxon who will reap the repercussions of this
case of segregation . . . it will be those of us who have yet to understand
that the only way to end discrimination and segregation is for us to integrate fully into society . . . making us part of the community and not
trying to live in an exclusive world reserved only for ourselves."[36] In the
pursuit of integration and equal opportunities, López broke with the idea
of an organic unity of the Mexican people on both sides of the border

supported by *La Opinión*. He did not believe, for example, that the economic interests of Mexican Americans and Mexican nationals necessarily coincided. López defended braceros and undocumented workers, but
recognized that they replaced and dislocated resident Mexican-American
workers. The right to a decent job was both a human and civil right and,
in certain cases, López found himself defending local workers against
Mexican nationals. In the Pomona Valley and throughout California, un-
scrupulous employers pitted one set of workers against the other and where
possible employed the cheaper braceros or *alambristas* [fence-jumpers].
Employers persistently declared that they could not find enough domestic agricultural workers and hence the need for braceros. Yet this claim
always worked against Mexican-American farmworkers. When local growers requested braceros in February of 1949, López replied that in his opinion braceros were not needed due to the availability of domestic workers
who often had to go without work during certain seasons. There were not
enough jobs for both Mexican Americans and braceros. Often, when
braceros arrived and discovered insufficient work, they abandoned their
camps and sought employment illegally. However, López viewed with
greater alarm the fact that the use of braceros lowered wage standards,
especially for Mexican Americans who could not compete with the cheaper
labor.[37]

In many instances, undocumented workers rather than braceros
harmed Mexican-American interests. *El Espectador* noted various cases
of employers illegally hiring *alambristas*, through illicit contraband traf-
fic in what the newspapers termed "human meat." López supported the
elimination of undocumented immigration and questioned the neutrality
of immigration and border patrol officers who often seemed invisible when
growers desired undocumented workers. "The only ones who can solve
this problem," López proposed, "are the resident workers of this region
who must take this issue to the highest officials and have them understand that this problem is one of the gravest facing labor in California and
is the problem of thousands of Mexican Americans who live exclusively
by doing farm labor."[38] He lamented opposing the employment of Mexican nationals and believed this dilemma to be a modern and tragic version of the Cain and Abel biblical story. Yet Mexican nationals replaced
Mexican-American workers, and López called for an end to this displacement. "It is unjust for those from the outside to come and take bread away
from our children, even if this is justified on the laws of Supply and Demand. The resident workers of this country should have priority over any
other group—even if this involves the painful case of that other group
being of our own race and tongue."[39] The migration of Mexican workers
across the border was a complex issue, but López suggested that the solu-

tion lay in Mexico establishing new agricultural centers that would be productive enough to retain workers in their own country.[40]

Politically, *El Espectador* differed from *La Opinión*. Whereas *La Opinión* applauded conationals retaining their Mexican citizenship and saw political organization as a means to ethnic solidarity and protection from American cultural contamination, López advocated the political integration of Mexican Americans within the United States. A fervent disciple of American democracy, López consistently encouraged his readers to vote. Voting expressed citizenship. During World War II, López reminded Mexican Americans that the war and the preservation of democracy would be won both in the battlefield and in the polling booth. "Remember that it is a patriotic obligation," he wrote, "to vote in the elections; register if you have not done so."[41] Through voting Mexican Americans could better assimilate into the political life of the nation. Unfortunately many Mexican Americans possessing the right to vote did not do so: "We refer to that large number of American citizens of Hispanic descent, men and women, who being able to vote and to actively participate in the civic life of their community fail to do so because they have not registered to vote."[42]

López viewed voting in more than idealistic terms. He realized that an electoral strategy could advance Mexican-American working and living conditions. In 1938, López editorialized concerning what Mexicans in the United States could do to improve their lives north of the border. Mexicans had two choices. They could either accept their second-class status, as many had done for almost one hundred years and through at least five generations, or they could begin to struggle to achieve equality. López believed that the time had arrived to demand the Mexicans' rightful place in American society. He observed that Mexicans now formed a sizable population in the Southwest, particularly in southern California. Statistics, however, would not generate changes. Mexican Americans alone could do this by directly participating in politics and, in a word, by voting. "If you want economic and social power," he told his audience, "then first acquire political power."[43] López even suggested that Mexican nationals in California think seriously about becoming American citizens so that, through voting, they could improve their material status. Mexican Americans should not complain about discrimination, López lectured, and then not vote. Only by voting in large numbers would Mexican Americans achieve respect and reforms.[44] "The vote is our most sacred right," López sermonized, "and at the same time the most powerful political weapon."[45] Indeed, the vote, "in the final analysis is the panacea for all our ills."[46] Politicians only understood organized political pressure. If Mexican Americans could achieve this through voting, they would be surprised at the "miracles" their votes would bring: paved and lighted streets, better police and fire [-fighting] service, better treatment by public officers, and more Mexican Americans in government.[47]

El Espectador also had to confront the cultural question in the United States. However, unlike *La Opinión*, which preached Mexican cultural nationalism, *El Espectador* opted for biculturalism and a modified form of Mexican-American nationalism. López supported the integration of Mexicans into the mainstream of American society, but not at the expense of cultural heritage. He took pride in being of Mexican descent and believed in pragmatic cultural retention. Moreover, López understood that the racial and cultural discrimination that bred insecurity among Mexican Americans had to be countered by ethnic pride. "Respect and pride in one's heritage," he advised young Mexican-American graduates in 1957, "is essential in order to feel proud in being American."[48] Hence, López cultivated a bicultural world view among Mexicans in the Pomona Valley. He promoted Mexican cultural traditions and accepted a process of acculturation that would pave the way for integration. Fearful of too much acculturation, especially among youth, López recognized cultural pluralism as a viable alternative. As one writer in *El Espectador* put it: "Continue united, for unity builds strength, and continue to be proud of being both in the United States and of having Mexican blood in your veins."[49]

López advocated Mexican cultural retention in several ways. Linguistically, he affirmed the use of Spanish and the development of a bilingual population. *El Espectador* itself was a predominantly Spanish-language organ. The paper also served as an outlet for local poets, who published their Spanish-language poems and *corridos* (ballads) in its pages. "Journalism has been my mission in life," López proclaimed in 1956. "And I have nothing to complain about. In publishing a Spanish-language newspaper we have contributed in a small way to fostering among our readers a love of our beautiful language and of our culture, which gives it life."[50] *El Espectador* paid particular attention to the celebration of the sixteenth of September—Mexican Independence Day—and Cinco de Mayo, the Mexican victory over an invading French army in 1862. López consistently prompted the Mexican communities to organize festivals for these key Mexican holidays. "The most important gift that we can leave our children," López editorialized, "is the pride in being Mexican." If parents retained their cultural traditions and passed them on to their offspring, the "Mexican soul" would survive north of the border.[51]

López, however, also recognized the importance and, indeed, the inevitability of acculturation. *El Espectador* reflected and even influenced this process. The paper's periodic use of a bilingual format underlined the cultural and linguistic changes experienced by Mexican Americans.

Between 1938 and 1959, López launched at least five bilingual versions of *El Espectador*. Each ran for several months before reverting again to a Spanish-language copy. Bilingualism in *El Espectador* consisted of an English-language page aimed at the growing number of Mexican-American youth in the public schools. "These young adults and children," López wrote in 1938, "preferring to read in English, in order to understand it better, and also because many cannot read in Spanish, have no interest in our newspaper. Hence, it is our intention (by publishing this English section) to interest our Mexican youth in *El Espectador*."[52] Nine years later, Larry Probasco, a World War II veteran and the second editor of the paper's English section, stressed the importance of learning English. It formed the common denominator linking all ethnic groups in the United States. One spoke English not just out of necessity but because it was a privilege.[53]

Supporting Mexican cultural traditions while understanding the attraction and pragmatic necessity of acculturation, López proposed a type of dual cultural citizenship. Mexican Americans could and should benefit from both cultures. Dual cultural citizenship was not only a goal but a growing reality. Adult Mexicans remained highly loyal to their language and culture, but among the young various forces pushed them to accept cultural compromises or what López termed "naturalization." However, this need not be feared. "Naturalization" remained distinct from forced Americanization, which had been tried earlier and failed. López opposed forced Americanization but accepted acculturation as inevitable and pointed out that customs, diet, marriage, education, jobs, and even wars helped socialize Mexican Americans to life in the United States.[54]

Acculturation was not wrong, but it had to be balanced. It should deprive Mexican Americans neither of their cultural heritage nor of their ethnic identity. Acculturation could not and should not be prevented, but this transformation could be eased by a sensitivity on the part of both Mexican Americans and Anglos to the benefits of cultural pluralism. World War II had proved, López editorialized in 1946, that people and nations had to cooperate and treat each other with respect. This also had to apply domestically in the postwar era. "The great hope for realization of a better world, instead of a planet of shattering holocausts," he wrote, "lies in our will to merge viewpoints and differing customs—to come to know its varying people as friends and neighbors. To have such opportunities here in our own communities is something we should seek ardently."[55] López recalled the unique cultural roots of California and of the distinct Spanish-Mexican heritage of the state. Cultural pluralism was real in California, but had to be more than simply the stereotypical "colorful Mexican." Mexican Americans had to be accepted as full citizens and integrated into all levels of California society. Only in this manner could a viable cultural pluralism flourish and a united society be forged or the "one world" López referred to: "The time has come—indeed it had to come— for 'one world' in our home communities. It is the time for friendliness and courtesy, for the merging of viewpoints and differing customs, for the sharing of civic responsibilities and problems. Not as newcomers, but as coworkers over many decades of community history, the descendants of Spain and Mexico, bearers of a great cultural heritage, come to take their place in civic life. They are ready to help bear its burdens and rejoice in its triumphs."[56]

The Chicano Era

Yet, despite certain advances, Mexican Americans such as Ignacio López failed to fully integrate Mexicans north of the border although this accommodating tendency continues to represent an important part of Mexican-American political thought. Consequently, out of the frustrated aspirations of the Mexican-American era a new and more militant politics emerged in the 1960s: the Chicano movement. A product of the historic exploitation of Mexicans in the United States, Chicanos as a generation were likewise the result of a decade of social conflict and questioning of American values and culture. Black civil rights struggles, the black power movement, antiwar protests, ethnic revivals, radical feminism, and youth alienation and rebellion influenced the birth of the Chicano generation. Chicanos rejected the politics of compromise and accommodation and, attracted to Third World struggles, called for political and cultural self-determination. Ironically more Americanized, educated, and occupationally mobile than their parents, Chicanos despaired of their acculturation and of American middle-class materialism. Instead, they sought roots and a new identity through the path of Chicano cultural nationalism and revived an image of a lost homeland in the Southwest: Aztlán.[57]

Cultural nationalism, however, soon proved to be politically and intellectually stifling for some Chicanos. It did not explain class contradictions among Mexicans in the United States. Culture and identity, they argued, could not be divorced from the predominant working-class character of most Mexicans. Cultural nationalism apart from class struggle could degenerate into an opportunistic reactionary movement. Hence, by the early 1970s an important wing of the Chicano movement had gravitated toward a synthesis of nationalism and working-class struggle. A leader of the Chicano left was CASA [El Centro de Acción Social Autónoma or the Center for Autonomous Social Action]—General Brotherhood of Workers [Hermandad General de Trabajadores]. Organized in

Los Angeles by long-time community organizer Bert Corona in the late 1960s for the protection of undocumented Mexican workers, CASA had been captured in the mid-1970s by young radical activists and intellectuals. Maintaining an emphasis on the increasing numbers of undocumented workers, CASA also saw itself as a political vanguard and symbolized an important evolution to the Left by young Chicano intellectuals, students, and particular sectors of workers. Moreover, in its development CASA inherited a radical current present in Mexican-American thought and expressed by earlier movements such as the followers of the anarcho-syndicalist Ricardo Flores Magón during the 1910s, the militant Spanish-Speaking Congress (1938–1943), and the Asociación Nacional México-Americana (ANMA) during the Cold War years of the early 1950s. In its analysis of the Mexican position in the United States and through its monthly and modestly circulated newspaper *Sin Fronteras* (1976–1979), CASA interpreted the border differently from *La Opinión* and *El Espectador*.

As its title indicated, *Sin Fronteras* (Without Borders) rejected the idea of a border. A political border existed, but *Sin Fronteras*, unlike *La Opinión* and *El Espectador*, considered it to be only an artificial creation that in time would be destroyed by the struggles of Mexicans on both sides of the border. In its version of the "National Question," *Sin Fronteras* regarded the Mexican War as a colonial conquest that had imposed a subordinate status on Mexicans. It sympathized with Chicano historians such as Rodolfo Acuña who proposed a theory of internal colonialism to explain the Chicano condition.[58] However, *Sin Fronteras* went one step further and included Mexicans south of the border as part of the colonized. "Occupied Mexico" was on both sides of the border. Yankee political, economic, and cultural colonialism victimized all Mexicans, whether in the United States or in Mexico. Like *La Opinión*, *Sin Fronteras* accepted Mexicans as one people, whether U.S. citizens or Mexican nationals and irrespective of which side of the border they lived on. "Presently, when we speak of the Mexican population, we speak of approximately 80 million people situated on both sides of the border," CASA proposed. "This means that we are the largest Spanish-speaking population in the world."[59] *Sin Fronteras* shunned terms such as Chicano and Mexican American that implied differences among Mexicans and, instead, used only the term "Mexicano." It rejected the narrow nationalistic concept of Aztlán, but agreed with the 1969 Plan de Aztlán that "we do not recognize capricious borders on the Bronze Continent."[60]

La Opinión, of course, had sponsored the organic unity of all Mexicans based on ethnic and cultural ties. *Sin Fronteras* differed by focusing on the national and class character of Mexicans. That is, Mexicans because of conquest were an oppressed nation and as a fundamentally working-class people they also formed an exploited class under capitalism. Consequently, the "Mexican worker" rather than *La Opinión*'s "universal Mexican" constituted the foundation for the organic unity that transcended the border. Mexicans were one people on both sides of the border because they were products of the same nation, Mexico, and possessed a common class character. Victims of oppression, Mexicanos could only achieve liberation and self-determination by engaging in a borderless struggle to defeat American international capitalism.[61] "Thus it is our responsibility," CASA stressed, "to fight exploitation and national oppression for our rights as workers and as a people."[62]

Because of this organic unity, *Sin Fronteras* in the 1970s concentrated on what it believed to be the most pressing issue facing Mexicans in the United States: the plight of the undocumented worker. It noted that those calling themselves Chicanos or Mexican Americans could not escape several fundamental factors that bound all Mexicans together. For example, Mexicans from both sides of the border were racially and ethnically one people. In his analysis of the Chicano movement, Carlos Vásquez observed that it had progressively evolved to include undocumented workers. "A segment of the Chicano Movement deepened its commitment to national identity and to class struggle and unified their efforts with those of the undocumented worker," he wrote. "Not as a solidarity to strangers, but as a direct responsibility to members of the same nationality, of the same people."[63] Vásquez criticized those Chicanos who, lacking historical and class consciousness, distanced themselves from the struggles of the undocumented. These Chicanos ironically withdrew from their own families, since many members often possessed no documents.[64] Unlike Ignacio López, who discerned political, economic, and cultural differences between Mexican Americans and Mexican nationals, *Sin Fronteras* idealistically dismissed such differences as minor and called on Mexicanos north of the border to reject such divisive proposals. "[W]e should not only resist the government's attempt to divide us by creating the conception that we are a different nationality from our compatriots born south of the border," CASA member Nativo López stressed, "we must also resist and combat these false notions among our people which are perpetuated by self-proclaimed vanguards, some intellectuals and assimilationists."[65]

Besides a common nationality, Chicanos and Mexican Americans needed to identify with the undocumented because any Mexican possessed a historic right to migrate to the Southwest. "To Mexicans," *Sin Fronteras* proclaimed, "it [migration] means we are concretely repopulating lands stolen from us in the Invasion of 1846."[66] CASA further emphasized that since most Chicanos and Mexican Americans descended from earlier immigrants, they should not now turn their backs on more recent arrivals.[67]

Chicanos and Mexican Americans likewise needed to pragmatically recognize that undocumented workers formed an indispensable component of the Mexican working class in the United States. Liberation and self-determination could not be achieved without the participation of the undocumented. Moreover, Chicanos and Mexican Americans, as a predominantly working-class people, possessed the same class position as the undocumented. Class interests, along with ethnic ones, produced one people. "Workers, with or without documents," CASA's Political Commission acknowledged, "only create the wealth that enriches the exploiting class. They [Mexicanos] are the exploited, and this is the common interest they have as a universal class."[68] Reversing *La Opinión*'s emphasis that Mexican workers in the United States would return to their homeland and introduce modernizing changes, *Sin Fronteras* believed that undocumented workers coming in the opposite direction could become a political vanguard among Mexicans north of the border. "The immigrant workers bring with them enormous experiences of struggle from their own countries," political exile José Jacquez Medina wrote: "An example of this is the concept of a 'strike' which immigrant workers have. When they participate in a strike, they are the first to openly propose the total shut-down of the factory and placing of the red-and-black flags over the gates. When North American workers tell them that it is against the law to do that, they usually answer that the only strike they know is when the workers stop the factory totally and do not allow scabs to replace them."[69]

Finally, Chicanos and Mexican Americans had to understand that their capitalist exploiters eyed all Mexicans as the same. It made no sense for Chicanos and Mexicans Americans to separate themselves from the undocumented since racism and class oppression affected them all. "Because we compose the majority of Latin workers in this part of the country," one CASA member explained, "racism is aimed at the Mexican worker. Although this capitalist government claims that we are all equal under the law, we are actually in an inferior position. In reality, there is no difference between those born here and those recently arrived, between those who have lived here for years."[70]

Because of this inescapable organic unity, *Sin Fronteras* urged Chicanos to protect undocumented workers from the antialien hysteria spreading during the 1970s. CASA in particular attacked President Carter's immigration plan as repressive legislation. The plan intended to curtail the right of Mexicans to enter the United States and would discriminate against all Mexicans north of the border. Like *El Espectador*, but for different reasons, *Sin Fronteras* opposed any reinstitution of the Bracero Program suggested by some proponents of immigration "reform." Ignacio López had primarily criticized the Program for harming Mexican-American farm workers, while *Sin Fronteras* considered it a system of "rented slaves" for the profit of agribusiness.[71] Moreover, *Sin Fronteras* disdained immigration legislation that sought to arbitrarily divide Mexicans. "Taken in parts or in its totality," Nativo López argued, "Carter's program is an affront to the very livelihood, the very existence of Mexican people, born on either side of the border, regardless of generation."[72]

Any Mexican who collaborated with Carter's plan, *Sin Fronteras* warned, betrayed his ethnic heritage and participated in the victimization of his own people. Such collaborators played the role of colonial administrators.[73] *Sin Fronteras* considered, for example, that Carter's appointment of Leonel Castillo as director of the Immigration and Naturalization Service (INS) fit this description. "If he becomes an apologist for the INS," it suggested, "he will be serving the interests of those who took our lands, who keep us in the condition under which we live, and who suck the lifeblood of Mexico with their multinational corporations and international investments."[74]

Instead of restricting immigration and deporting undocumented workers, *Sin Fronteras* advocated unconditional amnesty for all Mexicans in the United States without papers. Mexicans producing wealth through their labor had earned the right to live and work here. Amnesty also validated the Mexicans' historic presence in the Southwest. "Amnesty," CASA member Felipe Aguirre underscored, "signifies the tacit acknowledgement of those rights taken away through violence, along with lands, and the aggression [*sic*] upon their culture, customs, and language of the Mexican people."[75] *Sin Fronteras* believed immigration restrictions and deportations against Mexicans to be historical hypocrisy. To consider Mexicans illegal in the Southwest was preposterous and a farce. "U.S. imperialists invaded and robbed our (Mexican) lands, put up fictitious borders and now want to treat us as illegals," stated Antonio Rodríguez, national coordinator of CASA. "It takes more than a treaty [of Guadalupe Hidalgo, 1848] to separate our people: no government can legislate our right to live in our own lands. We demand complete and total amnesty for all immigrants, and an end to deportations."[76]

Self-determination, however, could not be limited to Mexicans north of the border. It could only be accomplished through the unified struggles of Mexicans on both sides. The same conditions, for example, that caused unemployment and subemployment on one side produced it on the other.

"Mexico is a classical example of North American economic intervention," Jacquez Medina stressed.[77] "We have seen . . .," columnist Magdalena Mora noted, "that the exploitation of workers is not limited by borders. Thus, the resistance of workers cannot be limited by national boundaries. Their struggle is one."[78] Mexican workers in the United States needed to join the anti-imperialist struggles of their "compañeros" in the factories and fields of Mexico. *La Opinión*, of course, had also opposed U.S. imperialism, but in support of a Mexican national bourgeoisie and not a society controlled by workers favored by *Sin Fronteras*. "Mexican people on both sides of the border," Jacquez Medina observed, "victims of worsening conditions, begin to understand that solutions to their problems are not found in the governments nor systems which rule on both sides of the borders."[79] Only the workers themselves could solve their problems by establishing a workers' state transcending the border. *Sin Fronteras* boldly concluded: "NO BORDER STOPS WORKERS' STRUGGLES."[80]

To achieve workers' unity, the borderless struggle for political liberation had to be accompanied by a movement for cultural self-determination. *Sin Fronteras*, like *La Opinión* and *El Espectador*, feared the dangers of Americanization. It disagreed, however, with *La Opinión* that self-enclosed Mexican cultural enclaves could be maintained. Instead, it pragmatically believed with Ignacio López that acculturation could not be avoided and that at best a bicultural, bilingual condition could be achieved. Yet, while López interpreted biculturalism as accommodation within the U.S. system, *Sin Fronteras* accepted it as a cultural base for national self-determination. *Mexicanos* had to protect their historic culture and language not only because of their heritage, but because they needed to form cultural links between Mexican Americans and Mexican nationals in the United States and between Mexicans on both sides of the border. Carlos Vásquez noted that a positive feature of the Chicano movement had been its emphasis on cultural self-determination. Unfortunately, the movement had not always put this into practice. Vásquez pointed out that many Chicano newspapers utilized English and avoided a bilingual format. Hence, they regrettably separated themselves from a large Spanish-speaking audience.[81] *Sin Fronteras* published bilingually. Moreover, without the right to use Spanish, many Mexican workers in the United States could not adequately defend themselves. *Sin Fronteras* particularly protested efforts by some labor unions in southern California to prohibit Spanish at their local meetings. This discriminated against Mexican members on the basis of language. "If members don't understand English, then they can't raise questions or engage in discussion; and if they can't do that, then corrupt union leaders will never be stopped."[82]

Consequently, cultural retention and promotion was needed to prevent such efforts by U.S. institutions or by unsympathetic Mexican Americans to deprive *Mexicanos* of a common culture and language as a way of dominating them. "[W]e must view all plans to assimilated [*sic*] us or portray us as assimilated as a conscious act to weaken our unity and our strength in numbers," *Sin Fronteras* editorialized: "It means that all attempts to divide us according to legal status, place of birth, language dominance, or whatever must be resisted. It does not matter whether it comes from the state or it comes from some of our own misguided and confused people who try to hide their assimilation and deculturation in pseudo-revolutionary rhetoric about multi-nationalism."[83] *Sin Fronteras* urged cultural maintenance, but did not advocate a separate Mexican educational system as earlier advanced by *La Opinión*. It aligned itself with *El Espectador*'s position favoring the right of Mexican-American students to equal educational opportunities in the public schools. However, *Sin Fronteras* also insisted on bilingual, bicultural education. Ignacio López and many other Mexican Americans of his era believed that bilingual education singled out Mexican Americans as different and hence they opposed it. They considered Spanish-language retention to be the responsibility of the home and community institutions. Chicanos in the 1960s rejected this view as assimilationist. Instead, they stressed bilingual education both as a methodology to assist Spanish-speaking students and for the cultivation of cultural nationalism. *Sin Fronteras* agreed and supported its implementation in the Los Angeles public schools. The issue of busing to desegregate schools only enhanced *Sin Fronteras*'s concern over bilingual education. Busing posed a difficult issue for CASA. It did not want to side with opponents of busing, yet CASA feared that busing could disperse the Mexican community and harm bilingual programs in predominantly Mexican-American schools. "Would forced busing be equivalent to forced assimilation?" it asked.[84] Discounting that true integration could be achieved under a racist capitalist system, *Sin Fronteras* aimed to protect the cultural integrity of *Mexicanos* as a way of advancing liberation struggles. Busing could endanger this effort. *Mexicanos* did not want integration, *Sin Fronteras* argued; they wanted cultural self-determination, and public education had to reflect this desire. "Busing does not resolve the demands of the Mexican people," Antonio Rodríguez explained: "It does not guarantee the respect to the practice and cultivation of our national rights, as reflected in the demand for bilingual and bicultural education. Without those rights equal education does not exist for us. The use of our language and culture forms part of the democratic struggle for our political survival faced with brutal Yankee cultural aggression and its attempt to destroy the use of our national language."[85] *Sin Fronteras* supported busing only if it did not adversely affect bilingual programs.

More radical than either *La Opinión* or *El Espectador*, *Sin Fronteras* pursued different long-range goals. *La Opinión* had looked toward the eventual return of Mexicans to their homeland south of the border and a better life under a Mexican capitalist state. *El Espectador* had hoped for the integration of Mexican Americans in an American bourgeois pluralist society. *Sin Fronteras*, however, believed in the achievement of socialism by *Mexicano* workers on both sides of the border. *Mexicanos* would repossess their lost lands in the Southwest and join with their compatriots in Mexico to establish a greater Mexican workers' state. Meanwhile, the struggles for the protection of the undocumented, for union democracy, for bilingual education, among others, formed a transitional phase for raising the political consciousness of Mexican workers and preparing them to achieve socialism and true democracy. In these efforts, *Mexicano* workers united with the larger working-class movement in the United States while retaining their right as a people to national self-determination.[86] "Although Mexican workers form part of the working class," CASA explained, "the oppression of the Mexican people goes beyond that experienced by other members of the working class under capitalism. We suffer both as workers and as a people."[87]

As socialists, CASA members encouraged a broader internationalist perspective. Besides rejecting a border between Mexico and the United States, *Sin Fronteras* also preached the borderless solidarity of all oppressed peoples, especially in Latin America and the Third World. This internationalism went beyond the more limited and elitist Pan-Americanism advocated by *La Opinión*. *Mexicano* workers, according to *Sin Fronteras*, could defeat U.S. imperialism not only by uniting with their brothers and sisters in Mexico but by joining with other workers throughout the world fighting the same enemy. "The revolutionary trend demands the intensification of the militant international solidarity and the support of the just struggles of national liberation which are being fought throughout the world," CASA's Political Commission concluded. "The international alliance of Capitalism must be opposed by proletarian internationalism and the people's international solidarity."[88] CASA sided with the Cuban Revolution and supported other movements for national liberation in Latin America. "Our organization is made up of Mexican and Latin American people that defeated colonialism," Antonio Rodríguez stated on his way to a Havana conference in solidarity with Puerto Rican independence. "We are part of a people that daily suffer racism, discrimination, exploitation under the same imperialists who today maintain Puerto

Rico as a colony."[89] *Sin Fronteras* recognized no borders between oppressed people in Latin America and called attention to its motto: "SOMOS
UNO PORQUE AMÉRICA ES UNO [*sic*]."

Conclusion

The different interpretations of the border by *La Opinión*, *El Espectador*,
and *Sin Fronteras* captured an important spirit within each of their historical periods. Although possessing unequal circulation and reaching by
and large different audiences, these newspapers reflected and shaped intellectual currents among opinion-makers and political activists, but, of
course, could not speak for all Mexicans. *La Opinión*, for example, was
distributed and read throughout the United States. On the other hand, *Sin
Fronteras* influenced primarily students, intellectuals, and young workers. Yet, each newspaper gives testimony to significant political and intellectual changes within the Mexican communities north of the border.
In its early years *La Opinión* spoke for the immigrants and political refugees who dominated most Mexican communities in the early twentieth
century. As such, *La Opinión* served and continues to serve as an immigrant institution. *El Espectador* articulated the voice of a people in search
of their place in the United States. Finally, *Sin Fronteras*, which ceased
publication by the late 1970s, transmitted the concerns of an important
segment of the new Chicano generation of the 1960s and 1970s that sought
to reconcile a renaissance of Mexican nationalism with working-class
ideological affiliation in the hope of militantly defending the interests of
Mexican workers on both sides of the border. Each of these newspapers
stressed central themes of the Mexican experience in the United States:
conquest, subjugation, immigration, racism, cultural nationalism, acculturation, integration, ethnic revival, alienation, and class consciousness.
Other ethnic groups in the country possessed somewhat similar intellectual traditions; yet, with the limited exception of French Canadians in the
United States, they did not confront a two-thousand-mile border between
the United States and the mother country that daily reinforced these
themes. Moreover, the persistence of such themes from one generation to
another among Mexicans attests to continued class and racial barriers
confronting Mexicans as well as the constant and relatively easy migration of Mexicans as economic refugees across the border into the United
States. In a fascinating departure from almost all other ethnic experiences
in this country, second- and third-generation U.S.-born Mexicans of varying class positions continue to coexist with thousands of recent arrivals
from Mexico. Consequently, different states of consciousness also coex-

ist: an immigrant consciousness steeped in *Mexicano* ethnic and cultural nationalism plus an abiding attachment to Mexico; a Mexican-American consciousness centered on integration and acculturation; and a Chicano consciousness stressing ethnic revival with elements of Marxism. These three political tempers and varying subtempers interact with one another in the 1980s and continue to influence Mexican-American political thought.

Clearly, with such heterogeneity no consensus has surfaced on the meaning of the border among Mexicans north of it. Still, each generation has had to directly or indirectly relate to *la frontera*. No viable political strategy among Mexican Americans or public policies affecting Mexican Americans can possibly succeed without being cognizant of the border. Unending immigration, Mexico's nearness, and the concentration of Mexicans in the Southwest have all given the border, as both symbol and reality, a major place in Mexican-American thought.

Notes

1. For the post-Mexican War period and the immigrant era see, for example: Mario Barrera, *Race and Class in the Southwest: A Theory of Racial Inequality* (Notre Dame, IN: University of Notre Dame Press, 1979); Albert Camarillo, *Chicanos in a Changing Society: From Mexican Pueblos to American Barrios in Santa Barbara and Southern California, 1848–1930* (Cambridge, MA: Harvard University Press, 1979); Lawrence Cardoso, *Mexican Emigration to the United States, 1897–1931* (Tucson: University of Arizona Press, 1980); Arnoldo De León, *The Tejano Community, 1836–1900* (Albuquerque: University of New Mexico Press, 1982) and *They Called Them Greasers: Anglo Attitudes toward Mexicans in Texas, 1821–1900* (Austin: University of Texas Press, 1983); Mario T. García, *Desert Immigrants: The Mexicans of El Paso, 1880–1920* (New Haven, CT: Yale University Press, 1981); Richard Griswold del Castillo, *The Los Angeles Barrio, 1850–1890: A Social History* (Berkeley: University of California Press, 1979); Leonard Pitt, *The Decline of the Californios: A Social History of the Spanish-Speaking Californians, 1846–1890* (Berkeley: University of California Press, 1966); Mark Reisler, *By the Sweat of Their Brow: Mexican Immigrant Labor in the United States* (Westport, CT: Greenwood Press, 1976); and Robert J. Rosenbaum, *Mexicano Resistance in the Southwest: The Sacred Right of Self-Preservation* (Austin: University of Texas Press, 1981). For an economic history of the U.S.-Mexican border, see Raul Fernández, *The United States-Mexican Border: A Politico-Economic Profile* (Notre Dame, IN: University of Notre Dame Press, 1977). For a good case study of border life, see Oscar J. Martínez, *Border Boom Town: Ciudad Juárez Since 1848* (Austin: University of Texas Press, 1978).

2. For a short content analysis of *La Opinión*, see Francine Medeiros, "La Opinión, A Mexican Exile Newspaper: A Content Analysis of Its First Years, 1926–1929," *Aztlán* 11 (Spring 1980): 65–88. *La Opinión*, of course, is still being published today, but for this study only the issues from 1926 to 1929 covering part of what I term the "immigrant era" were considered.

3. See *Sin Fronteras* for the 1970s.

4. See David Weber, ed., *Foreigners in Their Native Land* (Albuquerque: University of New Mexico Press, 1973).

5. *La Opinión*, 10 June 1928, p. 37. The types of questions posed by *La Opinión* indirectly dealt with what is termed the "National Question." That is, do Mexicans in the United States constitute a separate nation, a national minority, or an oppressed nationality. One writer suggests that the debate on the "National Question" is only of recent origin; however, Mexicans in the United States in one form or another have addressed this question for some time, even though in a less theoretical fashion than in recent years. See Antonio Ríos Bustamante, *Mexicans in the United States and the National Question* (Santa Barbara, CA: Editorial La Causa, 1978).

6. *La Opinión*, 15 November 1926, p. 3.

7. Ibid., 25 August 1927, p. 3.

8. Ibid., 20 February 1927, p. 1.

9. Ibid., 3 January 1927, p. 3.

10. Ibid., 10 September 1927, p. 1.

11. Ibid., 18 March 1928, p. 1.

12. Ibid., 15 November 1926, p. 3; 1 January 1927, p. 3; 6 November 1928, p. 1.

13. Ibid., 29 November 1926, p. 3.

14. Ibid., 25 August 1927, p. 3.

15. Ibid., 5 November 1927, p. 3.

16. Ibid., 3 October 1928, p. 1.

17. Ibid., 26 March 1927, p. 3.

18. Ibid., 30 October 1926, p. 1.

19. Ibid., 19 September 1926, p. 1; 28 October 1926, p. 1; 18 March 1927, p. 1.

20. Ibid., 24 August 1927, p. 1.

21. Ibid., 2 March 1928, p. 1.

22. Ibid., 21 March 1928, p. 3.

23. Ibid.

24. Ibid., 8 December 1927, p. 1; 6 March 1928, p. 1.

25. Ibid., 9 June 1927, p. 1.

26. Ibid., 20 August 1927, p. 1.

27. Ibid., 2 April 1928, p. 1; 3 March 1927, p. 1; 28 January 1928, p. 1; 16 November 1926, p. 1; 15 February 1928, p. 3; 23 January 1928, p. 3; 6 January 1928, p. 3; 4 March 1927, p. 3; 11 February 1927, p. 3; 14 June 1927, p. 3.

28. Ibid., 27 February 1928, pp. 1 and 6; 13 August 1927, p. 3; 11 October 1926, p. 3; 8 October 1926, p. 3; 4 March 1928, p. 1.

29. Ibid., 10 June 1928, pp. 3 and 10.

30. Ibid., 12 October 1927, p. 3; 7 June 1927, p. 3; 9 June 1927, p. 3; 1 December 1927, p. 3; 12 December 1927, p. 3; 31 January 1928, p. 3.

31. For the Mexican-American era, see for example: Carl Allsup, *The American G.I. Forum: Origins and Evolution* (Austin: Center for Mexican-American Studies, University of Texas, 1982); Luis Arroyo, "Chicano Participation in Organized Labor: The CIO in Los Angeles, 1938–1950, An Extended Research Note," *Aztlán* 6 (Summer 1975): 277–303; Albert Camarillo, "Research Note on Chicano Community Leaders: The G.I. Generation," *Aztlán* 2 (Fall 1971): 145–50; Richard A. García, "The Mexican American Mind: A Product of the 1930s," in Mario T. García and Francisco Lomeli, eds., *History, Culture, and Society:*

Chicano Studies in the 1980s (Ypsilanti, MI: Bilingual Press, 1983), 67–94; Edward Garza, "L.U.L.A.C." (master's thesis, Southwest State Teachers College, 1951); Ralph Guzmán, *The Political Socialization of the Mexican American People* (New York: Arno Press, 1976); Beatrice Griffith, *American Me* (Boston: Houghton Mifflin, 1948); Pauline K. Kibbe, *Latin Americans in Texas* (Albuquerque: University of New Mexico Press, 1946); Raúl Morín, *Among the Valiant: Mexican Americans in World War II and Korea* (Los Angeles: Borden Publishing, 1963); Alonso S. Perales, *Are We Good Neighbors?* (San Antonio, TX: Arte Gráficas, 1948); Guadalupe San Miguel, "Mexican American Organizations and the Changing Politics of School Desegregation in Texas, 1945–1980," *Social Science Quarterly* 63 (December 1982): 701–15; and Frances Jerome Woods, *Mexican Ethnic Leadership in San Antonio, Texas* (Washington, DC: Catholic University of America Press, 1949).

32. For a short biography of López, see Ignacio López Collection Folder of information in Ignacio López Collection in Special Collections, Stanford University. The López Collection consists of original as well as microfilm copies of *El Espectador*.

33. *El Espectador*, 17 February 1939, pp. 1 and 2; 24 February 1939, pp. 1 and 7; 3 March 1939, pp. 1, 9, and 11.

34. Ibid., 13 December 1947, p. 2.

35. Ibid., 23 October 1942, p. 1.

36. Ibid., 11 August 1950, pp. 2 and 3.

37. Ibid., 18 February 1949, p. 17. Also see 5 October 1945, pp. 1, 2, and 10; 7 December 1945, pp. 1 and 4; 5 April 1946, p. 1; 10 January 1947, pp. 1 and 8; 28 May 1948, p. 1; 13 May 1949, p. 1; August 1950, p. 2; 28 September 1951, p. 1; 25 April 1952, pp. 1 and 7; 20 July 1956, p. 8; 29 March 1957, p. 1.

38. Ibid., 1 September 1952, p. 2.

39. Ibid., 6 October 1950, pp. 1 and 15.

40. Ibid., 22 June 1951, p. 1.

41. Ibid., 3 July 1942, p. 1.

42. Ibid., 27 January 1939, p. 1.

43. Ibid., 18 February 1938, p. 3.

44. Ibid., 19 May 1939, p. 2; 7 March 1950, p. 1; 28 April 1950, p. 1.

45. Ibid., 8 September 1950, p. 2.

46. Ibid., 3 November 1950, p. 3.

47. Ibid., 22 February 1952, pp. 1 and 8.

48. Ibid., 14 June 1957, p. 1.

49. Ibid., 24 April 1959, p. 2.

50. Ibid., 17 August 1956, p. 1.

51. Ibid., 16 September 1949, p. 1.

52. Ibid., 4 November 1938, pp. 1 and 7.

53. Ibid., 13 June 1947, p. 4.

54. Ibid., 7 July 1949, p. 1.

55. Ibid., 1 March 1946, p. 12.

56. Ibid. For a leftist contrast on the Mexican-American era, see Emma Tenayuca and Homer Brooks, "The Mexican Question in the Southwest," *The Communist* 18 (March 1939): 257–68. Tenayuca and Brooks saw all Mexicans north of the border as one people, but no longer an organic part of Mexico. They called for a united front of Mexicans and progressive Anglos to achieve basic democratic rights.

57. For the Chicano era, see F. Chris García, ed., *La Causa Política: A Chicano Political Reader* (Notre Dame, IN: University of Notre Dame Press, 1974); Juan Gómez Quiñones, *Mexican Students Por La Raza: The Chicano Student Movement in Southern California, 1967–1977* (Santa Barbara, CA: Editorial La Causa, 1978); Carlos Muñoz, "The Politics of Protest and Chicano Liberation: A Case Study of Regression and Cooptation," *Aztlán* 5, nos. 1 and 2 (Spring and Fall 1974): 119–41; Armando Rendón, *Chicano Manifesto* (New York: Macmillan, 1971); Gerald Paul Rosen, *Political Ideology and the Chicano Movement: A Study of Political Ideology of Activists in the Chicano Movement* (San Francisco: R and E Research Associates, 1975); Richard Santillan, *La Raza Unida* (Los Angeles: Tlaquilo Publications, 1973); John Shockley, *Chicano Revolt in a Texas Town* (Notre Dame, IN: University of Notre Dame Press, 1974); and Stan Steiner, *La Raza: The Mexican Americans* (New York: Harper, 1970).

58. See Rodolfo Acuña, *Occupied America: The Chicano's Struggle toward Liberation* (San Francisco: Canfield Press, 1972). For other views on Chicano internal colonialism, see Mario Barrera, Carlos Muñoz, and Carlos Ornelas, "The Barrio as an Internal Colony" in García, ed., *La Causa Política*, 281–301; Robert Blauner, *Racial Oppression in America* (New York: Harper and Row, 1972); Tomás Almaguer, "Toward the Study of Chicano Colonialism," *Aztlán* 2 (Spring 1971): 7–21; Guillermo Flores, "Race and Culture in the Internal Colony: Keeping the Chicano in His Place," in Frank Bonilla and Robert Girling, eds., *Structures of Dependency* (Stanford: Nairobi Bookstore, 1973); and Mario T. García, "Internal Colonialism: A Critical Essay," *Revista Chicano-Riqueña* 6 (1978): 38–41.

59. See "Who We Are," special supplement to *Sin Fronteras* (no date), p. 1.

60. *Sin Fronteras*, July 1977, p. 10. For a comparison of CASA's position on the "National Question" with that of other leftist organizations, see Ríos Bustamante, *Mexicans in the United States*. See also August Twenty-Ninth Movement, *Fan the Flames: A Revolutionary Position on the Chicano National Question*, and "The Struggle for Chicano Liberation," special issue of *Forward* 2 (August 1979). For a discussion of CASA's political action, see Richard A. García, "The Chicano Movement and the Mexican American Community, 1972–1978: An Interpretive Essay," *Socialist Review* 8 (July–October 1978): 117–36; and Tomás Almaguer, "Chicano Politics in the Present Period: Comments on García," *Socialist Review* 8 (July–October 1978): 137–41.

61. *Sin Fronteras*, September 1975, p. 6.

62. "Who We Are," p. 4.

63. *Sin Fronteras*, July 1977, p. 10.

64. Ibid.

65. Ibid., August 1977, p. 9.

66. Ibid., January 1977, p. 8.

67. Ibid., May 1977, p. 4.

68. Ibid., September 1975, p. 7.

69. Ibid., March 1977, p. 8.

70. Ibid., August 1977, p. 10.

71. Ibid., December 1976, p. 8.

72. Ibid., March 1977, p. 9.

73. Ibid.

74. Ibid., May 1977, p. 8.

75. Ibid., December 1976, p. 9.

76. Ibid., September 1975, p. 1.

77. Ibid., February 1977, p. 9.
78. Ibid., January 1976, p. 8.
79. Ibid., September 1977, p. 9.
80. Ibid., May 1977, p. 10.
81. Ibid., February 1977, p. 10; June 1977, p. 8; September 1977, p. 10.
82. Ibid., September 1975, p. 3.
83. Ibid., June 1977, p. 8.
84. Ibid., February 1977, p. 8.
85. Ibid., April 1977, p. 9.
86. Ibid., January–February 1978, p. 9; December 1976, p. 9.
87. Ibid., "Who We Are," p. 5.
88. Ibid., January 1976, p. 7.
89. Ibid., September 1975, p. 2.

5

Caravans of Sorrow: Noncitizen Americans of the Southwest

Luisa Moreno

The Zoot Suit Riots and similar anti-Mexican incidents stimulated an immediate response in Mexican-American and Mexican immigrant communities thoughout the southwestern United States. Forming new organizations or expanding existing community groups, Mexican Americans began a concerted civil rights campaign that continues in many ways to the present day. Most of the activists associated with these civil rights organizations employed the rhetoric of political integration and cultural assimilation during the war era, believing that demonstrating their "Americanism" in this manner would help legitimate their claim to equal rights.

Not all ethnic Mexicans, however, agreed with this point of view. Although most, if not all, Mexican Americans and Mexican immigrants probably would have applauded the efforts of these reformist organizations, other political perspectives were also espoused by ethnic Mexicans during this volatile period. One of the most prominent of the advocacy organizations espousing alternative political views was El Congreso de Pueblos que Hablan Español (Spanish-Speaking Peoples' Congress). Founded in the late 1930s by a broad coalition of labor, civil rights, and community activists, the Congress broke new ground in the struggle to win basic civil and human rights for ethnic Mexicans in the United States. Encouraging Mexican Americans, Mexican immigrants, and other Latinos to disregard differences in nationality or formal citizenship status, the Congress sought to organize a strong pan-Latino coalition. In the process, the innovative organization articulated radical new positions on

From an address delivered at the panel of Deportation and Right of Asylum of the Fourth Annual Conference of the American Committee for Protection of the Foreign Born, Washington, DC, March 3, 1940. Box 1, Folder 1, Carey McWilliams Collection, University Research Library, Department of Special Collections, University of California, Los Angeles.

the increasingly interrelated issues of immigration, citizenship and natu-
ralization, and the general status of the Spanish-speaking minority. In
this chapter, Luisa Moreno, who spent years working as an organizer of
ethnic Mexican and other Spanish-speaking workers, explains the
Congress's vision for the future of Mexican immigrants and other Latinos
in the United States.

One hears much today about hemisphere unity. The press sends special correspondents to Latin America, South of the Border songs are
wailed by the radio, educational institutions and literary circles speak the
language of cultural cooperation, and, what is more important, labor unions
are seeking the road of closer ties with the Latin American working people.

The stage is set. A curtain rises. May we ask you to see behind the
scenery and visualize a forgotten character in this great theater of the
Americas?

Long before the "grapes of wrath" had ripened in California's vine-
yards a people lived on highways, under trees or tents, in shacks or railroad sections, picking crops—cotton, fruits, vegetables—cultivating sugar
beets, building railroads and dams, making a barren land fertile for new
crops and greater riches.

The ancestors of some of these migrant and resident workers, whose
home is this Southwest, were America's first settlers in New Mexico,
Texas, and California, and the greater percentage was brought from Mexico
by the fruit exchanges, railroad companies, and cotton interests in great
need of underpaid labor during the early postwar period. They are the
Spanish-speaking workers of the Southwest, citizens and noncitizens
working and living under identical conditions, facing hardships and mis-
eries while producing and building for agriculture and industry.

Their story lies unpublicized in university libraries, files of government, welfare and social agencies—a story grimly titled the "Caravans of
Sorrow."

And when in 1930 unemployment brought a still greater flood of human distress, trainloads of Mexican families with children born and raised
in this country departed voluntarily or were brutally deported. As a result
of the repatriation drive of 1933, thousands of American-born youths returned to their homeland, the United States, to live on streets and highways, drifting unattached fragments of humanity. Let the annals of juvenile
delinquency in Los Angeles show you the consequences.

Today the Latin Americans of the United States are seriously alarmed
by the "antialien" drive fostered by certain un-American elements; for
them, the Palmer days [referring to the mass arrests and expulsions of
suspected Communist subversives conducted under the direction of Attorney General A. Mitchell Palmer during the height of the infamous "Red

Scare" of 1919–20] have never ended. In recent years while deportations in general have decreased, the number of persons deported to Mexico has constantly increased. During the period of 1933 to 1937, of a total of 55,087 deported, 25,135 were deportations of Mexicans. This is 45.5 percent of the total and does not include an almost equal number of so-called voluntary departures.

Commenting on these figures, the American Committee for Protection of Foreign Born wrote to the Spanish-Speaking Peoples' Congress in 1939: "One conclusion can be drawn, and that is, where there is such a highly organized set-up as to effect deportations of so many thousands, this set-up must be surrounded with a complete system of intimidation and discrimination of that section of the population victimized by the deportation drive."

Confirming the fact of a system of extensive discrimination are university studies by Paul S. Taylor, Emory Bogardus, and many other professors and social workers of the Southwest. Let me state the simple truth. The majority of the Spanish-speaking peoples of the United States are victims of a setup for discrimination, be they descendants of the first white settlers in America or noncitizens.

I will not go into the reasons for this undemocratic practice, but may we state categorically that it is the main reason for the reluctance of Mexicans and Latin Americans in general to become naturalized. For you must know, discrimination takes very definite forms in unequal wages, unequal opportunities, unequal schooling, and even through a denial of the use of public places in certain towns in Texas, California, Colorado, and other Southwestern states.

Only some 5 or 6 percent of Latin American immigrants have become naturalized. A number of years ago it was stated that in a California community with fifty thousand Mexicans only two hundred had become citizens. An average of one hundred Mexicans out of close to a million become citizens every year. These percentages have increased lately.

Another important factor concerning naturalization is the lack of documentary proof of entry, because entry was not recorded or because the immigrants were brought over en masse by large interests handling transportation from Mexico in their own peculiar way.

Arriving at logical conclusions, the Latin American noncitizens, rooted in this country, are increasingly seeing the importance and need for naturalization. But how will the thousands of migrants establish residence? What possibility have these people had, segregated in "Little Mexicos," to learn English and meet educational requirements? How can they, receiving hunger wages while enriching the stockholders of the Great Western Sugar Company, the Bank of America, and other large interests, pay high naturalization fees? A Mexican family living on relief in Colorado would have to stop eating for two and a half months to pay for the citizenship papers of one member of the family. Is this humanly possible?

But why have "aliens" on relief while the taxpayers "bleed"? Let me ask those who would raise such a question: what would the Imperial Valley, the Rio Grande Valley, and other rich irrigated valleys in the Southwest be without the arduous, self-sacrificing labor of these noncitizen Americans? Read *Factories in the Fields*, by Carey McWilliams to obtain a picture of how important Mexican labor has been for the development of California's crop after the world war. Has anyone counted the miles of railroads built by these same noncitizens? One can hardly imagine how many bales of cotton have passed through the nimble fingers of Mexican men, women, and children. And what conditions have they had to endure to pick that cotton? Once, while holding a conference for a trade union paper in San Antonio, a cotton picker told me how necessary a Spanish paper was to inform the Spanish-speaking workers that FSA [Farm Security Administration] camps were to be established, for she remembered so many nights, under the trees in the rain, when she and her husband held gunny sacks over the shivering bodies of their sleeping children—young Americans. I've heard workers say that they left their shacks under heavy rains to find shelter under trees. You can well imagine in what condition those shacks were.

These people are not aliens. They have contributed their endurance, sacrifices, youth, and labor to the Southwest. Indirectly, they have paid more taxes than all the stockholders of California's industrialized agriculture, the sugar beet companies and the large cotton interests that operate or have operated with the labor of Mexican workers.

Surely the sugar beet growers have not been asked if they want to dispense with the skilled labor cultivating and harvesting their crops season after season. It is only the large interests, their stooges, and some badly misinformed people who claim that Mexicans are no longer wanted.

And let us assume that 1.4 million men, women, and children were no longer wanted, what could be done that would be different from the anti-Semitic persecutions in Europe? A people who have lived twenty and thirty years in this country, tied up by family relations with the early settlers, with American-born children, cannot be uprooted without the complete destruction of the faintest semblance of democracy and human liberties for the whole population.

Some speak of repatriation. Naturally there is interest in repatriation among thousands of Mexican families in Texas and, to a lesser degree, in other states. Organized repatriation has been going on, and the net results in one year has been the establishment of the Colonia "18 de Marzo" in

Tamaulipas, Mexico, for two thousand families. There are 1.4 million Mexicans in the United States according to general estimates, probably including a portion of the first generation. Is it possible to move those many people at the present rate, when many of them do not want to be repatriated?

What then may the answer to this specific noncitizen problem be? The Spanish-Speaking Peoples' Congress of the United States proposes legislation that would encourage naturalization of Latin American, West Indian, and Canadian residents of the United States and that would nurture greater friendships among the peoples of the Western Hemisphere.

The question of hemispheric unity will remain an empty phrase while this problem at home remains ignored and is aggravated by the fierce "antialien" drive.

Legislation to facilitate citizenship to all natural-born citizens from the countries of the Western Hemisphere, waiving excessive fees and educational and other requirements of a technical nature, is urgently needed.

A piece of legislation embodying this provision is timely and important. Undoubtedly it would rally the support of the many friends of true hemispheric unity.

You have seen the forgotten character in the present American scene—a scene of the Americas. Let me say that, in the face of greater hardships, the "Caravans of Sorrow" are becoming the "Caravans of Hope." They are organizing in trade unions with other workers in agriculture and industry. The unity of Spanish-speaking citizens and noncitizens is being furthered through the Spanish-Speaking Peoples' Congress of the United States, an organization embracing trade unions and fraternal, civic, and cultural organizations, mainly in California. The purpose of this movement is to seek an improvement of social, economic, and cultural conditions, and for the integration of Spanish-speaking citizens and noncitizens into the American nation. The United Cannery, Agricultural, Packing, and Allied Workers of America, with thousands of Spanish-speaking workers in its membership, and Liga Obrera of New Mexico, were the initiators of the Congress.

This Congress stands with all progressive forces against the badly labeled "antialien" legislation and asks the support of this Conference for democratic legislation to facilitate and encourage naturalization. We hope that this Conference will serve to express the sentiment of the people of this country in condemnation of undemocratic discrimination practiced against any person of foreign birth and that it will rally the American people, native and foreign born, for the defeat of un-American proposals. The Spanish-speaking peoples in the United States extend their fullest support and cooperation to your efforts.

6

"Star Struck": Acculturation, Adolescence, and the Mexican-American Woman, 1920–1950

Vicki L. Ruiz

In this chapter, Vicki Ruiz, professor of history and women's studies at Arizona State University explores one of the most intriguing and provocative elements of the Mexican diaspora—the tensions created between Mexican immigrants and their U.S.-born-and-reared children. Although these immigrants often considered themselves part of México de afuera *(that is, Mexicans outside Mexico) and sought to inculcate and preserve their own culture in their offspring, they invariably found it difficult, if not impossible, to insulate their children from the powerful forces of acculturation and socialization to American norms. Based on oral history interviews, contemporary ethnographic accounts, and a close reading of other pertinent sources, Ruiz's analysis focuses on the heavy influence that employment experiences, public education, and exposure to American popular and material culture (particularly Hollywood movies) exerted on the Mexican-American children of Mexican immigrants.*

Ethnic identity, Americanization, and generational tension first captured the historical imagination during the 1950s with the publication of Oscar Handlin's *The Uprooted* and Alfred Kazin's *A Walker in the City*.[1] These issues continue to provoke discussion among both humanists and social scientists. Within the last decade, feminist scholars have expanded and enriched our knowledge of acculturation through the study of immigrant daughters. Cross-class analysis of adolescent culture provides another window onto the world of ethnic youth.[2] This vibrant discourse

From *Building with Our Hands: New Directions in Chicana Studies*, ed. Adela de la Torre and Beatríz M. Pesquera (Berkeley: University of California Press, 1993), 109–29. Reprinted by permission of The Regents of the University of California and the University of California Press.

on generation, gender, and U.S. popular culture has a decidedly East Coast orientation. Are patterns typical of working-class immigrants in New York City applicable to those in Los Angeles? . . .

The Spanish-speaking population in the United States soared between 1910 and 1930 as over one million Mexicanos migrated northward. Pushed by the economic and political chaos generated by the Mexican Revolution and lured by jobs in U.S. agribusiness and industry, they settled into existing barrios and forged new communities both in the Southwest and the Midwest, in small towns and cities. For example, in 1900 only three thousand to five thousand Mexicans lived in Los Angeles, but by 1930 approximately one hundred fifty thousand persons of Mexican birth or heritage had settled into the city's expanding barrios.[3] On a national level, by 1930 Mexicans, outnumbered only by Anglos and blacks, formed the "third largest 'racial' group."[4]

Pioneering social scientists, particularly Manuel Gamio, Paul Taylor, and Emory Bogardus, examined the lives of these Mexican immigrants, but their materials on women are sprinkled here and there and at times are hidden in unpublished field notes. Among Chicano historians and writers, there appears a fascination with second-generation Mexican-American men, especially as *pachucos*.[5] The life-styles and attitudes of their female counterparts have gone largely unnoticed, even though women may have experienced deeper generational tensions.[6] "Walking in two worlds," they blended elements of Americanization with Mexican expectations and values.[7] To set the context, I will look at education, employment, and media as agents of Americanization and assess the ways in which Mexican-American women incorporated their messages. Drawing on social science fieldwork and oral interviews, I also will discuss the sources of conflict between adolescent women and their parents as well as the contradictions between the promise of the American dream and the reality of restricted mobility and ethnic prejudice.

This study relies extensively on oral history. The memories of thirteen women serve as the basis for my reconstruction of adolescent aspirations and experiences (or dreams and routines). Of the thirteen full-blown life histories, ten are housed in university archives, eight as part of the *Rosie the Riveter* collection at California State University, Long Beach. I became familiar with most of these interviews during the course of my research for *Cannery Women, Cannery Lives*, and two surfaced as student oral history projects. I personally interviewed three of the informants.

The women themselves are fairly homogeneous by nativity, class, residence, and family structure. With one exception, all are U.S. citizens by birth and attended southwestern schools. Ten of the interviewees were born between 1913 and 1929.[8] Although two came from families once considered middle class in Mexico, all can be considered working class in the United States. Their fathers' typical occupations included farm worker, day laborer, and busboy. Two women had fathers with skilled blue-collar jobs (butcher and surveyor), and two were the daughters of small family farmers. The informants usually characterized their mothers as homemakers, although several remembered that their mothers took seasonal jobs in area factories and fields. The mother of the youngest interviewee (Rosa Guerrero) supported her family through domestic labor and fortune-telling. Eleven grew up in urban barrios, ten in Los Angeles. Most families were nuclear rather than extended, although kin usually (but not always) resided nearby. Rich in detail, these interviews reveal the complex negotiations across generation and across culture.

Education and employment were the most significant agents of Americanization. Educators generally relied on an immersion method in teaching the English language to their Mexican pupils. In other words, Spanish-speaking children had to sink or swim in an English-only environment. Even on the playground, students were enjoined from conversing in their native Spanish. Admonishments such as "Don't speak that ugly language, you are an American now," not only reflected a strong belief in Anglo conformity but denigrated the self-esteem of Mexican-American children and dampened their enthusiasm for education.[9] Ruby Estrada remembered that corporal punishment was a popular method for teaching English. "The teacher was mean and the kids got mean."[10] At times children internalized these lessons, as Mary Luna reflected: "It was rough because I didn't know English. The teacher wouldn't let us talk Spanish. How can you talk to anybody? If you can't talk Spanish and you can't talk English, what are you going to do? . . . It wasn't until maybe the fourth or fifth grade that I started catching up. And all along that time I just felt I was stupid."[11]

Students also became familiar with U.S. history and holidays (e.g., Thanksgiving). In recounting her childhood, Rosa Guerrero elaborated on how, in her own mind, she reconciled the history lessons at school with her own heritage. "The school system would teach everything about American history, the colonists, and all of that," she explained. "Then I would do a comparison in my mind of where my grandparents came from, what they did, and wonder how I was to be evolved and educated."[12]

Schools, in some instances, raised expectations. Imbued with the American dream, young women (and men) believed that hard work would bring material rewards and social acceptance. In fact, a California grower disdained education for Mexicans because it would give them "tastes for things they can't acquire."[13] Some teenage women aspired to college while others planned careers as secretaries. "I want to study science or be a stenographer," one Colorado adolescent informed Paul Taylor. "I thinned beets this spring, but I believe it is the last time. The girls who don't go to school will continue to top beets the rest of their lives."[14] Courses in typing and shorthand were popular among Mexican-American women, even though few southwestern businesses hired Spanish-surnamed office workers. In 1930, only 2.6 percent of all Mexican women wage earners held clerical jobs. Anthropologist Ruth Tuck noted the contradiction between training and placement. When she asked one teacher why Mexican women were being trained for clerical positions largely closed to them, the educator replied, " 'To teach them respect for the white-collar job.' " Skin color also played a role in obtaining office work. As one typing teacher pointed out to young Julia Luna, " 'Who's going to hire you? You're so dark.' "[15]

Many young Mexican women never attended high school but took industrial or service-sector jobs directly after the completion of the eighth grade. Like the East European and French Canadian workers studied by John Bodnar and Tamara Hareven, they gave family needs priority over individual goals. Family obligations and economic necessity propelled Mexican women into the labor force. One government study appearing in a 1931 issue of *Monthly Labor Review* revealed that in Los Angeles over 35 percent of the Mexican families surveyed had wage-earning children.[16] By 1930, approximately one-quarter of Mexicana and Mexican-American female wage earners in the Southwest obtained employment as industrial workers. In California, they labored principally in canneries and garment firms.[17] Like many female factory workers in the United States, most Mexican operatives were young, unmarried daughters whose wage labor was essential to the economic survival of their families. As members of a "family wage economy," they relinquished all or part of their wages to their elders. According to a 1933 University of California study, of the Mexican families surveyed with working children, the children's monetary contributions comprised 35 percent of total household income.[18]

At times working for wages gave women a feeling of independence. Historian Douglas Monroy asserted that outside employment "facilitated greater freedom of activity and more assertiveness in the family for Mexicanas." Some young women went a step further and used their earnings to leave the family home. Facing family disapproval, even ostracism, they defied parental authority by sharing an apartment with female friends.[19] Conversely, kin networks, particularly in canneries and packing houses, reinforced a sense of family. Working alongside female kin, adolescents found employment less than liberating. At the same time, the work environment did give women an opportunity to develop friendships with other Spanish-surnamed operatives and occasionally with their ethnic immigrant peers. They began to discuss with one another their problems and concerns, finding common ground both as factory workers and as second-generation ethnic women. Teenagers chatted about fads, fashions, and celebrities.[20]

Along with outside employment, the media also influenced the acculturation of Mexican women. Movie and romance magazines enabled adolescents (and older women as well) to experience vicariously the middle-class and affluent life-styles heralded in these publications and thus could nurture a desire for consumer goods. Radio, motion pictures, and Madison Avenue advertising had a profound impact on America's cultural landscape. According to historians John D'Emilio and Estelle Freedman, "corporate leaders needed consumers . . . who were ready to spend their earnings to purchase a growing array of goods designed for personal use." They continue: "Americans did not automatically respond to factory output by multiplying their desire for material goods; an ethic of consumption had to be sold."[21] The Mexican community was not immune to this orchestration of desire, and there appeared a propensity toward consumerism among second-generation women. In his 1928 study on Mexican women in Los Angeles industry, Paul Taylor contended that, second to economic need, the prevalent motive for employment among single women was a desire to buy the "extras"—a radio, a phonograph, jazz records, fashionable clothes. As Carmen Escobar revealed, "After I started working, I liked the money. I loved clothes—I used to buy myself beautiful clothes."[22] As members of a "consumer wage economy," daughters also worked in order to purchase items for their families' comfort, such as furniture, draperies, and area rugs.[23] Other teenagers had more modest goals. After giving most of her wages to her mother, Rosa Guerrero reserved a portion to buy peanut butter and shampoo. "Shampoo to me was a luxury. I had to buy shampoo so I wouldn't have to wash my hair with the dirty old Oxydol. I used to wash my hair with the soap for the clothes."[24]

The American cinema also made an impression. Although times were lean, many southern California women had dreams of fame and fortune, nurtured, in part, by the proximity to Hollywood. Movies, both Mexican and American, provided a popular form of entertainment for barrio residents. It was not uncommon on Saturday mornings to see children and young adults combing the streets for bottles, so that they could afford the price of admission—ten cents for the afternoon matinee. Preteens would frequently come home and act out what they had seen on the screen. "I was going to be Clara Bow," remembered Adele Hernández Milligan. Another woman recounted that she had definitely been "star struck" as a youngster and attempted to fulfill her fantasy in junior high by "acting in plays galore." The handful of Latina actresses appearing in Hollywood films, such as Dolores Del Rio and Lupe Velez, also whetted these aspirations. Older "star struck" adolescents enjoyed afternoon outings to Hollywood, filled with the hope of being discovered as they strolled along Hollywood and Vine with their friends.[25]

The influential Spanish-language newspaper *La Opinión* encouraged these fantasies, in part, by publishing gossipy stories about movie stars, like Charlie Chaplin and Norma Shearer, as well as up-to-the-minute reports on the private lives and careers of Latino celebrities. It also carried reviews of Spanish-language films, concerts, and plays.[26] Although promoting pride in Latino cultural events, the society pages reflected the public fascination with Hollywood. One week after its first issue, *La Opinión* featured a Spanish translation of Louella Parsons's nationally syndicated gossip column. Furthermore, the Los Angeles-based newspaper directly capitalized on the dreams of youth by sponsoring a contest with Metro-Goldwyn-Mayer. "Day by day we see how a young man or woman, winner of some contest, becomes famous overnight," reminded *La Opinión* as it publicized its efforts to offer its readers a similar chance. Touted as "the unique opportunity for all young men and women who aspire to movie stardom," this promotion held out the promise of a screen test to one lucky contestant.[27]

For many, show business had obvious appeal; it was perceived as a glamorous avenue for mobility. One could overcome poverty and prejudice as a successful entertainer. As an article on Lupe Velez optimistically claimed, "Art has neither nationalities nor borders."[28]

Americanization seemed to seep into the barrios from all directions—from schools, factories, and even their ethnic press. Parental responses to the Americanization of their children can be classified into two distinct categories: accommodation and resistance. These responses seem more rooted in class than in gender. In the sample of thirteen interviews and in my survey of early ethnographies, I can find no indication that intergenerational tension occurred more frequently among fathers and daughters than among mothers and daughters. While parents cannot be viewed as a monolithic group, certainly both took an active interest in the socialization of their children. Although resistance was the norm, some parents encouraged attempts at acculturation, and at times entire families took adult education courses in a concerted effort to become "good Americans." Paul Taylor argues that middle-class Mexicans desiring to dissociate themselves from their working-class neighbors had the most fervent aspirations for assimilation. Once in the United States, middle-class Mexicanos found themselves subject to ethnic prejudice that did not dis-

criminate by class. Because of restrictive real estate covenants and segregated schools, these immigrants had lived in the barrios with people they
considered inferiors.[29] By passing as "Spanish," they cherished hopes of
melting into the American social landscape. Sometimes mobility-minded
parents sought to regulate their children's choice of friends and later marriage partners. "My folks never allowed us to go around with Mexicans,"
remembered Alicia Mendeola Shelit. "We went sneaking around, but my
dad wouldn't allow it. We'd always be with whites." Interestingly, Shelit
was married twice, both times to Anglos. As anthropologist Margarita
Melville has concluded in her contemporary study of Mexican women
immigrants, "aspirations for upward mobility" emerged as the most distinguishing factor in the process of acculturation.[30] Of course, it would be
unfair to characterize all middle-class Mexican immigrants as repudiat-
ing their mestizo identity. As one young woman cleverly remarked, "Lis-
ten, I may be a Mexican in a fur coat, but I'm still a Mexican."[31]

Although enjoying the creature comforts afforded by life in the United
States, Mexican immigrants retained their cultural traditions, and parents
developed strategies to counteract the alarming acculturation of their
young. Required to speak only English at school, Mexican youngsters
were then instructed to speak only Spanish at home. Even when they permitted the use of English, parents took steps to ensure the retention of
Spanish among their children. Rosa Guerrero fondly remembered sitting
with her father and conjugating verbs in Spanish, "just for the love of
it."[32] Proximity to Mexico also played an important role in maintaining
cultural ties. Growing up in El Paso, Texas, Guerrero crossed the border
into Ciudad Juárez every weekend with her family in order to attend traditional recreational events, such as the bullfights. Her family, moreover,
made yearly treks to visit relatives in central Mexico. Those who lived
substantial distances from the border resisted assimilation by building
ethnic pride through nostalgic stories of life in Mexico.[33] As one San José
woman related: "My mother never . . . tired of telling us stories of her
native village in Guanajuato; she never let us children forget the things
that her village was noted for, its handicrafts and arts, its songs and its
stories. . . . She made it all sound so beautiful with her descriptions of the
mountains and the lakes, the old traditions, the happy people, and the
dances and weddings and fiestas. From the time I was a small child I
always wanted to go back to Mexico and see the village where my mother
was born."[34] While many youngsters relished the folk and family lore
told by their parents or grandparents, others failed to appreciate their elders' efforts. "Grandmother Perez's stories about the witches and ghosts
of Los Conejos get scant audience, in competition with Dick Tracy and
Buck Rogers."[35]

In bolstering cultural consciousness, parents found help through youth-oriented community organizations. Church, service, and political clubs reinforced ethnic awareness. Examples included the "Logia 'Juventud Latina' " of the Alianza Hispano Americana; the Mexican-American movement, initially sponsored by the Young Men's Christian Association; and the youth division of El Congreso de Pueblos que Hablan Español [Spanish-Speaking Peoples' Congress]. Bert Corona, a leading California civil rights advocate for over four decades, began his career of activism as a leader in both the Mexican-American movement and the youth auxiliary of the Spanish-Speaking Peoples' Congress.[36]

Interestingly, only two of the thirteen women mentioned Catholicism as an important early influence. The Catholic church played more of a social role; it organized youth clubs and dances, and it was the place for baptisms, marriages, and funerals.[37] For others, Protestant churches offered a similar sense of community. Establishing small niches in Mexican barrios, Protestant missionaries envisioned themselves as the harbingers of salvation and Americanization. Yet some converts saw their churches as reaffirming traditional Mexican values. "I was beginning to think that the Baptist church was a little too Mexican. Too much restriction," remembered Rose Escheverria Mulligan. Indeed, this woman longed to join her Catholic peers who regularly attended church-sponsored dances. "I noticed they were having a good time."[38] Whether gathering for a Baptist picnic or a Catholic dance, teenagers seemed more attracted to the social rather than the spiritual side of their religion. Certainly, more research is needed to assess the impact of Protestant social workers and missionaries on the attitudes of adolescent women. Mary Luna, for example, credited her love of reading to an Anglo educator who converted a small house in the barrio into a makeshift community center and library. The dual thrust of Americanization, education and consumerism, can be discerned in the following excerpt from Luna's oral history: "To this day I just love going to libraries. . . . There are two places that I can go in and get a real warm, happy feeling; that is, the library and Bullock's [department store] in the perfume and makeup department."[39] Blending new behavior with traditional ideals, young women also had to balance family expectations with their own need for individual expression.

Within families, young women, perhaps more than their brothers, were expected to uphold certain standards. Indeed, Chicano social scientists have generally portrayed women as "the 'glue' that keeps the Chicano family together" and as the guardians of "traditional culture."[40] Parents, therefore, often assumed what they perceived as their unquestionable prerogative to regulate the actions and attitudes of their adolescent daughters. Teenagers, on the other hand, did not always acquiesce in the boundaries set down for them by their elders. Intergenerational tension flared along several fronts.

Generally, the first area of disagreement between a teenager and her family would be over her personal appearance. During the 1920s, a woman's decision "to bob or not to bob" her hair assumed classic proportions in Mexican families. After considerable pleading, Belen Martínez Mason was permitted to cut her hair, though she soon regretted her decision. "Oh, I cried for a month."[41] Differing opinions over fashions often caused ill feelings. One Mexican-American woman recalled that, when she was a young girl, her mother dressed her "like a nun" and she could wear "no makeup, no cream, no nothing" on her face. Swimsuits, bloomers, and short skirts also became sources of controversy. Some teenagers left home in one outfit and changed into another at school. Once María Fierro arrived home in her bloomers. Her father inquired, " 'Where have you been dressed like that, like a clown?' " "I told him the truth," Fierro explained. "He whipped me anyway. . . . So from then on whenever I went to the track meet, I used to change my bloomers so that he wouldn't see that I had gone again."[42] The impact of flapper styles on the Mexican community was clearly expressed in the following verse, taken from a *corrido* appropriately entitled "Las Pelonas" (The Bobbed-Haired Girls):

> Red bandannas
> I detest,
> And now the flappers
> Use them for their dress.
> The girls of San Antonio
> Are lazy at the *metate*.
> They want to walk out bobbed-haired,
> With straw hats on.
> The harvesting is finished,
> So is the cotton;
> The flappers stroll out now
> For a good time.[43]

With similar sarcasm, another popular ballad chastised Mexican women for applying makeup so heavily as to resemble a piñata.[44]

Once again, bearing the banner of glamour and consumption, *La Opinión* featured sketches of the latest flapper fashions as well as cosmetic ads from both Latino and Anglo manufacturers. The most elaborate layouts were those of Max Factor. Using celebrity testimonials, one advertisement encouraged women to "FOLLOW THE STARS" and purchase "Max Factor's Society Makeup." Factor, through an exclusive arrangement with *La Opinión*, went even further in courting the Mexican market by answering beauty questions from readers in a special column—"Secretos de Belleza" (Beauty Secrets).[45]

The use of cosmetics, however, cannot be blamed entirely on Madison Avenue ad campaigns. The innumerable barrio beauty pageants—sponsored by *mutualistas*, patriotic societies, churches, the Mexican Chamber of Commerce, newspapers, and even progressive labor unions—encouraged young women to accentuate their physical attributes. Carefully chaperoned, many teenagers did participate in community contests from La Reina de Cinco de Mayo to Orange Queen. They modeled evening gowns, rode on parade floats, and sold raffle tickets.[46] Carmen Bernal Escobar remembered one incident where, as a contestant, she had to sell raffle tickets. Every ticket she sold counted as a vote for her in the pageant. Naturally, the winner would be the woman who had accumulated the most votes. When her brother offered to buy twenty-five dollars' worth of votes (her mother would not think of letting her peddle the tickets at work or in the neighborhood), Escobar, on a pragmatic note, asked him to give her the money so that she could buy a coat she had spotted while window-shopping.[47]

The commercialization of personal grooming made additional inroads into the Mexican community with the appearance of barrio beauty parlors. Working as a beautician conferred a certain degree of status, "a nice, clean job," in comparison to factory or domestic work. As one woman related: "I always wanted to be a beauty operator. I loved makeup; I loved to dress up and fix up. I used to set my sisters' hair. So I had that in the back of my mind for a long time, and my mom pushed the fact that she wanted me to have a profession—seeing that I wasn't thinking of getting married."[48] Although further research is needed, one can speculate that neighborhood beauty shops reinforced women's networks and became places where they could relax, exchange *chisme* (gossip), and enjoy the company of other women.

Conforming to popular fashions and fads cannot be construed as a lack of ethnic or political consciousness. In 1937, Carey McWilliams spoke before an assembly of fifteen hundred walnut workers in Los Angeles and was "profoundly stirred" by this display of grass-roots labor militancy on the part of East European and Mexican women. In describing the meeting, he wrote, "And such extraordinary faces—particularly the old women. Some of the girls had been too frequently to the beauty shop, and were too gotten up—rather amusingly dressy."[49] I would argue that dressing up for a union meeting could be interpreted as an affirmation of individual integrity. Although they worked under horrendous conditions (actually cracking walnuts with their fists), their collective action and personal appearance gave evidence that they did not surrender their self-esteem.

The most serious point of contention between an adolescent daughter and her parents, however, regarded her behavior toward young men. In both cities and rural towns, girls had to be closely chaperoned by a family member every time they attended a movie, a dance, or even church-related events. Recalling the supervisory role played by her "old maid" aunt, María Fierro laughingly explained, "She'd check on us all the time. I used to get so mad at her." Ruby Estrada recalled that in a small southern Arizona community, "all the mothers" escorted their daughters to the local dances. Even talking to male peers in broad daylight could be grounds for discipline.[50] Adele Hernández Milligan, a resident of Los Angeles for over fifty years, elaborated: "I remember the first time that I walked home with a boy from school. Anyway, my mother saw me and she was mad. I must have been sixteen or seventeen. She slapped my face because I was walking home with a boy."[51] Describing this familiar protectiveness, one social scientist aptly remarked that the "supervision of the Mexican parent is so strict as to be obnoxious."[52]

Faced with this type of situation, young women had three options: they could accept the rules set down for them; they could rebel; or they could find ways to compromise or circumvent traditional standards. "I was *never* allowed to go out by myself in the evening; it just was not done." In rural communities, where restrictions were perhaps even more stringent, "nice" teenagers could not even swim with their male peers. "We were ladies and wouldn't go swimming out there with a bunch of boys." Yet many seemed to accept these limits with equanimity. "It wasn't devastating at all," reflected Ruby Estrada. "We took it in stride. We never thought of it as cruel or mean. . . . It was taken for granted that that's the way it was."[53] In Sonora, Arizona, as in other small towns, relatives and neighbors kept close watch over adolescent women and quickly reported any suspected indiscretions. "They were always spying on you," Estrada remarked. Women in cities had a distinct advantage over their rural peers in that they could venture miles from their neighborhood into the anonymity of dance halls, amusement parks, and other forms of commercialized leisure. With carnival rides and the Cinderella Ballroom, the Nu-Pike amusement park of Long Beach proved a popular hangout for Mexican youth in Los Angeles.[54] It was more difficult to abide by traditional norms when excitement loomed just on the other side of the streetcar line.

Some women openly rebelled. They moved out of their family homes and into apartments. Considering themselves freewheeling single women, they could go out with men unsupervised, as was the practice among their Anglo peers. "This terrible freedom in the United States," one Mexicana lamented. "I do not have to worry because I have no daughters, but the poor señoras with many girls, they worry."[55] Those Mexican-American adolescents who did not wish to defy their parents openly would "sneak out" of the house in order to meet their dates or to attend dances with female friends. A more subtle form of rebellion was early marriage. By marrying at fifteen or sixteen, these women sought to escape parental supervision; yet it could be argued that many of these child brides exchanged one form of supervision for another, in addition to taking on the responsibilities of child rearing.[56]

The third option sometimes involved quite a bit of creativity on the part of young women as they sought to circumvent traditional chaperonage. Alicia Mendeola Shelit recalled that one of her older brothers would always accompany her to dances, ostensibly as a chaperon. "But then my oldest brother would always have a blind date for me." Carmen Bernal Escobar was permitted to entertain her boyfriends at home, but only under the supervision of her brother or mother. The practice of "going out with the girls," though not accepted until the 1940s, was fairly common. Several Mexican-American women, often related, would escort one another to an event (such as a dance), socialize with the men in attendance, and then walk home together. In the sample of thirteen interviews, daughters negotiated their activities with their parents. Older siblings and extended kin appeared in the background as either chaperons or accomplices. Although unwed teenage mothers were not unknown in the Los Angeles barrios, families expected adolescent females to conform to strict standards of behavior.[57] As can be expected, many teenage girls knew little about sex other than what they picked up from friends, romance magazines, and the local theater. As Mary Luna remembered, "I thought that if somebody kissed you, you could get pregnant." In *Singing for My Echo*, New Mexico native Gregorita Rodriguez confided that on her wedding night she knelt down and said her rosary until her husband gently asked, " 'Gregorita, *mi esposa*, are you afraid of me?' " At times this naïveté persisted beyond the wedding. "It took four days for my husband to touch me," one woman revealed. "I slept with dress and all. We were both greenhorns, I guess."[58]

Of course, some young women did lead more adventurous lives. A male interviewer employed by Mexican anthropologist Manuel Gamio recalled his "relations" with a woman he met at a Los Angeles dance hall. Though born in Hermosillo, Elisas "Elsie" Morales considered herself Spanish. She helped support her family by dancing with strangers. Although she lived at home and her mother and brother attempted to monitor her actions, she managed to meet the interviewer at a "hot pillow" hotel. To prevent pregnancy, she relied on contraceptive douches provided by "an American doctor." Although Morales realized her mother would not approve of her behavior, she noted that "she [her mother] is from Mexico. . . . I am from there also but I was brought up in the United States, [so] we think about things differently." Just as Morales rationalized her actions as "American," the interviewer also regarded her as "American," though in a distinctly less favorable sense of the word. "She seemed very coarse to me. That is, she dealt with one in the American way."[59] In his field notes, Paul Taylor recorded an incident in which a young woman had moved in with her Anglo boyfriend after he had convinced her that such living arrangements were common among Americans. Popular *corridos*, such as "El Enganchado" and "Las Pelonas," also touched on the theme of the corrupting influence of U.S. ways on Mexican women.[60]

It is interesting to note that Anglo and Mexican communities held almost identical preconceptions of each other's young female population. While Mexicans viewed Anglo women as morally loose, Latina actresses in Hollywood found themselves typecast as hot-blooded women of low repute. For example, Lupe Velez starred in such films as *Hot Pepper*, *Strictly Dynamite*, and *The Mexican Spitfire*.[61]

The image of loose sexual mores as distinctly American probably reinforced parents' fears as they watched their daughters apply cosmetics and adopt the apparel advertised in fashion magazines. In other words, "If she dresses like a flapper, will she then act like one?" Seeds of suspicion reaffirmed the penchant for traditional supervision.

Tension between parents and daughters, however, did not always revolve around adolescent behavior. At times, teenagers questioned the lifestyles of their parents. "I used to tell my mother she was a regular maid," Alicia Shelit recalled. "They [the women] never had a voice. They had to have the house clean, the food ready for the men . . . and everything just so."[62] As anthropologist Tuck observed: "Romantic literature, still more romantic movies, and the attitudes of American teachers and social workers have confirmed the Perez children in a belief that their parents do not 'love' each other; that, in particular, Lola Perez is a drudge and a slave for her husband."[63]

However, I would argue that the impact of Americanization was most keenly felt at the level of personal aspiration. "We felt if we worked hard, proved ourselves, we could become professional people," asserted Rose Escheverria Mulligan.[64] Braced with such idealism, Mexican Americans faced prejudice, segregation, and economic segmentation. Though they considered themselves Americans, others perceived them as less than desirable foreigners. During the late 1920s, the *Saturday Evening Post*, exemplifying the nativist spirit of the times, featured inflammatory characterizations of Mexicans in the United States. For instance, one article portrayed Mexican immigrants as an "illiterate, diseased, pauperized" people who bear children "with the reckless prodigality of rabbits."[65] Racism was not limited to rhetoric; between 1931 and 1934, an estimated one-third of the Mexican population in the United States (over five hundred thousand people) were either deported or repatriated to Mexico, even though many were native U.S. citizens. Mexicans were the only immigrants targeted for removal. Proximity to the Mexican border, the physical distinctiveness of mestizos, and easily identifiable barrios influenced immigration and social welfare officials to focus their efforts solely on the Mexican people, people whom they viewed as foreign usurpers of American jobs and as unworthy burdens on relief rolls. From Los Angeles, California, to Gary, Indiana, Mexicans were either summarily deported by immigration agencies or persuaded to depart voluntarily by duplicitous social workers who greatly exaggerated the opportunities awaiting them south of the border.[66] According to historian George Sánchez: "As many as seventy-five thousand Mexicans from southern California returned to Mexico by 1932. . . . The enormity of these figures, given the fact that California's Mexican population was in 1930 slightly over three hundred and sixty thousand . . . , indicates that almost every Mexican family in southern California confronted in one way or another the decision of returning or staying."[67]

By 1935, the deportation and repatriation campaigns had diminished, but prejudice and segregation remained. Historian Albert Camarillo has demonstrated that in Los Angeles restrictive real estate covenants and segregated schools increased dramatically between 1920 and 1950. The proportion of Los Angeles-area municipalities with covenants prohibiting Mexicans and other minorities from purchasing residences in certain neighborhoods climbed from 20 percent in 1920 to 80 percent in 1946. Many restaurants, theaters, and public swimming pools discriminated against their Spanish-surnamed clientele. In southern California, for example, Mexicans could swim at the public plunges only one day out of the week (just before they drained the pool).[68] Small-town merchants frequently refused to admit Spanish-speaking people to their places of business. "White Trade Only" signs served as bitter reminders of their second-class citizenship.[69]

In 1933, a University of California study noted that Mexicans in southern California were among the most impoverished groups in the United States. Regardless of nativity, they were often dismissed as cheap, temporary labor and were paid "from 20 to 50 percent less per day for . . . performing the same jobs as other workers."[70] This economic segmentation did not diminish by generation. Writing about San Bernardino, California, in the 1940s, Ruth Tuck offered the following illustration: "There is a street . . . on which three families live side by side. The head of one family is a naturalized citizen, who arrived here eighteen years ago; the head of the second is an alien who came . . . in 1905; the head of the third is the descendant of people who came . . . in 1843. All of them, with their families, live in poor housing; earn approximately $150 a month as un-skilled laborers; send their children to Mexican schools; and encounter the same sort of discriminatory practices."[71]

Until World War II, Mexicans experienced restricted occupational mobility as few rose above the ranks of blue-collar labor. Scholars Mario García and Gilbert González have convincingly argued that the curricula in Mexican schools helped perpetuate this trend. Emphasis on vocational education served to funnel Mexican youth into the factories and building trades.[72] In the abstract, education raised people's expectations, but in practice, particularly for men, it trained them for low-status, low-paying jobs. Employment choices were even more limited in rural areas. As min-ers or farmworkers, Mexicans usually resided in company settlements, where almost every aspect of their lives—from work schedules to wage rates to credit with local merchants—was regulated. In 1925, a newspa-per editor in Greeley, Colorado, bluntly advocated "a caste system," even though, he alleged, such a system "will be worse upon us, the aristocracy, than upon the Mexicans in the serfdom."[73] Both in urban and rural areas, ethnicity became not only a matter of personal choice and heritage but also an ascribed status imposed by external sources.[74]

Considering these circumstances, it is no surprise that many teenag-ers developed a shining idealism as a type of psychological ballast. Some adolescents, such as the members of the Mexican-American movement, believed that education was the key to mobility, while others placed their faith in the application of Max Factor's bleaching cream.[75] Whether they struggled to further their education or tried to lighten their skin color, Mexican Americans sought to protect themselves from the damaging ef-fects of prejudice.

Despite economic and social stratification, many Mexicanas believed that life in the United States offered hope and opportunity. "Here woman has come to have place like a human being," reflected Señora————.[76] More common perhaps was the impact of material assimilation, the pur-chase of an automobile, a sewing machine, and other accoutrements of U.S. consumer society. The accumulation of these goods signaled the realization of (or the potential for realizing) the American dream. As Margaret Clark has eloquently commented: "In Sal Si Puedes [a San José barrio] where so many people are struggling to escape poverty and want, a 'luxury item' like a shiny new refrigerator may be the source of hope and encouragement—it may symbolize the first step toward the achievement of a better way of life."[77] One of Clark's informants made the point more directly: "Nobody likes to be poor."[78]

The World War II era ushered in a set of new options for Mexican women. In southern California, some joined unions in food-processing plants and negotiated higher wages and benefits. Still others obtained more lucrative employment in defense plants. As "Rosie the Riveters," they gained self-confidence and the requisite earning power to improve their standard of living. A single parent, Alicia Mendeola Shelit purchased her first home as the result of her employment with Douglas Aircraft.[79] The expansion of clerical jobs also provided Mexican-American women with additional opportunities. By 1950, 23.9 percent of Mexican women workers in the Southwest held lower white-collar positions as secretaries or sales clerks.[80] They could finally apply the office skills they had acquired in high school or at storefront business colleges. Intermarriage with Anglos, although beyond the scope of this study, may have been perceived as a potential avenue for mobility.[81]

Most of the thirteen interviewees continued in the labor force, combining wagework with household responsibilities. Only the oldest (Ruby Estrada of Arizona) and the youngest (Rosa Guerrero of Texas) achieved a solid, middle-class standard of living. While one cannot make a facile correlation, both women are the only informants who attained a college education. Six of the eleven California women took their places on the shop floor in the aerospace, electronics, apparel, and food-processing industries. Two became secretaries and one a sales clerk at Kmart. The remaining two were full-time homemakers. Seven of these eleven informants married Anglo or Jewish men; yet their economic status did not differ substantially from those who chose Mexican spouses.[82] With varying degrees of financial security, the California women are now working-class retirees. Their lives do not exemplify rags-to-riches mobility but, rather, upward movement within the working class. Though painfully aware of prejudice and discrimination, people of their generation placed faith in themselves and in the system. In 1959, Margaret Clark asserted that the second-generation residents of Sal Si Puedes "dream and work toward the day when Mexican Americans will become fully integrated into American society at large."[83] The desire to prove oneself appears as a running theme in twentieth-century Mexican-American history. I should hasten to add that, in the process, most people refused to shed their cultural heritage. "Fusion is what we want—the best of both ways."[84]

In this essay, I have attempted to reconstruct the world of adolescent women, taking into account the broader cultural, political, and economic environment. I have given a sense of the contradictions in their lives— the lure of Hollywood and the threat of deportation. The discussion gives rise to an intriguing question. Can one equate the desire for material goods with the abandonment of Mexican values? I believe that the ideological impact of material acculturation has been overrated. For example, a young Mexican woman may have looked like a flapper as she boarded a street-car on her way to work at a cannery; yet she went to work (at least in part) to help support her family, as part of her obligation as a daughter. The adoption of new cultural forms certainly frightened parents, but it did not itself undermine Mexican identity. The experiences of Mexican-American women coming of age between 1920 and 1950 reveal the blending of the old and the new, fashioning new expectations, making choices, and learning to live with those choices.

Notes

1. Oscar Handlin, *The Uprooted* (New York: Grosset and Dunlap, 1951); Alfred Kazin, *A Walker in the City* (New York: Harcourt Brace, 1951).

2. Examples of this rich literature include John Bodnar, *The Transplanted* (Bloomington: University of Indiana Press, 1985); Kathy Peiss, *Cheap Amusements: Working Women and Leisure in Turn-of-the-Century New York* (Philadelphia: Temple University Press, 1986); Paula S. Fass, *The Damned and the Beautiful: American Youth in the 1920's* (New York: Oxford University Press, 1977); and Estelle B. Freedman and John D'Emilio, *Intimate Matters* (New York: Harper and Row, 1988).

3. The word *Mexicano(a)* designates someone of Mexican birth residing in the United States (either temporarily or permanently), while *Mexican American* denotes a person born in the United States with at least second-generation status. *Mexican* is an umbrella term for both groups. I use the term *Chicano(a)* only for the contemporary period, since most of the older women whose oral interviews contributed to this study did not identify themselves as Chicanas. *Latino(a)* denotes someone of Latin American birth or heritage.

4. Albert Camarillo, *Chicanos in a Changing Society: From Mexican Pueblos to American Barrios in Santa Barbara and Southern California, 1848–1930* (Cambridge, MA: Harvard University Press, 1979), 200–201; Ricardo Romo, *East Los Angeles: History of a Barrio* (Austin: University of Texas Press, 1983), 61; T. Wilson Longmore and Homer L. Hitt, "A Demographic Analysis of First and Second Generation Mexican Population of the United States: 1930," *Southwestern Social Science Quarterly* 24 (September 1943): 140.

5. Manuel Gamio, *Mexican Immigration to the United States: A Study of Human Migration and Adjustment* (Chicago: University of Chicago Press; rpt. New York: Arno Press, 1969); Paul S. Taylor, *Mexican Labor in the United States*, 2 vols. (Berkeley: University of California Press, 1928, 1932); Emory S. Bogardus, *The Mexican in the United States* (Los Angeles: University of Southern California Press, 1934). *Pachucos* were young men who adopted the zoot suit, a badge of adolescent rebellion in Mexican- and African-American communities during World War II. Because of their dress and demeanor, they were subject to verbal and physical abuse by law enforcement officials and servicemen. Mauricio Mazón's *The Zoot Suit Riots: The Psychology of Symbolic Annihilation* (Austin:

University of Texas Press, 1984), and the Luis Valdez play and feature film *Zoot Suit* provide examples of literature on *pachucos.*

6. Works that focus on Mexican women during this period include Rosalinda M. González, "Chicanas and Mexican Immigrant Families, 1920–1940: Women's Subordination and Family Exploitation," in *Decades of Discontent: The Women's Movement, 1920–1940,* ed. Lois Scharf and Joan Jensen (Westport, CT: Greenwood Press, 1983), 59–83; and Vicki L. Ruiz, *Cannery Women, Cannery Lives: Mexican Women, Unionization and the California Food Processing Industry, 1930–1950* (Albuquerque: University of New Mexico Press, 1987).

7. Ruth Zambrana, "A Walk in Two Worlds," *Social Welfare* 1 (Spring 1986): 12.

8. The age breakdown for the thirteen interviewees is as follows: two women were born between 1910 and 1912; six between 1913 and 1919; four between 1920 and 1929; and one after 1930.

9. Adelina Otero, "My People," *The Survey* 63 (May 31, 1931), rpt. in *Aspects of the Mexican American Experience,* ed. Carlos Cortés (New York: Arno Press, 1976), 150; Ruth Tuck, *Not with the Fist* (New York: Harcourt, Brace, 1946; rpt. New York: Arno Press, 1974), 185–88; Vicki L. Ruiz, "Oral History and La Mujer: The Rosa Guerrero Story," in *Women on the United States–Mexico Border: Responses to Change,* ed. Vicki L. Ruiz and Susan Tiano (Boston: Allen and Unwin, 1987), 226–27; interview with Belen Martínez Mason, in *Rosie the Riveter Revisited: Women and the World War II Work Experience,* ed. Sherna Berger Gluck (Long Beach, CA: CSULB Foundation, 1983), 23: 24–25.

10. Interview with Ruby Estrada, August 4, 1981, conducted by María Hernández, "The Lives of Arizona Women" Oral History Project (On File, Special Collections, Hayden Library, Arizona State University, Tempe), 6.

11. Interview with Mary Luna, in *Rosie the Riveter,* 20: 10. During the 1940s, bilingual education appeared as an exciting experiment in curriculum reform. See George I. Sánchez, ed., *First Regional Conference on the Education of Spanish-Speaking People in the Southwest* (Austin: University of Texas Press, 1946), 1–22; rpt. in *Aspects of the Mexican American Experience.*

12. Margarita B. Melville, "Selective Acculturation of Female Mexican Migrants," in *Twice a Minority: Mexican American Women,* ed. Margarita B. Melville (St. Louis, MO: Mosby, 1980), 161; Ruiz, "Oral History and La Mujer," 222.

13. Interview with Rose Escheverria Mulligan, in *Rosie the Riveter,* 27: 16–17, 24; Ruiz, "Oral History and La Mujer," 227–28; Taylor, *Mexican Labor,* 1: 79, 205–6. Text quotation is from Taylor, 1: 79.

14. Tuck, *Not with the Fist,* 162–63, 190–91; Paul S. Taylor, "Women in Industry," field notes for his book *Mexican Labor in the United States, 1927–1930,* Bancroft Library, University of California, 1 box; Estrada interview, 10–15; Escheverria Mulligan interview. Text quotation is from Taylor, *Mexican Labor,* 1: 205. See also Paul S. Taylor, "Mexican Women in Los Angeles Industry in 1928," *Aztlán* 11 (Spring 1980): 99–131.

15. Lois Rita Helmbold, "The Work of Chicanas in the United States: Wage Labor and Work in the Home, 1930 to the Present" (seminar paper, Stanford University, 1977), 53; Taylor field notes; Tuck, *Not with the Fist,* 190–91; interview with Julia Luna Mount, November 17, 1983, conducted by the author.

16. John Bodnar, "Immigration, Kinship and the Rise of Working-Class Realism in Industrial America," *Journal of Social History* 14 (Fall 1980): 53–55; Tamara K. Hareven, "Family Time and Industrial Time: Family and Work in a

Planned Corporation Town, 1900–1924," in *Family and Kin in Urban Communities*, ed. Tamara K. Hareven (New York: New Viewpoints, 1977), 202; Taylor field notes; U.S. Department of Labor, Bureau of Labor Statistics, "Labor and Social Conditions of Mexicans in California," *Monthly Labor Review* 32 (January–June 1931): 89.

17. Mario Barrera, *Race and Class in the Southwest* (Notre Dame, IN: University of Notre Dame Press, 1979), 131; Taylor field notes. The percentage of Mexican women workers employed in industry was comparable to that of European immigrant women in the Eastern states, where one-third of ethnic women who worked outside the home labored as blue-collar employees. See Alice Kessler-Harris, *Out to Work: A History of Wage Earning Women in the United States* (New York: Oxford University Press, 1982), 127.

18. Heller Committee for Research in Social Economics of the University of California, and Constantive Panuzio, *How Mexicans Earn and Live*, University of California Publications in Economics 13, no. 1, Cost of Living Studies 5 (Berkeley: University of California, 1933), 11, 14–17; Taylor field notes; Luna Mount interview; interview with Alicia Shelit, in *Rosie the Riveter*, 37: 9. For further delineation of the family wage and the consumer wage economy, see Louise A. Tilly and Joan W. Scott, *Women, Work and Family* (New York: Holt, Rinehart, and Winston, 1978).

19. Taylor field notes; Helmbold, "The Work of Chicanas," 15, 30–31, 36; Douglas Monroy, "An Essay on Understanding the Work Experience of Mexicans in Southern California, 1900–1939," *Aztlán* 12 (Spring 1981): 70; González, "Chicanas and Mexican Immigrant Families," 72.

20. Discussing popular magazines and movies helped build important cross-cultural bridges—bridges that would facilitate union organizing drives among southern Californian food-processing workers during the late 1930s and early 1940s. See Ruiz, *Cannery Women, Cannery Lives*.

21. Roland Marchand, *Advertising the American Dream: Making Way for Modernity, 1920–1940* (Berkeley: University of California Press, 1985), 197–99, 219; Freedman and D'Emilio, *Intimate Matters*, 278.

22. Taylor field notes; Richard G. Thurston, "Urbanization and Sociocultural Change in a Mexican-American Enclave" (Ph.D. diss., University of California, Los Angeles, 1957; rpt. San Francisco: R and E Research Associates, 1974), 128; Helmbold, "The Work of Chicanas," 42–44; interview with Carmen Bernal Escobar, June 15, 1986, conducted by the author.

23. Elizabeth Fuller, *The Mexican Housing Problem in Los Angeles*, Studies in Sociology 5, Sociological Monograph no. 17 (Los Angeles: Southern California Sociological Society, 1920; rpt. New York: Arno Press, 1974), 4–5.

24. Ruiz, "Oral History and La Mujer," 226.

25. Shelit interview, 4; interview with Adele Hernández Milligan, in *Rosie the Riveter*, 26: 14; Martínez Mason interview, 85–86; Luna interview, 18, 26; Clint C. Wilson II and Felix Gutiérrez, *Minorities and Media* (Beverly Hills, CA: Sage, 1985), 85–86.

26. For examples, see *La Opinión*, September 16 and 18, 1926; May 13 and 15, 1927; June 3 and 4, 1927.

27. Ibid., September 23, 24, 27, and 30, 1926.

28. Ibid., March 2, 1927.

29. Taylor field notes. Referring to Los Angeles, two historians have argued that "Mexicans experienced segregation in housing in nearly every section of the

city and its outlying areas" (Antonio Ríos-Bustamante and Pedro Castillo, *An Illustrated History of Mexican Los Angeles, 1781–1985* [Los Angeles: Chicano Studies Research Center, University of California, 1986], 135). Ruth Tuck (in *Not with the Fist*, 142–143) noted that Anglo-Americans also employed the term *Spanish* in order to distinguish individuals "of superior background or achievement."

30. Shelit interview, 32; Escheverria Mulligan interview, 14; Melville, "Selective Acculturation," 155, 162.

31. Tuck, *Not with the Fist*, 133.

32. Gamio, *Mexican Immigration*, 172–73; Bogardus, *The Mexican in the United States*, 75; Romo, *East Los Angeles*, 142; Ruiz, "Oral History and La Mujer," 224. "Some adolescents are stimulated to play the dual roles of being good Mexicans at home and good 'Americans' at school" (Bogardus, 75).

33. Ruiz, "Oral History and La Mujer," 221, 224–25; Margaret Clark, *Health in the Mexican American Culture* (Berkeley: University of California Press, 1959), 21.

34. Clark, *Health in the Mexican American Culture*, 21.

35. Tuck, *Not with the Fist*, 108. The term "Los Conejos" refers to a village in Mexico.

36. Ríos-Bustamante and Castillo, *An Illustrated History*, 139; George Sánchez, "The Rise of the Second Generation: The Mexican American Movement" (unpublished paper, 1986), 26–27; interview with Luisa Moreno, August 12–13, 1977, conducted by Albert Camarillo.

37. Sociologist Norma Williams contends that contemporary Mexican Americans view the Catholic church almost solely in terms of social, life-cycle functions, such as baptisms and funerals (see *The Mexican American Family: Tradition and Change* [Boston: G. K. Hall, 1990].

38. Vicki L. Ruiz, "Dead Ends or Gold Mines? Using Missionary Records in Mexican American History," *Frontiers* 12 (1991): 33–56. Escheverria Mulligan interview, 24. For an interesting collection of Protestant missionary reports during this period, see Carlos Cortés, ed., *Church Views of the Mexican American* (New York: Arno Press, 1974).

39. Luna interview, 9.

40. George Sánchez, " 'Go after the Women': Americanization and the Mexican Immigrant Woman, 1915–1929," in *Unequal Sisters: A Multicultural Reader in U.S. Women's History*, ed. Ellen Carol DuBois and Vicki L. Ruiz (New York: Routledge, 1990), 250–63.

41. Bogardus, *The Mexican in the United States*, 74; Martínez Mason interview, 44. During the 1920s, Mexican parents were not atypical in voicing their concerns over the attitudes and appearance of their "flapper adolescents." A general atmosphere of tension between youth and their elders existed—a generation gap that cut across class, race, ethnicity, and region. See Fass, *The Damned and the Beautiful*.

42. Shelit interview, 18; Taylor, *Mexican Labor*, 2: 199–200; interview with María Fierro, in *Rosie the Riveter*, 12: 10.

43. Gamio, *Mexican Immigration*, 89. The verse taken from "Las Pelonas" in the original Spanish follows:

Los paños colorados
Los tengo aborrecidos

> *Ya hora las pelonas*
> *Los Usan de vestidos.*
> *Las muchachas de S. Antonio*
> *Son flojas pa'l metate*
> *Quieren andar pelonas*
> *Con sombreros de petate.*
> *Se acabaron las pizcas,*
> *Se acabó el algodón*
> *Ya andan las pelonas*
> *De puro vacilón.*

44. Taylor, *Mexican Labor*, 2: vi–vii.

45. *La Opinión*, September 18, 1926; May 3, 1927; June 5, 1927. Using endorsements from famous people was a common advertising technique (see Marchand, *Advertising the American Dream*, 96–102).

46. Rodolfo F. Acuña, *A Community under Siege: A Chronicle of Chicanos East of the Los Angeles River, 1945–1975* (Los Angeles: Chicano Studies Research Center, University of California, 1984), 278, 407–8, 413–14, 418, 422; FTA *News*, May 1, 1945; Escobar interview. For an example of the promotion of a beauty pageant, see issues of *La Opinión*, June–July 1927.

47. Escobar interview.

48. Sherna B. Gluck, *Rosie the Riveter Revisited: Women, the War and Social Change* (Boston: Twayne, 1987), 81, 85.

49. Letter from Carey McWilliams dated October 3, 1937, to Louis Adamic, Adamic File, Carton 1, Carey McWilliams Collection, Special Collections, University of California, Los Angeles.

50. Martínez Mason interview, 29–30; Escobar interview; Fierro interview, 15; Estrada interview, 11–12. Chaperonage was also common in Italian immigrant communities. Indeed, many of the same conflicts between parents and daughters had surfaced a generation earlier among Italian families on the East Coast (Peiss, *Cheap Amusements*, 69–70, 152).

51. Hernández Milligan interview, 17.

52. Evangeline Hymer, "A Study of the Social Attitudes of Adult Mexican Immigrants in Los Angeles and Vicinity: 1923" (M.A. thesis, University of Southern California, 1924; rpt. San Francisco: R and E Research Associates, 1971), 24–25.

53. Escobar interview; Estrada interview, 11, 13.

54. Estrada interview, 12; also Shelit interview, 9; Ríos-Bustamante and Castillo, *An Illustrated History*, 153.

55. Taylor field notes; Thurston, "Urbanization," 118; Borgardus, *The Mexican in the United States*, 28–29, 57–58.

56. Martínez Mason interview, 30; interview with Beatrice Morales Clifton, in *Rosie the Riveter*, 8: 14–15.

57. Shelit interview, 9, 24, 30; Escobar interview; Martínez Mason interview, 30; Hernández Milligan interview, 27–28; Taylor field notes.

58. Luna Mount interview; Fierro interview, 18; Luna interview, 29; Gregorita Rodriguez, *Singing for My Echo* (Santa Fe, NM: Cota Editions, 1987), 52; Martínez Mason interview, 62.

59. "Elisa Morales," Manuel Gamio field notes, Bancroft Library, University of California, Berkeley, 1 box.

60. Taylor field notes; Taylor, *Mexican Labor*, 2: vi–vii; Gamio, *Mexican Immigration*, 89. The *corrido* "El Enganchado" (in *Mexican Labor*, vol. 2) offers an intriguing glimpse into attitudes toward women and Americanization.

61. Wilson and Gutiérrez, *Minorities and Media*, 86.

62. Tuck, *Not with the Fist*, 115; Shelit interview, 26.

63. Tuck, *Not with the Fist*, 115.

64. Taylor, *Mexican Labor*, 1: 205–6; Ruiz, "Oral History and La Mujer," 227–28; Sánchez, "The Rise of the Second Generation," 7–10, 12; Escheverria Mulligan interview, 17.

65. Kenneth L. Roberts, "The Docile Mexican," *Saturday Evening Post*, March 10, 1928, as quoted in Sánchez, " 'Go After the Women,' " 8.

66. Rodolfo Acuña, *Occupied America: A History of Chicanos*, 2d ed. (New York: Harper and Row, 1980), 138, 140–41; Albert Camarillo, *Chicanos in California* (San Francisco: Boyd and Fraser, 1984), 48–49; Abraham Hoffman, *Unwanted Mexican Americans in the Great Depression* (Tucson: University of Arizona Press, 1974), 16–20; Neil Betten and Raymond A. Mohl, "From Discrimination to Repatriation: Mexican Life in Gary, Indiana, during the Great Depression," in *The Chicano*, ed. Norris Hundley (Santa Barbara, CA: ABC-Clio Press, 1975), 132, 138–39.

67. Sánchez, "The Rise of the Second Generation," 10.

68. Albert Camarillo, "Mexican American Urban History in Comparative Ethnic Perspective," Distinguished Speaker Series, University of California, Davis, January 26, 1987; Acuña, *Occupied America*, 310, 318, 323, 330–31; Romo, *East Los Angeles*, 139; Tuck, *Not with the Fist*, 51, 53; Shelit interview, 15.

69. Taylor, *Mexican Labor*, 1: 221–24; interview with María Arredondo, March 19, 1986, conducted by Carolyn Arredondo.

70. Heller Committee, *How Mexicans Earn and Live*, 68–69, 72. Text quotation is from Camarillo, *Chicanos in a Changing Society*, 215.

71. Tuck, *Not with the Fist*, 209–10.

72. Barrera, *Race and Class in the Southwest*, 82–91; Mario T. García, *Desert Immigrants: The Mexicans of El Paso, 1880–1920* (New Haven, CT: Yale University Press, 1981), 110–26; Gilbert González, "Racism, Education, and the Mexican Community in Los Angeles, 1920–30," *Societas* 4 (Autumn 1974): 287–300.

73. González, "Chicanas and Mexican Immigrant Families," 63–66; Taylor, *Mexican Labor*, 1: 162–66, 176–79, 190–91, 217, 220, 227–28 (quotation from p. 220).

74. Melville, "Selective Acculturation," 159–60; John García, "Ethnicity and Chicanos," *Hispanic Journal of Behavioral Sciences* 4 (1982): 310–11.

75. Sánchez, "The Rise of the Second Generation," 7–9; Guadalupe San Miguel, Jr., "Culture and Education in the American Southwest: Towards an Explanation of Chicano School Attendance," *Journal of American Ethnic History* 7 (Spring 1988): 15, 17; *La Opinión*, June 5, 1927.

76. "Sra.———," Manuel Gamio field notes.

77. Clark, *Health in the Mexican American Culture*, 92.

78. Ibid.

79. Ruiz, *Cannery Women, Cannery Lives*; Shelit interview, 52–55; Sherna Berger Gluck, "Interlude or Change: Women and the World War II Work Experience," 14, 32–34 (rev. version of paper originally published in *International Jour-*

nal of Oral History 3 [1982], courtesy of author); see also Gluck, *Rosie the Riveter Revisited.*

80. William H. Chafe, *The American Woman: Her Changing Social, Economic, and Political Roles, 1920–1970* (New York: Oxford University Press, 1972), 137–43, 146; Barrera, *Race and Class in the Southwest*, 131, 140–45.

81. Shelit interview, 32; Escheverria Mulligan interview, 14; Richard Griswold del Castillo, *La Familia: Chicano Families in the Urban Southwest, 1848 to the Present* (Notre Dame, IN: University of Notre Dame Press, 1984), 120–22.

82. Many of the husbands were skilled workers in the aerospace industry. The highest occupation for a spouse was firefighter.

83. Clark, *Health in the Mexican American Culture*, 20.

84. Tuck, *Not with the Fist*, 134. According to historian Richard Griswold del Castillo (in *La Familia*, 126), "present-day Chicano families are a bridge between the social and cultural heritages of Anglo and Latin America."

7

From *Ranchero* to *Jaitón*: Ethnicity and Class in Texas-Mexican Music (Two Styles in the Form of a Pair)*

Manuel Peña

Texas has always had a unique relationship with Mexico. Sharing a common border of more than twelve hundred miles, the state has served as a conduit through which millions of Mexican migrants have passed in both directions across the international frontier. In addition, the development over time of a number of "twin cities" on the border (El Paso-Ciudad Juárez, Laredo-Nuevo Laredo, McAllen-Reynosa, Brownsville-Matamoros) speaks to the intimate intercourse that has bound tejanos *to neighbors, friends, relatives, and business partners "on the other side."*

*Like California, however, Texas also has always been a site of cultural and social conflict not only between Anglo-Americans and ethnic Mexicans but also between and among ethnic Mexicans themselves. Ethnomusicologist Manuel Peña of the University of Texas, Austin, explores a different source of conflict than those examined in Chapter 6—the growing class differences among ethnic Mexicans in Texas. Peña argues that the intraethnic conflicts caused by the increasing class stratification of the ethnic Mexican population after World War II were often acted out in symbolic ways, particularly in matters of cultural tastes. Focusing on the musicians who played, and the audiences who danced to, two popular forms of regional Mexican music—*orquesta *and* conjunto—*Peña demonstrates that a preference for one or the other style reveals volumes about the forces of cultural change and conflict facing ethnic Mexicans in the United States.*

From *Ethnomusicology* 29, no. 1 (Winter 1985): 29–55. The original text has been slightly modified. Reprinted by permission of the Society for Ethnomusicology.

*The subtitle was inspired by Gilbert Chase's "Two Lectures in the Form of a Pair."

Two popular musical styles were forged by *tejano* [Texas-Mexican] musicians during World War II. The styles are known as *orquesta tejana*, or simply *orquesta*, and *norteño*. Among *tejanos* the latter is more commonly referred to as *conjunto*, and that is the label that will be used here. Each style, though intricately related to the other, actually merits its own study.[1] Nonetheless, the relationship between the two types of music presents a challenging subject for interpretation, not only to students of musical culture, but to social scientists generally.

The essay focuses mainly on the period 1935–1965, with particular emphasis on the decade or so after the war. Additionally, the primary interest is to explain the dynamics that sustained the *conjunto-orquesta* relationship, particularly the series of contrasts the two [kinds of] music came to articulate and, indeed, embody: working vs. middle class,[2] ethnic resistance vs. cultural assimilation, continuity vs. change, and folk vs. "sophisticated." Moreover, underlying these contrasts, or oppositions, was the key factor operating in the emergence of both *conjunto* and *orquesta*— namely, the shift in *tejano* society from a Mexicanized, rural, folk, and proletarian group to a class-differentiated, urban, and increasingly Americanized and literate population.

In two earlier works devoted mainly to *conjunto*, this author noted two questions that are raised in considering the emergence of this folk style among Texas-Mexicans. Since these questions (and their answers) impinge directly on the emergence of *orquesta* as well, they are worth recalling here. The first question had to do with the musical evolution of the *conjunto*, i.e., how such a style could crystalize so rapidly into a mature artistic form. The second dealt with the social and cultural significance of the music; the *timing* of the style's appearance and development, and, specifically, why a well-defined style should emerge among this particular group of people at this precise moment in their history (1935–1960). The problem of *conjunto*'s emergence holds as well for *orquesta*, since, in a doubly remarkable accident of history, at the very same time that the former was establishing itself as a formidable artistic expression, the latter was likewise coming into its own.

Thus, keeping in mind the contrasts mentioned above—and by way of moving to resolve the question of the *orquesta-conjunto* nexus—there are two hypotheses on the relationship between the two [kinds of] music. The remainder of the essay will be devoted to an explanation of the two hypotheses. First, at the historical level the two [kinds of] music unfolded within a framework of emerging class difference and conflict among Texas-Mexicans, and as such they have signified an intrinsic class dialectic working itself out within Texas-Mexican society. The second hypothesis is linked to the first, but builds on a more "synchronic" base, as it were.

That is, it posits *orquesta* and *conjunto* as symbolic projections of a Texas-Mexican social structure that was solid enough to survive both the disruptive effects of interethnic contact with American society and the fragmentation introduced by class differences. To put it another way, from a synchronic ("structural") perspective the two styles should be considered dual expressions of a unitary musico-symbolic whole that emerged out of the conflict between an ethnic *tejano* culture and a dominant, often hostile Anglo-American social order. . . .

At least one sociologist of music has addressed the need for an approach that makes "intelligible for us why a certain style may have emerged in the social and cultural structure of a given period, and thus clarify the sociological prerequisites and conditions involved."[3] A similar line of thought is pursued by James Ackerman, who proposes that the creative impulse out of which new styles spring may be thought of as "a class of related solutions to a problem—or responses to a problem."[4] Following Ackerman's notion, this essay argues that the changes wrought by World War II and its aftermath posed a challenge to Texas-Mexican society that demanded solutions to a number of problems. Artistic expression offered one solution, and, as we shall see, stylistic developments in *conjunto* and *orquesta* suggest themselves as specific examples.

Distinguishable stylistic elements coalesced first around the accordion ensemble that Texas-Mexicans forged between 1935 and 1960. The *orquesta tejana*, whose instrumentation was a simplified version of the big American dance band, began to acquire its unique qualities after the war. Groping for direction at first, both *conjunto* and *orquesta* had gained coherent and expressive forms by the mid-1950s. By this time each ensemble had gravitated toward its respective social context: *conjunto* toward the mass of proletarian workers, *orquesta* toward a small but growing and influential middle class.

Nonetheless, despite their social and musical differences, . . . the two ensembles and their musical styles are best described as tending to diverge at the level of class (or, at least, occupational) consciousness, but to converge at the level of ethnic consciousness. This is to say, that in modern Texas-Mexican society musical culture has not been strictly determined by socioeconomic factors; rather, ethnic conflict has played a critical role as well. In any case the tendency to converge, both stylistically and socially, was much stronger after the mid-1960s, a result of the closer alignment (for reasons to be explored later) of *orquesta* with the musical preferences of the working class. In the decade immediately following the war, however, the tension between convergence and divergence was much more pronounced, a state of affairs that reflected the inevitable contradictions that Texas-Mexican society faced as a consequence of the contrasts noted earlier, especially the contrast between cultural assimilation and ethnic resistance. . . .

Conjunto: "A Folk Music, of the People"

Briefly, the development of *conjunto* music was, in every sense of the concept, a folk phenomenon. As one *orquesta* musician observed (personal interview), "La música de conjunto es una música vernácula, del pueblo" (*Conjunto* music is a folk music, of the people). Without exception, its contributors had two characteristics in common: they were totally or for the most part illiterate, and they belonged to a proletarian class. In short, *conjunto* musicians were members of a society that was characterized by strong folk elements: a deep oral tradition, a lack of socioeconomic differentiation, a collective sense of ethnic identity, and a relative isolation from other groups.[5]

By the 1930s, however, when the modern *conjunto* first began to take shape, the *tejanos*' participation in an expanding American political economy had begun the irreversible erosion of their traditional culture. The modern *conjunto* thus emerged at a critical moment in Texas-Mexican history, when many of the folk traditions were beginning to yield to the pressures of social change. Grounded in those traditions, the *conjunto* became a strong musical symbol for the folk, working-class Texas-Mexicans, a symbol, moreover, that was part of a larger response to the challenges of a new era. . . .

One other observation should be made about the *conjunto* and its relationship to earlier folk music practices. Its rapid standardization, which resulted in a highly uniform style with fixed relationships between the component instruments, undeniably set it apart from its predecessors. Nonetheless, certain continuities did persist. To begin with, the *conjunto*'s principal member, the diatonic button accordion, had been a part of Texas-Mexican music since the 1880s, at least, although prior to World War II the one- and two-row models were the rule, rather than the three-row model commonly used today.[6]

The early accordion (and the ad hoc ensembles that were built around it) shared another important attribute with the modern *conjunto*: Historically, accordion music in northern Mexico and South Texas has been firmly linked to folk, working-class elements of *norteño* society, both in Mexico and in Texas. The "respectable" class of Mexicans, meanwhile—as well as the Anglo-Americans—have looked with disfavor upon the instrument and the celebrations traditionally associated with it. For example, an early report in the *San Antonio Express* (August 20, 1880) referred to the dances where accordion music was often featured as "a great curse to the country." "The respectable class of Mexicans," the report concludes, "do not attend them." Until recently this harsh attitude was shared by middle-class or upwardly mobile *tejanos*. Arnaldo Ramírez, head of Falcon, the largest Mexican-American record company today, and a man intimately familiar with Texas-Mexican music, summed up the attitude of "society" *tejanos* succinctly: "A la gente de sociedad," he said, "mencionar el acordeón era mentarles la madre" (To people of 'society,' to mention the accordion was to call their mother a name) (personal interview).

Two other factors that have remained more or less constant during the accordion's history among Texas-Mexicans are related to performance context and repertory. Both the early accordion and the modern *conjunto* have relied heavily on the dance—weddings and other domestic celebrations before World War II and public, paid-admission dances (as well as domestic celebrations) since the war. Repertorially, the changes that occurred after the war as part of the *conjunto*'s emergence involved a streamlining of genre selection, more than anything else. That is, in addition to the *huapango tamaulipeco*, genres derived from nineteenth-century instrumental salon music—the polka, redowa, mazurka, and schottische—were the mainstays of the early accordionists. After the war only the polka and the *huapango* retained a strong presence, though the former was superseded by the *canción ranchera*, the latter performed for the most part in tempo di polka. As one musician explained, "La canción ranchera es una polka, pero cantada" (The *canción ranchera* is a polka, only sung [i.e., with lyrics added]).[7] Since the war only two genres have gained an appreciable presence in the *conjunto*'s basic repertory—a *ranchero* version of the Mexican bolero, introduced in the late 1940s, and the Colombian *cumbia*, introduced in the mid-1960s.

Besides the continuities in the history of accordion music among Texas-Mexicans, there are some important discontinuities. First, of course, is the matter of style, especially ensemble style, for it is here that the modern *conjunto* differed radically from earlier accordion music. To begin with, playing technique changed drastically during the mid-1930s (see below); moreover, until the 1920s the accordion was for the most part an instrument played solo (see, e.g., the *San Antonio Express*, June 18, 1881). Its incorporation into an ensemble should thus be considered a major break from past tradition. There is evidence, however, that as early as the 1890s the accordion had been randomly combined with sundry instruments, especially the *tambora de rancho* (ranch drum).[8] The latter was a makeshift instrument that made use of homemade materials—goat-skin heads, mallets, and drumsticks—as well as manufactured parts (metal rims, old parade drum carcasses). Moreover, in the late nineteenth century the *bajo sexto*, an instrument which evidently made its way to South Texas from the *bajío* region in Mexico (Martín Macías, personal interview), also began to come into use with the accordion. The *bajo* is a bass guitar with twelve strings in six double courses; it is ordinarily played with a plectrum. By the 1920s the accordion-*bajo sexto* duet was quite common, as was, indeed, the inclusion of the *tambora* (see Arhoolie Records, *Border Music* series, vol. 4).

Yet, despite the fact that the accordion-*bajo sexto-tambora* ensemble contained all the elements for at least a rudimentary *norteño* style, no stylistic uniformity existed, of the kind that involves set relationships between instruments. In fact, prior to the 1930s the above combination was not in any way standardized. Other instruments were often featured with the accordion, in particular the clarinet (*Border Music* series, vol. 4).[9] Thus, the early accordion ensembles, such as they were, should be considered improvisational in nature. It was not until the 1930s, when the accordion and *bajo sexto* became the anchors for a more permanent ensemble, that the stage was set for the formation of a new and lasting *norteño* style. Coincident with this development was the disappearance of the ad hoc accordion groups of an earlier day. . . . One major reason why no uniform ensemble, with its own style, emerged sooner was the lack of strong socioesthetic impulse, of the type that World War II engendered.

The mid-1930s, then, marks the juncture when the modern *conjunto* first emerged. The history of the ensemble and its style can be divided into two phases. The first is represented by those musicians who established themselves before the war—"*los músicos viejos*," as accordionist Narciso Martínez called them. The second phase belongs to *la nueva generación*, under whose direction the music reached stylistic maturity.

Of the many musicians who contributed to the creation of the emergent style, three first-generation accordionists stand out in a retrospective assessment. These are Narciso Martínez (unanimously called *el primero*), Pedro Ayala, and Santiago Jiménez. The first two were born in 1911, in Mexico, the latter in 1913, in San Antonio. All three, however, shared the same socioeconomic background: they descended from poor, farmworking families, and all had to work in menial jobs to support themselves, despite the fact that as recording artists they were in great demand for dance performances.

The importance of these three performers lies in the contributions that each made to the emerging ensemble and its style. Martínez is an especially pivotal figure because from the beginning of his commercial career (1935), he was the first to exploit the capabilities of the right-hand, or "treble," side of the button accordion. In so doing, he initiated a radical departure from the earlier technique that the Mexicans shared with the Germans: He virtually stopped using the lefthand bass/accompaniment elements, leaving the rhythmic and chordal accompaniment to the very capable Santiago Almeida, one of the best of the early *bajo sexto* players. Jiménez deserves recognition because he was the first (in 1936) to make regular use of the contrabass (known among Mexicans as the *tololoche*), while Ayala fashioned a style in the years immediately following the war that adumbrated strongly the changes that the new generation of musicians was about to introduce.

The second generation of musicians included a number of outstanding performers, accordionists in particular, but, again, three of the latter may be acknowledged in this brief sketch. In the order of their rise to prominence, they are: Valerio Longoria, Tony de la Rosa, and Paulino Bernal. Longoria's accomplishments are many, but among the most notable is his introduction in 1947 of two vocal genres into the *conjunto*—the *canción ranchera* and the bolero (the latter, again, considerably simplified, or "rancheroized"). His most important contribution, however, was his enlistment of the modern drum set, in 1949. The drums had been in use in *orquestas* for some time, but *conjuntos* had generally avoided them because they were considered "too noisy" for the accordion and *bajo sexto* (Pedro Ayala, Tony de la Rosa, personal interviews).

Longoria's experiment soon caught on, however, and with the addition of the drums the modern *conjunto*'s development was almost complete. By the early 1950s the ensemble was essentially in place, except that the contrabass, which had never been widely adopted for dance performances, was still confined to the recording studio. In the mid-1950s, however, in response to the shift toward complete amplification of the music (a significant development in itself), the electric bass not only replaced the *tololoche* in the studio, but became a regular member in what has since become the standard four-man ensemble: accordion, *bajo sexto*, drums, and electric bass.

Tony de la Rosa is known for his superb polkas, which featured an extremely staccato style on the accordion and a considerably slower tempo than hitherto common (see *Border Music* series, vol. 13). This style was deemed to be admirably suited to *el tacuachito*, a new polka dance that had recently been introduced in the working-class dance halls of San Antonio, and de la Rosa consequently became very influential with younger accordionists. He became so popular, in fact, that he was one of the first *conjunto* musicians to rely solely on his music for economic support. By 1952 he was criss-crossing the state of Texas in pursuit of what one *orquesta* leader called the "taco circuit"—large public dances that attracted thousands of cottonpickers who followed the seasonal harvest.

This brings us, finally, to the last and most famous exponent of *conjunto* music during its formative years—Paulino Bernal. *El Conjunto*

Bernal is generally recognized as the "greatest of all time," as one *orquesta* musician described it. The group draws the praise of other musicians (and laymen) because, first, it was able to synthesize the stylistic elements that had been coalescing around the accordion ensemble since Martínez's initial emphasis on the treble end. Second, Bernal succeeded in attracting the best musicians available in the tradition, an accomplishment that enabled the group to bring the kind of finesse to the music that was unmatched before or after. Lastly, *El Conjunto* Bernal launched several innovations of its own—for example, the introduction of three-part vocalizations (1958) and the chromatic accordion (1964). In fact, in the mid-1960s two such accordions were featured. In sum, *El Conjunto* Bernal represented the apex of the *conjunto* tradition; no other group since then has been able to duplicate its innovative spirit.

Indeed, since the experiments of Paulino Bernal the music has remained virtually static, especially with respect to its most unique and characteristic genre—the *canción ranchera* in polka tempo. The question, of course, is why *conjunto* suddenly reached such a stylistic dead end. In other words, how could a vital, unfolding tradition do such a drastic about face after *El Conjunto* Bernal became so rigidly conservative? . . .

Orquesta Music: Squeezed between *Ranchero* and "High Class"

Although the modern *orquesta tejana* was originally patterned after the American swing bands of the 1930s and 1940s, it did have important precursors, in both Texas-Mexican and Mexican music. In fact, the *orquesta tejana* had not one but two predecessors, one of which was principally a string (violin), the other a wind (clarinet, trumpet, etc.) ensemble. The development of early Texas-Mexican orquestas (or *orquesta*-like groups), especially prior to the 1920s, remains to be investigated. . . . Such *orquestas* did exist, and, moreover, in many instances, particularly among the workers, the organization of the two types of ensemble remained highly diffuse, in terms of instrumentation and stylistic development.[10] More often than not, depending on the availability of often scarce instruments and musicians, among working-class folk the two types of instrument were actually combined to form makeshift *orquestas*. Under the patronage of a small middle class, however, better-organized *orquestas* apparently operated, especially in urban areas such as San Antonio and El Paso.[11]

A noteworthy variant of the Texas-Mexican string *orquesta* was the so-called *orquesta típica*, modeled after the Mexican *orquestas* of the same name that [sprang] up in Mexico in the late nineteenth century.[12] The latter, in turn, were bourgeois versions of the rural folk *típicas* that had existed among the Mexican proletarians throughout the nineteenth century.[13] The bourgeois *típicas* were the product of the romantic nationalism that swept through Mexico after the expulsion of the French, when, according to historians Meyer and Sherman, "self-esteem replaced the sense of shame of the introspective diagnoses of the past."[14] In short, *orquestas típicas* symbolized the upper classes' attempts to invoke *lo mexicano* (discussed below) by appropriating selected elements of the true *típicas* of proletarian origin—especially those elements (e.g., stylized *charro* costumes) that evoked the simplicity of an idyllic, rural (*ranchero*) life. Thus, as Baqueiro Foster observed of the first officially designated *típica*: "We must speak, of course, of the founding of the Orquesta Típica Mexicana [as] a monument of musical nationalism in Mexico."[15]

Judging from Baqueiro Foster's statement, it is evident that *orquestas típicas* were made to order for the kind of romantic nationalism, or *costumbrismo*, that the Mexican bourgeoisie was imbued with in the late nineteenth century. But, as Behague has noted, "popular [folk] music had to be clothed [in genteel "garb"] to make it presentable to concert audiences."[16] *Orquestas típicas* were perfect examples of this. Ultimately, however, the contradiction between the romantic ideology these *orquestas* gave voice to and the unavoidable reality of class cleavage could not be reconciled. The seeds for the ambivalence of *lo ranchero*, a concept linked to *lo mexicano* and critical for understanding the formation of Texas-Mexican orquestas, were being sown in the Conservatorio Nacional de Música, where the first *típica* was founded in 1884. Half a century later, the modern mariachi and *orquesta tejana* would emerge as the principal heirs to that contradiction.

In Texas, meanwhile, *orquesta*-like ensembles of sundry types, including the *típica* variety, were in abundance by the early twentieth century, as is evidenced by the frequent reference to them in various sources (Peña, 1985)—for example, an enthusiastic report on the founding of a "Nueva Típica Mexicana en Houston" in the March 6, 1930, edition of *Excelsior*, Mexico City's largest newspaper. Again, among the working class these *orquestas* were of an ad hoc, improvisational nature, since that is how they were founded as late as the 1930s (cf. note 10 above). As mentioned, under the patronage of merchants, professionals, and other groups of financial means, a few well-organized *orquestas* did exist.[17] A variety of *orquestas*, then, some consisting of string, others of wind instruments (and some combinations) continued to operate in Texas until the 1930s, when they were finally supplanted by the *conjunto*, which emerged as the preferred ensemble among the common workers, and by the modern *orquesta*, which began to take hold among the more "respectable" (i.e., upwardly mobile) segments of *tejano* society.

It was thus in the 1930s that more permanent and better-organized wind *orquestas*—the new type, modeled after the American big bands—began to appear with increasing frequency. On the basis of informants' reports and the course that *orquesta* music subsequently took, it is clear that the new *orquestas* articulated the strategies of a nascent group of Texas-Mexicans, usually upwardly mobile, who wanted to distance themselves from the mass of proletarian workers, and who desired at the same time to imitate the life-style of middle-class America. Highly symbolic of this desire, in my estimation, was the demand for American music, which was generously represented in the *orquesta* repertories (Beto Villa, Reymundo Treviño, personal interviews). Indicative of the sentiments that underlay the preference for things American, including music, are the words of a middle-class Texas-Mexican of the time: "We have American ways and think like Americans. We have not been able to convince some [American] people that there is a difference between us [and the old Mexicans]."[18]

By the mid-1930s several well-established *orquestas* were playing in cities like San Antonio, Corpus Christi, Kingsville, and in the Rio Grande Valley. These were the immediate predecessors of the modern *orquesta tejana*, as it came to be known by the 1950s. The man who, more than anyone else, was responsible for the creation of an *orquesta tejana* style began his professional career in the early 1930s. It was in 1932 that Beto Villa, Narciso Martínez's counterpart in the *orquesta* tradition, organized his first group. Since culturally and socioeconomically he belonged to the new middle class, and since his name became synonymous with *orquesta* music in Texas, it is worth discussing his life and career at some length.[19]

Villa was born in 1915 but, unlike Narciso Martínez and the other early accordionists, he was fortunate enough to remain in school until he was seventeen. This is a critical fact about Villa's life, because his educational accomplishments were the exception rather than the rule for the Mexicans of his time, and also because Villa's musical experience in high school had a profound influence on his subsequent career. One more point about Villa's early life should be noted, and that is the fact that he was able to stay in school as long as he did because of his family's economic stability. His father was a prosperous tailor, as well as a musician of some note, having learned his art in Monterrey, a city in northern Mexico that until recently enjoyed special prestige among Texas-Mexicans as a center of musical culture.[20]

It is interesting that the first group Villa organized was known as "The Sonny Boys." Although the members were all Mexican high school students, the band emulated the style of the American swing bands then in fashion—Benny Goodman, the Dorsey brothers, and others. It is important to note, however, that Villa was exposed to Mexican music too, since he also played with his father's group as well as others active in the Falfurrias area, where Villa was born and raised. Through these the young saxophonist became familiar with Mexican or Mexicanized styles and genres, which ranged from salon music to Latin pieces such as the *danzón* and bolero.

Villa's opportunity to enter the commercial recording market came in 1946, at almost the same time that the first Mexican-American recording companies appeared on the scene. Indeed, Ideal Records, for a time the most active of these early companies, owed much of its initial success to the popularity of Villa's own music. Yet, Villa's commercial debut was inauspicious at best. For one thing, by 1946 the "father" of modern *orquesta tejana* seems to have postponed his pursuit of an American musical ideal. Instead, in his first recordings Villa opted for the *ranchero* sound then associated with *conjunto* music. That is, he restricted himself mostly to the polkas and waltzes that had become a part of Texas-Mexican folk music since the late nineteenth century. More than that, however, the "folklorization" (or "*ranchero*-ization," we might say) of Villa's music points to the likelihood that Villa realized that only by adopting a *ranchero* style would he be able to reach a wide audience. But this is not surprising since in 1946 at least three-quarters of the Mexicans in Texas were members of a working class that subscribed overwhelmingly to the *ranchero* music that *conjuntos* and the Mexican mariachi had so thoroughly popularized.

In any case, when Villa approached Ideal, Paco Betancourt, one of the owners, objected because he felt the band was not "professional" enough. It was a minimal *orquesta*, consisting of alto saxophone, trumpet, piano-accordion, and rhythm section of electric guitar, contrabass, and drums. Consonant with its *ranchero* orientation, the group featured simple melodies, with unsophisticated harmonies. Indeed, it was the generally unpolished sound of the *orquesta* that prompted Betancourt to object. In the end, however, Villa prevailed, and at his own expense Ideal released two 78 RPM sides: "Porque te ries," a *vals*, and "Las Delicias Polka." According to Armando Marroquín, Ideal's other owner, here is what happened: "So then the record came out—Boy! About a month after Betancourt started distributing it, he called me and said, 'Say, tell him to record some more.' They were asking for it in bunches. It was

like a *conjunto*; it wasn't even an *orquesta* yet. . . . There were only
five or six—real small, *ranchero*-like" (personal interview, the author's
translation).

With this first recording, Villa's position in Texas-Mexican music
was assured; but Marroquín's statement on the group's *ranchero* quality
and its similarity to the *conjunto* is provocative. It confirms the link between *orquesta* and *conjunto*, a link made possible by the *ranchero* sound
that all *conjuntos* shared and that many *orquestas*, including that of Beto
Villa, were beginning to incorporate into their repertories. This brings up
an important point: . . . it was the *ranchero* sound complex that served as
the common denominator between the two ensembles, although in other
critical features they did differ—and sharply, both in style and social acceptance. We may be certain that Villa never lost sight of the *ranchero*,
ethnic origins of his music. This is clearly demonstrated, for example, in
his willingness to collaborate with none other than Narciso Martínez on
several recordings. Especially fruitful was their recording of "Rosita
Vals," an immensely popular tune whose success Ideal was never able to
duplicate.

Yet, it soon became obvious that, despite his successes with Martínez,
Villa was hardly interested in becoming permanently associated with
conjunto music. In fact, by 1949 he had decided on a drastic change. First,
he weeded out the "folk" musicians—those who had no formal training—
from his fledgling *orquesta*. Raymundo Treviño, a long-time associate of
Villa's, recalled what happened: "Those of us who could not read music—we were fired" (personal interview). Second, as is evident from the
post-1949 recordings, he began to deemphasize the *ranchero* sound
(though not to abandon it altogether) in favor of more cosmopolitan styles
that would amalgamate American, Mexican, and more generalized Latin
genres. In short, Villa was ready to return to his first love—the big American band sound, though he aimed to retain a Latin flavor as well, including the indispensable *ranchero* style. But above all, . . . Villa was striving
for a combination of styles that would mediate the contradictions between
the ethnic nature of his audience, which was inescapably tied to the *ranchero* roots that the *conjunto* epitomized, and the class aspirations of that
same audience—aspirations that aimed at cutting all links with *conjunto*
music and the "low-class" life it symbolized. . . .

The concept of *lo ranchero* has been firmly linked historically to the
ideology of romantic nationalism, or *mexicanismo*. . . . To grasp the
concept's significance in *tejano* (as well as Mexican) culture, we need,
first, to understand that the bulk of Mexican society has traditionally been
folk and agrarian, and only in recent times has it moved forward with
"modernization."[21] Second, ever since romantic nationalism first made

its appearance in Mexico (after the expulsion of the French), it has been endemic among Mexicans, manifesting itself in numerous facets of national life. Particularly germane for this discussion is the heavy commercialization since the 1930s of some of the symbols of that nationalism, as capitalists began to convert them into profitable mass commodities, principally through radio and film. It was, in fact, in the 1930s that the *ranchero* label was first attached to the Mexican *canción*.[22] Moreover, it is evident that such labeling was a conscious effort by commercial promoters to capitalize on the ideology of romantic nationalism.[23]

The symbols . . . belong to the vast collective consciousness that is Mexico's cultural heritage, symbols that have been selectively chosen for exaltation as representative of the glory of Mexico's history and culture. A number of these symbols have long enjoyed currency—for example, the Virgin of Guadalupe and the familiar Aztec warrior—but two encompass the concept of *lo ranchero* especially well, although they have become somewhat stereotyped. These are the *charro/vaquero* figure, which symbolizes the arrogant manliness (machismo) of the Mexican male, and the person of the campesino, which signifies the humble but perseverant spirit of that same Mexican.

These last two have been singled out for intensive exploitation in both music and film (often simultaneously) since the 1930s.[24] As a result of this commercial exposure, the twin symbols of the *charro* and campesino have succeeded admirably in imparting to the concept of *lo ranchero* its visual substance. The one's dauntless machismo and penchant for action coexists with the other's stoicism and humility, which actually border on inertia and diffidence. But this juxtaposition creates tension, as the two symbols, representing opposite qualities, pull in different directions. In fact, they threaten the integrity of the concept itself. But this is precisely what Victor Turner as suggested about "root metaphors," which our symbols clearly are. Attached to concepts that are "linked analogically to the basic problems of an epoch," they are subject to great ambiguity and contradiction. Such is the case with *lo ranchero* and its symbols, especially among Mexicans in the United States, where the contradictions are painfully apparent.[25]

On this side of the border the ambiguities attached to *lo ranchero* are compounded by the pressures for assimilation and conformity. For example, to espouse *lo ranchero*, as many Chicanos do through their advocacy of *música ranchera*, is to overvalue their Mexican "roots": to ennoble the culture of pastoral, agrarian life, which is presumed unspoiled by social snobbery. Yet, this mystified vision can quickly turn into disillusion when jarred by the reality of modern life, especially in the United States, where the campesino (the sleeping man with the wide-brimmed sombrero) is a stereotype for fatalism and laziness. Thus, to the "progressive" Mexican American the negative side of *lo ranchero* is never completely hidden. It lies ready to spring into consciousness to transform nostalgia into rejection, for the romanticized *rancho* also happens to harbor the *arrancherado*—the "low-class," coarse, excessively Mexicanized peon who cannot possibly appreciate the subtleties of modern, civilized life. There is an apt folk expression that captures the acculturated Mexican-American's indignations: "México recoge a tu gente" (Mexico, reclaim your people). An appeal is made in this well-worn refrain for Mexico to reclaim its vagabonds, who are a source of embarrassment to the "respectable" Mexican American.

Yet, despite the paradox, if there is one encompassing musical symbol among Texas-Mexicans, it is that conveyed by *música ranchera* (as is true among Mexicans generally, for that matter). A sound that spans several styles, *música ranchera* compresses a wide range of feelings and attitudes into a single esthetic moment. People immediately recognize a *ranchero* sound, whether it be interpreted by a *conjunto*, *orquesta*, or any other group, although it is true that some types of ensemble are considered more "naturally" *ranchero* than others—for example, the *conjunto* and the mariachi. But invariably, the music stirs vaguely defined but deeply experienced feelings of *mexicanismo*—or, in other words, romantic nationalism.

Thus, *ranchera* music has always been an integral part of Texas-Mexican musical consciousness, even among the upwardly mobile urbanites. That fact was never lost on Beto Villa and other *orquesta* musicians. Consequently, even in the immediate postwar years, a *ranchero* style was cultivated by all but the most Americanized (i.e., culturally assimilated) *orquestas*. As one *orquesta* musician put it, "I think we have always included rancheras because it goes back to our ancestors and the type of music they liked and we listened to when we were little." And, as Armando Marroquín observed in discussing Beto Villa's popularity: "What helped Beto Villa was that he had everything—*ranchero* and 'high class.' "

But the negative side of *lo ranchero* was not lost on *orquestas* either, and it helps explain why *orquesta* musicians were so caught up in what one of them called *lo moderno*—the modern, which on closer examination turns out to be a code phrase for the assimilation of middle-class elements, not only from American bands, but from similarly situated groups in Mexico. Thus, in comparing *conjunto* and *orquesta* music, one prominent musician observed that while *conjunto* was the music of the farmworker, "the so-called upper crust demanded big bands and sophisticated music"—i.e., foxtrots, boleros, etc.

However, the *orquesta tejana* was also powerfully affected by developments in *conjunto* music, and it was never able to free itself completely from the latter's influence. Indeed, one of the problems we face in analyzing *orquesta* as a cultural expression its extreme stylistic fluctuations—its many faces, as it were. To a far greater extent than any of the other musics that influenced it, *orquesta tejana* has always been a multidimensional musical expression, as even a cursory listening of the recordings made since the 1940s will reveal. Marroquín's comments on Beto Villa's oscillation between *ranchero* and "high class" should make it clear that, unlike *conjunto*, which adhered to a strongly homogeneous style, *orquesta* encompassed a broad spectrum of styles, only one of which, properly speaking, stamped the "*tejana*" label on it.

Thus, most *orquestas* attempted to amalgamate any number of disparate types of music, including those associated with the big American dance bands (e.g., foxtrots, swings, etc.), Mexican and Latin American dance bands (boleros, *danzones*, mambos), and, of course, the *ranchero*, regional style of the *conjunto*. Within this spectrum of styles and genres there were some *orquestas*—particularly the most culturally assimilated and middle-class oriented—that emphasized cosmopolitan music. They played, in the words of working-class *tejanos*, "*música mas jaitona*" (more high-toned music). However, the most commercially popular were those that, like Beto Villa's, succeeded in accommodating both the *ranchero* and the "sophisticated," or "high class."

Villa's success encouraged a spate of imitators, though, again, some pursued a more cosmopolitan style than others. Among the more "*jaitón*" *orquestas* was that of Balde González, the blind singer-pianist from Victoria, Texas. A highly acclaimed performer in the early 1950s, González, much more than Villa, attempted to project a smooth, sophisticated sound, one that blended American foxtrots with romantic boleros. In fact, a measure of González's assimilation of American musical ideas (tempered, nonetheless, by the limitations of his ethnic background) was his habit of adapting Mexican vocals to American rhythms, especially the foxtrot.

A more *ranchero* approach was taken by González's most popular successor in the rapidly expanding *orquesta* music market—singer-saxophonist Isidro López, from Corpus Christi. Born in 1933, López learned to play alto saxophone and clarinet in high school, as many other *orquesta* musicians did. In the meantime he was gaining experience by playing with various local groups. A significant development in López's career was his association with Narciso Martínez. For a time in the early 1950s he accompanied the latter on some of his tours around the state. This experience convinced López that, at bottom, there has never been much difference between *orquesta* and *conjunto*. However, López also played for Balde González shortly before he organized his own *orquesta* (in 1955), and that association did leave its influence on his subsequent style.

In any case, although Isidro López clearly belongs in the *orquesta* tradition, he was acutely aware that the future of *orquesta tejana* music lay with the traditional working class, and its strong affiliation with the *norteño* variety of Mexican culture. Thus, although he did incorporate a variety of styles. López nevertheless leaned heavily toward the *ranchero* sound—one that he claims combined elements from both *conjunto* and mariachi. He labeled it *texachi*, López's own neologism, derived from the terms "Texas" and "mariachi." The synthesis worked; adapting the *canción ranchera* to the idiosyncrasies of the *orquesta*, López surpassed all his competitors in public appeal from the mid-1950s until 1965, when two new *orquestas* entered the picture: Little Joe (Hernández) and the Latinaires, and Sunny (Ozuna) and the Sunliners.

In a retrospective assessment it is clear that Isidro López was the man most responsible for setting in motion the final shift of *orquesta* music toward that of *conjunto*. However, that shift did not proceed in an uninterrupted sweep—an indication of the conflicting currents that determined the course of *orquesta* music. Thus, Little Joe, who most personifies the next phase of *orquesta tejana*, and Sunny Ozuna, who also ranks among the leading personalities, began their careers in pursuit of the exploding rock-and-roll market of the late 1950s. Like many of the younger—and usually better educated—*tejano* musicians, Little Joe and Sunny were caught up in the rock-and-roll wave that swept the United States at the end of the 1950s. This was a time when, according to one *orquesta* musician, "*mexicano* wasn't in"—when young musicians shunned not only *conjunto* but even the music of a Beto Villa and Isidro López. They preferred to emulate American rock-and-roll groups. Little Joe and Sunny were no exceptions.

Clearly, what was taking place among the Mexicans in Texas was the inexorable assimilation of American culture. . . .[26] The post-depression babies—the first generation of Mexicans to enjoy a measurable upgrading in their education—were responding to the pressures of cultural assimilation, even if the barriers that effectively prevented them from complete integration into American society (i.e., through "primary" associations achievable principally through intermarriage) remained firmly in place. With cultural assimilation came a desire to adopt the life-styles of American mass society. What Rubel observed about upwardly mobile *tejanos* in South Texas who had fought in World War II and Korea certainly applied to an increasing number of *tejanos* born after the depression. These also aspired "toward life goals which include[d] social equality with Anglos."[27] They felt entitled to "clean" occupations, "high school and college education, and possession of such other status markers as automobiles, refrigerators, television sets."[28] In short, they demanded the amenities of middle-class citizenship. Lastly, among the symbols that signified upward mobility was music—specifically music that approximated the ideal of mainstream American life.

Thus—to discuss his rise to prominence first—Little Joe's first recording was a rock tune with the title "Safari." This was followed by a number of sporadic efforts throughout Little Joe's career (and that of his brother, Johnny) to break into the "top forty" music charts. That proved to be an impossible task, and by 1965, perhaps discouraged by his failure, Little Joe finally decided to try his fortune on the *tejano* music circuit. He signed on with Sarape Records, a small label from Dallas, which produced an album titled "Amor Bonito" in 1965. It was a phenomenal success, catapulting Little Joe and the Latinaires into the forefront of *orquesta tejana* music. As trumpetist Tony Guerrero, who later was to become a mainstay in Little Joe's *orquesta*, recalled (personal interview), "I was in California when I heard about this new band out of Texas that was called Little Joe and the Latinaires, and a promoter told me, 'These guys are kicking Isidro López's ass all over the place.'"

Of the utmost significance, however, was the sound Little Joe had fashioned. It was thoroughly *ranchero*, down to the familiar duet singing, in parallel thirds, that became the hallmark of Little Joe and his brother, Johnny. Clearly, "Amor Bonito" signaled Little Joe's newfound interest in *tejano* music, but more than that, it marked the revival of *ranchero* music among the younger generation of Texas-Mexicans. In short, Little Joe's new style symbolized the final step in the "*ranchero*-ization" of *orquesta* music. Thereafter, despite *orquestas*' conspicuous forays into non-*ranchero* music (e.g., the always popular Mexican bolero), the staple genre, now played in what became *the* typical *tejano* style, was the *canción ranchera*, sung solo or duet and backed by increasingly standardized obbligatos from the horn section. This was, or course, the very same *canción* set to the tempo di polka (and sometimes waltz) that had earlier become the hallmark of the *conjunto* style. After 1965, then, with the exception of a few local *jaitón orquestas*, the convergence of *orquesta* and *conjunto* was all but an accomplished fact.

Sunny Ozuna deserves our attention because, first, for a fleeting instant in 1963 the former carhop did manage to break into the "top forty" charts with a rhythm-and-blues tune titled "Talk to Me." It was, however, a short-lived glory, as Ozuna quickly faded from the pop music scene. Second, although Ozuna soon discovered that his only real alternative was to pursue a career in the *orquesta tejana* field, to this day, as his manager once revealed to me, Sunny and the Sunliners have always tried to "cater to a more middle-class crowd"—that is, to those *tejanos* who think of themselves as a cut above the common workers. Like many other *orquestas*, Ozuna has done this by consciously maintaining a delicate balance between *ranchero* and "high class" (to recall Marroquín's statements about Beto Villa). Ozuna has been successful: like Little Joe he has maintained a visible presence in *tejano* music since the mid-1960s.

As the comments of Ozuna's manager indicate . . . there have been two discernable (and contradicting) trends in *orquesta tejana* music since its inception. One is obviously *ranchero* and heavily influenced by the *conjunto* style. The other is difficult to classify neatly, since it has always aimed at amalgamating a number of disparate styles. We may, however, label it collectively as "sophisticated," "cosmopolitan," or "modern." Or, we may follow the native, working-class usage and call it "high class" or "*jaitón*"—terms . . . heard many times . . . in Texas in the 1950s. In either case, some *orquestas* have not hesitated to shift back and forth between *ranchero* and *jaitón*. Moreover, the consensus among initiated laypersons and musicians is that the distinguishing characteristic between *ranchero* and non-*ranchero* is harmonic complexity and, to a lesser extent, genre selection.

For example, a *canción* set in tempo di polka and arranged with relatively simple harmony—say, a I-IV-V-I (e.g., C-F-G^7-C) chord progression—is unequivocally *ranchera*, especially if, as is often the case, certain preestablished obbligato licks are used, as in the following phrase with the eight-sixteenth-note figure:

On the other hand, the same *canción* may be substantially transformed by elaborating on the harmony: adding seventh and altered chords (e.g., Cmaj^7-Fmaj^7-G^9-C^{6+9}), alternating keys, introducing syncopation, and so on. The resulting sound would then be considered "sophisticated," rather than *ranchero*, depending on the degree of complexity. In sum, the more harmonic and rhythmic complexity introduced, the more "modern" the style is judged to be. Conversely, the simpler the harmony, rhythm, and obbligato backgrounds, the more a piece falls in the *ranchero* category.

The first of the *ranchero orquestas* was undoubtedly that of Isidro López, followed by those of Augustín Ramírez, Freddie Martínez, and Joe Bravo, to name three of the most popular to this day.

On other other hand, *orquestas* such as Sunny and the Sunliners, Latin Breed, and Jimmy Edwards's have chosen to deemphasize the *ranchero* mode, incorporating more diverse genres, including rhythm and blues and a host of others derived from Afro-Hispanic traditions (e.g., salsa). At the same time even when they perform the *canción ranchera*, the latter groups are easily distinguishable from the former by their use of the "sophisticated" elements.

One more point needs to be brought out in connection with the stylistic variation within *orquestas tejanas*. Since the mid-1960s, when the bulk of them committed themselves to working-class audiences, they have had to limit their range of musical expression, insofar as they have become sensitive to the dictates of their new constituency (not to mention their economic survival). This means that experimentally minded *orquestas* must thread a thin needle, indeed. For if they exceed the stylistic limits imposed on them by working-class tastes, then they threaten to dissolve the slender threads that link them to *tejano* musical culture. This they cannot afford to do, since, as one *orquesta* musician put it, "We can't afford to experiment too much anymore. The *orquesta* crowd is getting smaller and smaller. We're squeezed in between the *conjuntos* and American music." Indeed, some *conjunto* musicians have predicted, with more than a trace of satisfaction, the imminent demise of *orquesta* music.

Predictions notwithstanding, *orquesta* is anything but dead. On the contrary, while it has faced adverse times, it has continued to hold its own through the years. In fact, beginning in the early 1970s the *orquesta tejana* witnessed a major resurgence and burst of innovation that has been unrivaled before or after. It is probably not premature, then, to label the 1970s as the "golden age" of *orquesta tejana* music. With the appearance in 1973 of an album by Little Joe y la Familia (the Latinaires renamed), titled "Para la Gente," an active new phase was ushered in. A score of productions by other *orquestas* followed in quick succession, each attempting to match La Familia's rather daring experiments, which included the addition of violins (sometimes a melotron), dense harmonies, and a constant assault on the basic polka beat of the *canción ranchera*. The experiments worked commercially because in the midst of the experimentation the basic *ranchero* sound was preserved.

More importantly, however, the experiments worked because *orquestas* had gained substantial support among a generation of high school and college students who were growing up in the shadow of the Chicano power movement and who were at that time reexamining their whole ethnic identity. These students were ripe for artistic expressions that reflected their newfound pride in things Chicano. *Orquestas* capitalized on this ethnic revivalism, of course. Indeed, they were themselves caught up in it. Little Joe's decision to change the name of his group from Latinaires to La Familia (in 1970) is a perfect case in point. Clearly, as Little Joe has many times demonstrated, this was a political decision, intended to identify his group with the tide of *chicanismo* that was surging among the younger generation.[29] With this aim in mind, what better label to link himself with the Chicano movement than the strongly evocative "La Familia"? Lastly, it is evident that much more than *conjunto* music (which perhaps smacked too much of the cotton sack), *orquesta* admirably fulfilled the esthetic preferences of the young Chicanos.[30]

Since about 1978 *orquesta* music has witnessed considerable stylistic retrenchment, as well as a decline—though *not* a demise—in its popularity. But, as one *orquesta* musician put it, "*Conjunto* music has its epochs, we have ours. We'll come back." Renamed *La onda chicana* (The Chicano wave), it has held its ground into the 1980s, thanks largely to the efforts of the indefatigable Little Joe Hernández. . . .

An Interpretive Summary

Tejano society experienced important—if not dramatic—socioeconomic changes during World War II. Indeed, the war ought to be considered a threshold for Texas-Mexican society. This was a period when the process of urbanization was greatly accelerated, when the native born for the first time outnumbered the immigrants, and when *tejanos* began to be absorbed into the American political economy in occupations that offered some upward mobility.[31] In addition, thousands of young men fought in the war, and they returned to civilian society with a new sense of purpose that contributed to the redefinition of citizenship, not only for them but for many other Mexican Americans as well.[32] In sum, these *tejanos* demanded—with some success—equal treatment in housing, education, employment, and so forth. But success had its ramifications for the structure of *tejano* society. Among other things, homogeneity of class gave way to differentiation, and its attendant distinctions (e.g., "clean" vs. "dirty" occupations). In short, the war changed the makeup of *tejano* society in an irrevocable way, presenting it with a set of challenges it had never before faced.

Perhaps the most far-reaching consequence of the changed nature of Texas-Mexican society was the increasing disparity in cultural assimilation between the middle and working classes, a disparity that was reflected in the undeclared rift that developed between them. For example,

even the old ethnic solidarity was called into question by upwardly mobile *tejanos* who were caught up in the assimilation of American middle-
class ideology.[33] It is important to note, however, that despite the internal
changes in *tejano* society that emerged during World War II, the formidable ethnic boundary that separated *tejano* and Anglo remained, posing
a nearly insurmountable obstacle against the complete structural (i.e.,
marital) assimilation of *tejanos* into Anglo-American society.

It was against this backdrop of *internal* socioeconomic differentiation and *external* ethnic segregation that *orquesta* and *conjunto* were cast.
Here it is worth recalling James Ackerman's comments on style formation as a response to the challenges of an age. These remarks are eminently applicable to the emergence of *conjunto* and *orquesta*. For what
tejano society witnessed was a fundamental shakeup of its infrastructural
composition, along with a high degree of social upheaval. . . . This social
upheaval could not be negotiated without profound cultural dislocation.
This dislocation, expressible in terms of social uncertainty and conflict,
necessitated solutions. This is where *conjunto* and *orquesta* fulfilled
their design: they were cultural solutions to infrastructurally generated
problems.

In the case of *conjunto*, we can explain its emergence in this way: In
the face of an unsympathetic middle class that saw the working class (both
native and immigrant) as an impediment to the acceptance of Mexicans
into American society because of its alleged "backwardness," the less-
acculturated workers felt obligated to respond in kind and to elaborate
cultural strategies in their defense. These strategies were intended to defend and also legitimize working-class existence and cultural sovereignty.
Thus, if upwardly mobile *tejanos* were critical of working-class life-styles,
then the latter countered with its own ridicule. Middle-class oriented
people were considered *agringados* (gringoized Mexicans), or worse,
agabachados, an even more caustic epithet for Mexicans who were seen
by traditional (usually) working-class people as snobs who pretended to
be what they were not. Worst, in so doing they not only demeaned themselves but also committed the contemptible act of denying their true cultural heritage—their *mexicanismo*.

Thus, working-class *tejanos*, convinced that only they and their kind
were true *mexicanos*, clung ever more tenaciously to their culture.
"Soy puro mexicano" (I am a real Mexican) was a popular phrase that
working-class *tejanos* certainly subscribed to. Underlying the working
class's displeasure with *agringado tejanos* was its unarticulated convic-
tion that the latter aimed to undermine long-standing Mexican traditions
that all *tejanos* were heir to (not without reason; cf. Taylor), and that they
had a duty to defend.[34] It mattered not that many of those traditions were

being seriously eroded by American cultural hegemony, or that many were in fact yielding to social change. To the working class they were immutable and imparted continuity to their threatened system of cultural values. . . .

It was out of this clash between change and continuity, between cultural assimilation and ethnic resistance, and between middle- and working-class ideology that *conjunto* music derived its cultural energy and symbolic power. By balancing innovation with tradition—by being subjected to changes strictly at the hands of working-class artists—*conjunto* music, as a symbolic expression, negotiated through esthetic means the conflicts and uncertainties that its constituency was experiencing in the socioeconomic sphere. In sum, the creation of this unique artistic expression was a symbolic solution to the conflicts. Lastly, once the original conflict between proletarians and their middle-class antagonists was mediated musically—that is, once *conjunto* music was seen as consummated—further innovation came to a halt. In short, as an esthetically satisfying expression, reflective of working-class sentiments, *conjunto* music was considered "perfected" by its practitioners. Thus, new accretions, such as the introduction of the piano-accordion, for example, were seen as superfluous and detracting from the singular beauty of the music.

A similar case can be made for *orquesta*. Just as the stylistic maturation of *conjunto* signified a working-class response to the challenges posed to it by the changing conditions of its existence, so did *orquesta* likewise correspond to the Texas-Mexican middle class's search for an appropriate expressive (artistic) response to its own emergence as an ideological bloc in *tejano* society. On the one hand, *orquesta*—at least in its first phase, up until 1965—was clearly an alternative mode of artistic expression to *conjunto*. . . . The statements of Moy and Delia Pineda, two veteran *orquesta* musicians, perhaps sum up the relationship between *orquesta* and the middle class—even today, when *orquesta* and *conjunto* are so much closer in form and substance. The following is an excerpt from a conversation the author had with them:

> *Peña*: Do *conjunto* and *orquesta* cater to the same people?
>
> *M. Pineda*: No, they're both different. *La gente que le gusta la orquesta* (people who like *orquesta*), they like something a little more sophisticated.
>
> *Peña*: Well, do you think class might have something to do with it?
>
> *M. Pineda*: There you go . . .
>
> *D. Pineda*: Yes, definitely.

Yet, the unavoidable reality of interethnic conflict and the subordination of Mexicans generally—especially before the civil rights gains of the 1960s—made middle-class status for Texas-Mexicans a rather precarious proposition.[35] Quite simply, the upwardly mobile *tejanos* were caught on the horns of a dilemma. On the one hand they aspired to be American, though Anglo society did not welcome them into its midst.[36] On the other hand, a retreat to the cultural position of the traditional proletarian class was out of the question, because the middle class's ideology, which was shaped, paradoxically, by American middle-class institutions such as the schools, clashed at many points with the ethnic culture of traditional *tejano* society. The middle class's position can be summed up succinctly: socially and culturally it lived in a state of contradiction.

Musically, this state of contradiction was mediated—and reflected—by *orquesta*'s extreme variations in style. For the sake of analysis, these variations may be reduced conceptually to simple bimusicality, with American styles on one side and Latin ones on the other. Moreover, the bimusicality was an extension of middle-class *tejanos*' increasing biculturalism, a biculturalism that straddled the interethnic boundary between Mexican and Anglo life experiences (see Paredes, 1968, on bicultural conflict in joking behavior). Beyond bimusicality there was also pervasive bilingualism and ambiguous attitudes about family, religion, and traditions generally—all a commentary on the contradictory position of the middle class. (Ambiguity crept into working-class life as well, but with far less unsettling results.) In short, the upwardly mobile *tejano* was caught in a bicultural bind that promoted considerable social stress. The stylistic flip-flopping *orquestas* engaged in—their struggle to mediate the differences between the Mexican and traditional vs. the American and "modern"—was a manifestation of that stress.

In summary, *orquesta* music represented a symbolic response by the middle class to the challenge of socioeconomic disparity and the pressures of cultural assimilation. This challenge was fraught with contradictions that were reflected in the music itself. Given these contradictions, middle-class *tejanos* in time came to respond with what was probably the only alternative available to them. Thus, preaching assimilation but frustrated in their attempts to gain full acceptance in the Anglo's world, they betrayed their own ideology by reverting to ethnic resistance. The musico-symbolic dimensions of this contradiction were clearly illustrated by Moy Pineda. Speaking of certain "elite" dances he played for, Pineda commented that "they want to show off by getting a big orchestra, and they have their daughters presented to society. It's supposed to be very exclusive. They want that big band, and we got those fancy tuxedos; but the music—the first hour we do, man, special arrangements ["Stardust,"

"Misty," etc.]—and nobody's dancing. But [after] about an hour—I take off with "Los Laureles," "El Abandonado" [*ranchero* tunes]. Ching! Everybody gets on the dance floor. . . . When they start drinking they go back to the roots."

In such ways have the bulk of middle-class *tejanos* attempted historically to validate their existence—by embracing selected aspects of American culture, while out of necessity retaining many of their antecedent symbols. As Pineda's statements attest, the middle-class Texas-Mexican has historically been bicultural, but not so much by choice as by default. And, in this betwixt-and-between position that the middle class has found itself, *orquesta* music has played its unique role by negotiating the contradiction between a frustrated assimilation, on the one hand, and a persistent ethnic allegiance, on the other. The musical solution has been: aspire for the *jaitón*, but keep the *ranchero* at hand. . . .

Notes

1. A preliminary assessment of *conjunto* music may be found in Manuel Peña, "The Emergence of *Conjunto* Music, 1935–1955," in *And Other Neighborly Names: Social Process and Cultural Image in Texas Folklore*, ed. Richard Bauman and Roger Abrahams (Austin: University of Texas Press, 1981), 280–99.

2. As used here, the terms "working class" (also "proletarians") and "middle class" have a specific meaning, derived in part from the writings of Eric O. Wright, "Class Boundaries in Advanced Capitalist Societies," *New Left Review* 98, no. 3 (1976): 41; and Nicos Poulantzas, "On Social Classes," *New Left Review* 78, no. 27 (1973): 54. Class is based on structural considerations: The working class is that sector which has no controlling access to the means of production, nor does it have any control over the labor power of others. It has only its own labor power to sell. Narrowly defined, the middle class shares attributes with both the capitalist (bourgeoisie) and the worker (e.g., managers who may not own a share of the means of production but who do control the labor power of others). However, in delineating the *tejano* middle class, I have also included the "labor aristocracy"—mainly white-collar workers—because ideologically they behaved much like the true middle class. This was a critical factor in the *orquesta-conjunto* nexus.

3. Quoted in Peter K. Etzkorn, *Music and Society: The Later Writings of Paul Honigsheim* (New York: John Wiley and Sons, 1973), 9.

4. James S. Ackerman, "A Theory of Style," *Journal of Aesthetics and Art Criticism* 20 (1962): 228.

5. Americo Paredes, *"With His Pistol in His Hand"* (Austin: University of Texas Press, 1958), 9ff.

6. Manuel Peña, *The Texas-Mexican Conjunto: History of a Working-Class Music* (Austin: University of Texas Press, 1985).

7. According to one *conjunto* musician's estimate, 80 percent of the modern *conjunto*'s repertory consists of *canciónes rancheras*, mostly played as *corridas*, i.e., in polka rhythm and tempo. The *canción* is occasionally performed in three-

quarter time (*valseada*) or, even less frequently, in six-eight time. On the other hand, prior to World War II *conjuntos* almost never performed vocal music. The reasons for this restriction had to do with social conventions. A combination of instrumental *and* vocal music was associated in the public mind with the disreputable atmosphere of the *cantina*. Thus, although accordion groups played in *cantinas* frequently, for "decent," that is, domestic, celebrations they were strictly prohibited from singing. The social upheaval ushered in by the war changed all that. See Peña, *Texas-Mexican Conjunto.*

8. One source of information on early accordion-*tambora* pairings is my father, who was born in 1895 and who clearly recalled the impression the two instruments made on him when he first noticed them around the turn of the century. He was raised in Salineño, a village on the Texas-Mexican border. Another source is the *San Antonio Express*, which occasionally featured articles on *tejano* dances where reference is made to the accordion and, in one, to the "beating of drums," though the label *tambora de rancho* is not specifically used (see June 18, 1881; August 3, 1890).

9. The LP cited is, of course, not the only source that illustrates the diffuse nature of accordion music to the 1920s. Chris Strachwitz of Arhoolie Records has in his possession over one hundred 78s that document the variety of early accordion music, at least as far back as the 1920s. To the author's knowledge no commercial recordings of accordion music were made prior to that period.

10. Thanks to Tom Kreneck of the Houston Public Library, the author has recently come upon a wealth of photographs dating back to 1915 that document this very point. The wild assortment of instruments found in these photographs is a graphic testimony to the variety of ensembles to be found in early Texas-Mexican society. Judging from the condition of instruments and the musicians' dress, it is obvious that many of these were of working-class origin.

11. Chris Strachwitz, jacket notes in *Texas-Mexican Border Music*, vol. 4 (Berkeley: Arhoolie Records, 1975).

12. Geronimo Baqueiro Foster, *La musica en el periodo independiente* (México, D.F.: Instituto Nacional de Bellas Artes, 1964), 546; Claes af Geijerstam, *Popular Music in Mexico* (Albuquerque: University of New Mexico Press, 1976), 83–84.

13. Otto Mayer-Serra, *Panorama de la musica mexicana* (México, D.F.: Fondo de Cultura Economica, 1941), 116ff; Baquiero Foster, *La musica en el periodo independiente*, 532.

14. Michael C. Meyer and William L. Sherman, *The Course of Mexican History* (New York: Oxford University Press, 1979), 466.

15. Baqueiro Foster, *La musica en el periodo independiente*, 546.

16. Gerard Behague, *Music in Latin America: An Introduction* (Englewood Cliffs, NJ: Prentice Hall, 1979), 100.

17. Strachwitz, jacket notes in *Texas-Mexican Border Music*.

18. Paul Taylor, *An American-Mexican Frontier* (Chapel Hill, NC: University of North Carolina Press, 1934), 245; brackets Taylor's.

19. This biographical sketch is derived in part from an interview that Linda Fregoso held with Villa in 1980. The author owes a special debt of gratitude to her for allowing him to share her information.

20. Peña, *The Texas-Mexican Conjunto.*

21. Charles C. Cumberland, *Mexico: The Struggle for Modernity* (London: Oxford University Press, 1968).

22. Juan Garrido, *Historia de la musica popular en Mexico* (México, D.F.: Editorial Contemporanees, 1974), 70.

23. Alex Saragoza, "Mexican Cinema in the United States, 1940–1952," in *History, Culture, and Society: Chicano Studies in the 1980s*, ed. Mario T. García et al. (Ypsilanti, MI: Bilingual Press, 1984).

24. Ibid.

25. Victor Turner, *Dramas, Fields, and Metaphors* (Ithaca, NY: Cornell University Press, 1974), 26.

26. Richard A. García, "The Mexican American Mind: A Product of the 1930s," in *History, Culture, and Society*.

27. Arthur Rubel, *Across the Tracks: Mexican Americans in a Texas City* (Austin: University of Texas Press, 1966), 12.

28. Ibid.

29. Joe Nick Patoski, "Little Joe," *Texas Monthly* (May 1978): 134–37; 211–14.

30. During three years that the author spent at the University of Texas at Austin (1977–1980), the Texas Union used to turn the tavern over to Chicano students every Thursday for "Chicano Night." Music for dancing was provided by a "disco" jockey. True to their designation, the events featured mostly "Chicano" music. More specifically, in accordance with what was a tacit consensus that a genuinely Chicano atmosphere prevail, *orquesta tejana* music was offered, de rigueur. In all the times that the author attended Chicano Night he does not recall hearing any *conjunto* music.

31. Robert G. Landolt, *The Mexican-American Workers of San Antonio, Texas* (New York: Arno Press, 1976); Douglas Foley et al., *From Peones to Politicos: Ethnic Relations in a South Texas Town* (Austin, TX: Center for Mexican-American Studies, University of Texas, Austin, 1977).

32. Leo Grebler, Joan Moore, and Ralph C. Guzmán have noted: "In our initial interviews throughout the Southwest, Mexican-Americans in the 30- to 50-year age class again and again referred to the new horizons opened up by the war itself and by postwar educational benefits. . . . Service abroad exposed Mexican-Americans to other peoples and cultures. . . . Thus, many Mexican-American veterans returned with a new sense of opportunities." See Leo Grebler, Joan Moore, and Ralph C. Guzmán, *The Mexican-American People: The Nation's Second Largest Minority* (New York: Free Press, 1970), 201.

33. Rubel, *Across the Tracks*; Taylor, *An American-Mexican Frontier*; William Madsen, *The Mexican-Americans of South Texas* (New York: Holt, Rinehart and Winston, 1964).

34. José Limón, "*Agringado* Joking in Texas-Mexican Society: Folklore and Differential Identity," in *New Directions in Chicano Scholarship*, ed. Ricardo Romo and Raymund Paredes (La Jolla: University of California at San Diego), 33–50.

35. Mario Barrera, *Race and Class in the Southwest* (Notre Dame, IN: University of Notre Dame Press, 1979).

36. This brings to mind the words of an Americanized Texas-Mexican friend who had been brought up on the Anglo side of our town in South Texas, and who, as a high school student, began to gravitate toward Mexican social circles and to reexamine his ethnic allegiance. In a poignant recognition of his dilemma, he once told the author, "I don't know where I belong anymore, but I can't ride the fence much longer." He eventually married a Mexican-American woman.

8

Sin Fronteras?: Chicanos, Mexican Americans, and the Emergence of the Contemporary Mexican Immigration Debate, 1968–1978

Although most people conversant in borderlands history recognize the 1960s as a period marked by the emergence of a series of intense political struggles that later became known as the Chicano movement, few associate the era with the resurgence of an similarly intense debate over Mexican immigration to the United States. David Gutiérrez, an historian at the University of California, San Diego, explores the relationship of the immigration controversy to the Chicano movement and the general Mexican-American civil rights campaign. Departing from much of the extant scholarship on the period, he argues that the reemergence of the immigration debate in the 1960s played a key role in the evolution of the movement. Indeed, Gutiérrez advances the thesis that the failure of Chicano activists to recognize and acknowledge the significance of large numbers of Mexican nationals in "Chicano" communities helped to expose serious flaws in their thinking on the issues of Mexican-American ethnicity and national identity and contributed to the fracturing and eventual dissolution of their political and cultural campaigns.

In October 1977, more than two thousand individuals assembled in San Antonio, Texas, for the First National Chicano/Latino Conference on Immigration and Public Policy. They represented a broad spectrum of Mexican-American and other Hispanic interests ranging from community groups and elected officials to militant ethnic separatist and Marxist

From the *Journal of American Ethnic History* 10, no. 4 (Summer 1991): 5–37. Reprinted by permission of the *Journal of American Ethnic History*.

organizations.[1] Called in response to President Jimmy Carter's recently announced immigration reform legislation, the conference provided dramatic evidence of the extent to which the immigration controversy had become a major civil rights issue in the 1970s. In three days of meetings, the conference participants passed a series of unanimous resolutions condemning the "Carter Plan" as discriminatory against both citizens and aliens of Latin descent. With Mexican-American organizations leading the way, the delegates specifically criticized the administration's call for the imposition of legal sanctions against habitual employers of illegal aliens, and lambasted other aspects of the proposal, including the provisions for extending a limited amnesty to hundreds of thousands of undocumented aliens already in the United States.[2]

The unanimous negative response to the Carter Plan by Mexican-American community groups, elected officials, and virtually every major national civil rights and political advocacy organization was a dramatic departure from traditional Mexican-American positions on the immigration issue. Indeed, dating from the first mass migrations of Mexicans into the United States after the turn of the century, most Mexican-American political activists and organizations had consistently demanded many of the same reforms that they now rejected. Accepting the premise that immigrants undermined the life chances of American citizens by competing with them for employment, depressing wages, and retarding their assimilation into the American social and cultural mainstream, most Mexican-American advocates traditionally had demanded that immigration from Mexico be tightly regulated, even though most Mexican Americans claimed descent from immigrants who had come north from Mexico.

Given this long history of restrictionist sentiment, the overwhelmingly negative Mexican-American response to the Carter Plan in 1977 was truly remarkable. In other ways, however, the united Mexican-American opposition to the government's immigration reform proposals was a logical outgrowth of the social ferment that transformed ethnic politics in the United States in the 1960s and 1970s. After a period of relative quiescence in the early 1960s, Mexican immigration reemerged as a national political issue at the same time that politically active Mexican Americans became embroiled in a complex debate over their cultural and ethnic identity. Paralleling developments in the black civil rights and the antiwar movements of the era, Mexican Americans also intensified their demands for equal rights in a series of disparate social protests that became known collectively as the "Chicano movement." Mexican-American activists—particularly students and youth—built a political campaign characterized by proclamations of cultural pride, ethnic solidarity, and a willingness to employ confrontational political tactics.

Though many Mexican Americans were alienated by the Chicano militants' ideology and rhetoric, the young activists helped change the political landscape by raising demands for social justice in aggressive new terms and drawing attention to the nation's second-largest minority group. In the process, Chicano militants also helped stimulate a far-reaching debate among Mexican Americans over complex issues concerning their own sense of ethnic identity, the nature of Mexican-American (or, as they termed it, "Chicano") culture in the United States, and the logic, potential efficacy, and desirability of a strident, ethnically based politics for the Mexican-American minority at large.

The immigration issue coincidentally reemerged after 1970 at the same time that Mexican-American and Chicano activists argued over the degree to which their ethnicity should be emphasized in Mexican Americans' political and social future in the United States. In this period, as had been true in previous periods when the immigration controversy intensified, many Mexican-American advocates initially supported the government's restrictionist reform proposals. However, as increasing numbers of young Mexican Americans began to reassess the significance of the ethnic heritage for their own sense of identity, they eventually began to develop new attitudes about the many hundreds of thousands of Mexican immigrants—and their children—who constituted such a large percentage of the total Mexican-origin population of the United States.[3] By the mid-1970s this broad-based process of reassessment had contributed to the emergence of a remarkable new consensus on the immigration controversy among Mexican-American and Chicano political activists. Indeed, by the late 1970s, most major Mexican-American and Chicano activists and civil rights organizations had reversed their traditional positions and now actively supported the civil and human rights of Mexican immigrants in the United States, a stance they maintained well into the 1980s. This essay is an exploration of the complex interplay between ethnic protest and immigration politics that resulted in this unprecedented realignment of Mexican-American and Chicano opinion on the Mexican immigration controversy in the 1960s and 1970s.

Mexican Americans have long held ambivalent attitudes about Mexican immigration. While strong historical, cultural, and kinship ties undeniably bound Mexican Americans to native-born Mexicans, some Mexican Americans expressed concern about these immigrants as early as the mid-nineteenth century.[4] Historically, much of this concern has been based upon Mexican Americans' belief that Mexican immigrants undercut their already tenuous socioeconomic position in the United States by depressing wages, competing for employment, housing, and social services, and reinforcing negative stereotypes about "Mexicans" among Anglo-

Americans. In addition, class stratification, regional attachments, and subtle differences in customs and language usage also tended to divide U.S.-born Mexican Americans from recent immigrants from Mexico.

Most Mexican-American political organizations and activists maintained an essentially negative outlook on Mexican immigration throughout the era of the Bracero Program, which ran from 1942 to 1964. Implemented in August 1942 as an emergency program designed to offset labor shortages caused by World War II, the Bracero Program provided for the temporary importation of thousands of Mexican agricultural and railroad laborers to work under contract in the United States. Although intended as a temporary wartime measure, the program was renewed several times in the 1940s and 1950s. During the peak years of the 1950s, more than 437,000 Mexicans worked under bracero contracts in the United States each year, primarily in large-scale corporate agriculture in the West.[5]

Critics of the program, which included a loose coalition of labor unions, religious organizations, Mexican-American groups, and the liberal wing of the Democratic Party, charged that the foreign labor program adversely affected the wages of citizen workers and that it encouraged the mass migration of Mexican workers who surreptitiously entered the country seeking employment. These groups argued that employers of Mexican workers often sought to circumvent the Bracero Program's regulations concerning wages, housing, and work conditions by hiring unauthorized Mexican workers, and that the presence of this large shadow labor force severely depressed agricultural wages and undermined American citizens' attempts to organize and bargain collectively.

The United States Immigration and Naturalization Service (INS) statistics on the apprehension of "deportable aliens" in the late 1940s and 1950s seemed to corroborate many of the critics' assertions. The INS reported rapid increases in the number of Mexican "wetbacks" (a derisive term used to describe aliens who purportedly waded across the Rio Grande) apprehended in each of the first twelve years of the Bracero Program. Arrests peaked in the period 1950–1955, when an average of 614,000 undocumented aliens were apprehended annually. These enforcement efforts gained national publicity during "Operation Wetback" in 1954, when the INS claimed to have apprehended nearly 1.1 million Mexican nationals.[6]

Throughout the life of the Bracero Program, Mexican-American groups such as the League of United Latin American Citizens (LULAC) and the American G.I. Forum in Texas, and the Community Service Organization (CSO) and the Mexican-American Political Association (MAPA) in California, and respected Mexican-American leaders such as George I. Sánchez of the University of Texas and Ernesto Galarza of the

National Agricultural Workers' Union argued that sanctioned and unsanctioned Mexican labor migration undermined their efforts to achieve economic and political justice for American citizens of Mexican descent. These advocates stated that while Mexican Americans understood the plight of Mexican immigrant workers, they were compelled to make hard choices on the issue. For example, in 1949, Sánchez expressed the frustrations of many concerned Mexican Americans when he observed: "The illegals are working not only in agricultural pursuits, but in the railroads, smelters, urban jobs [and] factories. Most of them work under conditions that border on peonage at dismally low wage rates. . . . More often than not each wetback displaces an entire resident family and causes those displaced persons to become migrants [and] inhabitants of the slums."[7] In Sánchez's view, the long-term cultural effects of unrestricted Mexican immigration were even more threatening. Quoted in a *New York Times* article in 1951, Sánchez asserted: "From a cultural standpoint, the influx of a million or more wetbacks a year transforms the Spanish-speaking people of the Southwest from an ethnic group which might be assimilated with reasonable facility into what I call a culturally indigestible peninsula of Mexico. The 'wet' migration tends to nullify processes of social integration going back 350 years, and I would say at the present time has set the whole assimilation process back at least twenty or thirty years."[8]

Other individuals and organizations expressed similar views. In a particularly strident broadside entitled "What Price Wetbacks?" published in 1954, the American G.I. Forum, a prominent Texas-based Mexican-American civil rights organization, argued that Mexican nationals "push . . . their blood brothers, American citizens of Mexican descent out of jobs . . . and push . . . wages down, down, down." In the Forum's view, the only solution to the "wetback crisis" was to amend U.S. immigration law "to provide an enforceable penalty for harboring or aiding an alien, to permit the confiscation of vehicles used to transport aliens, and to provide an enforceable penalty for the employment of illegal aliens."[9] As a historian of the G.I. Forum succinctly noted, by the mid-1950s the Forum and most other Mexican-American organizations "sincerely believed that the native Mexican American came first and priority lay with his welfare. If the bracero (or *mojado*) [Spanish for "wet one" or wetback] had to suffer because of this belief, that was unfortunate, but so was the [Mexican American] who could not feed his family because of their presence."[10]

The proponents of the Bracero Program were successful in their efforts to renew the program throughout the 1950s, but by early 1960s opponents had begun to make headway. The Kennedy administration was open to considering farm labor reform proposals, and as groups such as the National Council of Churches, the Catholic Rural Life Conference, the Bishops' Committee for the Spanish-Speaking, and Americans for Democratic Action stepped up their criticism, Secretary of Labor Arthur Goldberg publicly announced doubts about the need to continue the Bracero Program. Corporate lobbyists convinced Congress to renew the Bracero Program twice during Kennedy's tenure as president, but opponents finally succeeded in ending the program at the end of 1964, when Congress refused to reauthorize the Mexican farm labor program.[11]

Following the demise of the Bracero Program, Mexican immigration virtually disappeared as an issue in national politics. By the mid-1960s, the intensifying civil rights movement, urban unrest, and the escalation of the war in Vietnam all served to push the immigration issue out of the political spotlight. Undocumented Mexican immigrants continued to enter the United States in this period, but the INS reported that the rate of apprehensions of "deportable aliens" recorded between 1960 and 1965 had dropped to one-tenth the rate recorded in the years immediately preceding Operation Wetback.[12]

The disappearance of the immigration issue in the early 1960s proved but a brief respite, however. The Mexican economy's inability to keep pace with population growth, combined with the attraction of the booming American economy of the Vietnam era, stimulated a slow but steady increase in the number of undocumented entries into the United States from Mexico. The INS reported that by 1967 apprehensions, while still only a fraction of the peak rates noted during the bracero era, had again exceeded the 100,000 mark. Apprehensions continued to rise steadily over the next decade. By 1970, the number approached 500,000, exceeded 680,000 in 1974, and neared the 1 million mark in fiscal 1977.[13]

A sharp recession in 1970 and 1971 rekindled concern among many Americans that "illegal aliens" were stealing jobs from American citizens. This impression undoubtedly was reinforced when prominent news publications including the *New York Times*, the *Washington Post*, the *Los Angeles Times*, and *U.S. News and World Report* began publishing stories describing the illegal alien influx as a "human flood" or "silent invasion."[14] In a series of particularly inflamatory articles and public statements, INS commissioner Leonard Chapman described the illegal alien issue in alarming terms, warning of dire long-term consequences to the national interest. In one widely publicized article, Chapman termed the illegal alien issue a "national disaster," claiming that illegal aliens were "milking the U.S. taxpayer of $13 billion annually by taking away jobs from legal residents and forcing them into unemployment; by acquiring welfare benefits and public services; by avoiding taxes." "Clearly," Chapman asserted, "the nation can no longer afford these enormous, growing costs."[15]

In response to the growing negative publicity and public outcry surrounding the illegal alien issue, in 1972 and 1973 the INS embarked upon a new effort to control undocumented immigration by instituting a series of "neighborhood sweeps" in which aliens were apprehended and returned to Mexico. These sweeps were concentrated in predominantly Mexican-American neighborhoods in the southwestern states and received extensive news coverage.[16]

In addition to these renewed enforcement efforts, both Congress and some state governments began to consider legislation designed to address the latest immigration "crisis." At the state level, perhaps the best-known legislative development unfolded in California in 1970, when State Assemblyman Dixon Arnett of Redwood City introduced a bill proposing to impose criminal sanctions on employers who "knowingly" hired an individual "not entitled to lawful residence in the United States."[17] Congress followed a similar approach in its deliberations on immigration reform. In early 1972, after more than a year of hearings and staff research, a House immigration subcommittee synthesized several proposals and drafted a series of recommendations which were then endorsed by the full Judiciary Committee. This legislation, which quickly became associated with House Judiciary Committee chairman Peter Rodino (D-NJ), provided the basis for much of the subsequent congressional debate on immigration policy in the 1970s and 1980s. Such legislative activity also served notice that the illegal immigration question had once again become a prominent national issue.

The centerpiece of the Rodino legislation was similar to the "employer sanctions" proposed in Arnett's bill in California. Acting on the assumption that the root of the problem of illegal aliens in the United States lay with employers who knowingly hired them for substandard wages, Rodino advocated imposing civil and criminal penalties on anyone hiring such workers. To overcome the obvious difficulties inherent in identifying "legal" workers, Rodino and others advocated the creation of improved Social Security cards, or the development of a new, counterfeit-proof national identification system. Most of the legislation introduced at this time also called for significantly increased appropriations for the INS. Finally, as a gesture to Mexican Americans and other Hispanic groups, some legislation proposed to extend a limited "amnesty" to aliens who could prove continuous residence in the United States from some arbitrarily set date.[18]

The increasingly negative national press coverage of the "illegal alien crisis," the policy debate in Congress, and the intensified and highly publicized enforcement efforts of the INS set the stage for renewal of debate among Mexican-American civil rights activists over the Mexican immigration issue. Unlike previous periods of antialien sentiment, however, the timing of the reemergence of the immigration controversy in the early 1970s soon led many politically active Mexican Americans to reevaluate their traditional positions on the issue. By 1971, and in some cases earlier, a broad range of individuals and organizations began to question and criticize both the media coverage of the issue and the government's approach to immigration policy reform and enforcement.

Numerous developments stimulated this process of reassessment, but it was clear that the intensification of the civil rights campaign of the previous few years strongly influenced Mexican-American activists' evolving positions on the question. Indeed, in some ways, the shift in opinion on the immigration issue can be traced as a direct offshoot of a larger debate raging among Mexican Americans over the outbreak of "Chicano" militance at the end of the 1960s.

Originating as a series of localized protests erupting in New Mexico, Colorado, Texas, and California early in the decade, by 1968 this militance had taken on the characteristics of a cohesive social movement. Inspired by the pioneering and widely publicized efforts of César Chávez and the United Farm Workers Union in California and Reies López Tijerina and his irredentist organization in New Mexico, the first stage of this period of accelerating social and political activism helped lay the foundation for the unprecedented politicization of thousands of Mexican Americans across the country.

By 1966, these initial efforts opened the way for a second phase of Mexican-American political activity. At this time, young Mexican Americans, particularly high school and college students, began to express increasing dissatisfaction with discrimination, inferior education, and what they perceived as severely limited life opportunities. In many ways, these students represented a paradox. Though their educational and occupational levels continued to lag behind those achieved by other Americans, young Mexican Americans growing up in the late 1950s and early 1960s had significantly outstripped the levels of education and employment their parents had been able to attain. However, in the context of rising expectations for social reform emanating from the "New Frontier" and "Great Society" rhetoric of the Kennedy and Johnson administrations, Mexican-American students grew increasingly impatient with the pace of social change. As the antiwar and "black power" movements intensified in the United States after 1965, young Mexican Americans also began to voice their frustrations and protests. To a certain extent emulating the style and rhetoric of these militant movements, in 1967 and 1968 Mexican-American students spontaneously walked out of classes in California,

Texas, Colorado, and New Mexico, thus signaling the birth of the Chicano student movement.[19]

One of the most important thrusts of this second stage of increasing political activism—and arguably the development which ultimately had the most impact in transforming Mexican-American opinion on the immigration issue—was the adoption and promotion among young Mexican Americans of a new, "Chicano" identity. Long used as a slang or pejorative in-group reference to lower-class persons of Mexican descent, in the 1960s the term "Chicano" was adopted by young Mexican Americans as an act of defiance and self-assertion, and as an attempt to redefine themselves along criteria of their own choosing. Similar to the dynamics involved in the shift from "Negro" to "black" as the preferred self-referent of young African Americans occurring at about this same time, young Mexican Americans soon adopted the term "Chicano" as a powerful symbolic code. The term implied pride in the Mexican cultural heritage of the Southwest and symbolized solidarity against what Chicano activists argued was a history of racial oppression and discrimination at the hands of Anglo-Americans. *Chicanismo*—the idea of "being Chicano"—established strong symbolic ethnic boundaries for young Mexican Americans who explicitly and stridently rejected the notion of inherent Anglo-American superiority. Although adopted and used primarily by young Mexican-American high school and university students, by 1970 the student movement had attracted sufficient attention that the term had entered fairly general usage as a descriptor of the Mexican-American population at large.[20]

This new assertion of ethnic solidarity was carried one step further in the concept of Aztlán, an idea first articulated and debated in 1969 at the landmark First National Chicano Youth Liberation Conference in Denver, Colorado. Sponsored by the Crusade for Justice, a Colorado community organization founded by Rodolfo "Corky" Gonzales in 1965, the meeting attracted more than two thousand delegates representing Chicano students, community organizers, and political organizations from across the country. The conference marked the first time a large group of Chicano activists had come together to discuss the goals and strategy of a broad-based national Chicano movement.

In the process of refining their new sense of ethnic identity, the participants at the Denver meeting proclaimed the idea of Aztlán in the conference's famous manifesto, "El Plan Espiritual de Aztlán." The Spiritual Plan of Aztlán drew its inspiration from Aztec origin myths and from the vivid expressions of Chicano cultural pride explored in the writings of Corky Gonzales and the Chicano poet Alurista. Aztlán referred to the presumed ancestral homeland of the Aztecs and thus, by extension, of the

Mexican people. Interpreted as the "lost territories" that Mexico had surrendered to the United States in 1848 after the Mexican-American War, to Chicano activists Aztlán represented the symbolic territorial base of the Chicano people.[21] The Plan of Aztlán presented an almost millennialist vision of the future, painting an image of a separate Chicano culture and nation that ultimately would be reclaimed by the Chicano descendants of the ancient civilization. Proclaiming, "We Are a Bronze People with a Bronze Culture," the participants at the First National Chicano Youth Liberation Conference declared, "Before the World, before all of North America, before all our brothers in the Bronze Continent, We are a Nation, We are a Union of free pueblos, We are Aztlán. Por La Raza todo, Fuera de la Raza nada" (For the [Chicano] people everything, for [non-Chicanos] nothing).[22]

The Plan of Aztlán marked an important turning point in young Chicanos' ongoing efforts to refine their conception of a collective Chicano identity and to build a political program based on that identity. In the idea of Aztlán the young activists presented a quasi-nationalist vision of the Chicano people which extolled a pre-Columbian, "native" ancestry, while simultaneously diminishing or even rejecting their connection with American culture and society. In so doing, they also dismissed traditional notions of "Americanization" and "assimilation" as nothing more than "*Gabacho*" (a derisive term for Anglo) attempts to maintain hegemony over Chicanos by destroying their culture. Pursuing a logic similar to that followed by black nationalists of the period, the Chicano nationalists at the Denver conference proposed to break Anglo hegemony by demanding "community control" or local autonomy over schools, elected offices, businesses, and even financial institutions located in areas of high Chicano concentration.[23]

Clearly, much of the ethnic separatism and nationalism expressed in the Plan of Aztlán represented a symbolic act of defiance, rather than a formal declaration of secession from American society. Nevertheless, the conference and its ringing manifesto galvanized the student delegates and stimulated a new level of activism and the formation of numerous new student and community groups throughout the Southwest. In addition, following the Denver conference, Chicano activists Corky Gonzales and south Texas organizer José Angel Gutiérrez attempted to implement their plans for achieving Chicano community control by building an alternative ethnically based political party in the Southwest, El Partido de La Raza Unida—La Raza Unida Party (LRUP).[24]

More importantly, the events surrounding the 1969 conference contributed to an intensifying debate among Mexican Americans over the wisdom of pursuing the politics of ethnic militancy. Despite Chicano militants' claim that they represented the "true" interests of the Mexican-descent people of the United States, their tactics and rhetoric often provoked strong hostile reactions from more moderate "old-line" Mexican-American political activists, who tended to view the militants' demands as unrealistic, counterproductive, or even racist.

Perhaps the best-known example of this increasingly volatile debate occurred in 1969 between José Angel Gutiérrez and Henry B. González, the veteran Mexican-American congressman representing San Antonio. Reflecting the views of many others of his generation who had grown up believing that Mexican Americans must "work within the system" to achieve social justice, Congressman González lambasted Gutiérrez and other Chicano militants. He characterized them as "professional Mexicans" who were attempting "to stir up the people by appeals to emotion [and] prejudice in order to become leader[s] and achieve selfish ends." In González's view, the militants' emphasis on Chicano ethnic distinctiveness and their espousal of separatist ideologies represented the "politics of hatred" and "racism in reverse." Articulating the views held by a great many Mexican Americans in that volatile period, González rejected the militants' appeals to ethnic solidarity because he felt that their campaign was based on "a new racism [that] demands an allegiance to race above all else."[25]

For his part, Gutiérrez derided González and Mexican-American moderates for denying the importance of their cultural heritage. Gutiérrez accused González of holding "gringo tendencies" and maintained that Mexican Americans who subscribed to the ideology of assimilation were "*vendidos*" (sellouts) who had abandoned their people and contributed to their oppression. Voicing a view prevalent among other Chicano militants in the late 1960s, Gutiérrez argued that Chicanos should consider the very idea of assimilation offensive, since it implied that Chicano culture was inferior to that of the "American mainstream." From Gutiérrez's and other militants' point of view, the key to the "liberation" of the Chicano people was "social change that will enable La Raza to become masters of their destiny, owners of their resources, both human and natural, and a culturally separate people from the gringo." "We will not try to assimilate into this gringo society," he declared, "nor will we encourage anybody else to do so."[26]

It is clear that a great many Mexican Americans like González profoundly disagreed with the rhetoric, ideology, and political tactics adopted by Gutiérrez and other militant Chicano activists. Nevertheless, few could deny that the Chicano movement, like the larger civil rights movement itself, was instrumental in raising public and government awareness of the chronic problems facing the Mexican-American population. Even if many Mexican Americans refused to accept a "Chicano" self-identity, much less the ethnic separatism espoused by the militants, the actions of Chicano activists undoubtedly helped convince at least some government officials that the militants' grievances warranted attention. This trend accelerated after 1971 when a U.S. District Court ruled in the landmark *Cisneros* case that Mexican Americans constituted an "identifiable minority group" entitled to special federal assistance.[27] By granting official recognition of Mexican Americans as a "disadvantaged minority," the court undoubtedly helped to encourage the trend among Mexican-American activists to pursue political reform as part of an organized ethnic lobby. Similarly, whether or not one agreed with the ideology and tactics of the militant young Chicanos, it was clear that by challenging the integrationist assumptions of assimilation ideology, Chicano activists in effect had forced Mexican-American moderates associated with older civil rights organizations to "prove their loyalties" and to justify their traditional approaches to achieving social change. Recognizing that the militants had achieved some credibility in Mexican-American communities—particularly among the young—many Mexican-American "mainstream" politicians eventually, if reluctantly, acknowledged that the Chicano militants articulated the frustrations of barrio residents impatient with the pace of social change. Consequently, some Mexican-American moderates began to acknowledge and act upon the militants' demands.[28] As one prominent scholar of this period has noted, "the success, albeit limited, of the movement . . . in focusing government attention on Mexican problems softened the initial resistance and pejorative attitudes of the established Mexican[-American] community leadership which realized its own interests could be served best by working in the 'movement' framework."[29]

One largely unforeseen effect of this internal debate over political ideology, ethnic identity, and the redefinition of the Chicano community was the profound influence it eventually exerted on Mexican Americans' attitudes about the Mexican immigration issue. This development was ironic in that very few Chicano or Mexican-American activists had recognized immigration as a significant political issue in the late 1960s. However, at the very same time Mexican Americans became embroiled in an escalating debate over such fundamental issues as the appropriate basis for political organization and activism, the sources and salience of ethnic identity in contemporary society, and the very nature of the "Mexican-American community," the immigration issue suddenly took on new significance, particularly for activists associated with the Chicano movement. Having attempted to redefine the "Chicano community" by rejecting the assimilationist model and emphasizing the central importance of Mexican culture, history, and language to contemporary Chicano society, Chicano activists had raised some complex questions as to the boundaries of their community. Few Chicano activists initially made the connection between their efforts to redefine Chicano identity and their need to adopt some position on the immigration issue. At the same time, however, their appropriation of Mexican cultural symbols as integral parts of "Chicano" culture seemed to open the door to establishing a new level of solidarity with immigrants from Mexico. Consequently, in the context of the significant "ethnic awakening" symbolized by the emergent Chicano movement, the immigration issue assumed much more complex dimensions and importance in Chicano political discourse.

Still, few of the early Chicano groups initially made any kind of connection between their objectives and the immigrant question. The important exception to this was a group known as El Centro de Acción Social Autónoma, Hermandad General de Trabajadores (The Center for Autonomous Social Action, General Brotherhood of Workers, or simply, CASA). Established in 1968 by veteran Mexican-American community activists and labor organizers Bert Corona and Soledad "Chole" Alatorre in Los Angeles, CASA was founded as a "voluntary, democratic mutual assistance social welfare organization" to provide needed services to undocumented Mexican workers in the United States. Patterned after the traditional Mexican *mutualista*, CASA had expanded by 1970 to include autonomous local affiliates in other California cities and in the states of Texas, Colorado, Washington, and Illinois. These locals provided undocumented workers with a variety of direct services including immigration counseling, notary, and legal assistance.[30] Moreover, in 1973, CASA helped established the National Coalition for Fair Immigration Laws and Practices, a coalition of a broad range of predominantly Mexican-American community and labor groups that played an important role in articulating Mexican-American opinion on the immigration controversy throughout the debate in the 1970s.[31]

What most distinguished CASA from other groups was that it was the first Chicano-era organization to explore systematically the significance of the relationship between immigration, Chicano ethnicity, and the status of Mexican Americans in the United States. Basing their political perspective on more than four decades of labor union organizing and activism in Mexican communities in the Southwest, CASA's founders, particularly Corona and Alatorre, argued that Mexican immigrant laborers historically represented an integral component of the American working class, and as such, had legitimate claim to the same rights as other workers in the United States. This assertion represented a significant departure from the views of most other contemporary Mexican-American and Chicano organizations, but CASA's organizing slogans, "Somos Un

PUEBLO SIN FRONTERAS" (We Are One People without Borders) and "SOMOS UNO PORQUE AMERICA ES UNA" (We Are One Because America Is One), had even more sweeping political connotations. From CASA's point of view, the historical and ongoing exploitation of both Mexican-American and Mexican immigrant workers in the United States made them virtually indistinguishable. CASA's overriding goal, therefore, was to "unite . . . immigrant workers with the rest of the working class in the United States who 'enjoy' citizenship." From CASA's leaders' perspective, there was "an immediate need to organize and educate the passive individuals who are the victims of these antihuman and antilegal [*sic*] practices so that they will incorporate physically and consciously to demand the rights and benefits all human beings are entitled to."[32] This statement not only called into question what the organization viewed as more than a century of American exploitation of the Spanish-speaking but, more significantly, it fundamentally challenged Mexican Americans' own responses to the exploitation of Mexican immigrants. Unlike other Mexican-American organizations of the period, CASA maintained that Mexican immigrant workers, by virtue of their sacrifices and contributions to American society, had the right to live and work in the United States without harassment from the government *or* from Mexican Americans.

The political demands that stemmed from these assertions were truly revolutionary in light of the assimilationist assumptions which had informed nearly two hundred years of American immigration policy and had deeply influenced Mexican-American political thought in the twentieth century. CASA asserted that naturalization, and surely "Americanization," were largely irrelevant in a society that refused to recognize the full rights of citizenship for its ethnic and racial minorities. CASA's spokespersons argued that immigrant workers had for too long suffered as scapegoats for social and economic dislocations in the United States. CASA members consistently argued that the inferior social, economic, and political position of Mexicans in the United States did not derive from their cultural backwardness and refusal to "assimilate" into American culture and society, but rather reflected the inherently exploitative nature of American capitalist development.

CASA's position, as expressed by Corona in a 1971 speech, squarely challenged attempts "to sell to the so-called 'Mexican Americans' the idea that the greatest threat to their well-being is not the capitalist system, not the corporations, not the bad wages, not discrimination, not exploitation . . . [but] our *carnales* [brothers and sisters], who in their poverty come from Mexico to find work." Rejecting what he considered to be a half-century of invidious Anglo-American corporate and governmental propaganda, Corona asserted that Chicanos themselves must reject the false distinctions that traditionally had divided them from other working-class Latin Americans. "Our unity has to include not only Chicanos born here," Corona argued, "but also those who come from Mexico and Central and South America with documents and those who come . . . without."[33] "The[se] workers never cause unemployment," argued another CASA representative, "it's the jobs that are disappearing to other countries and which are being eliminated due to corporate greed." "The aliens contribute much, much more than they remove," he concluded, "they have not only built our country but continue to contribute to it by being taxed super-heavily and by consuming, utilizing, and paying for services in this country."[34] Following this logic, CASA maintained that the basic guarantees of American law represented only the bare minimum to which undocumented workers were entitled. CASA's leaders proposed, much as the Spanish-Speaking Peoples' Congress had thirty years before, that the undocumented be granted the "right of access to public bodies," a statute of limitations of one year on deportations, eligibility for citizenship after one year's residence, and the right "to be offered employment on equal terms with workers native to the host country."[35]

In many ways, CASA's views represented an extreme position on the growing controversy in the early 1970s. However, the government's recent actions in immigration policy and enforcement, the tenor of media coverage on immigration, and Mexican Americans' growing impatience with the pace of social change soon led others to join in a spirited critique of American immigration policy. Moreover, CASA's strong advocacy of working-class solidarity with Mexican immigrants held great appeal to Chicano student activists, who by 1972 had begun to explore Marxian class analyses to help explain the subordination of Mexicans in American society. Employing these more sophisticated conceptual frameworks to analyze Chicanos' historical experience, Chicano students and a small but growing number of Mexican-American academicians developed a new understanding of the close correspondance between the historical exploitation of both Mexican and Mexican-American workers in the American labor market.[36]

Such analyses soon spilled over into Chicanos' evaluation of the immigration debate. On the most basic level, young Chicano students, activists, and community organizers began developing a new perspective on immigration by rejecting the government's contention that undocumented workers represented a threat to the Mexican-American working class. As one young activist stated in the militant Los Angeles Chicano newspaper *Regeneración* in 1972: "It is claimed that illegals cause high unemployment of residents; that they oppose the formation of unions; that they drain residents' incomes by adding to welfare costs; that they add to the tax burden by needing special programs." "These are fake claims," he argued, "illegals . . . do not create unemployment of Chicanos, employers desiring to pay the lowest possible wages do."[37]

Over the coming months the combination of INS sweeps, legislative action in Congress, and what Chicano militants perceived as intensifying anti-Mexican rhetoric in the media, led other Chicano activists to step up their criticisms of the government's reform efforts, and their increasingly strident rhetoric clearly reflected these trends. In July 1972, La Raza Unida Party in California issued a statement describing undocumented workers as "refugees from hunger" and called upon the government to issue a blanket amnesty to those aliens already in the United States. Like CASA, LRUP also demanded that the law be amended so that all aliens would be eligible for American citizenship after three years with no language requirements.[38] In Denver, a coalition of Mexican-American groups led by the Crusade for Justice went further by issuing a press statement decrying the Rodino proposal as an attempt to "perpetuate racism" against all Latinos. The coalition charged that if the Rodino bill passed, "all Latinos, Chicanos, [and] Mejicanos [Mexicans] will be obligated to produce identity papers, and many applicants for jobs will be denied a chance for employment based solely on the fact that we may 'appear' alien."[39]

Although activists of the Chicano movement led the growing clamor against the government's proposals for immigration reform, some politically moderate and even conservative old-line organizations such as LULAC and the American G.I. Forum began to be pulled toward a new position on the question. For example, during the initial Rodino hearings in 1971, even LULAC began to express growing ambivalence on the issue. Before this time, most LULAC spokesmen seemed to support the government's general approach to the issue. Over the course of the hearings, however, some LULAC leaders seemed to be having second thoughts on the question of undocumented Mexican workers.

During the Rodino hearings, for example, some LULAC members criticized proposed legislation by stressing the adverse effects such laws might have on American citizens of Mexican descent. This marked a significant change because LULAC's representatives had shifted the target of their criticism from undocumented workers themselves to the proposed *legislation.* Though LULAC at this point still tended to favor the proposals for employer sanctions contained in the Rodino legislation, their testimony indicated a growing concern over the impact this particular reform might have on American citizens of Mexican descent. Consequently, LULAC representatives repeatedly admonished the committee to see to it that the law "did not become a tool of oppression on those people who have a right to live and work here," a concern LULAC would emphasize with increasing frequency in the coming months.[40]

On the other hand, LULAC's rhetoric during the Rodino hearings betrayed a growing sensitivity to the plight of undocumented aliens who entered the country seeking work. While not nearly as strident on the issue as Chicano militants would soon prove to be, LULAC members nevertheless began to use rhetoric expressing a new level of empathy with Mexican immigrants in the United States. Albert Armendáriz, Sr., who had been president of the organization when these issues surfaced within LULAC during Operation Wetback, attempted to explain LULAC's changing position to the Rodino committee. He summarized LULAC's shifting point of view when he stated that Mexican Americans were "torn between two desires, the desire to be good to our brothers who come from across the border and suffer so much when they are here trying to get ahead, and our desire to have those that are here as citizens advance in our society and become better adjusted to American life with the benefits of American life."[41] Another LULAC leader expressed similar sentiments. While he made sure to point out that Mexican Americans remained "very much concerned with the problem because our people are . . . in competition with illegal aliens for jobs," he concluded his remarks by flatly asserting that "they are our brothers, we speak the same language . . . we are the same, the same people."[42]

At the same time that LULAC was advancing this rather startling departure from traditional "mainstream" Mexican-American opinion on the immigration question, other organizations were beginning to make the same kind of arguments. For example, the Mexican-American Political Association (MAPA) also revised its position at this time. Established as an organizational offshoot of the Community Service Organization in 1959, MAPA, like LULAC and the G.I. Forum, had been among the strongest critics of the Bracero Program and had lobbied extensively for stricter enforcement of laws against undocumented immigration. During the debate over the Dixon Arnett bill in the California assembly, however, MAPA executed a reversal in its position on immigration reform that was every bit as remarkable as LULAC's shift.

In testimony before Arnett's subcommittee in late 1971, MAPA's state president, Armando Rodríguez, detailed the logic behind his organization's change in position. Though MAPA had once supported employer sanctions as an effective means of controlling undocumented immigration, he explained, his organization now intended to oppose the Arnett legislation because it would open the door to discrimination against anyone who "looked" Latino. While Mexican Americans had made this argument before (most notably during Operation Wetback in 1954), Rodríguez took this criticism a significant step further. Reminding the committee that MAPA traditionally had "favored employment for legal aliens and [American] citizens as opposed to employment of illegal aliens," MAPA's president went on to insist that the proposed legislation "should not be used by employers to continue harassing Mexican American people seeking employment, be they legals, illegals, citizens or otherwise."[43]

Rodríguez's statement is particularly enlightening because it provides a clear, though in all probability unintentional, indication of the extent to which even Mexican-American moderates were beginning to reassess their thinking on the relationship of Mexican immigrants to Americans of Mexican descent. MAPA, LULAC, and similar Mexican-American advocacy organizations previously had based much of their civil rights programs on their constituencies' American citizenship and had consistently attempted to emphasize the distinctions separating Mexican Americans from Mexican nationals. Now, MAPA's California state president rhetorically referred to a "Mexican-American people" that included both legal and undocumented aliens from Mexico along with American citizens of Mexican descent. It must be emphasized that Rodríguez's remarks represented only the views of an activist minority of the Mexican-American population (MAPA claimed a membership of twenty-three thousand in 1971), but his comments reflected a changing awareness of the civil rights implications of the immigration issue, one that was occurring among a growing number of diverse Mexican-American interests.[44] Although it was still common to hear Mexican-American citizens voice the opinion that "illegal aliens have no rights, and should be rounded up, and booted back across the border," Mexican-American political and civil rights advocates were beginning to see the issue from a new perspective.[45] Clearly, moderate Mexican-American advocacy organizations continued to base much of their revised position on their growing concern over the potential employer sanctions held for creating job discrimination against Americans of Latin descent. Their changing rhetoric suggests, however, that Mexican-American advocates were also beginning to recognize a new level of convergence between their civil rights efforts and the issue of the rights of Spanish-speaking immigrants in the United States, a concern Chicano activists were articulating with growing vehemence. Though most Mexican-American moderates would not admit that Chicano militants had influenced their thinking on the issue, the changing tenor of debate over the civil rights and social identity of the "Chicano" people in the past decade had laid the foundations for a fundamental reassessment of the immigration issue. As Albert Armendáriz recently recalled, the combined efforts of the militants and "mainstream" Mexican-American civil rights groups had contributed to a growing realization "that our previous position was not a realistic goal in our society. We realized that we needed to include noncitizens—both legal and illegal—in our [civil rights] efforts."[46]

The change in LULAC's and MAPA's positions marked a significant shift in Mexican-American opinion on the Mexican immigration controversy, but the most dramatic evidence of the change occurring in the 1970s was provided by a dispute that developed over the United Farm Workers [UFW] union's position on the question. Established in California in 1962 by César Chávez and Dolores Huerta, the UFW undoubtedly had been most instrumental in publicizing the plight of Mexican Americans to a national public. Chávez's farm workers' movement had begun as a modest struggle merely to gain collective bargaining rights and union recognition for Mexican-American and Filipino farm workers in California. But by skillfully employing nonviolent tactics and utilizing emotionally charged ethnic symbols such as the union's stylized black Aztec eagle insignia and banners of Mexico's patron saint, the Virgin of Guadalupe, to attract members and garner publicity, Chávez succeeded in capturing the imagination of Mexican Americans across the Southwest. He cultivated the image of a modest, pious man committed to using the powers of civil disobedience on behalf of his downtrodden people, and, more than any other individual, Chávez gave Mexican Americans a nationally recognized role model and champion. Moreover, by winning the support of priests, nuns, ministers, and a multiethnic horde of idealistic young student volunteers, Chávez imbued his movement with a moral dimension that transcended traditional labor union politics. His ability to gain mass media attention during the 1960s was also instrumental in eventually gaining the public support of national celebrities such as comedian/musician Steve Allen, writer Peter Matthiessen, labor leader Walter Reuther of the powerful United Autoworkers Union, and liberal politicians such as Robert F. Kennedy, Eugene McCarthy, and George McGovern.[47]

Chávez was convinced, however, that in order to achieve the UFW's goals, the union's energies needed to be expended exclusively on behalf of American citizens and resident aliens. Consequently, from its inception in 1962, the UFW lobbied for strict control of the Mexican border. Like Ernesto Galarza before him, César Chávez argued that the presence of a large pool of politically powerless noncitizen workers severely hampered efforts to unionize American citizen workers. Moreover, the UFW stressed that American employers had always used undocumented Mexican workers to break strikes by American citizens. Chávez therefore stubbornly argued for the repeal of the Bracero Program and was among the most vocal critics of "illegal" immigration. The UFW consistently maintained this position in its early years, going so far as to report undocumented Mexican farm workers to the INS.[48] In 1971, the UFW's leadership quietly supported the Dixon Arnett bill, later justifying its position by insisting that the use of undocumented workers was a "massive, well-organized black market in slave labor."[49] A Chicano UFW worker on strike for higher wages summarized his union's position when he told a reporter, "I know these people [i.e., undocumented workers] want to work. But we can't let them break our strike, in the end we will benefit and they too will benefit. We are suffering for them, they should suffer a little for us."[50]

By 1973 it was apparent, however, that Chávez's stated position on the immigration issue was seriously out of line with the public views expressed by other Chicano and Mexican-American groups. In the spring of that year, CASA and the National Coalition for Fair Immigration Laws and Practices led a growing chorus of criticism against the UFW's apparent continued support of the Arnett and Rodino legislation.[51] Such criticism was remarkable in that it simultaneously marked the erosion of support for an individual leader and a political cause that up to this point had enjoyed the overwhelming support of Mexican-American and Chicano activists, and the crystallization of opinion on the immigration issue.[52]

The UFW's vacillation on the immigration issue renewed conflict among Chicano groups to such a point that the National Coalition issued an open letter to the union in July 1974. Incensed over an Associated Press story which quoted UFW officials as stating aliens were "depriving jobs [from] farm workers and posing a threat to all people," the coalition's letter was the clearest statement yet as to the new position of Mexican-American and Chicano activists. The coalition insisted that "all workers have the right to seek work in order to support themselves and their families. When we ask for the deportation of all of the workers who have no visas," the letter stated, "we are attacking many good union brothers and sisters that have no visas but would never break a strike." The coalition concluded by pointedly observing: "The [employers'] traditional response has been to deport not only the leaders of strikes but the workers themselves. Thus, when a union calls on the U.S. Immigration [Service] to help them it is calling on a traditional tool of the employers and the United States [government]."[53]

If Chávez remained unconvinced of the strength of Mexican-American and Chicano advocates' position on the immigration issue, he was made painfully aware of it when the controversy made newspaper headlines again that autumn. The controversy was reignited when Attorney General William B. Saxbe announced the Justice Department's intention of deporting "one million" illegal aliens from the country. Saxbe's announcement was particularly inflammatory in light of the increasing

Mexican-American sensitivity to the INS raids of the previous eighteen months, but when Saxbe claimed the full support of the United Farm Workers, the issue exploded. Within days, a coalition of organizations including CASA, MAPA, the American G.I. Forum, LULAC, and the Los Angeles-based Chicana organization Comisión Feminil angrily denounced the government's plan and demanded Saxbe's immediate resignation.[54]

Chávez gamely tried to defend his policies by flatly asserting that "most of the [Chicano] left attacking us has no experience in labor matters. They don't know what a strike is." "They don't know," Chávez continued, "because they're not workers. They don't know because they've never felt the insecurity of being on strike. And they don't know because really they haven't talked to the workers."[55] Aware, however, that he desperately needed to maintain his base of support among urban Mexican Americans—particularly Chicano activists and students—Chávez was compelled to reassess his union's position on the increasingly explosive issue. In a letter to the editor of the *San Francisco Examiner* dated November 22, 1974, Chávez detailed the UFW's latest stand on the question. While reiterating the UFW's long-term objections to the use of undocumented workers as strikebreakers, Chávez subtly altered his position by laying primary responsibility for "the mass recruitment of undocumented workers for the specific purpose of breaking our strikes and jeopardizing the rights of all farm workers" on the Justice Department and the INS. Chávez flatly denied supporting Saxbe's proposal and charged that the government's plan for mass deportation was nothing but "a ploy toward the reinstatement of a Bracero Program, which would give government sanction once more to the abuse of Mexican farm workers and, in turn, of farm workers who are citizens." Treading a very fine line between his earlier public support of restrictive legislation and his need to mend fences with other Mexican-American and Chicano organizations, Chávez further asserted that "the illegal aliens are doubly exploited, first because they are farm workers, and second because they are powerless to defend their own interests. But if there were no illegals being used to break our strikes, we could win those strikes overnight and then be in a position to improve the living and working conditions of all farm workers." Chávez promised that the farm workers would advocate "amnesty for illegal aliens and support their efforts to obtain legal documents and equal rights, including the right of collective bargaining." Concluding with a clear overture to militant Chicano groups, Chávez pledged his support to the undocumented because "the illegals [are] our brothers and sisters."[56]

The United Farm Workers' shifting position on the immigration question provided a good barometer of the extent to which Mexican-

American thinking on immigration had changed by the mid-1970s. The debate between the Farm Workers and Chicano and Mexican-American activists over Mexican immigration now seriously affected support for Chávez's movement—and for what up to that point had been the most successful and unified political effort in Mexican-American history. Clearly, many Mexican Americans continued to believe that political efforts on behalf of immigrants must remain secondary to efforts made on behalf of American citizens. But by 1975, Chicano activists and most major Mexican-American advocacy organizations—including the United Farm Workers Union—had come to a new understanding of the relationship of the immigration controversy to the ongoing struggle to achieve equal rights for Americans of Mexican descent. A Mexican-American labor union official in Los Angeles captured the spirit of this new position when he insisted that Mexican Americans who continued to support restrictive immigration policies "should realize that they would not be here if their fathers had not been illegal aliens"; an assertion that was certainly true for a large proportion of the Mexican-American population.[57] Reflecting this new awareness, these diverse organizations and individuals had reconstructed earlier positions. Even the farm workers, arguably the group most directly affected by undocumented immigration, expressed solidarity with undocumented workers while excoriating the federal government for proposing many of the same reforms they had once advocated. Although CASA's claim that its view on immigration had gone "from a minority position in the Mexican and Latin communities to the position of the overwhelming majority" was overstated, by 1975 a significant realignment had indeed occurred.[58] Given the ideological gulf separating politically moderate organizations such as LULAC, MAPA, and the G.I. Forum, on the one hand, and CASA and Chicano student groups, on the other, this united front on the immigration controversy was remarkable.

If anything, this united front solidified among Chicano and Mexican-American advocates when President Jimmy Carter announced his immigration reform package in the summer of 1977. Having overwhelmingly supported Carter in the 1976 presidential campaign, many Mexican-American and Chicano political activists had expected the president-elect to bring a new perspective to the controversial issue. Thus, when Carter announced his immigration reform package in the summer of 1977, Mexican-American and Chicano civil rights advocates were shocked to learn that the administration's plan closely resembled Rodino's. Indeed, in arguing that illegal aliens "had breached [the] Nation's immigration laws, displaced many American citizens from jobs, and placed an increased financial burden on many state and local governments," President Carter restated virtually all the assumptions that had shaped congressional consideration of immigration policy reform since the turn of the century.[59]

In response to the president's announcement, virtually every major Mexican-American and Chicano organization immediately protested the "Carter Plan." In Washington, DC, national organizations including LULAC, the American G.I. Forum, the Mexican-American Women's National Association (MANA), the National Council of La Raza, the Mexican-American Legal Defense and Education Fund (MALDEF), and a broad range of at least ten other national and local groups established an ad hoc coalition to work against the Carter proposals.[60] The drama of the reaction was underscored when LULAC, completing a process of re-evaluation on the issue that had begun in 1971, now expressed its unequivocal opposition to the Carter plan. In an almost complete departure from the organization's founding principles, LULAC's national headquarters issued a statement arguing it "unconscionable and objectionable" to subject resident Mexican nationals to the "second-class citizenship" that would be established under Carter's "amnesty" proposal. LULAC's Texas state director, Ruben Bonilla, elaborated on his organization's position, charging that the aliens' impact on American society had been "unduly sensationalized, grossly distorted, and vastly misrepresented." Bonilla expressed LULAC's particular opposition to Carter's proposed development of a national identification system, the reinstitution of some sort of "limited" foreign worker program, and the imposition of employer sanctions, arguing that such provisions would create "a dual system of employment [in which] hiring will be based largely on a prospective employee's pigmentation and English-speaking ability."[61] The American G.I. Forum, next to LULAC perhaps the most politically conservative of the organizations in the ad hoc coalition, also derided the Carter plan, passing a resolution which strongly criticized the administration's proposals at its national convention.[62]

However, the single most dramatic manifestation of the broad-based agreement on the issue was the landmark First National Chicano/Latino Conference on Immigration and Public Policy, held in San Antonio in October 1977. Organized primarily under the auspices of José Angel Gutiérrez and the Texas La Raza Unida Party, the conference attracted nearly two thousand participants representing groups and individuals as diverse as LULAC, the American G.I. Forum, MALDEF, La Raza Unida Party, the Crusade for Justice, CASA, the Socialist Workers Party, and numerous Latino elected and appointed government officials. In the weeks preceding the conference and during the three-day meeting itself, the conference participants made it clear that the government's proposals would meet with widespread Hispanic opposition. The conference's "Call to Action" rejected virtually all of the government's stated premises on immigration reform, charging that "the truth of the matter [was] that Latinos are to be made the scapegoat for this administration's ineptness at solving economic problems of inflation, unemployment, wage depression and rising consumer frustration." Voicing their dismay with a president from whom they had expected support, the conference organizers protested that "the very same man our Raza supported for the Presidency now seeks to deport us. The Carter administration is designing a new immigration policy. We are the main target."[63]

The significance of such unprecedented unity among the Mexican-American, Chicano, and other Hispanic organizations and individuals represented at San Antonio was not lost on the participants. Peter Camejo, a Chicano representative of the Socialist Workers Party, observed: "I am speaking. So is LULAC, an organization I have disagreements with. We can disagree. But we can also sit down and talk to each other. Because when they come to deport us, we're all in the same boat."[64] Reflecting just how far Mexican-American opinion on the issue had evolved since 1969, LULAC's national leaders now made corresponding claims. LULAC's national director, Edwin Morga, argued that the issue of undocumented workers in the United States represented a fundamental question of human rights. "We should show the world," he asserted, "that we are aware of the continuing political repression, the repression of human rights that is ongoing not only against Blacks, but certainly against Chicanos, against Mexicanos, and other brother Latins."[65]

Acting on this new-found unity, the conference delegates passed a series of resolutions demanding "full and unconditional" amnesty for undocumented workers already in the country, and the extension of full constitutional rights to resident aliens. Furthermore, the conference demanded that the government guarantee aliens the right to unionize, to receive unemployment compensation, and to educate their children in the United States.[66] After nearly six years of intense debate, Chicano and Mexican-American activists had achieved an unprecedented consensus on the immigration controversy, a consensus that would last well into the debate over the Simpson-Rodino immigration proposals in the 1980s.

In many ways, the First National Chicano/Latino Conference on Immigration and Public Policy marked the culmination of nearly a half century of Mexican-American debate on Mexican immigration. Though the delegates remained ideologically divided on other issues, the meeting's resolutions demonstrated just how far Mexican-American and Chicano activists had come on the complex question of the political, social, and cultural relationships between Mexican Americans and immigrants from

Mexico. The conference also demonstrated the degree to which immigration had become a central issue in Mexican-American politics.

This state of affairs was the outcome of a complicated historical process in which Chicano and Mexican-American activists, in their separate pursuits of equal rights for the Mexican-descent minority in the United States, came to recognize how closely linked their campaigns were to the plight of Mexican immigrants. Forced to confront the recurrent issue of the mass immigration of relatively impoverished Mexican laborers into their communities, Mexican-American political activists were also constantly compelled to assess and define their own sense of social and cultural identity vis-à-vis the recent arrivals. In the late 1960s, few militant Chicano organizations and activists considered Mexican immigration a pressing concern, but the media's depiction of the "illegal alien crisis" and the government's subsequent actions in the immigration arena, combined with their own awakened sense of ethnic identity, soon stimulated a strong response among them. In the context of the ethnic catharsis symbolized by the rise of the Chicano movement, young Chicanos tended to view these reform efforts as yet another attack on the Mexican minority in the United States. By the early 1970s, their central concern with exploring the sources of Chicano identity, their attempts to redefine the "Chicano community," and a growing recognition that Mexican immigrants were "Chicanos in the making," led them to adopt a new, empathic stance on the issue. By 1975, most Chicano organizations had come to accept the view, as CASA's San José, California, affiliate succinctly put it, that "to learn how to protect the rights of workers without papers is to learn how to protect ourselves."[67]

Mexican-American moderates had also come to a new understanding of the immigration dilemma. Indeed, by almost any measure, the shift in Mexican-American activists' opinion on the immigration issue in the 1970s represented a fundamental realignment on one of the most historically vexing and divisive issues in Mexican-American politics. Though initially not nearly as aggressive as their Chicano counterparts, Mexican-American moderates responded to what they too had come to perceive as an unwarranted campaign of anti-Mexican hysteria. Once they realized that the proposed immigration policy held potentially grave civil rights implications for American citizens of Mexican descent, organizations spanning the political spectrum began to soften their traditional restrictionist positions on the question. And although few Mexican-American advocates would admit it, the rhetoric of Chicano militants on both immigration and ethnic politics contributed to their growing awareness of the close relationships that bound Mexican immigrants to American citizens of Mexican descent.

The unprecedented show of unity on the immigration question should not obscure, however, the paradoxes and disagreements that continued to divide Mexican-American and Chicano political activists on the related issues of ethnic identity, ideology, and the direction of Mexican-American/Chicano politics. Indeed, when all was said and done, Mexican Americans' changing positions on the immigration controversy in many ways served to magnify what were already very old ideological and philosophical cleavages. Despite their newly sympathetic stand on immigration, moderate Mexican-American political activists and organizations generally continued to adhere to a vision of America which, while modifying the traditional assimilationist/"Americanization" perspective so prevalent in Mexican-American politics since World War II, still emphasized achieving political and social reform by working within the confines of the existing American political system. For such individuals and organizations, and presumably for a large percentage of the U.S.-born Mexican-American population as well, a militant ethnic-based politics held little appeal. Similarly, while Mexican-American moderates had substantially altered their thinking on supporting the rights of Mexican workers in the United States, few were willing to accept the premise that distinctions between American citizens and Mexican nationals should disappear entirely. As one LULAC member expressed it: "Mexico and its people know, and readily admit, that no one born in the United States is a Mexican, even if his parents were Mexican. . . . We have never been Mexicans nor Mexican Americans . . . much less Chicanos. Wake up, Spanish-speaking Americans—claim your rightful heritage, your real nationality. Tell the world, with the rest of our fellow citizens—I AM AN AMERICAN—don't call me anything else!"[68]

For the more militant wing of the Chicano movement, consideration of ethnic nationalist ideology in conjunction with the immigration issue helped expose some of the most glaring conflicts and contradictions of leaders who advocated Chicano nationalism without fully and critically examining the sources of their ethnicity, their relationship to Mexicans who had arrived from the other side of the border, or their relationship to other Americans. Though the process of refining and reshaping their cultural identity and political ideology led Chicano activists to reject "assimilation" and "Americanization" as sterile strategies that contributed to Chicano oppression, their ultimate inability to provide an alternative vision by precisely defining the parameters of Chicano culture and the ethnocultural boundaries of the community they claimed to represent spoke to an ideological dilemma that is yet to be resolved.

In broader terms, the ability of Mexican-American and Chicano movement activists and organizations to achieve consensus on the immigration issue while continuing to disagree deeply over issues of culture, ethnic identity, political ideology, and "community" during the 1960s and 1970s was symptomatic of the fractured nature of the Mexican-American experience throughout the twentieth century. These issues all revolved around the fundamental and ultimately inextricable questions of Mexican Americans' and Mexican immigrants' self-perceived place in American society. Was it reasonable to expect that either or both groups could ultimately achieve sociocultural and political assimilation into that society, or was it possible to maintain distinct and viable ethnic cultures in the larger society? Or could some as yet undefined "middle path" be followed? By the late 1970s, internal debate among Mexican Americans and Chicanos over the most basic questions of ethnic and cultural identity, the steadily increasing class, generational, and regional diversity of the population, and fundamental historical disagreements over the best political strategy for the United States' ethnic Mexican minority combined to foil concerted Mexican-American/Chicano action. The rapid growth of the Mexican-American/Mexican immigrant population of the United States since then, the attendant social dislocations accompanying that growth, and the continuing and increasing pressures inducing emigration from Mexico (and increasingly, from other Latin American "sending nations") are all clear indications that such fundamental questions will continue to be pressing concerns facing Americans of Mexican descent in the years to come.

Notes

1. I have taken care in this study to use terminology to describe various subgroups of the Mexican-origin population as they labeled themselves, or to make clear distinctions among the various cohorts. Thus immigrants from Mexico are referred to as "immigrants," "Mexican aliens," "Mexican nationals," or simply "Mexicans." I have attempted to restrict use of the term "Chicano" to that group of American citizens of Mexican descent who used this term to describe themselves. The term "Mexican American" is more problematic, but again, for the purposes of this essay, the term refers specifically to those individuals who labeled themselves as such. However, as a matter of convenience, I also occasionally use the term to describe all American citizens of Mexican descent, regardless of their political orientation. The term "Hispanic" came into vogue in the 1970s—especially among agencies of the federal government—as a descriptor of the total "Spanish-heritage" population of the United States. As used in this essay the term refers to the combined resident population of "Latin American" descent, including those from Mexico, Puerto Rico, Cuba, and the predominantly Spanish-speaking nations of Central and South America. For discussion of the recent evolution of such nomenclature, see Leo F. Estrada, José Hernández, and David Alvirez, "Using Census Data to Study the Spanish Heritage Population

of the United States," in Charles H. Teller et al., eds., *Cuantos Somos: A Demographic Study of the Mexican American Population*, monograph no. 2 (Austin: Center for Mexican-American Studies, University of Texas, Austin, 1977); Martha E. Giménez, "The Political Construction of the Hispanic," in *Estudios Chicanos and the Politics of Community*, ed. Mary Romero and Cordelia Candelaria (Boulder, CO: National Association for Chicano Studies, 1989), 66–88; and Ramón A. Gutiérrez's provocative "Unraveling America's Hispanic Past: Internal Stratification and Class Boundaries," *Aztlán* 17, no. 1 (Spring 1986): 79–102.

2. The various terms used by the government and the media to describe Mexican immigrants in the 1960s and 1970s were themselves politically charged. Persons believing that Mexican nationals surreptitiously entering the United States had broken U.S. law tended to label these migrants "illegal aliens." Others, seeking to emphasize the complexity of international migration phenomena, tended to use the phrase "undocumented aliens" or "undocumented workers" to describe these immigrants. In this essay, I have tried to use the specific terminology employed by the various actors to describe immigrants from Mexico.

3. According to U.S. Census figures, of the estimated 3,464,999 Spanish-surname persons residing in the Southwest in 1960 nearly 55 percent were natives of native parentage, 15 percent had been born in Mexico, and approximately 30 percent were U.S. natives of "mixed" parentage (i.e., children having at least one parent born in Mexico). By 1970, these percentages had changed very little. Of the 4,532,435 persons of Mexican descent enumerated in the 1970 census, 3,715,408 (nearly 82 percent) were native-born American citizens and 817,027 were resident Mexican nationals. However, of the native-born Mexican-American component, 1,579,440 (approximately 35 percent of the total Mexican-descent population and almost 43 percent of the U.S.-born Mexican-American cohort) were the children of foreign or mixed parentage. For discussion of the demographics of the Mexican-descent population of the Southwest in 1960, see Leo Grebler, Joan W. Moore, and Ralph C. Guzmán, *The Mexican American People: The Nation's Second Largest Minority* (New York: Free Press, 1970), 30; and Richard L. Nostrand, "The Hispanic-American Borderland: Delimitation of an American Culture Region," *Annals of the Association of American Geographers* 60, no. 1 (December 1970): 640. For 1970 see U.S. Bureau of the Census, *Census of Population, 1970: Subject Reports*, Final Report PC (2)-1C, "Persons of Spanish Origin" (Washington, DC, 1973), table 4, p. 32; and *Census of Population, 1970: Subject Reports*, Final Report PC (2)-1A, "National Origin and Language" (Washington, DC, 1973), table 10, p. 70.

4. For discussion of the ambivalent historical relationship between immigrants and Mexican Americans in the nineteenth and early twentieth centuries, see Albert Camarillo, *Chicanos in a Changing Society: From Mexican Pueblos to American Barrios in Santa Barbara and Southern California, 1848–1930* (Cambridge, MA: Harvard University Press, 1979), 182–92; Leonard Pitt, *Decline of the Californios: A Social History of the Spanish-Speaking Californians, 1846–1890* (Berkeley: University of California Press, 1966), 6–7, 53; and Manuel Gamio, *The Life Story of the Mexican Immigrant: Autobiographical Documents* (Chicago: University of Chicago Press, 1930). For a more comprehensive view, see David G. Gutiérrez, *Walls and Mirrors: Mexican Americans, Mexican Immigrants, and the Politics of Ethnicity* (Berkeley: University of California Press, 1995).

5. See Richard B. Craig, *The Bracero Program: Interest Groups and Foreign Policy* (Austin: University of Texas Press, 1971); Ernesto Galarza, *Merchants of Labor: The Mexican Bracero Story, An Account of Managed Migration of Mexican Farmworkers in California, 1942–1960* (Charlotte, NC: McNally & Loftin, 1964); and Manuel García y Griego, "The Importation of Mexican Contract Laborers to the United States, 1942–1964: Antecedents, Operation, and Legacy," in *The Border That Joins: Mexican Migrants and U.S. Responsibility*, ed. Peter G. Brown and Henry Shue (Totowa, NJ: Rowman & Littlefield, 1983).

6. Though undocumented migration is by nature difficult to measure, some scholars have estimated that undocumented migration during the bracero era may have outstripped "legal" immigration by a ratio of 4:1. See James Cockcroft, *Outlaws in the Promised Land: Mexican Immigrant Workers and America's Future* (New York: Grove Press, 1986), 69. For a critical overview of Operation Wetback, see Juan Ramón García, *Operation Wetback: The Mass Deportation of Mexican Undocumented Workers in 1954* (Westport, CT: Greenwood Press, 1980).

7. George I. Sánchez to Ernest Schwarz, Executive Secretary, Committee on Latin American Affairs, Congress of Industrial Organizations, January 19, 1949, Ernesto Galarza Collection, Immigration/1, Department of Special Collections, Stanford University Libraries, Stanford, California (hereafter SUL).

8. "Peons in West Lowering Culture," *New York Times*, March 27, 1951.

9. American G.I. Forum of Texas and the Texas State Federation of Labor, *What Price Wetbacks?* (Austin: G.I. Forum of Texas, 1954; reprinted in Carlos Cortés, ed., *Mexican Migration to the United States* [New York: Arno Press, 1974]).

10. Carl Allsup, *The American G.I. Forum: Origins and Evolution* (Austin: University of Texas Press, 1982), 119.

11. For succinct discussions of the demise of the Bracero Program, see Ellis Hawley, "The Politics of the Mexican Labor Issue, 1950–1965," *Agricultural History* 40 (July 1966): 157–76; and García y Griego, "The Importation of Mexican Contract Laborers."

12. For INS estimates of apprehensions of "deportable Mexican aliens," refer to U.S. Department of Justice, Immigration and Naturalization Service, *Annual Report, 1954* (Washington, DC, 1955), and tables 24 and 24a for each *Annual Report*, 1965–1970 (Washington, DC, 1965–1971); and Immigration and Naturalization Service, "Deportable Aliens Located, Aliens Deported, and Aliens Required to Depart—Years Ended June 30, 1892–1976, July–September 1976, and Years Ended September 30, 1977–78," cited in U.S. Congress, Senate, Committee on the Judiciary, *Selected Readings on U.S. Immigration Law and Policy*, 96th Cong., 2d sess. (Washington, DC, 1980), 16.

13. INS, "Deportable Aliens." See also U.S. Congress, Senate, Committee on the Judiciary, "U.S. Immigration Law and Policy: 1952–1979" (Washington, DC, 1979), 34.

14. All of these publications provided extensive coverage of the evolving immigration controversy during the 1970s, but *U.S. News and World Report* paid special attention to the issue. For examples of the tenor of the *USN&WR* reportage during this period, see "Why Wetbacks Are So Hard to Control," October 18, 1971, p. 50; "Surge of Illegal Immigrants across American Borders," January 17, 1972, pp. 32–34; " 'Invasion' of Illegal Aliens and the Problems They Create,"

July 23, 1973, pp. 32–35; "How Millions of Illegal Aliens Sneak into the U.S.," July 22, 1974, pp. 27–30; and "Rising Flood of Illegal Aliens," February 3, 1975, pp. 27–30.

15. Leonard F. Chapman, "Illegal Aliens: Time to Call a Halt!" *Readers Digest* (October 1976), 189. See also Chapman's statements to the *New York Times*, October 22, 1974; and Chapman, "Illegal Aliens—A Growing Population," *Immigration and Naturalization Reporter* 24 (Fall 1975): 15–18.

16. See, for example, "600 More Aliens Rounded Up in Continuing L.A.-Area Raids," *Los Angeles Times*, May 30, 1973; "U.S. Roundup of Suspected Aliens Hit in Suit," *Los Angeles Times*, June 23, 1973; "Roundup of Illegal Aliens Stirs Angry Charges," *Los Angeles Times*, June 27, 1973, "Suit Asks Curb on Questioning of Suspected Aliens," *Los Angeles Times*, June 21, 1974.

17. See Kitty Calavita, "California's 'Employer Sanctions': The Case of the Disappearing Law," Center for U.S.-Mexican Studies, University of California, San Diego, *Research Report Series* 39 (La Jolla, CA: The Center, 1982).

18. The development of the Rodino and similar legislation is summarized in Donald C. Hohl and Michael G. Wenk, "Current U.S. Immigration Legislation: Analysis and Comment," *International Migration Review* (*IMR*) 5, no. 3 (Fall 1971): 339–56; Austin T. Fragomen, "Legislative and Judicial Developments," *IMR* 6, no. 3 (Fall 1972): 296–302; Donald C. Hohl and Michael G. Wenk, "The Illegal Alien and the Western Hemisphere Immigration Dilemma," *IMR* 7, no. 3 (Fall 1973): 323–32; Donald C. Hohl, "United States Immigration Legislation: Prospects in the 94th Congress," *IMR* 9, no. 1 (Spring 1975): 59–62; and U.S. Congress, House Committee on the Judiciary, *House Report 94–506: Amending the Immigration and Nationality Act, and for Other Purposes*, 94th Cong., 1st sess., September 24, 1975.

19. The best discussions of the evolution of the Chicano student movement are Gerald Paul Rosen, "The Development of the Chicano Movement in Los Angeles, from 1967 to 1969," *Aztlán* 4, no. 1 (Spring 1973): 155–84; Juan Gómez-Quiñones, *Mexican Students por La Raza: The Chicano Student Movement in Southern California 1967–1977* (Santa Barbara, CA: Editorial La Causa, 1978); Carlos Muñoz, Jr., and Mario Barrera, "La Raza Unida Party and the Chicano Student Movement in California," *Social Science Journal* 19, no. 2 (April 1982): 101–20; Mario Barrera, *Beyond Aztlán: Ethnic Autonomy in Comparative Perspective* (New York: Praeger, 1988); Carlos Muñoz, Jr., *Youth, Identity, Power: The Chicano Movement* (London: Verso, 1989); and Juan Gómez-Quiñones, *Chicano Politics: Reality and Promise, 1940–1990* (Albuquerque: University of New Mexico Press, 1990).

20. For differing interpretations on the origins and significance of the term "Chicano," see Tino Villanueva, "Sobre el termino 'chicano,' " *Cuadernos Hispano-Americanos* (1978): 387–410; and José Limón, "The Folk Performance of 'Chicano' and the Cultural Limits of Political Ideology," in Richard Bauman and Roger Abrahams, eds., *"And Other Neighborly Names": Social Process and Cultural Image in Texas Folklore* (Austin: University of Texas Press, 1980), 197–225. Evidence that awareness of the Chicano movement was growing in the media and in government is scattered, but trends in this direction were clearly evident by 1969. See, for example, "Mexican Americans and 'La Raza,' " *The Christian Century* 5 (March 1969): 325–28; Patrick H. McNamara, "Rumbles along the Rio," *Commonweal* 14 (March 1969): 730–32; and "Chicanos Stirring with New Ethnic Pride," *New York Times*, September 20, 1970. For a discussion of the evo-

lution and use of different self-referents in the Mexican-descent population of the Southwest, see Gutiérrez, "Unraveling America's Hispanic Past."

21. The background to the 1969 Chicano Youth Liberation Conference is assessed in Barrera, *Beyond Aztlán*, Chapter 4. For an interpretation of the historical evolution of the concept of Aztlán, see John R. Chávez, *The Lost Land: The Chicano Image of the Southwest* (Albuquerque: University of New Mexico Press, 1984); and Rudolfo A. Anaya and Francico Lomelí, eds., *Aztlán: Essays on the Chicano Homeland* (Albuquerque, NM: El Norte Publications, 1989).

22. First National Chicano Youth Liberation Conference, "El Plan Espiritual de Aztlán," in Luis Valdez and Stan Steiner, eds., *Aztlán: An Anthology of Mexican American Literature* (New York: Bantam, 1972), 403–4; and Barrera, *Beyond Aztlán*, 37.

23. For elaboration of the concept of "community control," as used by Chicano activists of this period, see Rodolfo "Corky" Gonzales, "Chicano Nationalism: The Key to Unity for La Raza," in Wayne Moquin, ed., *A Documentary History of the Mexican Americans* (New York: Bantam, 1972), 488–93; and John C. Hammerback, Richard J. Jensen, and José Angel Gutiérrez, *A War of Words: Chicano Protest in the 1960s and 1970s*, Contributions in Ethnic Studies, no. 12 (Westport, CT: Greenwood Press, 1985), particularly 53–100. Compare the similarities in black militants' rhetoric on this point in Raymond L. Hall, *Black Separatism in the United States* (Hanover, NH: University Press of New England, 1978).

24. See Gómez-Quiñones, *Chicano Politics*, 128–38; and Ignacio M. García, *United We Win: The Rise and Fall of La Raza Unida Party* (Tucson: Mexican-American Studies and Research Center, University of Arizona, 1989).

25. Henry B. González to Jake Rodríguez, June 5, 1967, Jake Rodríguez Papers, Box 11, Folder 4, LULAC Archives, Benson Library, University of Texas, Austin. See also González's remarks in the *Congressional Record*, 91st Cong., 1st sess., March 3, 1969, vol. 115., pt. 6, p. 8590; and March 15, 1969, p. 9058. For a succinct overview of González's critique of Chicano militants, see "The Rhetorical Counter-Attack of Mexican American Political Leaders," in Hammerback et al., eds., *A War of Words*, 101–20. See also Ruben Salazar's insightful analysis, "Chicanos vs. Traditionalists," *Los Angeles Times*, March 6, 1970.

26. José Angel Gutiérrez quoted in the *Congressional Record*, 91st Cong., 1st sess., April 15, 1969, vol. 115, pt. 7, p. 9059.

27. Cabinet Committee on Opportunity for the Spanish Speaking, "Judge Identifies Mexican Americans in School Suit" (news release, June 1970), Ernesto Galarza Papers, Box 14, Folder 5, Stanford University Libraries. On the far-reaching significance of *Cisneros* v. *Corpus Christi Independent School District*, see Guadalupe San Miguel, Jr., *"Let All of Them Take Heed": Mexican Americans and the Campaign for Educational Equality in Texas, 1910–1981* (Austin: University of Texas Press, 1987), 177–81.

28. Edward R. Roybal, the veteran moderate Mexican-American politician, by then a congressman representing East Los Angeles, acknowledged the influence Chicano militants exerted on Mexican-American politics of the period when he complained in a House subcommittee hearing that "[Chicano] students are asking questions. The militants in our community are on our backs almost every moment of the day. And the question that is being asked of me . . . and other elected officials is, 'Is it necessary for us to riot? Is it necessary for us to burn a

206 *Between Two Worlds*

town before the Government looks at our problems objectively? What are we to do if our community is not recognized?' " See U.S. Congress, House Committee on Government Operations, *Hearings on Establishing a Cabinet Committee on Opportunities for the Spanish-Speaking People*, 91st Cong., 1st sess., November 25–26, 1969, 18.

29. Gómez-Quiñones, "Mexican Students," 14.

30. Author interview with Bert Corona; CASA, "Articles of Incorporation, Article II" (1969), CASA Papers, Box 7, Folder 14; CASA, "What Is CASA?" mimeo (ca. 1974), CASA papers, Box 31, Folder 13; and CASA, "History of CASA" (typescript draft, ca. 1978), CASA Papers, Box 4, Folder 4, Department of Special Collections, SUL. For an interpretation of CASA's role in immigration politics and the Chicano movement in southern California, see David G. Gutiérrez, "CASA in the Chicano Movement: Ideology and Organizational Politics in the Chicano Community, 1968–1978," *Working Paper Series*, no. 5 (Stanford University: Stanford Center for Chicano Research, 1984); and Arturo Santamaría Gómez's insightful study, *La izquierda norteamericana trabajadores indocumentados* (Sinaloa, Mexico: Ediciónes de Cultura Popular, S.A., Universidad Autónoma de Sinaloa, 1988).

31. National Coalition for Fair Immigration Laws and Practices, "A Call to Action" (December 1973), CASA Papers, Box 32, Folder 11, SUL.

32. CASA, "What Is CASA?"

33. Bert Corona, *Bert Corona Speaks!* (New York: Pathfinder Press, 1972), 13–14.

34. Letter from Steve Hollopeter, vice president, CASA, to editor, *Los Angeles Times*, November 8, 1972.

35. CASA, "What Is CASA?"

36. Employing variants of the "internal colonial model" in attempts to analyze the historical position of minorities in American society, Chicano scholars of this period built on the early work of sociologists Robert Blauner and Joan W. Moore to develop new class-based interpretations of the Chicano experience. For examples of early Chicano scholarship along this vein, see Tomás Almaguer, "Toward the Study of Chicano Colonialism," *Aztlán* 2, no.1 (Spring 1971): 137–42; and Mario Barrera, Carlos Muñoz, Jr., and Charles Ornelas, "The Barrio as an Internal Colony," in Harlan Hahn, ed., *People and Politics in Urban Society* (Los Angeles: Sage Publications, 1972). For an insightful review and critique of the evolution of the internal colonial model in Chicano studies, see Tomás Almaguer, "Ideological Distortions in Recent Chicano Historiography: The Internal Colonial Model and Chicano Historical Interpretation," *Aztlán* 18, no. 1 (Spring 1987): 7–28.

37. Steve Teixeira, "Dixon Arnett Bill," *Regeneración* 2, no. 2 (1972).

38. "La Raza Platform Prohibits Support of Non-Chicano," *Los Angeles Times*, July 4, 1972.

39. "Rodino Immigration Proposal Protested," *Denver Post*, October 4, 1974.

40. Albert Armendáriz, Sr., testimony before U.S. Congress, House Committee on the Judiciary, Subcommittee no. 1, *Hearings: Illegal Aliens*, pt. 2 (El Paso, TX, July 10, 1971), Serial No. 13, 92nd Cong., 1st sess., 596.

41. Ibid., 592.

42. Statement of Manny Villareal, Past District Director, LULAC, in ibid., 596–97, 600. For an expression of similar sentiments, see also *LULAC News* 35, no. 12 (November–December 1973): 9.

43. *La Voz de MAPA* (February 1972), Manuel Ruiz Collection, Box 8, Folder 17, Department of Special Collections, SUL. See also "The Vicious Circle of the Illegal Alien Hiring Ban," *Los Angeles Times*, January 23, 1973.

44. See "Latin Political Unit Elects President in Stormy Session," *Los Angeles Times*, August 2, 1971.

45. See published letter to the editor, *Los Angeles Times*, July 1, 1973. For the range of opinion on the issue expressed by members of the public see the letters to the editor, *Los Angeles Times*, November 8, 1974.

46. Author's telephone interview with Albert Armendáriz, Sr., September 18, 1989.

47. For the evolution of the UFW, see Peter Matthiessen, *Sal Si Puedes: César Chávez and the New American Revolution* (New York: Random House, 1969); Jacques Levy, *César Chávez: Autobiography of La Causa* (New York: Norton, 1975); Ronald B. Taylor, *Chávez and the Farmworkers: A Study in the Acquisition and Use of Power* (Boston: Beacon Press, 1975); and J. Craig Jenkins, *The Politics of Insurgency: The Farm Worker Movement in the 1960s* (New York: Columbia University Press, 1985).

48. For the UFW's position on braceros and undocumented workers, see Taylor, *Chávez and the Farmworkers*, 218–19, 287–89; Jenkins, *The Politics of Insurgency*, 108–9, 144–46; and the statement of Len Avila, Colorado Labor Council, United Farm Workers Organizing Committee, in U.S. Congress, House Judiciary Subcommittee no. 1, *Hearings: Illegal Aliens* (June 24–25, 1971, Denver), 403–16. The UFW's official newspaper, *El Malcriado*, published many articles during the 1970s decrying the use of "illegal alien labor." For some representative stories, see, for example, "Hiring Illegals Challenged," December 1, 1972, p. 11; "Growers Use Illegals for Scabs," July 27, 1973, p. 4; "Illegal Aliens—Million Dollar Import Business," August 24, 1973, 5; "New Proposal for 'Bracero' Slave Labor," December 14, 1973, p. 3; "Chávez Assails Use of 'Illegals'in Mendota Rally," and "The 'Illegals' and the Growers," July 31, 1974, pp. 3, 10.

49. "UFW Campaign against Illegal Aliens—Farm Workers Ask for Citizens' Drive against Illegal Workers," *Accion!* (UFW newsletter, July 1974). See also Calavita, "California's 'Employer Sanctions,' " 29–30.

50. See "UFW Border Patrol," in *El Malcriado*, November 18, 1974, p. 5.

51. By the end of 1973, the National Coalition claimed the support of a broad range of Mexican-American and Chicano groups and individuals including chapters of LULAC, the American G.I. Forum, labor unions, and numerous Hispanic government officials.

52. The growing divisions between Chávez and other Chicano activists is summarized in "Chicanos Divided by Sympathy for Aliens, Fear for Own Jobs," *Los Angeles Times*, March 25, 1972; "Chávez Union Does Turnabout, Opposes Alien Worker Bill," *Los Angeles Times*, March 27, 1973; and "Why Citizen Chicanos Fear Fresh Turmoil," *Los Angeles Times*, February 23, 1975.

53. National Coalition for Fair Immigration Laws and Practices and CASA, "Open Letter to Our Brothers and Sisters of the United Farm Workers of America, AFL-CIO" (July 20, 1974), CASA Papers, Box 32, Folder 11, SUL.

54. "Saxbe Calls Illegal Aliens a U.S. Crisis," *Los Angeles Times*, October 31, 1974; "Chicanos Criticize Saxbe on Alien Deportation Proposal," *Los Angeles Times*, November 8, 1974; "Chicanos Criticize Saxbe on Alien Deportation Proposal," *Los Angeles Times*, November 8, 1974; "Chicano Activists Ask Ford to Seek Saxbe's Resignation," *Los Angeles Times*, November 18, 1974.

55. See "UFW Leader Talks with *El Malcriado*," *El Malcriado*, October 18, 1974, p. 11.

56. Chávez to *San Francisco Examiner*, November 22, 1974. See also his very similar statement in *El Malcriado*, September 9, 1974, p. 10. Chávez and the UFW maintained this new position throughout the rest of the decade and into the 1980s, as was evident in the union's forceful opposition to President Jimmy Carter's immigration reform proposals in 1977. For the union's revised position, see "UFW Denounces Carter Program on Illegal Aliens," *Los Angeles Times*, August 28, 1977; and United Farm Workers of America, AFL-CIO, Third Constitutional Convention, "Resolution 73" (August 1977), CASA Papers, Box 32, Folder 11, SUL.

57. Trinidad Flores, President, Los Angeles Mexican-American Labor Council, to Antonio Rodríguez, CASA [n.d., ca. 1975], CASA Papers, Box 31, Folder 6, SUL.

58. National Coalition for Fair Immigration Laws and Practices, "Stop Inhuman Rodino Bill" (1975), CASA Papers, Box 32, Folder 11, SUL. The American G.I. Forum's position during this period provides further evidence that even Mexican-American moderates were changing their views on the immigration issue. As late as March 1974 the Forum was supporting legislation such as Rodino's bill because the use of braceros and undocumented workers "pits *Mexicanos* from south of the border and Chicanos del norte against each other in . . . the farm labor market . . . [and because] it hampers César Chávez's farmworkers union in their organizing efforts." *The Forumeer* (March 1974): 3. By May of the following year, however, the *Forumeer* reported that the G.I. Forum was actively advising undocumented workers about their legal rights in the United States. By October 1975, the Forum's position had changed sufficiently so that the organization's national chairman, Tony Morales, publicly demanded the ouster of INS Commissioner Leonard Chapman. "Maybe we should give amnesty to illegal aliens and let them vote," argued Morales. "Then maybe we could remove people like Mr. Chapman from our government." See *The Forumeer* (May 1975): 3; and "Morales Asks Ouster of U.S. 'Migra' Boss," *The Forumeer* (October 1975): 1–2.

59. See President Jimmy Carter, "Communication to Congress," *Congressional Record*, August 4, 1977; "Carter Asks Congress to Let Illegal Aliens Stay," *Los Angeles Times*, August 5, 1977; "President Seeks Legalized Status for Many Aliens," *New York Times*, August 5, 1977.

60. Hispanic Ad Hoc Coalition on Immigration, "Response by Hispanics to Changes in Immigration Law Proposed by President Jimmy Carter," mimeo (Washington, DC: February 15, 1978), in author's personal files. Constituents of the ad hoc coalition included the American G.I. Forum, LULAC, the Mexican-American Legal Defense and Education Fund (MALDEF), the Mexican-American Women's National Association (MANA), the National Coalition of Hispanic Mental Health and Human Services Organizations (COSSMHO), the National Congress of Hispanic-American Citizens, the National Council of La Raza, National IMAGE, and La Raza National Lawyers Association. Local endorsers included the Bishop's Committee for the Spanish Speaking (East Chicago, Indiana), Centro Cultural Aztlán (San Antonio, Texas), Centro de Immigración (Georgetown University Law Center, Washington, DC), the Hispanic Advisory Committee, Immigration and Naturalization Service (Washington, DC), the National Association of Farm Worker Organizations (Washington, DC), and others. See also Mexican-American Legal Defense and Education Fund,

"Statement of Position Regarding the Administration's Undocumented Alien Legislative Proposal" (Washington, DC, September 26, 1977), in author's personal files. A summary of MALDEF's statement can be found in Senate Judiciary Committee, *Selected Readings*, 133–34. For the broad-based nature of the Hispanic response to the Carter Plan, see Congressman Roybal's and the Congressional Hispanic Caucus's criticism in "Carter Asks Congress," *Los Angeles Times*, August 5, 1977, and "President Seeks Legalized Status," *New York Times*, August 5, 1977; "Southland Group Assails Plan for Aliens," *Los Angeles Times*, August 5, 1977; Art Hernández, "The Peril Peering in on Us—A Hungry Human," *Los Angeles Times*, August 22, 1977; and "Latins Ready Lobby Effort," *Los Angeles Times*, October 16, 1977.

61. LULAC, Office of the Texas State Director, "Analysis of the Immigration Proposals—A Civil Rights Dilemma" (September 12, 1978), LULAC Archives, Box 3, Folder 3, University of Texas, Austin (hereafter UTA). See also "Alien Plan Criticized by LULAC," *San Antonio Express*, August 6, 1977.

62. See "G.I. Forum Knocks Alien Plan," *El Paso Times*, August 15, 1977; and "Resolutions Seek Equality for Aliens, Advancement for Women," and "The American G.I. Forum Continues to Fight for Human Rights," *The Forumeer*, September 1, 1977, pp. 1, 4. This constituted a complete reversal of the G.I. Forum's position presented in the Rodino hearings just six years earlier. Compare the G.I. Forum's testimony in United States Congress, House Judiciary Subcommittee no. 1, *Hearings: Illegal Aliens*, pt. 1 (Los Angeles, June 21, 1971), 254–55.

63. National Chicano/Latino Conference on Immigration and Public Policy, "A Call for Action" (ca. August 1977), CASA Papers, Box 34, Folder 2, SUL. The conference organizers' political perspective is further elaborated in Estevan Flores and the Research Task Force, Conference on Immigration and Public Policy, "A Call to Action: An Analysis of Our Struggles and Alternatives to Carter's Immigration Program," CASA Papers, Box 34, Folder 2, SUL.

64. Pedro Camejo, "Human Rights for Immigrants," *The Militant* 41, no. 46 (December 9, 1977).

65. "Latino Leadership Rips Carter Deportation Plan," *The Militant* 41, no. 43 (November 18, 1977).

66. See "Chicanos Will Fight Carter's Alien Plan," *Los Angeles Times*, October 31, 1977; "Hispanics Rap Amnesty Plan," *San Antonio Express*, October 31, 1977. For contemporary Chicano assessments of the San Antonio Conference, see Richard A. García, "The Chicano Movement and the Mexican American Community, 1972–1978: An Interpretive Essay," and Tomás Almaguer, "Chicano Politics in the Present Period: Comment on García," *Socialist Review* 40–41 (July–October, 1978): 117–41.

67. CASA—San José, *El Inmigrante Militante*, August 24, 1974. Or, as a UFW supporter put it in a letter to the union in 1974, "There is no such thing as an illegal worker. These so-called 'illegal aliens' are your brothers and sisters. . . . If you allow the brothers and sisters to be divided, I'm afraid your struggle will be in vain, the movement will be ripped apart." See Thomas J. Morgan to editor, *El Malcriado*, October 18, 1974, p. 9.

68. Jake Rodríguez, "Exploring and Analyzing 'Mexican' Misnomers and Misconceptions" (typescript, 1971), and Rodríguez, draft typescript correspondence addressed to Associated Press [n.d.], Jake Rodríguez Collection, LULAC Archives, Benson Library, UTA.

III

Contemporary Perspectives

9

U.S. Immigration Policy toward Mexico in a Global Economy

Saskia Sassen

Since the late 1970s, many scholars have sought to understand Mexican migration patterns in relation to larger international economic, political, and social trends. Keenly attuned to the fact that the dynamics of advanced capitalism have profoundly affected international migration patterns, these scholars have called for reconceptualizations of transnational migrations that take into account far-reaching trends such as the increasing economic domination of multinational corporations, the influence on local labor markets of foreign investment practices, and the development of instant global communications networks.

Columbia University sociologist Saskia Sassen attempts to shift traditional discussions of Mexican emigration processes by locating them as part of a general trend toward what she terms "economic internationalization." Comparing Mexico-United States migration patterns and structural changes in the American economy since World War II with similar patterns unfolding elsewhere in the world, Sassen advances the provocative argument that by allowing and encouraging massive foreign labor migration to the United States, policymakers unwittingly set into motion powerful forces that may be beyond the ability of the traditional nation-state to manage.

The concern here is to examine Mexican immigration within a broader global context. The central thesis is that the failure of U.S. immigration policy to meet its explicit objectives, particularly in regard to Mexico, rests on the insistence in treating immigration as a process autonomous from other major international processes. In the last few decades, domestic financial markets have been opened to foreign firms and multiple

From the *Journal of International Affairs* 43, no. 2 (Winter 1990): 369–83. Reprinted by permission of the *Journal of International Affairs* and the Trustees of Columbia University in the City of New York.

regulations lifted. U.S. firms have set up offshore manufacturing facilities in the Caribbean and Southeast Asia. Twin-plant manufacturing programs, which allow U.S. (and other non-Mexican) manufacturers to set up assembly facilities in Mexico, have expanded rapidly, and various restrictions on the inflow of direct foreign investment have been eliminated both in the United States and in Mexico. In brief, major areas of economic activity have become increasingly internationalized and deregulated. Yet U.S. policymakers insist on trying to maintain strict control over the flow of people and on treating immigration as a domestic issue. But is this viable?

In the 1960s and 1970s, the United States played a crucial role in the development of a world economic system. It passed legislation aimed at opening its own and other countries' economies to the flow of capital, goods, services, and information. The central military, political, and economic role the United States played in the emergence of a global economy contributed, I will argue, both to the creation of conditions that mobilized people into migrations, whether local or international, and to the formation of links between the United States and other countries that subsequently were to serve as bridges for international migration. Measures commonly thought to deter emigration—foreign investment and the promotion of export-oriented growth in developing countries—seem to have had precisely the opposite effect. After Mexico, the leading suppliers of immigration to the United States in the 1970s and 1980s have been several of the newly industrialized countries of South and Southeast Asia whose extremely high growth rates are generally recognized to be a result of foreign direct investment in export manufacturing.

If the new immigration to the United States from Southeast Asia and the Caribbean Basin is indeed part of a broader process of internationalization, it invites an examination of the possibility that factors other than the territorial continuity of a shared border account for some of the movement of workers from Mexico to the United States. In this context, it is worth examining the other major migration streams into the United States since 1965, all of which originated in areas lacking a common border with the United States. I would like to examine the possibility that in the case of U.S.-Mexican migration, concentration on the shared border has overshadowed the many different elements that create international migrations, many of which may be unrelated to the existence of a shared border, but are nevertheless routinely attributed to its influence.

Japan, for instance, now has a new illegal immigration of workers from several Asian countries—Pakistan, Bangladesh, South Korea, Taiwan, the Philippines, and Thailand—with which it has no shared border, but with which it has strong economic ties and investments in offshore manufacturing. In Japan we are seeing an immigration process just beginning in a country that has always been proud of its homogeneity and kept its doors closed to immigration.

In what ways has the internationalization of the U.S. economy created conditions for international migration? My perspective is not that of a specialist on Mexican immigration, but rather, of a specialist on the global economy. The new immigration to the United States and the conditions that have contributed to it raise questions about the possibility that there may also be a new immigration from Mexico. That is to say, while many flows of Mexican immigrants into the United States have occurred over the last thirty years, there may be new conditions, notably the Border Industrialization Program, that have promoted the formation of a new Mexican immigration, distinct from those of the past. If this is the case, it clearly carries policy implications, insofar as U.S. activities in Mexico, and not merely the latter's poverty and unemployment, may be a key element in the formation of such migrations.

This article will briefly examine the main immigration flows into the United States since 1965 in the light of major immigration policy objectives, the impact of the internationalization of production on the formation of migration flows, transformations in the U.S. labor market, particularly those that may contribute to the absorption of the post-1965 immigration, and finally, what all this means for policy.

Immigration Policy since 1965

There is, it would seem, a troubled relation between the understanding of immigration underlying policymaking and the objective processes that constitute what we usually refer to as immigration. U.S. policies, while carefully devised, have consistently failed to limit or regulate immigration in the intended way. The 1965 Amendment to the Immigration and Naturalization Act[1] contained a rather elaborate system of quotas meant to open the country to more immigration but to do so in a way that would allow the government to control entries and reduce illegal immigration. For instance, the emphasis on family reunification meant that the majority of new immigrants should have come from the European countries that had already sent large numbers of immigrants to the United States. Immigration did rise dramatically after 1965 as intended, but it consisted not of Europeans but of a new set of migrations mostly from the Caribbean Basin and South and Southeast Asia (henceforth referred to as Southeast Asia).[2] Annual entries increased from 1965 on, reaching 373,000 in 1970; 531,000 in 1980; and 602,000 in 1986, with more than half these entries being women. As recently as 1960, more than two-thirds of all immigrants entering the United States came from Europe. By 1985, Europe's share of annual entries had shrunk from almost 140,000 in 1960 to 63,000, one-ninth of annual entries. Hispanics form the single largest foreign-language population in the United States (and probably the largest population of undocumented immigrants as well), but Asians are the fastest-growing group of legally admitted immigrants with annual entries rising to 236,000 in 1980 and to 264,700 in 1985. While these figures include Southeast Asian refugees admitted in the aftermath of the Vietnam War, refugees account for only a small proportion of the overall rise in Asian immigration. In fact, the Philippines, South Korea, and Taiwan, not the refugee-sending countries of Vietnam and Cambodia, are the largest Asian sources of immigrants. And in the 1980s several new migration flows began from Southeast Asian nations such as Singapore, Malaysia, and Indonesia that had not previously experienced emigration to the United States. Furthermore, undocumented immigration from Mexico increased sharply in this period as did undocumented immigration from the same countries that were the source of legal immigration flows.[3]

Rising illegal immigration led to a series of congressional proposals that culminated in the 1986 Immigration Reform and Control Act. This law contains a limited legalization program whereby undocumented aliens who can prove their continuous residence in the United States since before January 1, 1982, and who meet certain other eligibility criteria, can legalize their status. It also contains sanctions on employers who knowingly hire undocumented workers, ostensibly in order to reduce employment opportunities for such workers. The third element of the 1986 law is an extended guest-worker program designed to ensure a continuing and abundant supply of low-wage workers for agriculture.

The 1986 law has had mixed results. About 1.8 million undocumented immigrants applied to legalize their status, less than expected but still a significant number. In addition, 1.2 million applied under special legalization programs for agriculture. Second, there is growing evidence of discrimination and abuses stemming from the employer sanctions program. Third, there is growing evidence of continuing undocumented immigration and the formation of new undocumented flows. Recently, there have been several proposals for revisions, partly in recognition of these problems.[4] Furthermore, congressionally mandated reviews of the employer sanctions provision by the General Accounting Office (GAO) question the statute's effectiveness. In brief, the 1986 law is not quite succeeding in regulating immigration in the ways it intended. Any policy that places immigrants and border control at its conceptual and operational center will keep failing in its purposes because it excludes the third central factor in the immigration process—the broader international forces, many generated or encouraged by the United States, that have helped give rise to immigration flows. The concept of "immigration" itself may be problematic in that it has come to be understood as the actions of individuals, the reasons for which are considered to be self-evident: People migrate to the United States because they are driven by poverty, economic stagnation, and overpopulation in their home countries. Immigration is seen as the direct result of unfavorable socioeconomic conditions in other countries. Yet an examination of the origins of most U.S. immigrants makes it evident that they come from a limited number of countries, not necessarily the poorest, and that most countries in the world that are poor and have stagnant economies do not have emigration.

The Internationalization of Production and Immigration

The main features of the new immigration—in particular the growing prominence of several Asian and Caribbean Basin countries as sources of immigrants—cannot be adequately explained under the prevailing assumptions of why immigration occurs. Even a cursory review of emigration patterns reveals that there is no systematic relationship between emigration and what conventional wisdom holds to be the principal causes of emigration, namely, high population growth, poverty, and economic stagnation. While these conditions cannot be disregarded in any analysis of emigration, it is clear that they alone do not explain large-scale emigration flows to the United States over the last two decades. Many countries with high population growth, vast poverty, and severe economic stagnation do not have large-scale emigration.

On the other hand, not all migrant-sending countries are poor, for example, South Korea and Taiwan. The utility of poverty in explaining emigration is further called into question by the fact that large-scale migration flows from most Asian and Caribbean Basin countries started only in the 1960s, despite the fact that many of these countries had long suffered from poverty. It is commonly assumed that economic stagnation in less-developed countries as measured by gross national product (GNP) growth rates is an important factor inducing individuals to emigrate. But the overall increase in emigration levels took place at a time when most countries had rather high economic growth according to conventional measures—annual GNP growth rates during the 1970s ranged from 5 to 9 percent for most of the leading migrant-sending countries. Even in Mexico, notwithstanding strong fluctuations, official GNP growth rates ranged between 4.2 and 7.5 percent in the early 1970s and then again in the late 1970s. In fact, most of the emigration countries were growing considerably faster than other countries that did not experience large-scale emigration. South Korea is the most obvious example. With a growth rate that was among the highest in the world during the 1970s, it was also a country with one of the fastest-growing levels of migration to the United States.

This is not to say that overpopulation, poverty, and economic stagnation do not create pressures for migration; by their very logic, they do. But it does make clear that the common identification of emigration with these conditions is overly simplistic. The evidence clearly suggests that these conditions are not sufficient by themselves to produce new large migration flows. At best, intervening factors need to be taken into account, factors that work to transform these conditions into migration-inducing situations. If the combination of high population growth, unemployment, and economic stagnation was a constant in each case long before emigration commenced, then what accounted for the sudden upsurge in immigration to the United States?

The emergence of political, military, and economic links with the United States seem to be the key factors that create conditions for the initiation of large-scale emigration. This is true in the case of the migration of Southeast Asians to the United States. In the period following the Korean war, the United States actively sought to promote economic development in order to stabilize the region politically. U.S. troops were stationed in Korea, the Philippines, and Indonesia, and these countries, along with Taiwan, received massive foreign investment. Together, U.S. business and military interests created a vast array of links with those Asians countries that subsequently developed large migration flows to the United States.

In most of the countries experiencing large migration flows to the United States, it is possible to identify a general set of conditions and ties with the United States that, together with overpopulation, poverty, or unemployment, induce out-migration. While these conditions vary from country to country, a common pattern of expanding U.S. political and economic involvement with emigrant-sending countries does emerge.

One significant common factor in this pattern over the last two decades is the presence of a specific type of foreign direct investment. It is recognized that the high growth rates of these countries are generally related to high levels of foreign investment, aimed at the development of production for export, especially in manufacturing and component assembly, that began in the late 1960s and increased rapidly in the 1970s. While total U.S. investment abroad increased between 1965 and 1980, with large amounts continuing to go to Europe and Canada, investment in the less-developed countries quintupled, much of it going to a few key countries in the Caribbean Basin and Southeast Asia. A large proportion of this investment in developing countries went into export industries which, because they tend to be highly labor intensive, are often located in low-wage countries. The result has been rapid employment growth, especially in manufacturing jobs, in these Asian and Caribbean Basin countries since 1965. To a lesser degree, this has also been the case in Mexico.

According to conventional explanations of why migrations occur, this combination of economic trends should have helped to deter emigration, or at least to keep it at relatively low levels. The deterrent effect should have been particularly strong in countries with high levels of export-oriented investment, since such investment is labor intensive and thus creates more jobs than other forms of investment. Yet it is precisely such countries, most notably the newly industrializing countries of Southeast Asia, that have been the leading senders of the new immigrants. To understand why large-scale migrations have originated in countries with high levels of job creation through substantial foreign investment in production for export, it is necessary to examine the impact of such investment on the economic and labor structure of developing countries.

Perhaps the single most important effect of foreign investment in production for export is that it uproots people from their traditional modes of existence. It has long been recognized that the development of commercial agriculture tends to displace subsistence farmers, creating a supply of rural wage laborers and mass migrations to cities. The recent large-scale development of export-oriented manufacturing in Southeast Asia, the Caribbean Basin, and Mexico's Border Industrialization Program has come to have a similar effect in that it has uprooted people and created an urban reserve of wage laborers. In both cases, the disruption of traditional work structures as a result of the introduction of modern modes of production plays a key role in transforming people into migrant workers and potential emigrants. Furthermore, export-led development generates a whole range of other jobs in occupations involving packaging, labeling, invoicing, clerical activities, loading, and shipping. The geographic concentration of much of this activity in a few areas raises its impact on employment.

In export manufacturing, the main cause of the disruption of traditional work structures is the massive recruitment of young women into jobs in the new industrial zones. Most of the manufacturing in these zones is of the sort that also employs women in the developed countries—apparel, electronics assembly, toys, textiles, and garments account for the largest share of all jobs in export zones and factories producing for export. Reducing labor costs and maximizing worker discipline in labor-intensive operations is the chief reason for developing offshore manufacturing facilities. In Mexico's case, proximity to U.S. markets gives added incentive for other countries, notably Japan, to invest in such facilities.

This mobilization of large numbers of women into wage labor has a highly disruptive effect on traditional, often unpaid, work situations in which women fulfill basic functions in the production of goods for family consumption or for sale in local markets. Village economies and rural households depend on a rather diversified labor input by women, ranging from food preparation to cloth weaving, basket making, and various other types of craftwork. Though conditions vary across regions and countries, typically women fulfill key functions in rural households.

One of the most serious—and ironic—consequences of the feminization of the new proletariat has been to increase the pool of wage laborers and thus contribute to male unemployment. Not only does competition from the new supply of female workers make it more difficult for men to find work in the new industrial zones, [but] the massive departure of young women has also reduced the opportunities for men to make a living in many rural areas where women are partners in the struggle for survival. More generally, in some of the poorer, less-developed regions or countries, export-led production has come to replace other, more diversified forms of economic growth oriented to the internal market and typically employing not only women but also men. The impressive employment growth figures for the main emigration countries do not reveal these disruptions.[5]

There is a relationship, then, between export-oriented foreign investment and the geographic, social, and political mobilization of certain populations. In addition to eroding traditional work structures and creating a pool of wage laborers, foreign investment contributes to the development of economic, cultural, and ideological connections with the industrialized countries. Now that Japan has become a leading global economic power and the major foreign investor in Southeast Asia, the same set of processes seem to have been put in motion: the creation of various political and economic ties that eventually come to operate as bridges for migration. The new illegal immigration to Japan comes from Thailand, Bangladesh, Taiwan, Pakistan, the Philippines, and South Korea—all countries where Japan has made major foreign direct investments.[6]

Though fragmentary, the evidence clearly points to a rapid increase over the last few years in the numbers of foreigners who have entered the country with tourist visas and are working illegally in Japan, mostly in the Tokyo metropolitan area, but also in Nagoya and Osaka. In Japan by mid-1988, there were an estimated two hundred thousand illegal workers, almost all of them from Asia, engaged in manual labor from construction to restaurant kitchens. Government figures recorded increases in arrests of illegal workers, from 51,268 in 1982 to 77,437 in 1987. There also has been an increase recently in the numbers of forced deportations, from 5,398 in 1987 to 13,771 in 1988.

As Japan internationalizes its economy and becomes a key investor in Southeast Asia, wittingly or not, it creates a transnational space for the circulation of its goods, capital, cultural products, technology, and services. In creating this space it has also created objective and cultural-ideological conditions for the circulation of workers, an early stage in the formation of an international labor market. The Japanese parliament has recently approved several amendments to the immigration law that seek to control immigration. On the one hand, the amendments expand the number of job categories for which the country will accept foreign workers. These are mostly in professional occupations such as lawyers, investment bankers, accountants with international expertise, and medical personnel. On the other hand, it seeks to restrict and control the inflow of unskilled and semiskilled workers. For the first time the law imposes sanctions on those employing illegal workers. Employers could be fined up to $14,000 and imprisoned for up to three years if they continue to employ illegal workers. Japan, then, is in many ways replicating the efforts of the United States to control those who cross its borders. It will be interesting to observe whether it succeeds in view of the growing internationalization of its economy.

Foreign Investment and Mexican Emigration

In the case of Mexico, the development of the Border Industrialization Program with the United States can be seen as part of a broader process. Migration northward began long before the program was implemented, and massive development of commercial agriculture had already put in motion many of the mechanisms for the disruption of traditional work structures and the mobilization of people into migrant labor streams. Furthermore, geographic proximity may have made a difference in the types of industries developed in the border zone, including auto parts manufacture, and hence in the somewhat higher incidence of male employment. Nonetheless, it is worth noting that while the total male labor force along the border grew more rapidly than the Mexican national average in the 1970s, by 1980 the labor force participation rate of men in the border zone was lower than the national average. On the other hand, women in the border zone had a higher participation rate than the national average. Using regression analysis, Brook has shown that a 1 percent increase in total manufacturing employment in the border municipalities raised the participation of women by 0.9 percent.[7] Women constituted 77 percent of production workers in the twin-plant program in 1980;[8] by 1986 their absolute numbers had increased although their share had declined to 68 percent.[9]

There is also evidence of increased migration inside Mexico due to the expanding border program. Between 1982 and 1987 there was a 23 percent increase in the number of plants and a 32 percent increase in the number of workers in the Border Industrialization Program.[10] The possibility that migration into the United States has been stimulated by these developments has been raised by several authors. Others argue, however, that the twin-plant program has not been the cause for northward migration to the border and into the United States.[11]

In addition to the direct impact on workers in the export sector, the links created by foreign direct investment of this sort have also had a generalized westernizing effect on the less-developed country and its people. The influence of such a cultural-ideological effect in promoting emigration should not be underestimated; it makes emigration an option not just for those individuals employed in the new industrial zones but for the wider population as well.

How different is the Mexican immigration of the last two decades from the new Southeast Asian and Caribbean Basin immigration to the United States? I would like to propose that there are many distinct Mexican immigrations and that part of the flow of immigration we see today belongs to the same broader process of internationalization that encompasses Asian and Caribbean migration to the United States, a dynamic that now we see emerging also in the case of Japan.

There is a distinction to be made between the Mexican immigration that has evolved out of the development of the Southwestern region, where there were once unrestricted flows of Mexican workers, and a new set of processes, epitomized by the Border Industrialization Program, that have engendered migration but are not necessarily a function of the joint border—that is, the same processes that are occurring in Southeast Asia and the Caribbean. It is evident that in practice contiguous territory may facilitate the flow of capital, manufactured components, and workers, but the broader dynamic of economic internationalization strengthens the regional dynamic of the border zone.

In both cases, the structures and mechanisms of international interaction, which cannot be reduced to the existence of a shared border, are at work. These structures and mechanisms change over time, respond to new conditions, expand or dissolve. At different times, they will reconstitute border areas as part of different dynamics of internationalization. For example, in the nineteenth century, the transatlantic economy was at the core of U.S. development. There were massive flows of capital, goods, and workers and specific structures that produced this transatlantic system. Today, the United States is at the heart of an international system of investment and production that has incorporated not only Mexico but areas in the Caribbean and Southeast Asia.

Hinojosa has proposed a series of models describing a range of possible forms that international systems can assume. He proposes that the North-South regime that was put into place during and after World War II is now in a state of crisis that began when import absorption in the Third World shrank, debt accumulated, and international competition among the developed countries rose rapidly after Japan and Western Europe had rebuilt their economies. Today the debt burden in the less-developed countries has reduced domestic demand, and export-led industrialization implies that the demand for production is not in the country of production but in the one sending the capital.[12]

The main implications of this analysis for a discussion on immigration policy are (a) the recognition of an international or transnational system that reproduces and regulates the economic and political processes that bind Mexico and the United States and within which immigration takes place, and (b) that insofar as the conditions supporting that system have changed, so perhaps should the terms of the immigration debate. The transformation of the organization of labor markets in the United States over the last decade, and hence, the transformation of the conditions for the demand and absorption of immigrant workers, is one key set of factors pushing for change in the international system which binds the two countries.

The Demand Side

Any analysis of the new immigration is incomplete without an explanation of the changes in labor demand in the United States. There has been a rapid expansion in the supply of low-wage jobs in the United States and a casualization of the labor market, both associated with the new growth industries, but also with the decline and reorganization of manufacturing. Such tendencies toward casualization are an important process facilitating the incorporation of illegal immigration into the labor market. Casualization opens up the hiring process, lifts restrictions on employers, and typically lowers the direct and indirect costs of labor. The increase in low-wage jobs in the United States is in part a result of the same international economic processes that have channeled investment and manufacturing jobs to low-wage countries. As industrial production has moved overseas or to low-wage areas in the South, the traditional U.S. manufacturing organization based on high wages has eroded and partly been replaced in many industries by a downgraded manufacturing sector characterized by a supply of poorly paid, semiskilled or unskilled production jobs, and extensive subcontracting. At the same time, the rapid growth of the service sector has created vast numbers of low-wage jobs in addition to the more publicized increase in highly paid investment banking, management, and professional jobs.

These trends have brought about growing inequality in the U.S. occupational and income structure. Along with a sharp decline in the number of middle-income blue- and white-collar jobs, there has been an increase in the number of high-paying professional and managerial jobs. This increasing inequality is clearly reflected in the transformation of the earnings distribution in the United States. Inflation-adjusted average weekly wages peaked in 1973, stagnated over the next few years, and fell in the decade of the 1980s.[13] Up to 1973 there was an increase in the degree of equality in the distribution of earnings. Since 1975, the opposite has occurred.[14] The data show an increase in low-wage, full-time, year-round jobs since the late 1970s and, though less pronounced, in high-income jobs.[15] But in the decade from 1963 to 1973, nine out of ten new jobs were in the middle earnings group[16] whereas after 1973 only one in two new jobs was in the middle earnings category. If one were to add the increase in the number of workers who are not employed full-time and year-round, then the inequality becomes even more pronounced. Part-time workers increased from 15 percent in 1955 to 22 percent in 1977; by 1986 they were a third of the labor force. Approximately 80 percent of these 50 million workers earn less than $11,000 a year.

The fact that the U.S. economy is generating a high proportion of low-income jobs suggests that the supply of such jobs and the casualization of many of these labor markets will probably continue. The growth of casual and informal labor markets also facilitates the absorption of undocumented immigrants. In this context, employer sanctions and an amnesty program that excludes a large number of undocumented workers will contribute to further erosion in their conditions of work and the consolidation of an underclass defined not only in economic but also in legal terms.

Conclusion

If immigration is understood as the act of individuals leaving their countries because of poor economic conditions, then the decision to accept immigrants can be understood as a generous act of a humane society willing to share its riches with the poor and the needy of the world. If, however, immigration is also a type of return on foreign economic and military activities by the U.S. government and business, then the decision to accept immigrants is part of a different equation.

Could it be that U.S. immigration policy has so often been overtaken by events that did not respond to its designers' aims because it has insisted on the first view? An examination of the conditions at work after the implementation of the 1965 Act shows that the vast majority of immigrants come from a limited number of countries, that these are all countries that have played a central role in the internationalization of production that began in the late 1960s, and, finally, that the vast majority of countries with high poverty and economic stagnation do not have mass labor migrations to the United States. This would seem to indicate that certain links or bridges need to be formed between countries of emigration and the United States before an emigration flow can begin. Moreover, only in these circumstances will an immigration policy that liberalizes entry conditions have the effect of raising immigration levels (as occurred after the 1965 Act).

Although it is ultimately individuals who make the decision to emigrate, clearly the vast majority of individuals chose not to do so, even in the leading emigration countries. Those who do choose to emigrate do not make this decision in a void, nor do they necessarily make this decision in response to policy. The case of Japan is of interest here. Japan is a closed country with no tradition of immigration. Yet now that it has emerged as a global power it has attracted a new illegal immigration, and it has drawn it from those countries that have received significant levels of investment and are part of its economic sphere of influence. These new immigrants are not coming from just any country.

The implications for the Mexican case are clear. Migrations are produced. The mere fact of a shared border and inequality in wages between the two countries is not sufficient in itself to account for immigration. The construction of railroads in the 1800s, the development of commercial agriculture, and now the development of the Border Industrialization Program are all processes which created a labor market. The fact that this labor market was eventually divided by a patrolled border led to contradictions in the legislation covering both halves. Secondly, if the United States, through its economic activities, has incorporated Mexican workers and Mexican areas into a broader international organization of production, and if, furthermore, these activities promote the formation of migrations, then the United States must assume some responsibility for immigration of Mexicans into North America.

At the same time, the transformation of the occupational and income structure in the United States—itself in good part a result of the globalization of production—has created an expanding supply of low-wage jobs.

The decline of manufacturing and the growth of services have contributed to make more jobs temporary and part-time, reduced advancement opportunities within firms, and weakened various types of job protection. The resulting casualization of the labor market facilitates the absorption of immigrants, including undocumented immigrants, a process also now evident in Japan as it becomes a global power.

These are powerful changes—in the United States, in Mexico, and in the conditions that bind the two countries. If we add to this the internationalization of many key markets and the growth of U.S. foreign investment, we must then ask whether a policy aimed at strict control of U.S. borders is viable or whether we should move toward a fundamental rethinking of the immigration question, one which would, for example, replace border control with protection of workers' wages and rights in both Mexico and the United States.

Notes

1. The 1965 Act sought to eliminate several highly discriminatory clauses of earlier immigration law and to regulate the influx of immigrants by settling up a system of preference categories within the general quota. Under the preference system, the primary mechanism for immigration was family reunification and, to a lesser extent, entry in the occupational categories with labor shortages, such as nurses and nannies.

2. The top ten immigrant-sending countries today are all in Latin America, the Caribbean Basin, and Asia. In the 1970s, Mexico, with more than half a million entries, was by far the largest source of legally admitted immigrants, followed by the Philippines with over 300,000, South Korea with 250,000, China (including both Taiwan and the People's Republic) with 200,000, India with 160,000, and Jamaica with 120,000.

3. See R. Warren and J. S. Passel, *Estimates of Illegal Aliens from Mexico Counted in 1980 U.S. Census* (Washington, DC: Bureau of the Census, Population Division, 1983).

4. In a departure from earlier immigration policy, the Senate recently approved a bill that seeks to give higher priority to applicants who satisfy labor needs in the United States. The 554,000-per-year limit placed on such immigrants is low, but it would (a) set an important precedent by acknowledging that immigrants, though only about 7 percent of the U.S. labor force, have accounted for 22 percent of the growth in the work force since 1970; and (b) respond to U.S. Department of Labor forecasts of impending labor shortages in a variety of occupations.

5. In a detailed examination of the employment impact of export-led industrialization, the United Nations Industrial Development Organization (UNIDO) found that, in general, this type of development eliminated more jobs than it created because of its disruptive effect on the national manufacturing sector, especially in the less-developed countries of the Caribbean and Southeast Asia. *World Industry since 1960: Progress and Prospects* (Vienna: UNIDO, 1979).

6. See Saskia Sassen, *The Global City: New York, London, Tokyo* (Princeton, NJ: Princeton University Press, 1990).

7. H. Brook, "Patterns of Labor Force Participation in the U.S.-Mexico Border Region, 1970 and 1980," *Journal of Borderlands Studies* 1, no. 1 (Spring 1986): 109–32.

8. M. P. Fernandez-Kelly, *For We Are Sold, I and My People: Women and Industry in Mexico's Frontier* (Albany: State University of New York Press, 1983).

9. G. K. Schoepfle and J. Perez-Lopez, "U.S. Unemployment Impact of TSUS 806.30 and 807.00 Provisions and Mexican Maquiladoras: A Survey of Issues and Estimates," Economic Discussion Paper 29 (Washington, DC: Bureau of International Labor Affairs, U.S. Department of Labor, 1988).

10. E. J. Williams, "Turnover and Recruitment in the *Maquiladora* Industry: Causes and Solutions in the Border Context" (a report submitted to the Office of Foreign Relations of the U.S. Department of Labor, September 1988).

11. E. R. Stoddard, *Maquila: Assembly Plants in Northern Mexico* (El Paso: Texas Western Press, 1987); and R. C. Jones, ed., *Patterns of Undocumented Migration* (Totowa, NJ: Rowman and Allenheld, 1984).

12. Ojeda R. Hinojosa, "The Political Economy of North-South Interdependence: Debt, Trade and Class Relations across Mexico and the U.S." (Ph.D. diss., University of Chicago, 1989).

13. Paul Blumberg, *Inequality in an Age of Decline* (New York: Oxford University Press, 1980), 67, 79.

14. Robert Z. Lawrence, "Sectoral Shifts and the Size of the Middle Class," *Brookings Review* (Fall 1984).

15. Bennet Harrison and Barry Bluestone, *The Great U-Turn* (New York: Basic Books, 1988).

16. A report by the staff of the House Ways and Means Committee found that, from 1979 to 1987, the bottom fifth of the population experienced a decline of 8 percent in its personal income, while the top fifth experienced an income increase of 16 percent.

10

Implications of the North American Free Trade Agreement for Mexican Migration into the United States

Dolores Acevedo and Thomas J. Espenshade

In January 1994, after extended and often acrimonious debate, the governments of Canada, Mexico, and the United States entered into the North American Free Trade Agreement (NAFTA). Designed to stimulate trade among the continent's three largest economies by gradually eliminating tariffs and other trade barriers, NAFTA already has significantly increased trade between the United States and Mexico. It is telling, and indicative of the complexity and political sensitivity of the immigration controversy, that negotiators generally chose not to include discussions of labor and migration issues during their deliberations over the regional trade agreement.

Princeton sociologist Thomas Espenshade and Dolores Acevedo, a doctoral candidate in the Woodrow Wilson School of Public Policy and International Affairs at Princeton, speculate about the short- and long-term effects NAFTA might have on migration trends between Mexico and the United States. Noting that deeply rooted, historically based migration circuits have not tended to respond to unilateral policy initiatives by the United States, the authors conclude that, barring further bilateral negotiations (and perhaps even then), NAFTA will probably not appreciably reduce migration flows "over the short to medium run." Over the long run, they suggest, only a dramatic improvement of Mexico's economy relative to that of the United States seems likely to reduce south-to-north migratory flows.

O n August 12, 1992, the governments of Canada, Mexico, and the United States concluded negotiations for the North American Free

From *Population and Development Review* 18, no. 4 (December 1992): 729–44. Reprinted by permission of the Population Council.

Trade Agreement (NAFTA). Approval by the legislature of each country, while far from certain, may come as early as the spring of 1993. The main provisions of NAFTA are the following:[1]

—Elimination of all import tariffs on manufactured goods and agricultural products traded among the three countries. Some tariffs will be eliminated as soon as the agreement becomes effective, while others will be phased out over five, ten, or fifteen years. A complex rules-of-origin system will ensure that only those goods entirely produced in North America will be exempt from tariffs.

—Most tariffs on agricultural products will be eliminated over a ten-year period. However, for those crops that are unusually sensitive to level of imports (for example, corn and beans in the Mexican case and peanuts, broccoli, cauliflower, onions, orange juice concentrate, sugar, and asparagus in the case of the United States), the phase-out period for tariffs will stretch over fifteen years.

—Tariffs on textiles and apparel will be eliminated over a ten-year period if the manufacture of these goods complies with the rules-of-origin stipulations described in NAFTA. For instance, textiles will be exempt from tariffs if they are made from North American thread, and apparel will be exempt if clothing is made from North American fabrics.

—The automobile market will gradually be opened over a ten-year period.

—Mexico's state-owned oil company (PEMEX) will allow foreign companies to bid for drilling, exploration, and service contracts, but Mexico will neither allow foreign ownership of its oil reserves nor guarantee the United States a specific annual allotment of oil.

—U.S. and Canadian companies operating in Mexico will have the same rights as Mexican companies, and vice versa.

—U.S. and Canadian banks and investment and insurance companies will be allowed to operate in Mexico, and vice versa.

We have stressed here those NAFTA provisions having the greatest potential bearing on migration behavior. But NAFTA contains numerous other conditions, including assurances that national and state environmental, health, and safety standards cannot by overridden by the trade pact.

NAFTA is likely to have broad implications in a wide variety of areas, both economic and noneconomic. This note explores the implications of NAFTA for south-north migration and, in particular, for migration from Mexico to the United States. It is divided into two sections. In the first, we consider the possible effects of free trade on migration. The discussion is based on a synthesis of the sparse literature on the links between trade and Mexico-U.S. migration. In the second, we provide estimates of the likely effect of NAFTA on the eventual flow of undocumented migrants from Mexico into the United States if the free-trade agreement results in an improvement in the Mexican economy relative to the U.S. economy.[2]

The Effect of Trade on Migration

It is well known from classical international trade theory that countries should concentrate on producing those goods in which they have a comparative advantage. A corollary view is that in the absence of protectionism, trade among countries with different factor endowments is a substitute for migration. In other words, if countries with an abundance of labor can specialize in the production of labor-intensive goods, there need not be labor migration to more developed countries.

On the basis of this theory, some scholars have contended that distorted trade and industrialization policies in both the economically more advanced and the developing countries of the world have stimulated south-north migration. Following a period of trade expansion that began after World War II, some industrialized countries insisted on protecting labor-intensive sectors (for example, textiles and clothing), and encouraged immigration to supply these sectors with sufficient workers. In the mid-1970s, however, as economic growth slowed and overall unemployment soared, political pressures to restrict the importation of foreign workers increased.[3]

Meanwhile, in sending countries, import substitution became the preferred industrialization strategy. Import substitution caused developing countries to deviate from comparative advantage principles and hindered the absorption of indigenous labor. Consequently, this strategy stimulated emigration. "Shifts in comparative advantage, which in a framework of competitive and open markets would have given rise to new patterns of world trade, in the context of protection-ridden economies had to be expressed in a greater international labor mobility."[4]

One implication of this reasoning is that unrestricted trade and international labor migration are substitutes. It follows that, by eliminating protectionism within North America and by increasing foreign investment in Mexico, Mexico's structural adjustment program and NAFTA will help reduce Mexican migration to the United States.

We turn next to recent research examining links between trade, development, and migration in the North American context.

The U.S. Immigration Reform and Control Act (IRCA), passed by Congress in 1986, has been criticized for trying to deal with undocumented (or illegal) migration solely through enforcement, by imposing sanctions on employers who knowingly hire undocumented workers and by allocating more resources to the U.S. Border Patrol. Most research concerning the effect of IRCA on the size of the undocumented flow has found that the Act had either a small effect during the first year or two after it was passed or no effect whatsoever.[5] The disappointment surrounding IRCA's effectiveness has led some Americans to suggest that, given the wide economic gap between Mexico and the United States, it is naive to think that tougher enforcement could be an effective solution to undocumented migration. Only economic development in Mexico and other sending countries can slow migration.[6]

A little-known provision of IRCA created a commission to examine the relationship between economic development and immigration. For the first time, Congress acknowledged that the United States might have to consider the immigration issue in nonenforcement terms. For three years the Commission for the Study of International Migration and Cooperative Economic Development (CSIMCED) sought to determine what kinds of economic policies in the sending and receiving countries would reduce the migratory flow.

In its final report the Commission praised the Mexican structural adjustment process but pointed out that the United States needed to open its markets to its southern neighbor.[7] It suggested that trade liberalization would mitigate the economic push factors generating outmigration from the Caribbean Basin. The main conclusion of the report was that, in the long run, economic development is the real solution to the immigration question and that "the most promising stimulus to future growth in sending countries is expanded trade between them and the industrialized countries—particularly the United States, which is their natural market."[8]

The Commission acknowledged that the United States has already taken some steps toward improving the access of Mexico and the Caribbean countries to its markets.[9] They added that the 1989 free-trade agreement (FTA) with Canada opened real prospects for a North American free-trade area including Mexico.[10] Mexico had by that time made clear its desire to negotiate a free-trade agreement with the United States, and negotiations between the two countries were under way. The Commission recommended that the United States expedite the development of a U.S.-Mexico free-trade area.

Surprisingly, the Commission's final report said little about the implications of an FTA for Mexican migration to the United States.[11] Of course, the fact that negotiations had just started prevented the analysis of specific questions. However, the Commission carefully noted that, in the short run, not just the FTA but any measure to foster Mexico's economic development would tend to increase migratory pressures.

Massey has argued that the way for developed countries to control immigration is to promote economic development in major sending countries. In the short run, however, development increases the impetus for migration because it destroys the peasants' social system through the substitution of capital for labor, the privatization and consolidation of land-holdings, and the creation of markets. Displaced rural dwellers become the source for the massive population movements that inevitably accompany development. In view of this statement, one could argue that some development initiatives—like the commercialization of agriculture that is implicit in Mexico's economic liberalization program—may stimulate out-migration.

Although Massey's reasoning is persuasive, one must take into account recent changes in the composition of the Mexican migratory flow. In the 1970s, about half the Mexican undocumented flow came from two states, Jalisco and Michoacán. But by 1988, owing to the pervasiveness of Mexico's economic crisis in the 1980s, the share of these two states had fallen to 17 percent, while six "nontraditional" states contributed about 40 percent of the undocumented flow.[12] Included among the nontraditional sending regions were Mexico City, Oaxaca, and Baja California. Thus, the majority of Mexican migrants to the United States no longer come from rural areas.[13]

The Commission pointed out that, because per capita income is about ten times higher in the United States than in Mexico, even if the FTA induced rapid economic growth in Mexico it would take decades for the two incomes to equalize. For example, if income per head grows at 3 percent annually in Mexico and 1 percent in the United States, equalization will take 116 years.[14] Nevertheless, a narrowing wage differential between the two countries reduces the expected gains from Mexico-U.S. migration and encourages more potential migrants to remain in Mexico.[15] Moreover, the existing wage differential will probably encourage some American businesses to move their operations to Mexico, thereby creating new job opportunities for would-be migrants.

Massey noted that, although emigration is a natural outcome of economic development under a market economy, there are large differences in the extent of out-migration among countries that have undergone economic development. In general, as two economies become more integrated and interdependent, the volume of migration between them grows.[16] Given that the FTA will logically increase the interdependence of the American and Mexican economies, one can predict that migratory pressures will increase.

Both Cornelius and Massey have argued that the existence of strong migrant networks has created a migration momentum. According to this view, regardless of domestic economic incentives Mexicans will continue to go to the United States, because a desire for the "norteño way of life" is already ubiquitous in many Mexican communities. Nevertheless, except for one case to be mentioned later, the Commission did not analyze the impact that a free-trade agreement might have on specific migrant circuits.

Because the FTA is bound to move Mexico even closer to export-oriented industrial development and privatization, one should look at the migration-related effects that structural adjustment policies so far have had in Mexico. The Commission asked several researchers to analyze this issue. The main conclusion of these studies is that, although production and employment have grown significantly faster in Mexican exports than in nonexports,[17] the direct employment effects may be small and will continue to pale beside the enormous pull that employment opportunities offer across the border.[18] Meanwhile, evidence on the employment effects of privatization is inconclusive due in part to the relative brevity of the Mexican experience. Thus far, it seems unwarranted to assert that privatization has either fostered or inhibited migration in any direct way.[19]

Liberalization policies in the agricultural sector are likely to exert migratory pressures. Mexico recently changed its constitution and its agrarian legislation to allow the privatization of communal landholdings (ejidos). Some observers have claimed that this measure has already caused a 10 percent jump in undocumented migration to the United States in recent months.[20] Regardless of the accuracy of this figure, it seems fair to say that the commercialization of agriculture will displace many rural workers, some of whom may become international migrants.

Under NAFTA Mexico has agreed to phase out its price supports for corn producers over a fifteen-year period. This measure will leave a large number of peasants unemployed. But in other crops the employment effects of liberalization need not be negative.[21] For example, a case study of the impact of trade liberalization on the production of fresh winter tomatoes in southern Florida (United States) and Sinaloa (Mexico) found that free trade might reduce hand-harvest jobs in Florida while providing more seasonal employment in Mexico.[22]

In addition, over the last decade, fruit, vegetable, and nursery (FVN) agriculture in the United States has expanded due to the availability of inexpensive immigrant labor. If NAFTA brings about a similar expansion of Mexican FVN agribusiness, financed by increased domestic and foreign investment, the jobs thereby created may not be adequate to offset the displacement effects of liberalization in such other crops as corn and beans. Even if FVN imports from Mexico rise, U.S. domestic production may also increase and with it the demand for immigrant laborers. The experience of America's tomato market in the 1980s shows that imports and domestic output can rise simultaneously. The process of "Mexicanization" of the U.S. agricultural work force and the existence of well-developed migrant networks will continue to foster migration.[23]

More generally, the trade-induced transfer of jobs from the United States to Mexico will not necessarily reduce migration, because (1) internal migration and international migration circuits are distinct; (2) production of vegetables creates only seasonal jobs, so workers can still migrate to the United States after the harvest season is over;[24] and (3) the wage differential remains large enough so that international migrants will not switch easily to the internal migration stream if employment in Mexico increases.[25]

NAFTA negotiators did not address the migration issue explicitly. One chapter in the agreement deals with the temporary entry of business persons.[26] But in contrast to the European Community scheme, the North American free-trade area is not a common market, and the free movement of labor is not allowed. However, it is not unlikely that in the future Mexico and the United States will initiate talks on immigration.

We have argued that some of NAFTA's effects on the Mexican economy may initially tend to increase migration to the United States. Trade-induced economic growth should eventually reduce the gap in living standards between the two countries, but in the short run development is likely to displace rural workers in certain crops. One presumes that jobs will be created in the industrial sector, but it is difficult to assess whether American firms based in Mexico or Mexican exporting firms will be able to absorb a significant number of potential migrants to the United States. More case studies showing the impact of free trade on specific migrant circuits are needed.

Free Trade and Undocumented Mexico-U.S. Migration

In this section, we present some illustrative calculations showing the possible effects of NAFTA on the size of the undocumented flow from Mexico to the United States. We concentrate on the undocumented flow because these migration links are of greater concern to policymakers, at least in the United States, and because neither NAFTA nor the U.S. Immigration Act of 1990 is designed to have appreciable effects on legal immigration.[27] Here we focus on wage rate and unemployment rate differentials between the two countries. Not only are these differentials key measures of relative economic performance that are likely to be affected by NAFTA;

they have also been shown to have important effects on the Mexico-U.S. undocumented migration flow.[28] The reader should keep in mind, however, that significant narrowing of the economic gap between Mexico and the United States will be a consequence of free trade only in the long run.

If NAFTA resulted in an improvement in the Mexican economy relative to the American economy, then it may be reasonable to assume that the flow of undocumented migrants will be reduced. This was a conclusion reached recently by the U.S. International Trade Commission: "An FTA [free-trade agreement] is likely to decrease slightly the gap between real United States wages and Mexican wages of both skilled and unskilled workers combined, but a greater share of the wage adjustment would occur in Mexico than in the United States. As wage differentials between the United States and Mexico narrow, the incentive for migration from Mexico will decline."[29]

But by how much might the flow be decreased? To answer this question, we present numerical estimates of the responsiveness of the annual gross undocumented migration flow across the southern U.S. border to a range of improvements in the relative performance of the Mexican economy. In particular, we show the likely response of the undocumented flow to possible changes in (1) the ratio of the U.S. unemployment rate to the Mexican unemployment rate and (2) the ratio of the hourly wage rate in the U.S. nonagricultural sector to the hourly earnings in the Mexican manufacturing sector.

The estimates shown in the table are based on a statistical model of undocumented migration from Mexico to the United States developed by Espenshade. The model was estimated using monthly data for the period January 1977 to September 1988. To produce the detailed annual estimates presented in the table, the model was applied for each month of fiscal year 1988 (October 1987–September 1988), and the predicted results were aggregated.[30] Other models also allow one to examine the effect of IRCA on the flow of undocumented migration to the United States,[31] but the model used here is the only one simultaneously to include seasonal and economic effects on the flow, to use a direct estimate of the undocumented flow rather than the number of apprehensions as the dependent variable, and to include a comprehensive analysis of flow across the entire southern border rather than at one particular entry point or from a few isolated villages in Mexico.

Our estimates may be briefly summarized. The baseline estimates shown in row 6 of the table assume during each month's calculation that the relative U.S.-Mexican unemployment rate and wage rate stay constant at their average values for the twenty-three-month post-IRCA period from November 1986 to September 1988. During this period, the

Estimated responsiveness of the Mexico-United States undocumented gross annual migration to stipulated levels of improvements in the Mexican economy relative to the U.S. economy

Row	Stipulated relative change factors for		Implied ratios of U.S. rates to Mexican rates		Estimated gross annual undocumented migration from Mexico to United States (millions)[a]		
	Col. 3 (1)	Col. 4 (2)	Male unemployment rate (3)	Hourly wage rate[b] (4)	If only relative unemployment rates change[c] (5)	If only relative wage rates change[d] (6)	If both relative unemployment and wage rates change (7)
1	0.5	1.5	0.80	10.77	2.23	2.59	2.89
2	0.6	1.4	0.96	10.06	2.18	2.46	2.68
3	0.7	1.3	1.13	9.34	2.14	2.33	2.49
4	0.8	1.2	1.29	8.62	2.09	2.22	2.32
5	0.9	1.1	1.45	7.90	2.04	2.10	2.15
6	1.0	1.0	1.61[e]	7.18[e]	2.00	2.00	2.00
7	1.2	0.9	1.93	6.47	1.91	1.90	1.82
8	1.4	0.8	2.25	5.75	1.83	1.80	1.65
9	1.6	0.7	2.57	5.03	1.75	1.71	1.50
10	1.8	0.6	2.89	4.31	1.68	1.63	1.36
11	2.0	0.5	3.21	3.59	1.60	1.54	1.24
12	2.2	0.4	3.54	2.87	1.53	1.47	1.13

[a]These figures do not include undocumented migrants returning to Mexico during the same year.

[b]United States: nonagricultural wages; Mexico: wages in manufacturing.

[c]The relative wage rate is held constant at its observed November 1986–September 1988 (post-IRCA) mean value of 7.18.

[d]The relative unemployment rate is held constant at its observed November 1986–September 1988 (post-IRCA) mean value of 1.64.

[e]Observed average monthly values over the twenty-three-month post-IRCA period, November 1986–September 1988.

American unemployment rate was about 1.6 times higher than the measured Mexican unemployment rate, and American hourly wages were more than seven times higher than Mexican wages. This combination of values for the two economic variables produces an estimated annual undocumented flow of 2 million, or an average of about 167,000 each month. The appropriateness of this figure as a baseline estimate is corroborated by the fact that the actual average monthly undocumented flow in the post-IRCA period is estimated at 176,000.[32] Readers should note that these estimates represent a *gross*, or one-way, flow into the United States. Other independent research is consistent with the position that the *net* undocumented flow is only about 10 percent as large as the gross flow on an annual basis.[33]

Most of the figures in the table indicate how the estimated annual undocumented gross flow could vary in response to changes between the United States and Mexico in relative unemployment rates and/or relative wage rates. The range of the stipulated changes in either component is somewhat arbitrary, yet sufficiently wide to encompass the likely effects of a free-trade agreement. For example, as shown by column 1, we have stipulated values for the relative unemployment rate ranging from 0.5 to 2.2 times its average value in the post-IRCA period. As shown in column 3, this variation corresponds to alternative values for the relative U.S./Mexico unemployment rate ranging from a low of 0.80 to a maximum of 3.54. Similarly, as column 2 indicates, stipulated relative wages range from 1.5 to 0.4 times their average post-IRCA value of 7.2. This produces a shift in the values used in the calculations between 10.8 and 2.9, as shown in column 4. The numbers in columns 3 and 4 are paired in the same direction so that reading down either column corresponds to progressive improvements in the Mexican economy relative to economic performance in the United States.

Column 5 shows estimates of the undocumented gross flow when relative unemployment rates are allowed to change and relative wage rates are held constant at a level of 7.2, the post-IRCA average. Alternatively, column 6 shows estimates of what would happen if relative wage rates varied, holding relative unemployment rates constant at their post-IRCA average value of 1.6. Finally, in column 7 relative wage and relative unemployment rates are assumed to change simultaneously, producing greater variations in the estimated undocumented flow. For example, the figures in the last column of row 11 indicate that the estimated gross annual undocumented flow would be slightly less than 1.25 million if the Mexican unemployment rate fell by one-half against the U.S. unemployment rate and if Mexican wages doubled relative to wages in the United States.

As noted above, we have calculated estimates of undocumented gross annual migration by stipulating various degrees of changes in the relative level of unemployment and of wage rates between the United States and Mexico. Thus, for example, if the unemployment rate in Mexico declines by roughly 30 percent relative to the U.S. unemployment rate (holding relative wages constant between the two countries), the estimated gross undocumented flow falls to 1.83 million each year, or to about 9 percent below the baseline estimate (row 8, column 5). Alternatively, if the relative decrease in the Mexican unemployment rate amounts to one-half (again holding relative wage rates constant), the estimated gross flow drops to 1.6 million annually, or to 20 percent less than the baseline (row 11, column 5).

On the other hand, if wage rates in Mexico rise by one-quarter with respect to American wages (holding constant the relative rates of unemployment between the two economies), the estimated annual undocumented flow falls from 2.0 million to 1.8 million, or by 10 percent below the baseline (row 8, column 6). Alternatively, if Mexican wages double relative to U.S. wages (again holding relative unemployment rates constant), then the estimated gross annual flow of undocumented migrants declines to slightly more than 1.5 million, or by close to 25 percent below the baseline (row 11, column 6).

Changes in the Mexican economy in response to NAFTA may result in improvements in both wages and unemployment rates relative to the United States. For example, if relative Mexican unemployment declines by 30 percent and relative Mexican wages increase by one-quarter, the estimates undocumented flow falls to 1.65 million annually, a decline from the baseline of nearly 20 percent (row 8, column 7). Alternatively, a doubling of Mexican wages and a halving of Mexican unemployment produces an estimated decline in the annual undocumented flow to less than 1.25 million, or nearly 40 percent below the baseline (row 11, column 7).

Discussion

The estimates in the table are useful in examining how a free-trade agreement between the United States and Mexico might affect the flow of the undocumented migrants across the Mexico-U.S. border. In particular, they show the responsiveness of the undocumented flow to alternative values of two indicators of relative economic performance between the two countries. It is often assumed that a free-trade agreement would improve Mexico's economy relative to that of the United States. If this supposition is correct, then estimates found below row 6 in the table are likely to capture the final outcome. Rows 1 through 5 correspond to situations in which either or both measures of relative economic performance indicate a deterioration in the Mexican economy from average post-IRCA values. These alternatives are included to allow for the possibility that a free-trade agreement might have unintended negative effects on the relative position of the Mexican economy vis-à-vis that of the United States.[34]

Finally, it is useful to comment on the implications of the figures in the table for the volume of illegal alien apprehensions along the Mexico-U.S. border. A repeated-trials model of undocumented migration implies that the ratio between the annual number of apprehensions and the annual undocumented flow is the same as the odds of being apprehended on any given attempt to cross over into the United States.[35] Moreover, the probability of being apprehended on any given attempt has fluctuated within a relatively narrow band during the past decade, with an average value of about 0.3.[36] Therefore, the estimated number of apprehensions associated with any annual undocumented flow may be calculated by multiplying the flow by (0.3/0.7). Performing these calculations implies that the annual number of apprehensions corresponding to the smallest and largest values in column 7 of the table is 482,000 and 1.24 million, respectively. During fiscal year 1986, just prior to IRCA's passage, the annual number of apprehensions was almost 1.8 million, and the current number is approximately 1.2 million.[37]

Conclusions

In the short to medium run, the North American Free Trade Agreement is likely to increase pressures for undocumented migration from Mexico to the United States. Although the literature on this topic is fragmentary, it suggests that the initial overall effect of free trade will be to foster migration. Some American observers agree, concluding that "the impending [free-trade agreement] will heighten the need for more effective immigration control."[38] On the other hand, given that NAFTA (if approved) will be phased in over fifteen years, the migration effect need not be sudden or overwhelming.

Even if NAFTA does result in a temporary increase in undocumented migration, government leaders in Canada, Mexico, and the United States are committed to the principle of free trade and believe that the overall net effects of NAFTA on employment and living standards in each of the three countries will be positive. As the evidence from the post-IRCA period shows, attempts to control the flow of undocumented migration by giving more resources to the U.S. Border Patrol or by policies that place the responsibility for enforcing immigration regulations on American employers have not worked.[39] Although the prospect of NAFTA has upset some anti-immigration lobbies in the United States, it also offers the opportunity for future bilateral talks on immigration.

In the long run, if free trade brings an improvement of the Mexican economy relative to the U.S. economy, the incentives for undocumented migration are likely to weaken. The model we have presented suggests that narrowing the large wage and unemployment differentials will substantially reduce the flow. It is important to note, however, that our estimates are only illustrative and are based on several assumptions. Future research needs to quantify more precisely how a free-trade agreement might affect relative unemployment and wage rates between the United States and Mexico.

Notes

1. México, Secretaría de Comercio y Fomento Industrial, 1992; Stuart Auerbach, "U.S., Canada and Mexico Agree to Form a Trade Bloc," *Washington Post*, 13 August 1992.

2. Although NAFTA involves Mexico, Canada, and the United States, in this note we consider only the Mexico-U.S. migratory flow, because the size of the Mexico-Canada flow is small by comparison. In 1990, 12.2 percent of all short-term (i.e., less than twelve months) temporary workers admitted to Canada, or 28,524, were Mexican. The figures for long-term temporary workers were just 2.3 percent, or 5,377. See Margaret Michalowski, "The Dynamics of Recent South-North Flows of Temporary Workers: A Canadian Case Study" (paper presented at the IUSSP Conference on the Peopling of the Americas, Veracruz, Mexico, May 1992), tables 1 and 3. The number of short-term temporary American workers admitted to Canada in 1990 was 160,386 (68.6 percent), and the number of long-term temporary workers admitted in the same year was 33,200 (14.2 percent). Throughout most of the 1980s Canadian legal migrants to the United States numbered no more than fifteen thousand annually, or less than 3 percent of total legal immigration. See U.S. Immigration and Naturalization Service, *Statistical Yearbook of the Immigration and Naturalization Service, 1990* (Washington, DC: GPO, 1991). In addition, the nature of the Mexico-Canada and Mexico-U.S. flows is very different from that of the U.S.-Canada flow. Mexican migrants to the other two North American countries are primarily unskilled workers, whereas U.S. and Canadian migrants are primarily skilled workers, managers, and professionals.

3. Juergen B. Donges, "International Migration and the International Division of Labor," in *Population in an Interacting World*, ed. William Alonso (Cambridge, MA: Harvard University Press, 1987), 129–48; Ulrich Humans and K. W. Schatz, *Trade in Place of Migration* (Geneva: International Labour Organisation, 1979).

4. Donges, "International Migration and the International Division of Labor," 137.

5. Thomas J. Espenshade, "Policy Influences on Undocumented Migration to the United States," *Proceedings of the American Philosophy Society* 136, no. 2 (1992): 188–207.

6. Wayne A. Cornelius, "Labor Migration to the U.S.: Development Outcomes and Alternatives in Mexican Sending Communities" (paper prepared for the Commission for the Study of International Migration and Cooperative Economic Development, 1990).

7. In 1982, Mexico faced a severe fiscal and economic crisis. Its import-substitution strategy was no longer sustainable, several state-owned enterprises had large deficits, and the price of oil—Mexico's main export—had collapsed. Under Presidents de la Madrid (1982–1988) and Salinas (1988–present), the country has undergone a radical economic reform based on trade liberalization, changes in foreign investment law, privatization, and elimination of subsidies.

8. Commission for the Study of International Migration and Cooperative Economic Development (CSIMCED), *Unauthorized Migration: An Economic Development Response*, Final Report of the Commission (Washington, DC: GPO, 1990), transmittal letter.

9. For example, in 1983 when it enacted the Caribbean Basin Initiative, in 1987 when the U.S.-Mexico Framework Agreement on Trade was negotiated, and in 1989 when the free-trade agreement with Canada came into effect. One of the studies done for the Commission pointed out that while no clear link exists between U.S. trade policy and international migration, there has been a policy tilt in favor of imports from Mexico, the Caribbean, and Central America in recent years. However, the driving force behind this change was not migration concerns. Stephen Lande and Nellis Crigler, "Trade Policy as a Means to Reduce Migration" (paper prepared for the Commission for the Study of International Migration and Cooperative Economic Development, 1989); Stephen Lande and Nellis Crigler, "Trade Policy Measures as a Means to Reduce Immigration in the 1990s: An Update" (paper prepared for the Commission for the Study of International Migration and Cooperative Economic Development, 1990).

10. CSIMCED, *Unauthorized Migration*, xvii.

11. The conclusions in the report were based on commissioned papers prepared by researchers in several universities in the United States, Mexico, and Central America. Of the approximately eighty papers that were finally published, only fifteen deal with the relationship between free trade and immigration in the Caribbean Basin. Ten of these refer to Mexico.

12. Leonardo Pimentel and Rafael López Vega, "Los Factores Económicos en los Cambios de Compartamiento Migratorio Externo de la Población Mexicana" (paper presented at the IUSSP Conference on the Peopling of the Americas, Veracruz, Mexico, May 1992).

13. Cornelius, "Labor Migration to the U.S."

14. CSIMCED, *Unauthorized Migration*, 5.

15. Michael P. Todaro, "A Model of Labor Migration and Urban Unemployment in the Less Developed Countries," *American Economic Review* 59, no. 1 (1969): 138–48; Michael P. Todaro and Lydia Maruszko, "Illegal Migration and U.S. Immigration Reform: A Conceptual Framework," *Population and Development Review* 13, no. 1 (1987): 101–14.

16. Douglas S. Massey, "Economic Development and International Migration in Comparative Perspective," *Population and Development Review* 14, no. 3 (1988): 383–413.

17. María de Lourdes de la Fuente Deschamps, "Manufacturing Exports and Commercial Policies in Mexico" (paper prepared for the Commission for the Study of International Migration and Cooperative Economic Development, 1990).

18. Alejandro Ibarra-Yunez and Chandler Stolp, "Exports and Employment Generation in Mexico: A Sectoral Study" (paper prepared for the Commission for the Study of International Migration and Cooperative Economic Development, 1990).

19. William Glade, "Privatization, Employment and Migration" (paper prepared for the Commission for the Study of International Migration and Cooperative Economic Development, 1990).

20. Diana Solis, "Migration Issue Reflects Free Trade's Cost," *The Wall Street Journal*, 13 July 1992.

21. In a study on the migration impact of NAFTA, David Simcox argued that the growth of jobs in Mexico's perishable crop sector will not offset the loss of jobs in other farms sectors (e.g., in grains). See David Simcox, "Immigration and Free Trade with Mexico: Protecting American Workers against Double Jeopardy," *Backgrounder*, no. 4–91 (Washington, DC: Center for Immigration Studies, 1991).

22. Gary D. Thompson and Philip L. Martin, "The Potential Effects of Labor Intensive Agriculture in Mexico on U.S.-Mexico Migration" (paper prepared for the Commission for the Study of International Migration and Cooperative Economic Development, 1989). Future studies of the impact of NAFTA on Mexico-U.S. migration should examine not only sectors of the American economy that employ Mexican workers but also the corresponding sending regions in Mexico. More sectoral accounts in the vein of Thompson and Martin's study of the fresh winter tomato market are needed. One could, for example, analyze the likely impact of NAFTA on the production of perishable crops that currently rely on immigrant labor for their harvest (e.g., raisin grapes, apples, and mushrooms). Furthermore, John Abowd and Richard Freeman provide valuable insights into the sectoral impacts that trade and migration have on the U.S. labor market. They find that immigrant ratios (percentages of immigrants in the labor force) are higher in traded-goods sectors than in nontraded sectors, and that within the traded-goods category, export-intensive industries employ relatively few immigrants compared with import-intensive industries. By determining which sectors are more likely to be affected by NAFTA and looking at the immigrant ratios within those sectors, one could begin to estimate the effect of free trade on the employment of immigrants. It would of course be useful to test Donges's (1987) and Humans and Schatz's (1979) hypothesis that free trade and labor migration are substitutes. See Monica L. Heppel and Sandra L. Amendola, *Immigration Reform and Perishable Crop Agriculture: Compliance or Circumvention?* (Washington, DC: The Urban Institute, 1991); John Abowd and Richard B. Freemen, eds., *Immigration, Trade and the Labor Market* (Chicago: University of Chicago Press, 1991).

23. Philip L. Martin, J. Edward Taylor, and H. Rosenberg, "The North American Free Trade Agreement and Rural Mexican Migration to the United States" (paper prepared for the University of California AIC Conference, Los Angeles International Airport, 5 March 1992).

24. Recruitment efforts and the composition of migrant groups play an important role in determining the proportion of "continuing migrants." For example, in Sinaloa, single, young, landless, male internal migrants are more likely to enter the U.S. migration circuit, whereas seasonal workers who bring their families with them to work in Sinaloa generally return to their states of origin in Central Mexico. See Thompson and Martin, "The Potential Effects of Labor Intensive Agriculture in Mexico on U.S.-Mexico Migration."

25. Philip L. Martin, "Labor Migration and Economic Development" (paper prepared for the Commission for the Study of International and Cooperative Economic Development, 1989).

26. México, Secretaría de Comercio y Fomento Industrial, *Tratado de Libre Comercio entre México, Canadá y Estados Unidos: Resumen* (Mexico, 1992), 18–19. The four categories of businesspersons considered in the NAFTA chapter are business visitors, traders and investors, intracompany transferees, and professionals.

27. Demetrios G. Papademetriou, "The Immigration Act of 1990: Overall Structure and Issues of Relevance to the Department of Labor" (Washington, DC: U.S. Department of Labor, Bureau of International Labor Affairs, 1990); Michael Fix and Jeffrey S. Passel, "The Door Remains Open: Recent Immigration to the United States and a Preliminary Analysis of the Immigration Act of 1990," *Program for Research on Immigration Policy*, PRIP-UI-14, January (Washington, DC: The Urban Institute, 1991). Between fiscal years 1980 and 1988 Mexican *legal* immigration to the United States ranged between 56,100 and 101,300 per year, with a median value of 61,000. No other country sent more legal immigrants during this period. Legal Mexican immigration jumped to 405,200 in 1989 and to 679,100 in 1990. This sudden increase reflects the large number of Mexican aliens with temporary resident status who were granted permanent residence under the legalization provisions of the 1986 Immigration Reform and Control Act (IRCA). "Nonlegalization" legal immigrants from Mexico numbered 66,400 in 1989 and 56,500 in 1990—not much different from the 1980–1988 figures. The balance is primarily made up of aliens who have been in the United States unlawfully since January 1, 1982 (legalization applicants), in addition to aliens who were employed in seasonal agricultural work for a minimum of ninety days in the year preceding May 1986 (Special Agricultural Worker, or SAW, applicants). Altogether in fiscal years 1989 and 1990, a total of nearly 1.36 million aliens gained permanent resident status in the United States under the IRCA provisions. Of the total of 3.04 million legalization and SAW applications filed by May 1991, more than 2.2 million, or roughly 75 percent, were from Mexican nationals. See U.S. Immigration and Naturalization Service, *Statistical Yearbook of the Immigration and Naturalization Service*.

28. Thomas J. Espenshade, "Undocumented Migration to the United States: Evidence from a Repeated Trials Model," in *Undocumented Migration to the United States: IRCA and the Experience of the 1980s*, ed. Frank D. Bean, Barry Edmonston, and Jeffrey S. Passel (Washington, DC: The Urban Institute Press, 1990), 111–58.

29. U.S. International Trade Commission, *The Likely Impact on the United States of a Free Trade Agreement with Mexico*, Investigation no. 332–297, USITC publication no. 2353 (Washington, DC: GPO, 1990), viii.

30. The prediction equation includes terms for the size of Mexico's population aged fifteen to thirty-four years, the cumulative number of SAW applications, U.S./Mexico ratios of wage and unemployment rates, and a series of dummy variables capturing monthly variations in seasonal labor demand, the deterrent effect of IRCA, the potential altered IRCA effect in the second year of the post-IRCA period, and spring and summer seasonality factors for both the entire post-IRCA period and for the second year of IRCA. Dummy variables were given their appropriate "0-1" value for each of the twelve monthly predictions during fiscal year 1988. Values for the Mexican population aged fifteen to thirty-four

and for SAWs were held constant at their most recently observed levels. Finally, for the baseline scenario, we used average monthly values for the relative wage and unemployment variables over the period November 1986 to September 1988. Estimates of the undocumented flow in the different rows of columns 5–7 in the table were derived by altering values for U.S./Mexico relative wage and/or relative unemployment rates, holding everything else constant.

31. See, for example, Wayne A. Cornelius, "Impacts of the 1986 U.S. Immigration Law on Emigration from Rural Mexican Sending Communities," *Population and Development Review* 15, no. 4 (1989): 689–705; Katharine M. Donato, Jorge Durand, and Douglas S. Massey, "Stemming the Tide? Assessing the Deterrent Effects of the Immigration Reform and Control Act," *Demography* 29, no. 2 (1992): 139–57; Sherrie A. Kossoudji, "Playing Cat and Mouse at the U.S.-Mexican Border," *Demography* 29, no. 2 (1992): 159–80.

32. Espenshade, "Undocumented Migration to the United States."

33. Previous analyses have found that undocumented immigration added an average of between one hundred thousand and three hundred thousand persons per year to the population of the United States for 1980–1986. See Karen A. Woodrow, Jeffrey S. Passel, and Robert Warren, "Preliminary Estimates of Undocumented Immigration to the United States, 1980–86: Analysis of the June 1986 Current Population Survey," *Proceedings of the Social Statistics Section of the American Statistical Association, 1987* (Washington, DC: American Statistical Association, 1987); Karen A. Woodrow and Jeffrey S. Passel, "Post-IRCA Undocumented Immigration to the United States: An Assessment Based on the June 1988 CPS," in *Undocumented Migration to the United States*, 33–75. If we take the midpoint (two hundred thousand) of this range as our estimate, then roughly 90 percent of each year's gross undocumented migration flow of two million leave the United States.

34. More generally, Sharon Stanton Russell and Michael S. Teitelbaum have noted that trade, aid, and development policies often work at cross purposes. In particular, one important development-migration paradox is that "although all industrialized countries have embraced explicit policies and formal mechanisms to further economic development in Third World countries, in practice their economic policies often tend, directly or indirectly, to neutralize these efforts." See Sharon Stanton Russell and Michael S. Teitelbaum, "International Migration and International Trade," World Bank Discussion Paper, no. 160 (Washington, DC, 1990), 33–75. Quotation is on page 34.

35. Espenshade, "Undocumented Migration to the United States," 111–58.

36. Ibid.

37. U.S. Immigration and Naturalization Service, *Statistical Yearbook of the Immigration and Naturalization Service*.

38. David Simcox, "Immigration and Free Trade with Mexico: Protecting American Workers against Double Jeopardy," *Backgrounder*, no. 4–91 (Washington, DC: Center for Immigration Studies, 1991), 11.

39. Espenshade, "Undocumented Migration to the United States," 111–58.

11

Mexican Migration and the Social Space of Postmodernism

Roger Rouse

As Chapters 9 and 10 indicate, one of the hallmarks of the best recent research on Mexican immigration to the United States has been the emphasis that scholars have placed on shifting analysis away from a narrowly defined national focus to one in which Mexican migration is contextualized within much larger international economic, political, and social transformations.

One of the most insightful of the researchers currently working in the field is University of Michigan anthropologist Roger Rouse. Drawing on his innovative research on a long-standing migration circuit between the Mexican municipio of Aguililla, Michoacán, and Redwood City, California, Rouse argues that the establishment and maturation of such circuits over several generations have created serious "challenge[s to] ways of 'reading' migration." In the process of "chronically maintaining two ways of life," he notes that members of Aguililla-Redwood City and similar migrant circuits have helped to destabilize and disorder traditional ways of conceiving of citizenship and nationality, settlers and sojourners, and the social construction of "community."

In a hidden sweatshop in downtown Los Angeles, Asian and Latino migrants produce automobile parts for a factory in Detroit. As the parts leave the production line, they are stamped "Made in Brazil."[1] In a small village in the heart of Mexico, a young woman at her father's wake wears a black T-shirt sent to her by a brother in the United States. The shirt bears a legend that some of the mourners understand but she does not. It reads, "Let's Have Fun Tonight!" And on the Tijuana-San Diego border Guillermo Gómez-Peña, a writer originally from Mexico City, reflects on

From *Diaspora* 1, no. 1 (1991): 8–23. Reprinted by permission of Oxford University Press.

the time he has spent in what he calls "the gap between two worlds": "Today, eight years after my departure, when they ask me for my nationality or ethnic identity, I cannot answer with a single word, for my 'identity' now possesses multiple repertoires: I am Mexican but I am also Chicano and Latin American. On the border they call me '*chilango*' or '*mexiquillo*'; in the capital, '*pocho*' or '*norteño*,' and in Spain '*sudaca*.' . . . My companion Emily is Anglo-Italian but she speaks Spanish with an Argentinian accent. Together we wander through the ruined Babel that is our American postmodernity."[2]

We live in a confusing world, a world of crisscrossed economies, intersecting systems of meaning, and fragmented identities. Suddenly, the comforting modern imagery of nation-states and national languages, of coherent communities and consistent subjectivities, of dominant centers and distant margins no longer seems adequate. Certainly, in [the] discipline of anthropology, there is a growing sense that our conventional means of representing both the worlds of those we study and the worlds that we ourselves inhabit have been strained beyond their limits by the changes that are taking place around us. Indeed, the very notion that ethnographers and their subjects exist in readily separable domains is increasingly being called into question.[3] But the problem is not confined to a single discipline, nor even to the academy at large. As Fredric Jameson has observed, the gradual unfolding of the global shift from colonialism and classic forms of dependency to a new transnational capitalism has meant that, during the last twenty years, we have all moved irrevocably into a new kind of social space, which our modern sensibilities leave us unable to comprehend. With appropriate dramatic flair, he calls this new terrain "postmodern hyperspace."[4]

Jameson suggests that, in order to locate ourselves in this new space, we must make two moves. First, to understand why the crisis in spatial representation exists, we must identify as clearly as possible the broad politico-economic changes that have undermined the verisimilitude of existing images; and second, to understand where we are and where we can go from here, we must develop new images, new coordinates, and a series of new and more effective maps. Jameson seeks to construct these alternative images through a critical reading of aesthetic forms such as novels, buildings, paintings, and films. But his focus seems unduly narrow. Given the ubiquity of the changes he describes and the profundity of their influence, the raw materials for a new cartography ought to be equally discoverable in the details of people's daily lives. And, from a radical perspective, the most significant materials surely lie in the circumstances and experiences of those working-class groups whose members have been most severely affected by the changing character of capitalist exploitation.[5]

In this article, I will develop these ideas by drawing on my work with rural Mexicans involved in migration to and from the United States. After outlining the images conventionally used to map the social terrain they inhabit, I will first build on their experiences to suggest new images better suited to charting their current circumstances and then indicate how these images may, in fact, be increasingly useful to us all as we try to map social landscapes found throughout Mexico and the United States.

Two socio-spatial images have dominated the modern discourse of the social sciences concerning the people of rural Mexico. I claim neither novelty nor insight for recognizing their influence. By underlining their importance and delineating their attendant assumptions, however, I hope to make it easier to understand both the nature of their limitations and the significance of the alternatives I shall propose.

The first image is one to which I shall attach the label "community."[6] The abstract expression of an idealized nation-state, it has been used concretely at numerous different levels, from the peasant village to the nation itself. It combines two main ideas.[7] First, it identifies a discriminable population with a single, bounded space—a territory or place. In so doing, it assumes that the social relationships in which community members participate will be much more intense within this space than beyond [it]. It also assumes that members will treat the place of community as the principal environment to which they adjust their actions and, correspondingly, that they will monitor local events much more closely than developments farther afield. Second, the image implies a certain commonality and coherence, generally expressed either in the functionalist dream of an entity whose institutional parts fit together neatly to form an integrated whole or in the structural-functionalist vision of a shared way of life that exists not only in a multiplicity of similar actions but, more profoundly, in a single and internally consistent set of rules, values, or beliefs. From the perspective that these two ideas establish, the heterogeneities and complexities of the worlds we actually encounter are normally understood in terms of either superficial interactions between distinct communities or transitional moments in the movement from one form of integrity and order to another.

The second image is one that I shall label "center/periphery."[8] The abstract expression of an idealized imperial system, it too has been realized concretely at many different levels, from the rural town to the entire world system. This image involves three main ideas. First, it suggests that differences are organized concentrically around a dominant core. Thus, power and wealth are greatest at the center and diminish gradually as one moves outward through a series of surrounding zones, and different locations are associated with different ways of life according to the zone in which they are found. Second, the image implies a process of change in which the center exercises a privileged capacity to shape outcomes, whether it is extending its influence to the margins or molding people from the periphery who enter its terrain. And third, it suggests that fields ordered in this way are autonomous: each peripheral site is oriented to a single center and each center is independent of all others at the same level.

In many ways, these images are opposed. Formally, the idea of community tends to privilege homogeneity and stasis while the idea of center/periphery privileges variations and change. And, in practice, they have frequently been used against one another, community being the principal socio-spatial image invoked by modernization theory and center/periphery, of course, serving as a crucial counterimage for dependency theory and the world systems approach. But their opposition should not be exaggerated. In many works they have been used in tandem and, in fact, the key tension between modernization theory and its critics lies less in frictions over spatial imagery than in disagreements about the intentions of the center and the nature of its influence.[9] Indeed, even when the two images have been in conflict, they have supported one another negatively, each being treated as the only viable alternative to the other. Opposed, combined, or alternating, they have long dominated work on rural Mexico with the casual authority of the commonsensical.

Migration has always had the potential to challenge established spatial images. It highlights the social nature of space as something created and reproduced through collective human agency and, in so doing, reminds us that, within the limits imposed by power, existing spatial arrangements are always susceptible to change. In practice, however, academics dealing with Mexican migration have rarely used it as the basis for a critical reappraisal of existing images. Instead, with a few notable exceptions, they have simply adapted the existing repertoire to make it fit the peculiarities of a mobile population. This is particularly apparent in the way they have used frameworks derived from the image of community to understand the experiences of the migrants themselves.

First, because migration is self-evidently a movement between places, it has commonly been treated as a movement from one set of social relationships to another. Thus, numerous studies have sought to gauge the changes that migrants have undergone by comparing the systems of family organization, kinship, and friendship dominant in their places of origin with those they have developed in the places to which they have moved.[10]

Second, as a movement between places, migration has also commonly been treated as a shift from one significant environment to another. Within a bipolar framework variously organized around oppositions between the rural and the urban, the traditional and the modern, and Mexico and the United States, many studies have examined how migrants take practices and attitudes adjusted to their original "niche" or setting and adapt them to the new locale in which they find themselves.[11]

And third, as a move between communities identified with distinct ways of life, migration has normally been seen as a process in which the migrants and their descendants experience a more or less gradual shift from one ordered arrangement to another, either fully converting to the dominant way of life or forging their own form of accommodation in an ordered synthesis of old and new. Such a perspective does recognize that contradictions can arise when people combine attitudes and practices associated with the place to which they have moved with others linked to their place of origin, but it has generally dealt with these in ways that sustain the primacy of order, treating them either as incongruities in form that disappear when viewed in terms of function or as temporary features peculiar to transitional situations. In the latter case, it has been particularly common to locate the contradictions within a widely used model of generational succession according to which the migrants themselves retain much of what they learned while growing up, they and their children balance traditional attitudes and practices maintained in intimate arenas such as the home and the ethnic neighborhood with other more appropriate to participation in the wider society, and a consistent sociocultural orientation appears only in the third generation.[12]

These ways of construing migration have faced a qualified challenge from accounts that treat it principally as a circular process in which people remain oriented to the places from which they have come. Under such circumstances, the patterns of social and cultural adjustment are clearly different.[13] But it is important to stress that the basic socio-spatial assumptions remain the same. As in accounts that emphasize a unidirectional shift, migrants are held to move between distinct, spatially demarcated communities and, in the long run, to be capable of maintaining an involvement in only one of them.

In recent years, however, this mobilization of modern socio-spatial images has become increasingly unable to contain the postmodern complexities that it confronts. Symptomatic of the unfolding shift to transnational capitalism, migration between rural Mexico and the United

States since World War II, and especially since the mid-1960s, has been obliging us ever more insistently to develop an alternative cartography of social space. I can elaborate this argument most effectively by drawing on the case that I know best, the U.S.-bound migration that has been taking place since the early 1940s from the rural *municipio* of Aguililla in the southwest corner of the state of Michoacán.[14]

At first sight, Aguililla seems to be an isolated community dedicated to small-scale farming and manifestly part of the Mexican periphery. The *municipio* is located in the mountains that form the southern limit of the west-central region; its administrative center, also known as Aguililla, lies at the end of a poor dirt road, one of those points where the national transport system finally exhausts itself; the land has been used principally for the subsistence-oriented production of basic foodstuffs and the raising of livestock; and trade with the interior has been limited. It is the kind of place onto which urban dwellers find it easy to project their fantasies of difference and danger.

But appearances can be deceptive. Aguililla's growing involvement in transnational migration has profoundly changed both its economic orientation and its socio-spatial relationships. By the early 1980s, when I carried out fieldwork in the *municipio*, it had come to operate largely as a nursery and nursing home for wage-laborers in the United States. Almost every family had members who were or had been abroad; the local economy depended heavily on the influx of dollars; and many of the area's small farming operations continued only because they were sustained by migrant remittances. Concomitantly, the *municipio* has become part of a transnational network of settlements and, in so doing, has significantly modified its status as a marginal site within a purely national hierarchy of places. Over the years, migrants have established several outposts in the United States, by far the largest being the one they have formed amid a rapidly growing Latino neighborhood in Redwood City, an urban area on the northern edge of California's famous Silicon Valley. There they now work principally in the service sector, as janitors, dishwashers, gardeners, hotel workers, house cleaners, and child minders—proletarian servants in the paragon of "postindustrial" society. Some Aguilillans have settled in Redwood City for long periods, but few abandon the *municipio* forever. Most people stay in the United States relatively briefly; almost all of those who stay longer continue to keep in touch with the people and places they have left behind, and even those who have been away for many years quite often return.

This pattern of migration must be understood as symptomatic of the way in which broad politico-economic developments involved in the unfolding of transnational capitalism have refracted themselves through the specificities of local circumstance. For many years, Aguilillans have placed a heavy emphasis on the capacity to create and maintain small-scale, family-run operations, ideally based in land, and, in relation to this goal, the broad developments have exerted contradictory pressures.

In the *municipio*, the nationwide diversion of capital to industry and commercial agriculture that has taken place since the 1940s has left the local economy without needed infrastructure, while the concentration of what government spending there has been in health and education has encouraged population growth and the broadening of people's horizons. As a result, it has become impossible for most Aguilillans to approach the realization of their goals solely through access to local resources. At the same time, however, the lack of large-scale land acquisitions in the *municipio* by commercially oriented owners, the periodic provision of small amounts of government aid to the area's farmers, and the entrepreneurial opportunities provided by the influx of dollars have all impeded full proletarianization. This, in turn, has meant that the old goals have not been abandoned and that migration has been seen principally as a way of raising outside funds to finance their local realization.[15]

Meanwhile, in the United States, the growing polarization of the labor market has created a mounting demand for Mexican workers to fill the bottom layers in agriculture, deskilled assembly, and, above all, services. Yet various factors have discouraged most Mexicans from staying permanently. In the case of Aguilillans, their cultural emphasis on creating and maintaining independent operations has led them to have deep-seated reservations about many aspects of life in the United States, prominent among them the obligation of proletarian workers to submit to the constant regulation of supervisors and the clock. In addition, the disappearance of many middle-level jobs and the attendant change in the shape of the labor market—from pyramid to hourglass—have made it increasingly difficult for people to see chances of upward mobility for themselves or, perhaps more significantly, for their children. And, finally, the economy's steady downturn since the mid-1960s has markedly increased both the hostility and the legal restrictions that many of the migrants face.[16]

Influenced by these contradictory developments, Aguilillans have forged socio-spatial arrangements that seriously challenge the dominant ways of reading migration. First, it has become inadequate to see Aguilillan migration as a movement between distinct communities, understood as the loci of distinct sets of social relationships. Today, Aguilillans find that their most important kin and friends are as likely to be living hundreds or thousands of miles away as immediately around them. More significantly, they are often able to maintain these spatially extended relationships as actively and effectively as the ties that link them to their neighbors. In this regard, growing access to the telephone has been particularly significant, allowing people not just to keep in touch periodically but to contribute to decision making and participate in familial events even from a considerable distance.

Indeed, through the continuous circulation of people, money, goods, and information, the various settlements have become so closely woven together that, in an important sense, they have come to constitute a single community spread across a variety of sites, something I refer to as a "transnational migrant circuit." Although the Aguilillan case undoubtedly has its local peculiarities, there is evidence that such arrangements are becoming increasingly important in the organization of Mexican migration to and from the United States.[17] Just as capitalists have responded to the new forms of economic internationalism by establishing transnational corporations, so workers have responded by creating transnational circuits.[18]

At the same time, as a result of these developments, it has become equally inadequate to see Aguilillan migration as a movement between distinct environments. Today, it is the circuit as a whole rather than any one locale that constitutes the principal setting in relation to which Aguilillans orchestrate their lives.[19] Those living in Aguililla, for example, are as much affected by events in Redwood City as by developments in the *municipio* itself, and the same is true in reverse. Consequently, people monitor what is happening in the other parts of the circuit as closely as they monitor what is going on immediately around them. Indeed, it is only by recognizing the transnational framework within which Aguilillans are operating that we can properly appreciate the logic of their actions. Thus, people in the United States may spend large amounts of time and money trying to obtain papers without ever seeking citizenship because it is as Mexican citizens with the right to "permanent residence" that they will be best equipped to move back and forth between the two countries. And they may send their children back to Mexico to complete their education or to visit during school vacations at least in part because they want to endow them with the bilingual and bicultural skills necessary to operate effectively on both sides of the border.

Finally, it is mistaken to see Aguilillan experiences in terms of an inexorable move towards a new form of sociocultural order. Although transnational migration has brought distant worlds into immediate juxtaposition, their proximity has produced neither homogenization nor synthesis. Instead, Aguilillans have become involved in the chronic maintenance of two quite distinct ways of life. More importantly, the resulting contradictions have not come simply from the persistence of past forms amid contemporary adjustments or from involvement in distinct lifeworlds within the United States. Rather, they reflect the fact that Aguilillans see their current lives and future possibilities as involving simultaneous engagements in places associated with markedly different forms of experience. Moreover, the way in which at least some people are preparing their children to operate within a dichotomized setting spanning national borders suggests that current contradictions will not be resolved through a simple process of generational succession.

The different ways of life that Aguilillans balance can be understood partly by reference to spatially demarcated national or local cultures, but they should also be understood in terms of class. In numerous combinations, Aguilillans have come to link proletarian labor with a sustained attachment to the creation of small-scale, family-based operations; and even though these ways of making a living may be reconcilable economically, in cultural terms they are fundamentally distinct, involving quite different attitudes and practices concerning the use of time and space, the conduct of social relationships, and the orchestration of appearances.[20] Indeed, one of the main considerations preserving the polarized relationship between Aguililla and Redwood City has been the fact that the latter has offered Aguilillans so few opportunities to create independent operations while the former, partly through the continued influx of remittances, has remained a place in which such opportunities are still available.

Obliged to live within a transnational space and to make a living by combining quite different forms of class experience, Aguilillans have become skilled exponents of a cultural bifocality that defies reduction to a singular order. Indeed, in many respects, Aguilillans have come to inhabit a kind of border zone, especially if we follow Américo Paredes in recognizing that a border is "not simply a line on a map but, more fundamentally, . . . a sensitized area where two cultures or two political systems come face to face."[21] Socioeconomically, the relationship between Aguililla and Redwood City is strikingly similar to the relationship along the international border between twinned cities such as Ciudad Juárez and El Paso or Matamoros and Brownsville. They are mutually implicated in numerous ways, but the line between them never disappears. And culturally, life within the circuit corresponds closely to the situation that Gómez-Peña describes for the border linking Tijuana and San Diego: "In my fractured reality, but reality nonetheless, live two histories, languages, cosmogonies, artistic traditions, and political systems dramatically opposed—the border is the continuous confrontation of two or more referential codes."[22] For many years, the U.S.-Mexican border seemed like a peculiar space, a narrow strip quite different from what lay at the heart of the two countries. But this is no longer the case. Ties such as those between Aguililla and Redwood City, places two thousand miles apart, prompt us to ask how wide this border has become and how peculiar we should consider its characteristics.

Socio-spatial frames derived from the image of the community no longer serve to represent the local terrain that Aguilillans inhabit. It seems that images such as those of the circuit and the border zone may be more appropriate. But these claims do not apply solely to small-scale settlements. Partly as a result of the migration that Aguilillans exemplify, they are becoming increasingly relevant to social landscapes found throughout Mexico and the United States.

It is scarcely a revelation to suggest that Mexico's dependent status renders problematic any assumption of functional integration or the presence of a singular sociocultural order. However, the shift to transnational capitalism has both intensified and changed the nature of national disarticulation, particularly during the last twenty years. Foreign capital plays a more significant role in Mexico than ever before, and, more critically, thanks to the rising use of offshore plants that carry out only a part of the production process and the growing ease with which these plants can be transferred to other underdeveloped countries, the ties linking foreign capital to the rest of Mexican society are becoming progressively weaker. Moreover, as the massive flight of domestic capital during the last few years illustrates only too well, the Mexican bourgeoisie is also orchestrating its actions increasingly within a transnational framework. At the same time, the growing institutionalization of migration to the United States through the medium of transnational circuits means that more of the Mexican population is oriented to developments outside the country and that this orientation is becoming steadily more pronounced. And finally, because of the expansion of a television system that carries numerous U.S. programs, the mounting of satellite dishes that tune directly into U.S. broadcasts, and the increasing exposure to U.S. ways of life through migration, foreign cultural influences are becoming rapidly more pervasive. The black T-shirt with its English exhortation, defying any attempt to read the wake as the textual expression of a coherent local culture, is emblematic of a process pervading rural Mexico.

What is perhaps more striking is that a similar kind of disarticulation is beginning to appear in the United States, particularly in its major cities. The U.S. economy, long dominated by domestic capital, is now increasingly influenced by transnationally orchestrated foreign investment, especially from Britain, Canada, Germany, the Netherlands, and Japan.[23] As regards labor, although immigrant workers have been an important factor for many years, they are today arriving under circumstances that distance them much more fully from the rest of society. In particular, the declining availability of those middle-level jobs that once encouraged hope of upward mobility, the increased scapegoating and legal restrictions that have accompanied economic decline since the mid-1960s, and the related development of transnational circuits are all serving to subvert the older possibilities of assimilation to a single national order. And partly as a result, ways of life commonly identified with the Third World are becoming increasingly apparent in a country often treated as the apogee of First World advancement. Extreme poverty, residential overcrowding and homelessness, underground economies, new forms of domestic service, and sweatshops exist side by side with Yuppie affluence, futuristic office blocks, and all the other accoutrements of high-tech postindustrialism.

Los Angeles is by no means typical, but the situation that had developed there by the mid-1980s offers a suggestive outline of emerging possibilities. In the downtown area, 75 percent of the buildings were owned wholly or in part by foreign capital, and as much as 90 percent of new multistory construction was being financed by investment from abroad.[24] In the larger conurbation, 40 percent of the population belonged to ethnic "minorities," many of them migrants from Asia and Latin America (estimates suggest that the figure will approach 60 percent by the year 2010).[25] And throughout the region, the growing contrasts between rich and poor and their increasingly apparent juxtaposition were prompting journalists to speculate about the "Brazilianization" of the city.[26] The hidden sweatshop in the heart of the metropolis, defying any attempt to claim a comfortable distance between Third World and First, calls attention to a trend that is gradually if unevenly affecting the whole of the country.[27]

Thus, in the United States as well as in Mexico, the *place* of the putative community—whether regional or national—is becoming little more than a *site* in which transnationally organized circuits of capital, labor, and communications intersect with one another and with local ways of life. In these circumstances, it becomes increasingly difficult to delimit a singular national identity and a continuous history, and the claims of politicians to speak authoritatively on behalf of this imagined community and its purported interests become increasingly hollow. But it is not just the image of the community which is compromised. The image of the center and periphery is also coming under increasing strain. U.S. capital increasingly intersects with capital from other core countries not only in peripheral areas such as Mexico but also in the United States itself. The growing influence of foreign investment means that, in both countries, people must accommodate themselves to a capital that is increasingly heteroglot and culturally diverse. And the concentric distribution of differences in power, wealth, and ways of life is breaking down, in large part because the United States no longer works as effectively to transform those who enter its terrain. Alongside the more familiar tale of capitalist penetration in the periphery, we are beginning to witness what Renato Rosaldo has called "the implosion of the Third World into the first," or what Saskia Sassen-Koob calls "peripheralization at the core."[28]

One of the results of these developments is that we are seeing a proliferation of border zones. The international border is widening, and, at the same time, miniature borders are erupting throughout the two countries. In Mexico, the provisions granting special tariff dispensations to offshore production have stretched and distended the border for capital, especially now that the offshore plants, first established in the northern part of the country, are steadily moving southward. At the same time, in the United States, the provisions regarding employer sanctions in the new immigration law have exploded the border for labor and relocated it in a multitude of fragments at the entrance to every workplace, while the recent amnesty has encouraged transnationally oriented migrants to extend their presence throughout the country. Moreover, the most readily dramatized juxtapositions of citizens and migrants are no longer confined to major urban sites such as downtown Los Angeles. They are also beginning to appear on the margins of suburbia as members of the native middle classes, scared by the real and imagined violence of these inner-city border zones, are developing residential enclaves in rural areas long inhabited by migrant farm workers.

Conditions in northern San Diego County illustrate the last of these trends in a particularly vivid way. Here, against the background of a burgeoning military-industrial economy, rapidly expanding middle-class suburbs have recently encroached on areas long filled with the ramshackle encampments of Latino migrants. In the words of the *Los Angeles Times*, the result has been a world where "squalid, plywood-and-cardboard hooches sit in the shadow of million-dollar mansions, where BMW and Volvo sets rub elbows at the supermarket with dusty migrants fresh from the fields." Put more pithily by an academic familiar with the area, "What you have . . . is the first of the First World intermixing with the last of the Third World. It's Nicaragua versus Disneyland." Or, as one local suburban resident observed, "It's like we're living in the Third World here. It doesn't seem to me that this is part of the American Dream."[29]

But these collisions and complaints are not the only markers of a newly emerging border zone. One man in a local trailer park, offended by migrants taking water from his spigot, put barbed wire on the chain-link fence behind his trailer, installed a set of floodlights, and armed himself with a twelve-gauge shotgun.[30] Other residents have hunted migrants with paintpellet guns and run them down with trucks. And, in November 1988, a local youth went one step further, shooting and killing two Latinos after confronting them near camps. Asked to explain his actions, he said simply that he hated Mexicans.[31] This is Nicaragua versus Disneyland, then, not simply as Latino versus Anglo or Third World versus First but as the savage implosion of frontline violence within the sanitized dreamworlds of middle-class escape.

The forces shaping Aguilillans' lives are thus coming to affect everyone who inhabits the terrain encompassed by Mexico and the United States. Throughout this fractured territory, transnationalism, contradictions in development, and increasingly polarized economies are stretching images of community beyond their limits, bringing different ways of life into vivid, often violent juxtaposition, and encouraging the chronic reproduction of their incongruities. The impact of these changes clearly varies with the circumstances of the people they affect, but their reach is increasingly broad.

Under such circumstances, images such as the circuit and the border zone may help us understand not only the specificities of Aguilillan experience but social landscapes increasingly familiar to us all. If this is true, it adds weight to the idea that, in our attempts to orient ourselves amid the complexities of postmodern hyperspace, we should look not only to art and literature but also to the lives of those "ordinary" people who inscribe their transient texts in the minutiae of daily experience. And this, in turn, suggests a pleasing irony with which to conclude, for it implies that, as in the case of Aguilillans and others like them, people long identified with an unworkable past may in fact be those from whom we have most to learn as we try to chart our way through the confusions of the present toward a future we can better understand and thus more readily transform.

Notes

1. See Charles Lockwood and Christopher B. Leinberger, "Los Angeles Comes of Age," *Atlantic Monthly* 261 (1988): 35. The assertion of a false point of origin is apparently used so that the manufacturers can participate in foreign delivery contracts. See Edward W. Soja, *Postmodern Geographies: The Reassertion of Space in Critical Social Theory* (London: Verso, 1989), 217.

2. "Hoy, ocho años de mi partida, cuando me preguntan por me nacionalidad o identidad étnica, no puedo responder con una palabra, pues mi 'identidad' ya posee repertorios multiples: soy mexicano pero tambien soy chicano y latinoamericano. En la frontera me dicen 'chilango' o 'mexiquillo'; en la capital 'pocho' o 'norteño' y en España 'sudaca.' . . . Mi compañera Emilia es angloitaliana pero habla español con acento argentino; y juntos caminamos entre los excombros de la torre de babel de nuestra posmodernidad americana" (author's translation).

3. See, for example, James Clifford and George E. Marcus, eds., "Introduction: Partial Truths," in *Writing Culture: The Poetics and Politics of Ethnography* (Berkeley: University of California Press, 1986), 22; and Renato Rosaldo,

Culture and Truth: The Remaking of Social Analysis (Boston: Beacon, 1969), 217.

4. Fredric Jameson, "Postmodernism, or the Cultural Logic of Late Capitalism," *New Left Review* 146 (1984): 83. Like Jameson, I find it useful to follow Ernest Mandel in arguing for the emergence since World War II of a new phase in monopoly capitalism, but I prefer to label this phase "transnational" rather than "late" partly to avoid the implication of imminent transcendence and, more positively, to emphasize the crucial role played by the constant movement of capital, labor, and information across national borders.

5. See Mike Davis, "Urban Renaissance and the Spirit of Postmodernism," *New Left Review* 151 (1985): 106–13; and George Lipsitz, "Cruising around the Hispanic Bloc: Postmodernism and Popular Music in Los Angeles," *Cultural Critique* 5 (1986–87): 161.

6. It is important to stress that I am concerned not with the various meanings of this particular term but instead with the image itself. The term serves merely as a convenient marker.

7. See Raymond Williams, *Keywords* (London: Fontana/Croom Helm, 1976), 65–66.

8. Ibid.

9. The combination of these images is readily apparent in the classic works on rural social organization by Robert Redfield and Eric Wolf [*The Little Community and Peasant Society and Culture*, and "Types of Latin American Peasantry: A Preliminary Discussion," *American Anthropologist* 57 (1955): 452–71], both of whom draw heavily on Mexican materials, and can also be seen in Immanuel Wallerstein's tendency [in *The Capitalist World Economy* (New York: Cambridge University Press, 1979)] to use nation-states as the constituent units of his world system, at least in the core.

10. This approach has been used in two related but different kinds of study. In work focusing on migration itself—especially on migration within Mexico—changes have commonly been gauged by comparing the forms of organization found in the points of destination with arrangements revealed by detailed research in the specific communities from which the migrants have come. See, for example, Douglas S. Butterworth, "A Study of the Urbanization Process among Mixtec Migrants from Tilaltongo in Mexico City," *América Indígena* 22 (1962): 257–74; Robert V. Kemper, *Migration and Adaptation: Tzintzuntzan Peasants in Mexico City* (Beverly Hills, CA: Sage, 1977); and Oscar Lewis, "Urbanization without Breakdown: A Case Study," *Scientific Monthly* 75 (1952): 31–41. In work on communities known to contain significant numbers of migrants and descendants of migrants—and especially in work on Mexican and Chicano communities in the United States—it has been more common to compare forms of organization found in these communities with arrangements discovered secondhand through reading literature on the general areas or types of society from which the migrants have come. See, for example, Shirley Achor, *Mexican Americans in a Dallas Barrio* (Tucson: University of Arizona Press, 1978); Ruth Horowitz, *Honor and the American Dream: Culture and Identity in a Chicano Community* (New Brunswick, NJ: Rutgers University Press, 1983); Norman D. Humphrey, "The Changing Structure of the Detroit Mexican Family: An Index of Acculturation," *American Sociological Review* 9 (1944): 622–26; William Madsen, *Mexican Americans of South Texas* (New York: Holt, 1964); Arthur J. Rubel, *Across the Tracks: Mexican-Americans in a Texas City* (Austin: University of

Texas Press, 1966); and Richard G. Thurston, *Urbanization and Sociocultural Change in a Mexican-American Enclave* (San Francisco: R & E Research Associates, 1974).

11. See, for example, Achor, *Mexican Americans in a Dallas Barrio*; Madsen, *Mexican Americans of South Texas*; and Rubel, *Across the Tracks*; Larissa A. Lomnitz, *Networks and Marginality: Life in a Mexican Shantytown*, trans. Cinna Lomnitz (New York: Academic, 1977); and Antonio Ugalde, *The Urbanization Process of a Poor Mexican Neighborhood* (Austin: Institute of Latin American Studies, University of Texas, 1974).

12. This approach has been manifested most commonly in work on migration to the United States, where the dominant tendency has been to challenge assumptions about full assimilation with analyses that stress the more or less gradual emergence of ethnic subcultures. See, for example, Achor, *Mexican Americans in a Dallas Barrio*; Horowitz, *Honor and the American Dream*; Madsen, *Mexican Americans of South Texas*; and Rubel, *Across the Tracks*.

13. See, for example, Michael J. Piore, *Birds of Passage* (New York: Cambridge University Press, 1979).

14. A more detailed account of the *municipio* and the history of its involvement in migration can be found in my "Mexican Migration to the United States: Family Relations in the Development of a Transnational Migrant Circuit" (Ph.D. diss., Stanford University, 1989). A *municipio* is a relatively small administrative unit occupying the rung immediately below the level of the state. In 1980, for example, the *municipio* of Aguililla, covering an area of roughly 630 square miles, was one of 113 such entities within the state of Michoacán. The term is difficult to gloss with any precision, however. "Municipality" is misleading because of its urban associations, while a gloss such as "county" runs the risk of suggesting something too large and too powerful. Given these difficulties, I use the term in its untranslated form.

15. For a fuller understanding of the broad processes affecting rural Mexico of the last forty years, see James Cockcroft, *Mexico: Class Formation, Capital Accumulation, and the State* (New York: Grove, 1983); Cynthia Hewit de Alcántara, *Modernizing Mexican Agriculture: Socioeconomic Implications of Technological Change, 1940–1970* (Geneva: UN Research Institute for Social Development, 1976).

16. For a fuller understanding of the changing character of the U.S. economy, particularly since the 1960s, see Saskia Sassen, *The Mobility of Labor and Capital: A Study in International Investment and Labor Flow* (New York: Cambridge University Press, 1988); and Mike Davis, *Prisoners of the American Dream: Politics and Economy in the History of the U.S. Working Class* (London: Verso, 1986), 181–230.

17. Such evidence can be found most readily in a series of studies that have appeared during the last decade charting the emergence of what are generally described as "binational migrant networks." See, for example, Reynaldo Baca and Dexter Bryan, "The 'Assimilation' of Unauthorized Mexican Workers: Another Social Science Fiction," *Hispanic Journal of Behavioral Sciences* 5 (1983): 1–20; Michael Kearney, "From the Invisible Hand to Visible Feet: Anthropological Studies of Migration and Development," *Annual Review of Anthropology* 15 (1986): 331–61; Douglas S. Massey et al., *Return to Aztlán: The Social Process of International Migration from Western Mexico* (Berkeley: University of California Press, 1987); and Richard Mines, *Developing a Community Tradition of*

Migration: A Field Study in Rural Zacatecas, Mexico, and in California Settlement Areas (La Jolla, CA: Program in U.S.-Mexican Studies, University of California at San Diego, 1981).

18. I use the term "transnational" in preference to "binational" partly to evoke as directly as possible the association between migrant forms of organization and transnational corporations. ("Transnational" is gradually replacing the more popular adjective "multinational," at least in academic discourse.) I also prefer it to "binational" because it allows for the possibility that a circuit might include sites in more than two countries. Specifically in the case of Aguilillans, there are indications that this may be coming about as migrants from particular places in Central America arrive in the Redwood City area and gradually attach themselves to the Aguilillan circuit. One of the advantages of such an attachment is that, if they need to leave the United States, they can go to Aguililla and call on social ties established there instead of having to make the longer, more expensive, and often more dangerous journey back to their own country. I use the term "circuit" in preference to "network" because it more effectively evokes the *circulation* of people, money, goods, and information, the pseudo-institutional nature of the arrangement (over purely individual ties), and the qualified importance of place (over purely social linkages). A fine analysis, sensitive to many of these issues, can be found in Michael Kearny and Carole Nagengast, *Anthropological Perspectives on Transnational Communities in Rural California*, Working Paper 3, Working Group on Farm Labor and Rural Poverty (Davis, CA: California Institute for Rural Studies, 1989).

19. For an account of the ways in which places linked by migration can come to form a single "field of activity," see Bryan Roberts, "The Interrelationships of City and Provinces in Peru and Guatemala," *Latin American Urban Research* 4 (1974): 208–9.

20. These ideas are developed more fully in my "Mexican Migration," and "Men in Space: Power and the Appropriation of Urban Form among Mexican Migrants in the United States" (manuscript, Department of Anthropology, University of Michigan, 1989).

21. Américo Paredes, "The Problem of Identity in a Changing Culture: Popular Expressions of Culture Conflict along the Lower Rio Grande Border," in *Views across the Border: The United States and Mexico*, ed. Stanley R. Ross (Albuquerque: University of New Mexico Press, 1978), 68. See also Rosaldo, *Culture and Truth*, 196–217.

22. "En mi realidad fracturada, pero realidad al fin, cohabitan dos historias, lenguajes, cosmogonías, tradiciones artisticas y sistemas politicos drásticamente opuestos (la frontera es el enfrentamiento continuo do dos o más códigas referenciales)" (author's translation). By quoting Gómez-Peña I do not mean to suggest that he and Aguilillans experience their particular border zones in exactly the same way. Clearly, people's experiences vary significantly according to their positions in local frameworks of power and as a function of the routes they have followed in reaching such positions.

23. See Sassen, *The Mobility of Labor and Capital*, 171–85.

24. Mike Davis, *"Chinatown*, Part Two? The 'Internationalization' of Downtown Los Angeles," *New Left Review* 164 (1987): 71–72; and Soja, *Postmodern Geographies*, 221.

25. Lockwood and Leinberger, "Los Angeles Comes of Age," 41. According to Soja, *Postmodern Geographies* (215), more than two million Third World

migrants settled in the Los Angeles area between the mid-1960s and the mid-1980s.

26. See Neal Richmen and Ruth Schwartz, "Housing Homeless Families: Why L.A. Lags Behind," *Los Angeles Times*, May 14, 1987 (quoted in Davis, "*Chinatown*, Part Two?" 77).

27. For a fuller picture of the changing political economy of Los Angeles, see Davis, "Urban Renaissance" and "*Chinatown*, Part Two?"; Sassen, *The Mobility of Labor and Capital*, 126–70; and Soja, *Postmodern Geographies*, 190–248. For reflections on these trends in other parts of the United States, see Jean Franco, "New York Is a Third World City: Introduction," *Tabloid* 9 (1985): 12–13; and Kristin Koptiuch, "Third Worlding at Home" (unpublished paper, University of Texas, Austin, 1989).

28. Renato Rosaldo, "Ideology, Place, and People Without Culture," *Cultural Anthropology* 3, no. 1 (1988): 85; see Saskia Sassen-Koob, "Recomposition and Peripheralization at the Core," *Contemporary Marxism* 5 (Summer 1982): 88–100.

29. All three quotations come from Eric Bailey and H. G. Reza, "Illegals, Homeless Clash in S.D. County," *Los Angeles Times*, San Diego County edition, June 5, 1988.

30. Eric Bailey, "Tempers Flare over Illegals in San Diego County," *Los Angeles Times*, San Diego County edition, June 6, 1988.

31. See Miriam Davidson, "Immigration Bashing: The Mexican Border War," *The Nation*, November 12, 1990, 556–57; and Seth Mydans, "Clash of Culture Grows Amid American Dream," *New York Times*, March 26, 1990.

Suggested Readings

Research on Mexican migration has increased exponentially over the past twenty-five years. Thus, rather than providing a comprehensive review of the literature, the following suggestions are meant to familiarize readers with the general contours of Mexican migration research. However, readers interested in gaining a broader sense of this large and growing body of work may begin by consulting the following items. Historical work on migration and ethnic Mexicans in the United States is critically examined in Arthur F. Corwin, "Causes of Mexican Emigration to the United States: A Summary View," *Perspectives in American History* 7 (1973): 557–635; and Silvia Pedraza-Baily, "Immigration Research: A Conceptual Map," *Social Science History* 14, no. 1 (Spring 1990): 43–67. For discussion of works in sociology and political science, see Douglas S. Massey, "Dimensions of the New Immigration to the United States and the Prospects for Assimilation," *Annual Review of Sociology* 7 (1981): 57–85; and Jorge Durand and Douglas S. Massey, "Mexican Migration to the United States: A Critical Review," *Latin American Research Review* 27, no. 2 (1992): 3–42. For work in anthropology see Michael Kearny, "From the Invisible Hand to Visible Feet: Anthropological Studies of Migration and Development," *Annual Review of Anthropology* 15 (1986): 331–61. Gendered analyses of migration are discussed in Silvia Pedraza, "Women and Migration: The Social Consequences of Gender," *Annual Review of Sociology* 17 (1991): 303–25; and Pierrette Hondagneu-Sotelo's insightful *Gendered Transitions: Mexican Experiences of Immigration* (Berkeley, 1994).

Scholars have found that merely gaining a sense of the magnitude of Mexican migration patterns presents a formidable challenge. For discussion of methodological problems involved in generating and analyzing demographic and migration data for ethnic Mexicans, see Arthur F. Corwin, "Quien Sabe? Mexican Migration Statistics," in *Immigrants—and Immigrants: Perspectives on Mexican Labor Migration to the United States*, ed. Arthur F. Corwin (Westport, CT, 1978), 108–35; and *Cuantos Somos: A Demographic Study of the Mexican American Population*, ed. Charles H. Teller et al. (Austin, 1977). For historical demographic analyses of the Mexican-American and Mexican migrant populations, see Oscar J. Martínez, "On the Size of the Chicano Population: New Estimates, 1850–

1900," *Aztlán* 6 (Spring 1975): 43–67; José Hernández Alvarez, "A Demographic Profile of the Mexican Immigration to the United States, 1910–1950," *Journal of Inter-American Studies* 8 (July 1966): 471–96; Moisés González Navarro, *Población y socieded en México (1900–1970)* (Mexico City, 1974); and Thomas J. Boswell, "The Growth and Proportional Distribution of the Mexican Stock Population in the United States, 1910–1970," *Mississippi Geographer* 7 (Spring 1979): 57–76. For discussion and analysis of more recent demographic trends, and projections for the future, see Frank D. Bean and Marta Tienda, *The Hispanic Population of the United States* (New York, 1987); David E. Lorey, ed., *United States-Mexico Border Statistics since 1900* (Los Angeles, 1990); John R. Weeks and Roberto Ham-Chande, eds., *Demographic Dynamics of the U.S.-Mexico Border* (El Paso, 1992); U.S. Bureau of the Census, Current Population Reports, series P-20, no. 455, *The Hispanic Population in the United States: March 1991* (Washington, DC, 1991); James Paul Allen and Eugene James Turner, *We the People: An Atlas of America's Ethnic Diversity* (New York, 1988); Mark T. Mattson, *Atlas of the 1990 Census* (New York, 1992); and Phillip Martin and Elizabeth Midgley, "Immigration to the United States: Journey to an Uncertain Destination," *Population Bulletin* 49, no. 2 (September 1994). For demographic projections for the pan-Latino population of the United States, see Thomas Exter, "How Many Hispanics?" *American Demographics* (May 1987): 36–39, 67.

Any serious student of Mexican migration history should begin work by consulting the classics in the field. For the earliest significant analysis, see Victor S. Clark, *Mexican Labor in the United States* (U.S. Bureau of Labor Statistics Bulletin, no. 78) (Washington, DC, 1908). Although ethnocentric and at times overly impressionistic, Emory S. Bogardus produced some of the more informative early research on Mexican migrants—see, in particular, *The Mexican in the United States* (Los Angeles, 1934). More nuanced early analyses of the Mexican diaspora were produced by the distinguished Mexican sociologist Manuel Gamio in *Mexican Migration to the United States: A Study of Human Migration and Adjustment* (Chicago, 1930); and *The Life Story of the Mexican Immigrant: Autobiographical Documents* (Chicago, 1931). A bit later, the noted journalist, social critic, and editor Carey McWilliams published a sensitive work of synthesis that has held up through the years: *North from Mexico: The Spanish-Speaking People of the United States* (New York, 1948). However, Berkeley economist Paul S. Taylor's research remains the best of the early work on the subject. Combining an obvious respect for Mexican workers with a particularly good ear for their stories, Taylor authored the foundational sources on the topic. See his magisterial multivolume *Mexican Labor in the United States* (University of California Publications in

Economics Series, vol. 6, no. 1: *Imperial Valley* [1928]; *Valley of South Platte, Colorado* [1929]; *Dimmitt County, Winter Garden District, South Texas* [1930]; *Chicago and the Calumet Region* [1932]); and his *An American-Mexican Frontier: Nueces County, Texas* (Chapel Hill, NC, 1934).

For historical discussion of the significance of mutually recognized regional and intraethnic distinctions among ethnic Mexicans in the nineteenth and the twentieth centuries, see, for example, Miguel León-Portilla, "The Norteño Variety of Mexican Culture: An Ethnohistorical Approach," in *Plural Society in the Southwest*, ed. Edward H. Spicer and Raymond H. Thompson (New York, 1972), 77–114; and *Mexico's Regions: Comparative History and Development*, ed. Eric Van Young (La Jolla, CA, 1992). For discussion of the significance of regional loyalties among ethnic Mexicans in the United States, see David J. Weber, *The Mexican Frontier, 1821–1846: The American Southwest under Mexico* (Albuquerque, NM, 1982); and Ramón A. Gutiérrez's provocative "Unraveling America's Hispanic Past: Internal Stratification and Class Boundaries," *Aztlán* 17 (Spring 1986): 79–102.

Much work remains to be done on the history of migration circuits between Mexico and the United States in the nineteenth century, but several studies have broken ground in this direction. For good syntheses see Arthur F. Corwin, "Early Mexican Labor Migration: A Frontier Sketch, 1848–1900," in *Immigrants—and Immigrants*, 25–37; and Lawrence A. Cardoso, *Mexican Emigration to the United States, 1897–1931* (Tucson, AZ, 1980). Several insightful community studies exploring nineteenth- and early twentieth-century patterns of Mexican migration, settlement, and interaction with Americans include Albert M. Camarillo, *Chicanos in a Changing Society: From Mexican Pueblos to American Barrios in Santa Barbara and Southern California, 1848–1930* (Cambridge, MA, 1979); Arnoldo de León, *The Tejano Community, 1836–1900* (Albuquerque, NM, 1982); Mario T. García, *Desert Immigrants: The Mexicans of El Paso, 1880–1920* (New Haven, CT, 1981); Robert R. Alvarez, *Familia: Migration and Adaptation in Baja and Alta California, 1800–1975* (Berkeley, 1985); and Thomas J. Sheridan, *Los Tucsonenses: The Mexican Community in Tucson, 1854–1941* (Tucson, AZ, 1986).

The intensification of the immigration debate in the early 1970s stimulated the production of a rich body of historical work on twentieth-century Mexican immigration. For example, in 1976, historian Mark Reisler published the standard political history of early migration in this period, *By the Sweat of Their Brow: Mexican Immigrant Labor in the United States, 1900–1940* (Westport, CT, 1976). For studies that revise and expand on Reisler's work while paying close attention to relationships between Mexican immigrants and Mexican Americans, see

David G. Gutiérrez, *Walls and Mirrors: Mexican Americans, Mexican Immigrants, and the Politics of Ethnicity* (Berkeley, 1995); George J. Sánchez, *Becoming Mexican American: Ethnicity, Culture, and Identity in Chicano Los Angeles, 1900–1945* (New York, 1993); and Emilio Zamora, *The World of the Mexican Worker in Texas* (College Station, TX, 1993). Excellent first-person accounts of the experiences of more recent migrants to the United States may be found in Ted Conover, *Coyotes: A Journey through the Secret World of America's Illegal Aliens* (New York, 1987); Marilyn Davis, *Mexican Voices, American Dreams* (New York, 1990); and Oscar J. Martínez, *Border People: Life and Society in the U.S.-Mexico Borderlands* (Tucson, AZ, 1994).

Although most Mexican immigrants historically have settled in one of the five southwestern states (California, Arizona, New Mexico, Colorado, and Texas), significant numbers also fanned out and established barrios and *colonias* in the Great Lakes region, other parts of the Midwest, and the Pacific Northwest. For good discussions of the development of these outlying ethnic Mexican communities, see, for example, Erasmo Gamboa, *Mexican Labor and World War II: Braceros in the Pacific Northwest, 1942–1947* (Austin, 1990); Dennis Nodín Valdés, *Al Norte: Agricultural Workers in the Great Lakes Region, 1917–1970* (Austin, 1991); and Zaragosa Vargas, *Proletarians of the North: A History of Mexican Industrial Workers in Detroit and the Midwest, 1917–1933* (Berkeley, 1993); and "Armies in the Fields and the Factories: The Mexican Working Classes in the Midwest in the 1920s," *Mexican Studies/Estudios Mexicanos* 7 (Winter 1991): 47–72.

Comparatively little work has been done exploring Mexican public sentiment and government action concerning permanent and cyclical emigration to the United States. For suggestive preliminary analyses of attitudes in Mexico concerning these issues, see Juan Gómez-Quiñones, "Piedras contra la luna, México en Aztlán y Aztlán en México: Chicano-Mexican Relations in the Mexican Consulates, 1900–1920," in *Contemporary Mexico: Papers of the IV International Congress of Mexican History* (Mexico City, 1975), 494–527; Arthur F. Corwin, "Mexican Policy and Ambivalence toward Labor Emigration to the United States," in *Immigrants—and Immigrants*, 176–224; *Views across the Border: The United States and Mexico*, ed. Stanley R. Ross (Albuquerque, NM, 1978); Francisco E. Balderrama, *In Defense of La Raza: The Los Angeles Mexican Consulate and the Mexican Community, 1929–1936* (Tucson, AZ, 1982); and Tom Barry, Harry Browne, and Beth Sims, *The Great Divide: The Challenges of U.S.-Mexico Relations in the 1990s* (New York, 1994).

The standard works on the mass repatriation of Mexican nationals and their U.S.-born children during the 1930s remain Mercedes Carreras de Velasco, *Los mexicanos que devolvió la crises, 1929–1932* (Mexico City, 1974); Abraham Hoffman, *Unwanted Mexican Americans in the Great Depression, Repatriation Pressures, 1929–1939* (Tucson, AZ, 1974); and Francisco E. Balderrama and Raymond Rodríguez, *Decade of Betrayal: Mexican Repatriation in the 1930s* (Albuquerque, NM, 1995). For more localized analyses, see Neil Betten and Raymond A. Mohl, "From Discrimination to Repatriation: Mexican Life during the Great Depression," *Pacific Historical Review* 52 (August 1973): 370–88; and D. H. Dinwoodie, "Deportation: The Immigration Service and the Chicano Labor Movement in the 1930s," *New Mexico Historical Review* 51 (July 1977): 193–206. For the best recent interpretations, see Camille Guerin-Gonzales, *Mexican Workers and American Dreams: Immigration, Repatriation, and California Farm Labor, 1900–1939* (New Brunswick, NJ, 1994); and Devra Weber, *Dark Sweat, White Gold: California Farm Workers, Cotton, and the New Deal* (Berkeley, 1994). The standard work on "Operation Wetback," a later episode of the mass repatriation of Mexican nationals, is Juan Ramón García's, *Operation Wetback: The Mass Deportation of Mexican Undocumented Workers in 1954* (Westport, CT, 1980).

The Bracero Program has attracted scholarly attention from historians, economists, political scientists, legal scholars, and sociologists. For overview discussions of the program from a public policy perspective, see Ellis Hawley, "The Politics of the Mexican Labor Issue, 1950–1965," *Agricultural History* 40 (July 1966): 157–76; Richard B. Craig, *The Bracero Program: Interest Groups and Foreign Policy* (Austin, 1971); and Otey M. Scruggs, *Braceros, "Wetbacks," and the Farm Labor Problem: Mexican Agricultural Labor in the United States, 1942–1954* (New York, 1988). Mexican-American scholars brought a unique perspective to the analysis of the program, paying particular attention to the adverse impact the braceros and undocumented workers had on U.S. citizens of Mexican descent. For example, labor activist-scholar Ernesto Galarza spent much of his life fighting for the abolition of the use of Mexican immigrant labor in the United States, an argument he advanced with great power in *Merchants of Labor: The Mexican Bracero Story; An Account of the Managed Migration of Mexican Farmworkers in California, 1942–1960* (Charlotte, NC, 1964), and *Farmworkers and Agribusiness in California, 1942–1960* (Charlotte, NC, 1964). Sociologist Julian Samora and his research team present a more empathetic analysis of undocumented workers during the bracero era in *Los Mojados—The Wetback Story* (Notre Dame, IN, 1971).

For more recent studies that attempt to analyze the Bracero Program in a broader context taking into account trends in the internationalization of capital and the global exploitation of labor, see Gilberto Cardenas,

"United States Immigration Policy toward Mexico: An Historical Perspective," *Chicano Law Review* 2 (1975): 66–91; Ellwyn R. Stoddard, "Illegal Mexican Labor in the Borderlands: Institutionalized Support of an Unlawful Practice," *Pacific Sociological Review* 19, no. 2 (1976): 175–210; Robert L. Bach, "Mexican Immigration and the American State," *International Migration Review* 12, no. 4 (Winter 1978): 536–58; James D. Cockcroft, *Outlaws in the Promised Land: Mexican Immigrant Workers and America's Future* (New York, 1986); Douglas S. Massey and Zai Liang, "The Long-Term Consequences of a Temporary Worker Program: The U.S. Bracero Experience," *Population Research and Policy Review* 8 (1989): 199–226; and Kitty Calavita, *Inside the State: The Bracero Program, Immigration, and the INS* (New York, 1992).

The body of scholarship on U.S. immigration history informed by some version of the "assimilationist" and "cultural deficiency" paradigms is a vast one. For recent critical reviews of this literature, see, for example, Charles Hirschman, "America's Melting Pot Reconsidered," *Annual Review of Sociology* 9 (1983): 397–423; Olivier Zunz, "American History and the Changing Meaning of Assimilation," *Journal of American Ethnic History* 5, no. 3 (Spring 1985): 53–84; and Peter Kivisto, "The Transplanted Then and Now: The Reorientation of Immigration Studies from the Chicago School to the New Social History," *Ethnic and Racial Studies* 13, no. 4 (October 1990): 455–81. For a recent rejoinder to such critiques, see Ewa Morawska, "In Defense of the Assimilation Model," *Journal of American Ethnic History* 13, no. 2 (Winter 1994): 76–87.

Since the late 1960s, Mexican-American scholars have mounted a withering critique of "cultural deficiency" explanations for social problems in ethnic Mexican communities. Again, this literature is too large to do more than touch on it here, but for examples of such critiques, see Octavio Romano, "The Anthropology and Sociology of Mexican Americans: The Distortion of Mexican American History," *El Grito* 2, no. 1 (Fall 1968): 13–26; "The Historical and Intellectual Presence of Mexican Americans," *El Grito* 2, no. 2 (Winter 1969): 32–46; and "Social Science, Objectivity, and the Chicanos," *El Grito* 4, no. 1 (Fall 1970): 4–16; Miguel Montiel, "The Social Science Myth of the Mexican American Family," *El Grito* 3, no. 4 (Summer 1970): 56–63; Nick C. Vaca, "The Mexican American in the Social Sciences, 1912–1970, Part 1," *El Grito* 3, no. 3 (Spring 1970): 3–24; and Part 2, *El Grito* 4, no. 1 (Fall 1970): 17–51; and David G. Gutiérrez, "Significant to Whom?: Mexican Americans and the History of the American West," *Western Historical Quarterly* 24, no. 4 (November 1993): 519–39.

Since the passage of the Immigration Reform and Control Act of 1986, there has been a marked resurgence in calls for immigration policy reform by individuals who tend to view Mexican migration as a domestic political issue subject to unilateral U.S. intervention and control. For recent examples of this kind of perspective see T. B. Morgan, "The Latinization of America," *Esquire* (May 1983): 47–56; Richard D. Lamm and Gary Imhoff, *The Immigration Time Bomb: The Fragmenting of America* (New York, 1985); Peter H. Schuck and Rogers M. Smith, *Citizenship without Consent: Illegal Aliens in the American Polity* (New Haven, CT, 1985); and Peter Brimelow, "Time to Rethink Immigration?" *National Review*, June 22, 1992.

A growing body of work critiques such narrow views of the sources and implications of transnational migration circuits between Mexico and the United States. For examples of such views in the social sciences, see Douglas Uzzell, "Ethnography of Migration: Breaking Out of the Bi-Polar Myth," in *New Approaches to the Study of Migration*, ed. David Guillet and Douglas Uzzell (Rice University Studies, vol. 62, no. 3, Houston, 1976), 45–54; Alejandro Portes and Robert L. Bach, *Latin Journey: Cuban and Mexican Immigrants in the United States* (Berkeley, 1985); "Transnational Migration," ed. Barbara Schmitter Heisler and Martin O. Heisler, *Annals of the American Academy of Political and Social Sciences* 485 (May 1986): 9–166; Douglas S. Massey, Rafael Alarcón, Jorge Durand, and Humberto González, *Return to Aztlán: The Social Process of International Migration from Western Mexico* (Berkeley, 1987); Michael Kearney, "Borders and Boundaries of State and Self at the End of Empire," *Journal of Historical Sociology* 4, no. 1 (March 1991): 52–74; Leo R. Chávez, *Shadowed Lives: Undocumented Immigrants in American Society* (Fort Worth, TX, 1992); and "Towards a Transnational Perspective on Migration: Race, Class, Ethnicity, and Nationalism Reconsidered," ed. Nina Glick Schiller, Linda Basch, and Christina Blanc-Szanton, in *Annals of the New York Academy of Sciences* 645 (1992): vii–258.

For suggestive discussions of the political and cultural implications of the maturation of complex binational and multinational social networks, see, for example, Gloria Anzaldúa, *Borderlands/La Frontera: The New Mestiza* (San Francisco, 1987); Guillermo Gómez-Peña, "The Multicultural Paradigm: An Open Letter to the Arts Community," *High Performance* 12 (Fall 1989): 18–27; Rubén Martínez, *The Other Side: Notes from the New L.A., Mexico City, and Beyond* (London, 1992); and "The Shock of the New," *Los Angeles Times Magazine*, January 30, 1994, 10–16, 39.